PRIVATE LABELS
Store Brands & Generic Products

RELATED AVI BOOKS

CONSUMER BEHAVIOR
Redman
FOOD AND ECONOMICS
Hungate and Sherman
FOOD AND THE CONSUMER
Revised Edition *Kramer*
FOOD LAW HANDBOOK
Schultz
FOOD PRODUCTS FORMULARY
VOL. 1, 2nd Edition, MEATS, POULTRY, FISH AND SHELLFISH
Long, Komarik, and Tressler
VOL. 2, CEREALS, BAKED GOODS, DAIRY AND EGG PRODUCTS
Tressler and Sultan
VOL. 3, FRUIT, VEGETABLE AND NUT PRODUCTS
Tressler and Woodroof
VOL. 4, FABRICATED FOODS
Inglett and Inglett
HANDBOOK OF PACKAGE MATERIALS
Sacharow
MICROECONOMICS: RESOURCE ALLOCATION AND PRICE THEORY
Redman and Redman
PACKAGE PRODUCTION MANAGEMENT
2nd Edition *Raphael and Olsson*
PACKAGING REGULATIONS
Sacharow
PRINCIPLES OF FOOD PACKAGING
2nd Edition *Sacharow and Griffin*
SCHOOL FOODSERVICE
2nd Edition *Van Egmond-Pannell*
STATISTICAL METHODS FOR FOOD AND AGRICULTURE
Bender, Douglass, and Kramer

PRIVATE LABELS
Store Brands & Generic Products

Philip B. Fitzell

Sponsored by *Private Label* Magazine

AVI Publishing Company, Inc.
Westport, Connecticut

Library of Congress Cataloging in Publication Data

Fitzell, Philip B.
Private labels.

"Sponsored by Private label magazine."
Bibliography: p.
1. Generic products. 2. Branded merchandise.
I. Title. II. Title: Store brands & generic products.
HF1040.7.F58 1982 658.8'27 82-20683
ISBN 0-87055-415-8

Printed in the United States of America

Contents

Foreword

It is particularly gratifying to me to introduce this book. It is the first textbook ever published about what is conservatively estimated to be at least a $100 billion industry, covering an almost unbelievable range of private and generic retail labels, growing with increasing momentum in food, drug, and general merchandising chains.

What a range this business covers! It includes soaps, detergents, canned and frozen foods, coffees, teas, and almost every popular grocery product; cheeses, health and beauty aids of all types, household cleaning supplies, pet foods, paper and plastic goods, photo films, razor blades, packaging, labeling, motor oils, vitamins, nutmeats, auto tires, mushrooms . . . yes, practically anything you can imagine.

From the national brand manufacturers' perspective, private labels were looked upon with some anxiety and consternation. How far was this movement to go? Until 1970, the national and regional brands had commanded the field. But the store labels caught on and gradually spread into every segment of retailing. This was not just a line of unadvertised labels, but another "brand" entirely. Private labels have been with us for many years, of course, but they were looked upon as stepchildren of retailing, kept in the closet, so to speak.

In April 1979, *Private Label* Magazine was published, the first publication ever to be devoted entirely to private labels and generics, reaching a circulation of 25,000 private label buyers in food, drug, and mass merchandising chains. Shortly thereafter, the first Private Label Directory in the industry was introduced. In October 1979, a group of private label manufacturers met and, a short time later, formed the Private Label Manufacturers Association, known now as PLMA. Like *Private Label* Magazine, PLMA's growth has been fantastic with nearly 350 member companies, mostly large and small private label manufacturers as active members, plus brokers, suppliers, retailers, etc., as associate members. What was until recently a widespread and fragmented industry has grown in 3 years to the point where a national convention was held in November 1982 with more than 1200 people in attendance, drawn in to visit 225 exhibitor booths in Chicago.

I can only predict a growth in the field of private and generic brands during the next several years which will easily exceed that of the past two decades. And it is to the future of the private label industry that this book is really dedicated.

E. W. Williams
Publisher
Private Label Magazine

Acknowledgments

This book has really been written by the people involved in the private label business. Through their cooperation in contributing to and supporting, first, *Private Label* Magazine and, second, the Private Label Manufacturers Association (PLMA), this study has been made possible. Without these two factors, this book would not exist.

Actually, there are hundreds of people responsible for this book's development. They appear on the pages of the magazine and belong to or have supported the association and its trade shows.

My appreciation goes out to a list of people long enough to fill another book. I cannot mention the many retailers, wholesalers, manufacturers, brokers, suppliers, distributors, and consultants, both in the United States and Canada, who have all played a role in shaping my perception of private labels. Every one of them shares the book by-line.

I must, however, single out Ed Williams, president of Private Label Publishing Co., who started the magazine and hired me to help launch it. He suggested that this book be written.

I would also like to thank a few people who took the time to review some of the chapters, in particular, Ken Gast of the Kroger Co.; Dr. Herb Shuster of Herbert V. Shuster, Inc.; Richard Kester of Ralph's Grocery Co.; and Ralph Behr, Esq., of Food Oils Corp.

Thanks also are extended to *Private Label* Magazine's Sam Martin, present editor—and an author in his own right—who has been especially helpful in advising me on this book.

Special, personal thanks go to my wife, Judith, who patiently tolerated the long months of research and writing needed to complete this work.

Overall, a hearty handshake is extended to the private label industry—the many people who have graciously and openly talked about their businesses. Without their help to augment the paucity of private label information available in books, magazines, etc., this project would never have been completed.

Philip B. Fitzell
Bloomfield, New Jersey

Part I

An Overview

1

What Is Private Label?

When something is called private, it belongs to someone; it is secret, not public. Private labels—the merchandise owned, controlled, and sold exclusively by a retailer, wholesaler, or distributor—no longer completely fit that description.

Not too long ago, many of these labels carrying a store's trademark name or a trade name created exclusively for the store, were kept secret, hidden on shelves without so much as a whisper of advertising. They were suspect, since no manufacturer's name appeared on the packaging: only the distributor's name was mentioned. In food stores, they blurred into a rainbow mix of many different private labels along with other brands and packer labels. In drugstores, they were barely visible, few and far between. The department store retailer or mass merchandiser treated them like any other brand, building equity into each trademark name, without giving them category status and sometimes using them as fill-in import merchandise. In fact, at one time it was almost sacrilegious to promote private labels, let alone compare them to the national brands: those products owned by a manufacturer who sells them publicly to the general trade.

Only in the past couple of decades have private labels truly come into their own. Out of the closet, private label value is no longer kept a secret. Retailers, wholesalers, and distributors now support their brands with money-back guarantees, much like the national brand manufacturers. Private label is now publicly recognized as a category comparable to national brands; in other words, it is an alternative choice usually sold for less money than the national brands. Private labels are not necessarily sold exclusively in a retailer's own stores; sometimes these products are sold, licensed, or exported to retailers in noncompetitive markets. In fact, some private labels are regionally or nationally advertised as brands, carrying the same marketing clout as the strong national brands.

Actually, private labels have come full circle in their evolution, which started in the nineteenth century. It was then that customers began to put their trust in local merchants who carried top quality merchandise, much of it under their own label. As national brands proliferated and took a commanding market share, private label products could only follow the leaders. Customers became more familiar with national brands, switching their trust from the merchant to the national brand name itself. The national brand manufacturers earned that confidence partly through product research and development, but also partly through creative advertising, effective promotions, and sophisticated packaging. Without the same national marketing clout or capital backing, private labels had to settle for a price image, selling up to 10% or more below the national brands.

Another important change in the marketplace was the exodus of many entrepreneurs in retailing—men who took pride first in selling quality merchandise and then in making a profit. They were replaced by professional managers, who focused their attention more on bottom-line profits.

As a price brand, a private label was often considered inferior or cheap. At best, it was given stepchild status in the marketing mix. Retailers and wholesalers gave it incidental support; store buyers devoted no more than a fraction of their time to sourcing products for private label. It was much easier for them to buy national brands than to bother about quality standards, consistency, packaging, etc. Product manufacturers (including national brand sources) would not admit to producing these so-called knock-off or copycat products. Besides their shoddy reputation, private labels carried legal implications.

In a landmark case, the Federal Trade Commission versus Borden Co. (383 U.S. 637—1966), Borden under the Robinson–Patman Act was accused of price discrimination, selling the same grade and quality of milk under its Borden label as under private label. Retailers and wholesalers paid more for the Borden brand. A U.S. Court of Appeals voted in 1967 that the price differential did not go beyond the "recognized consumer appeal of the Borden label." Competition was not hurt, yet that label appeal to the customer was never spelled out.

The argument is that the national brand manufacturer pays more to develop, market, and advertise his branded products. Those costs are built into the wholesale and retail costs. The consumer pays extra for the "sizzle," but could get the same "steak" under private label.

Of course, not all private labels are equal in quality to the national brands. Some products are manufactured like the national brands, but not exactly duplicating them. There are commodities purchased at grades above, equal to, or below national brand standards—in tiers of quality under private label names. It is also true that not all national brands are equal to so-called national brand quality. Knock-off national brands exist, too. It is all part of the free enterprise system that allows for competition—a freedom of choice that prevents a monopoly or discourages a manufacturer from becoming too greedy in taking the full market share with his product.

Today, retailers and wholesalers set their own quality specifications in private label; frequently, that quality is no different from the manufacturer's brand, especially in a top quality private label line. One of the major reasons why national brands outsell private labels is that the consumer is familiar with the national brand through the influence of advertising and years of usage. Consumers know and recognize that quality and respect the brand trademark.

In its 1976 annual report, Pet Inc. of St. Louis talked about this attitude:

> A brand name stands as a character witness for a manufacturer and his product. Consumers don't buy companies, they buy products—products with brand names found to be consistent in quality. Each of Pet's many brands and marks symbolizes this dedication to quality. Some of the brands are more than a century old; some barely infants. Their common bond is a worth that has been proven in the marketplace, and a resulting loyalty and trust built among the buying public.

The private label position is no different. One of the important ingredients in a strong private label program is consistent quality. When retailers locate a good manufacturing source, they keep their relationship active for decades. Quality standards for some retailers go back to their founding—unwavering from day one. Some retailers have established vendor relations as long as their own history.

J. C. Penney opened his first Golden Rule Store in 1902 in Kemmerer, Wyoming, a mining town of about 1000 people. One of his guiding principles was to give customers value, quality, and satisfaction for their dollar. On Penney's buying trips, he would take fabric swatches back to his hotel room and wash them by hand, testing to his own satisfaction the manufacturer's claims. He did this because of his insistence that he had to be fully satisfied with the quality before the product would go on sale in his stores. Once the right sources of supply were found, he cemented a relationship that lasted for years. A shoe supplier who has been filling

Penney's orders since 1907 eventually became one of the largest suppliers of any single category of merchandise for J. C. Penney Company, Inc., New York. Around 1910, a glove company began another long-term relationship with the retailer.

It is a symbiotic relationship, favorable to both parties. As the company puts it:

> We have helped them to develop new products at lower prices to the consumer; we have offered them a wider market, and we have helped them to reduce their costs by minimizing seasonal production dips. And they, in turn, have contributed immeasurably in helping to insure the continued confidence customers have placed in our products.
>
> While not on the books in dollars and cents, we regard our vendors as one of our most priceless assets. (Batten 1967).

Other retailers, too, are protective with their established private label suppliers.

The unknown labels—the private labels—carrying that same consistent quality and proven worth claimed by national brands are now becoming bolder or less private in the marketplace. Retailers and wholesalers have modernized their label packaging and consolidated their label names and now are moving aggressively into advertising and merchandising private labels.

GENERICS

Since 1977, a new category of private label, the generics, has revolutionized the marketplace and, in fact, given new status to private label. Awareness levels of both private label and generics have virtually skyrocketed in a short time, thanks to reports in newspapers, TV, and radio. Consumers listen to discussions about generic value in these current inflated economic times.

People change, thinking changes. Today's shopper is growing smarter out of economic necessity. Brand loyalty is not as strong today as it was in decades past. In surveys of consumer attitudes, high percentages of respondents now check off "no brand preference." Consumers also are beginning to notice private labels and generics on their shopping trips.

Customers are turning their trust back to the retailer, who now listens to their wants and needs. The retailer's attitude and marketing philosophy are changing. A large retailer once confided: "The old attitude about not rocking the boat, just pulling in the national brand leaders and pounding them out in promotional activity, no longer applies. We've got to use some push. Procter & Gamble uses the pull. We're not going to just sit out there and pull for them. We have more push than they have. And we now use that push to get sales in private label."

It takes time for the customer and the retailer to change, but they do. The country's first supermarket chain, King Kullen Grocery Co., Westbury, New York, established in 1930, was the last in its market area to adopt generics, in April 1981.

In the past, merchants and manufacturers were guilty of listening mostly to their own needs. When a revolutionary idea like the supermarket came along, giving the customer low-price, high-quality national brands, it turned the food industry upside down. When discount department stores adopted the same formula in the 1950s, the consequences were the same in the mass merchandising market, as well as in the drug and food markets.

Now, another revolutionary idea, a sleeper for decades, is turning the marketplace inside out. It carries the same theme: give the customer low-price, top-quality merchandise; in other words, give shoppers value for their dollar. This idea, pioneered by entrepreneurs in the last century, is called private label.

In the past five years, food retailers and wholesalers have embraced the new generation of so-called generic labels as an extension of private label. Generic products are usually positioned at a lower quality and price level than national brands and private labels, but still offer customers value in terms of nutrition and acceptable quality.

At first, generics evolved in the marketplace not as a private label (belonging to a single retailer or wholesaler) but as a category label. While each generic label belonged to a specific retailer or wholesaler, they were perceived en masse by the consumer as a common category of low-priced products—an alternative to high-priced national brands. In newspaper ads, the shopper was often told of the dramatic savings realized with generics, an average of 30–40% below the national brand pricing. While the strength of private label might be traced partly to consistently high quality, the strength of generics derived from its consistently low price—lower than private label, which usually is positioned up to 10% below national brands. Price differentials, however, can range from pennies up to many dollars and vary widely from region to region in the country.

When customers asked their retailers to stock generics, they did. That brought King Kullen into the fold, as it did many others, primarily as a defensive strategy against the competition, which was already carrying generics and drawing more traffic to their stores.

Today, generics are evolving more into a private label identity, as retailers and wholesalers seek to distinguish their generic lines from the competition, using color (sparingly) and specific economic-sounding names. A&P, for example, recently changed from the basic no-name, black-and-white generic label to a "P&G" logo (borrowed from its Price and Quality merchandising slogan) featuring two shades of green against a white background. Each label also carries the A&P identity as distributor of the product. Other examples are Safeway markets "Scotch Buy," Kroger sells "Price Cutter," Winn Dixie has "Price Breaker," and so on.

A CLOSER LOOK

Private labels are recognizable by their name; frequently, it is the same as the store name—the Kroger brand at the Kroger Co., Cincinnati, for example. A private label also can be a trademark name created exclusively for the store or chain—J. C. Penney's newest private label lines are Windsor Bay raincoats and Pick 'n' Post mix-and-match jackets, skirts, tailored pants, and blouses. Private labels also can be a controlled label, a name or names created by a wholesaler or a buying co-op for the exclusive use of its membership (retailers), such as the wholesaler United Grocers, Ltd., Oakland, California, with its Bonnie Hubbard label and Shurfine-Central Corp., Northlake, Illinois, a nonprofit buying co-op owned by independent food retailers, with the Shurfine and Shurfresh labels. Private labels can even be generated by a broker, who establishes labels for his customers, the retailer, or wholesaler. Alliance Associates, a food broker in Coldwater, Michigan, has 25 private labels for its customers. Alliance distributes its own label, Family Fare, and also provides a multiple label program, including store name labels, for customers.

Some private label names are as well known as some national brands. Sears products, Sherwin Williams paint, Thom McAn shoes, and Baskin-Robbins ice cream are private labels sold only in stores carrying the same name. Thom McAn does license its brand to other stores for their exclusive use. Famous retailers have put their names onto private label lines: Brooks Brothers, Macy's, John Wanamaker, T. Eaton (Toronto), etc. Private labels also can be traded without the store name. At Sears, for example, there are Kenmore appliances, Craftsman tools, Die-Hard car batteries, and Cheryl Tiegs jeans; at A&P, there are Eight O'Clock Coffee, Ann Page groceries, and Jane Parker bakery items; at Woolworths there are Primrose panty hose, Pata Cake diapers, Audition electronic items, Lorraine hair nets, and Herald Square stationery; at Walgreen Drug there are Chambly milk bath, Jeri cologne, and Nature's Finest vitamins; at K mart there are Challenger men's wear, Changing Scene women's wear, Texas Steer work shoes, Trax running shoes, Performer paint, and Focal film.

Identities as generic as "Our Own," "Our Finest," "Our Best," etc., can often represent private label lines. (In Europe, private labels generally are referred to as "own labels.") Often initials signal a private label: A&P, S brand at Safeway Food Stores, Oakland, California; D at Dominion Stores, Toronto, Canada; FM at FedMart General Stores, San Diego,

California; FM tires at K mart, Troy, Michigan; GNC at General Nutrition Health Food Stores, Pittsburgh, Pennsylvania; CVS at CVS Pharmacies, Consumer Value Stores, Woonsocket, Rhode Island, etc.

Any time a product is packaged under a label owned exclusively by a retailer, it can be called private label. That retailer can operate in the food, drug, or general merchandise markets or a combination of the three. The retailer also can be involved in the foodservice business. McDonald's Big Mac, for example, is a private label owned by McDonald's Corp., Oak Brook, Illinois. As one of the largest restaurant chains in the country, McDonald's sells its own products, all protected by trademarks, only through its owned, franchised, or licensed stores. In fact, the only national brands it sells chainwide in the United States are Coca-Cola and Tab, and Dr Pepper on a regional basis.

Sometimes a foodservice retailer will extend sale of its private brands to outside sources. Howard Johnson Co. of Boston, for example, sells its private label products through grocery stores primarily in the Northeast; but the bulk of the Howard Johnson product line is sold through its restaurants for on-premises consumption or for take-out service.

The private label business in foodservice retailing—products packaged under the operator's private trademarks—is gaining momentum. Dunkin' Donut, Randolph, Massachusetts, which in the past packaged donuts and fresh ground coffee under its store name for take out, has expanded the selection to brownies, muffins, and cookies, becoming in effect a chain of private label bakeries.

In 1980, Bonanza family budget restaurants, Dallas, established a new meat division to supply pre-portioned cuts of meat, poultry, and seafood (purchased from outside suppliers and processors) for wholesale distribution under the Bonanza label to its franchised restaurants. The result: Bonanza is in the private label meat business.

Chain foodservice operators in particular see potential in developing product specifications under their own label for better quality control. The larger foodservice distributors also maintain a strong commitment to their own private label. Many distributors as members of major foodservice distributor marketing/buying groups pick up their group's controlled label: Nifda, CODE, Frosty Acres, etc.

The private label business also encompasses other types of retailing. Gasoline service stations, for example, sell a number of different products—gasoline, motor oil, tires, grease, waxes, auto accessories—under a dealer's name: Exxon, Mobil, Shell. In the home-center store, numerous do-it-yourself products carry a retailer's private label in such areas as paint, lumber, hardware, electrical supplies, plumbing equipment and seasonal merchandise.

Traditionally, the key ingredient for a private label has been its exclusivity. A retailer, wholesaler, or distributor limits the sale and distribution of its own brands to its operation: a store, a chain of stores, or a group of unrelated stores or distributors belonging to a co-op buying service. In each case, the label is controlled within the parameters of that operation. The label owner may manufacture his own private label products or have them manufactured and packaged to certain specifications by outside sources, including imports.

There are cases where private label exclusivity is stretched into a licensing agreement. Such an arrangement is made often to extend the market of a retailer (or foodservice operator), for example, development of foreign markets. Other circumstances can bring about a licensing deal. Fisher Foods Inc., Bedford Heights, Ohio, for example, in selling off its Dominick's Finer Foods division, allowed the Dominick's chain to continue carrying Fisher's Heritage House label under a licensing agreement. Early in 1982, Fisher took a step further by establishing a Heritage Wholesaling operation in order to license the Heritage House label to other chains and independents. Fisher's other supermarket division, Fazio's, continues to carry Heritage House as its private label along with several other store brands.

Those who sell or distribute their private label products to outside sources, feel that their label does not lose its exclusivity, since it is usually sold to noncompetitive retailers in other marketing areas or outside the country. Of course, there is no law that restricts their label to "private" use only, especially when greater profits can be realized through expanded distribution. The extension of private label distribution is another manifestation of its move toward national brand status.

Private labels also are moving toward greater consolidation—fewer labels—often categorized by quality grades or tiers—good, better, and best; or standard, extra standard, choice and fancy; or grade C, grade B, and grade A—with different trademark names for each level. For example, Stop & Shop Supermarkets, Boston, offers Stop & Shop brand as grade A, Sun Glory as extra standard, and Economy as standard grade or generic. Stop & Shop also carries an "Our Own" label, top grade, which is shared by other divisions operated by the parent company. There are cases, of course, where several different labels, representing different product categories are within the same quality grade.

In a certain sense, private labels are house brands; that is, they are kept in-house and not sold elsewhere. When private labels expand distribution to ouside users, then the labels tend to move toward a regional or national brand status. But the label still is owned and controlled by the retailer, wholesaler, or distributor.

Recently, there has been an increase in export activity by retailers who manufacture their own private labels. Safeway Brands by Safeway Stores are now exported to the Far East and more recently to the Middle East. Also, Safeway's Canadian Division in Eastern Canada is looking to expand distribution to Western Canada. In 1981, The Kroger Co. began exporting its food items to Japan, where they are picked up by The Daiei, Inc., Japan's largest food and general merchandise retailer.

The Great Atlantic & Pacific Tea Company, Inc. (A&P), Montvale, New Jersey, however, has been by far the most aggressive—traditionally so—in flexing the potential of private label. In the 1930s, that firm advertised and merchandised private label in the way many other retailers have begun to adopt only in the 1980s. A&P's efforts, unfortunately, were premature and costly in terms of market share. Recently, the company slipped to the number three or four position in the food market segment.

Recently, A&P has embarked on some interesting private label activities at a time when private label is more acceptable and recognized by the consumer. In 1979, A&P started a chain of private label Plus Discount Foods stores, a limited assortment unit of about 1000 items, featuring from 60 to 70% private label stock under the new Plus label. This concept is still being tested and refined.

Through the standard A&P supermarket, the company became the first major U.S. chain to launch a generics program early in 1978, picking up a plain black-and-white, no-brand-name label. That label recently was updated, reidentified as P&Q, representing Price and Quality in A&P's marketing slogan. The old plain label was identified only as distributed by Compass Foods, which most customers would not recognize as an A&P subsidiary. The new P&Q label carries two shades of green in the logo and a green stripe pattern along with A&P's name as the distributor.

A&P's private label brands have been cut back today to about eight trademarks: A&P, Ann Page, Jane Parker, Eight O'Clock, Our Own, Marvel, and Plus, with a few other brands, including the P&Q label. Compass Foods, A&P's outside sales organization, draws on the manufacturing might of the company to provide more than 8000 items for export, selling A&P, Ann Page, and other private brands to some 30 foreign countries. Compass also sells some of those brands to other U.S. retail chains in non-A&P markets, giving the private labels a double role: private label in the A&P operations and regional brand outside A&P's marketing areas. (At this writing, A&P, because of its financial difficulties, is planning to sell some of its manufacturing facilities.)

CHANGING STATUS

Private labels are not static in the marketplace. They adapt to changing consumer habits, reform to competitive or strategic maneuvering by retailers. Private labels have broken away from their in-house or house brand status. These brands now are licensed or exported. They copy not only national brand formulations, packaging, and marketing developments, but also to a degree their distribution strategies.

It is interesting to note that perhaps the oldest private label coffee, Eight O'Clock Coffee, introduced by A&P in 1882 (just about the time Joel Cheek created a coffee brew for patrons at the Maxwell House Hotel in Nashville, Tennessee), is now breaking out of its private label frame and taking on a national brand status. In June 1979, A&P through Compass began franchising the Eight O'Clock Whole Bean Coffee Program, complete with coffee mills (for fresh in-store grinding), competitive pricing, promotions, point-of-sale materials, and field assistance. In A&P marketing areas, the retailers are offered Compass' packer label, Compass Gold Coffee, the same product under a different label.

In another development, A&P's new investor-partner, the Tengelmann Group of West Germany, has adopted the A&P logo on its private label products sold in Europe. The A&P line, translated as "Attractive and Priced right," is being sold in the Tengelmann and Kaiser's chains.

These efforts together with Compass Foods' export program make the A&P label one of the most international private labels today.

A&P, however, has suffered economic setbacks recently, forcing the company to close its 1.5 million-square-foot manufacturing facility in Horsehead, New York, called the world's largest food plant, covering some 35 acres. This facility, operational since 1965, has produced a wide variety of items, such as condiments, dressings, soups, pudding mixes, fruit drinks, etc. A&P continues to operate three coffee roasting plants and several dairies and bakeries.

The role of private label is changing in other respects, too. As retailers expand their operations, diversifying into other businesses, they have promoted private label to corporate label status. Stop & Shop Supermarkets serves as a good example. The company started as a food chain in 1914, followed the industry movement into supermarkets in the 1930s and 1940s, married up with the discount store concept in the 1960s first by acquiring Bradlees department stores and then MediMart drug stores, and then diversified more by acquiring Charles P. Perkins and by developing a new concept, Off the Rax women's specialty stores. Different market segments sometimes lend themselves to common products. There is no problem with adopting national brands, but what about selling a Stop & Shop label in a Bradlee's department store? As mentioned previously, the Stop & Shop Companies are now experimenting with a corporate label, "Our Own," a fourth private label that covers items in general merchandise and health and beauty aids. The private label line can be stocked in Stop & Shop, Bradlee's, and MediMart, all operations draw from the same inventory. The company achieves better inventory control, as products move out of the warehouse quicker. In the past, any item with a slow turnover in the supermarket segment might require large inventories held in stock. Now that product, under Our Own label, can be turned more quickly, allowing the company to continue buying large quantities for greater savings.

Steinberg Inc., Montreal, has picked up an "Our Own for you" label in its line of health and beauty aids and general merchandise products, both in its Steinberg supermarkets and its Miracle Mart department stores.

Corporate labels have also been developed by Lucky Stores, Dublin, California, which calls itself "a well-balanced company . . . having achieved both geographic and store-type diversity," with operations in food, department, specialty, fabric, and automotive stores. Lucky Stores once carried the Lucky label; but through diversification into other businesses (Gemco, Eagle, Kash & Karry, etc.) its warehousing and brand identity problem forced a change. So Lucky developed a premium line, Lady Lee, and a secondary value line, Harvest Day, both identified not as Lucky Store products but as "distributed by Markets, Inc." These private labels, now established as corporate labels, can be distributed to all chains in the Lucky family that carry that type of merchandise. They become more like brands. In fact, these labels sometimes are mistaken for national brands. Brokers from the east coast have called Markets, Inc. (Lucky's headquarters), asking for orders for their customers or asking if they can represent those brands in their markets. Recently, Lucky has developed a new yellow-and-black generic line, which is being marketed systemwide in its different operations. As part of that activity, Lucky in mid-1981 set up an office in Dublin, headed by Donald R. McPherson, the firm's first corporate private brands manager. (Previously, some divisions in the Lucky system never recognized Lady Lee and Harvest Day as exclusive labels, but instead regarded them as just another "brand.") The company also reidentified all its private labels (in small print) as "distributed by LKS Products, Dublin, California." This acronym of Lucky Stores ties all the corporate labels—Lady Lee, Harvest Day, generics, etc.—into a single merchandising program.

A perfect example of the corporate label phenomenon is Loblaw Companies Limited, Toronto. This $5 billion operation encompasses three food distribution businesses and four wholesale food distribution companies spread across North America. In efforts to centralize and standardize its food distribution network, Loblaw in 1975 created Intersave Canada, a buying and merchandising service. First, all national brand buying was coordinated from that operation. Then Intersave began drawing private labels out of the Loblaw Ontario supermarket chain—strong labels that had equity built in over the years, such as Pride of Arabia coffee, Red Label tea, and Jack and Jill natural peanut butter—for distribution to its other Canadian food distributors: Zehrmart; National Grocers; Atlantic Wholesalers; and Kelly, Douglas & Company, Ltd. It also created wholesale labels, Sunspun and Better Buy, for coast-to-coast distribution in Canada through its wholesalers. The recent success of No Name generics in Loblaws Ontario has pushed that yellow-and-black label out into the Loblaw network under the corporate identity, No Name, with Sunfresh Canada identified as distributor. Loblaws Ontario has kept its Loblaw name as a private label, which actually has taken a secondary role to the No Name generic program.

In 1980, Loblaw created Intersave USA to coordinate similiar activities for its U.S. operations, beginning with the development of a No Name yellow-and-black label, distributed by Sunfresh USA. It is being marketed as a national corporate label for National Tea, Peter J. Schmitt Co., and Western Grocers, all located in the United States.

PRIVATE LABEL INDUSTRY STATISTICS

It is nearly impossible to determine the dollar volume of the private labels. It is a problem of semantics: Not everyone thinks or speaks in terms of private label.

In the supermarket business, for example, huge volumes of sales are generated in perishable meats, produce, dairy, deli, and bakery departments; yet a retailer does not always count these product categories under private label. Some packaging is less critical in these areas; the label identity is not that important because national brands are not always a competitive factor. A private label reference point does go on grocery, health and beauty aids, household cleaning supplies, and general merchandise, where packaging and identity are critical up against national brand competition.

In the drug store business, generic prescription drugs are not considered private label, primarily because of the packaging aspect. A prescription usually is filled in a nondescript container, often a hand-written label. Yet, these products are private label, prepared and controlled by the pharmacist.

In the mass merchandising market, many soft and hard goods are imported with no more than a generic label—"made in Taiwan", for example. This merchandise is not recognized as private label, yet the sourcing and control of quality standards follow the private label buying pattern, falling under the control of the retail buyer.

In the foodservice business, fast food and family restaurants often package products under their own labels—hamburgers, chicken, french fries. Also, foodservice distributors, serving the commercial and institutional markets, often group products (from outside sources) under their controlled labels in institutional packs.

In gasoline service stations, dealers sell gasoline, tires, batteries, oil, grease, and auto accessories under the retailer's name. These products may be advertised nationally as brands. Exxon, for example, sells some 140 product items under its Exxon and Atlas trademarks through some 22,000 stations in the United States. While Atlas tires, batteries, and auto accessories are sold in some competitive service stations and Exxon motor oil and automatic transmission fluid are sold also in mass merchandise stores, the major portion of its station products are exclusively private label. Exxon also does contract packing in some products, selling to retailers for their private labels. Through Exxon Chemical, the company is also a supplier of plastic bags and wraps to retailers wishing to sell that type of product under private label. In fact, Exxon Chemical claims to be the first generic bag producer in the United States and the first private label bag supplier of the new gas phase resin.

In the lumber, building materials, and hardware market segment, many products are packaged under a retailer's brand name, sometimes sold generically without a package identity—all of it private label. Rickel, a division of Supermarkets General Corp., Woodbridge, New Jersey, has store brand representation in its "core departments": lumber, paint, hardware, electrical, and plumbing.

Specialty stores sometimes are exclusively private label. Thom McAn, through some 1260 stores, sells its brand of footwear only. Three years ago, Sherwin Williams stores (1400 total) began stocking Sherwin Williams label paints and supplies exclusively. The company continues to carry private label paints for retailers under their brands as well as selling Martin Senour paints as a brand and other brands; but Sherwin Williams labeled items are restricted to the firm's retail outlets only. The same holds true at its 70 automotive service centers for Sherwin Williams refinishing products.

Any time a retailer's brand name appears on products, they can be called private label. This does not necessarily mean that those products must be sold only in the retailer's stores. Private label is too strong today for such a restrictive definition. In effect, private label not only copies national brands but also becomes a brand itself, but from a different source—the retailer, wholesaler, or distributor—and not exclusively the manufacturer, as in national brands.

According to Standards & Poor, the U.S. retail market amounted to $942.4 billion in 1980. Even the most conservative estimate of private label volume, say, 15%, would amount to $140 billion. Penetration in each market segment varies; there are no hard data isolating private label sales. Most analyses do not consider private label at all. Government reporting sources do not track it. It is not indexed in libraries. There is no dictionary definition. Books rarely mention the subject; indeed, this book may very well be the only private label book in existence. Companies barely mention it in their annual reports and rarely break out private label sales. Industry trade shows previously have paid little, if any, attention to private label, selling it mostly under the table or out of sight. At best, there have been only educated guesses and fragmented studies projecting private label penetration and growth. A 15% private label penetration is perhaps grossly understated, especially when weighed against developments in recent years.

In 1969, SAMI (Selling Areas-Marketing, Inc., New York) began biannual reports of national projected share trends of private label brands in food stores, during a recession economy. Private label's market share nationally was put at 13.65% for the year ending December 24, 1971. In 10 years, private label's market share has crept forward by only 0.84% to a current share of 14.19% for the year ending December 11, 1981, according to SAMI. Not too impressive. But when SAMI adds in the 1981 generic market share of 1.77%, bringing total private label market share to 16.26% for the current year, the penetration is significant. (Generics, of course, have only been around in food stores since 1977.)

SAMI breaks down its private label data by product departments, showing a slight drop off in dry groceries (food and nonfood) during the decade 1971s (12.78%) to 1981s (12.27%), while frozen/refrigerated climbs from 21.78% to 25.77%, and health and beauty aids advance from 2.05% to 3.16% market share. When generics are added to these departments, dry groceries in 1981 picks up to 14.34% total private label market share, while frozen/refrigerated increases to a 26.80% share, and health and beauty aids advance to 3.69% share. (See Appendix for detailed current charts on private label and generic market share data provided by SAMI.)

In summary, private label with the help of generics has advanced its market share by 2.61% from 1971 to 1981, nibbling away at the market share of national brands in food stores. This activity is underscored by a recent generics report (October 1981) where SAMI traced total private label market share (including generics) for the 12-week period ending May 1, 1981, versus the comparable period a year earlier (May 2, 1980). On a national projected basis for 444 product categories, covering dry groceries, frozen and refrigerated foods, and health and beauty aids, SAMI showed private label and generics gaining at the expense of national brands (Table 1).

This 12-week comparison, taken from SAMI food operators who handle generics (where reported), shows generics biting hard into national brand market share. The overall private label share (including generics) has gained at the expense of national brands.

Table 1

Category	Year ago $ share	Current $ share	Year ago unit share	Current unit share
Regular Private Label	15.8%	16.8%	19.0%	19.7%
Generics	1.0%	1.8%	1.5%	2.7%
Total Private Label	16.7%	18.6%	20.5%	22.4%
vs.				
All Other Brands	83.3%	81.4%	79.5%	77.6%

SAMI (1981) projected these data out on a volume basis (Table 2).

On a projected basis, private labels down the line gain at the expense of other brands—the total category gaining 24.3% in dollar volume versus 34.5% gain for national brands, while total private label unit volume increases 10.2% versus a 1.4% decline in brands. Percentage-wise, generics alone gain 108.5% in dollars and 81.6% in units. The trend is obvious: generics are rattling the food industry and eroding national brand market share, while pushing the total private label category upward.

Manufacturers of national brands have attacked the so-called bargain brands (private labels, specifically) and the no-name brands (generics) in their TV ads; they have introduced more invoice and advertising allowances to make their brands more attractive to retailers (and ultimately, the consumer); they have stepped up trade dress fights seeking to protect their national brand labels from design infringements; they have introduced unadvertised brands to fight back at generics on the same ground, that of low price; and they have moved steadily into production of private label and generic products. Most of the major manufacturers, with few exceptions, are now involved in producing private labels. One of the strongest opponents and, in fact, the largest national brand advertiser in the country, Procter & Gamble, recently acquired a private label firm, Ben Hill Griffin, Inc., Frostproof, Florida (frozen and canned juices). Campbell Soup also purchased a private label firm, Snow King Frozen Foods, Inc., Pottstown, Pennsylvania (uncooked frozen specialty meat products).

Table 2

Category	Year ago $ volume	Current $ volume	Year ago unit volume	Current unit volume
Regular Private Label	2,771,233	3,299,897	3,933,213	4,118,586
Generics	171,159	356,805	304,874	553,692
Total Private Label	2,942,392	3,656,702	4,238,087	4,672,078
vs.				
All Other Brands	14,637,807	19,682,008	16,419,693	16,183,901

Tetley Tea has taken control of Tenco, Kinden, New Jersey, a major supplier of private label and generic tea, coffee, and flavored drinks.

Business Week (1981) reported that, overall, generics now take 5% of the grocery market and could climb to a 25% market share in the 1980s. Estimates of the total retail food store sales volume in 1980 are $211.9 billion. If total private label market share exceeds 20%, then private label sales account for more than $42 billion in that market segment.

It is estimated that general merchandise stores account for $116.2 billion in 1980. Private label share of that market exceeds 30%, which gives a total private label volume of $35 billion-plus.

In a third retail market segment, drug and proprietary stores, where private label also is readily identified, its market share very likely approaches 10%. Estimates of this market are put at close to $30 billion, giving private label $3 billion in sales. When generic prescription drugs are added—estimated at $2 billion-plus in volume—the private label share climbs to $5 billion.

In other retail market segments—apparel, automotive, gasoline service stations, lumber building materials, hardware, furniture and appliances, foodservice, liquor, and durable and nondurable goods—there is sketchy information about private label penetration. Private label is not always an acceptable category definition in these markets.

Instead of gazing at the universe, it is more informative to blink at its stars.

Sears, Roebuck & Co., Chicago, carries nearly 99% of its sales in private label. As the country's leading merchandiser, at $16.9 billion, nearly every dollar derives from private label. In its 1981 fall catalog, Sears offered some 105,000 items, including all color and size options.

Safeway Stores, Inc., Oakland, California, the country's leading supermarket chain, lists more than 5000 private label items. Of its $15 billion in sales, private label captures nearly 30%, or $4.5 billion.

The Kroger Co., Cincinnati, second largest supermarket chain, carries more than 4000 private label items. Of its $9.6 billion sales volume, approximately 25% or $2.4 billion is generated in private label.

K mart, Troy, Michigan, the country's second largest mass merchandiser in the discount store segment, generates sales in excess of $13.6 billion. More than 1600 private label items account for an estimated $4.1 billion or 30% of those sales.

J. C. Penney Company, Inc., New York, with recent sales of $11.4 billion, has an estimated 60%-plus of its volume or nearly $7 billion in private label sales.

Montgomery Ward & Co., Inc., Chicago, reported sales of $5.5 billion, of which an estimated 80%-plus or roughly $4.5 billion was in private label sales.

Revco D.S., Inc., Twinsburg, Ohio, the leading drug chain, produced sales in excess of $1 billion, 7% or $70 million coming from private label merchandise. Another large drug chain, Rite Aid Corp., Shiremanstown, Pennsylvania, grossing $944 million, reports some 11% or $103.8 million in private label.

The leaders in each market segment all are committed to private label. Volumes in private label filter down to multimillion levels in each retail or wholesale business. Private label usually captures from 5 to 30% or more of total sales, depending on the market segment. For example, A&P with a $6.9 billion volume in fiscal 1981 has an estimated 25% or $1.7 billion in private label, roughly 3000 private label items. T. Eaton in Canada has 25% or $250 million of its total $1 billion volume in private label, about 5000 items. A number of chains in the supermarket segment carry 2000-plus private label items, including Pathmark (Supermarkets General), Grand Union, and IGA.

THE PRODUCT CYCLE

In the private label business, suppliers of raw product—paper, overwraps, cans, ingredients, flavors, type/printing, and so on—provide private label manufacturers with the material to produce products. The private label manufacturer may be in business exclusively in private label, or he may be a retailer who manufactures products. He also may be a national or regional brand manufacturer who uses idle production time either for contract packing or to compensate for a fall-off in business (a secondary brand losing market share, for example) by filling in with private label work. In so doing, the manufacturer can be more productive with his facilities and also avoid possible loss of talented workers, who when laid off during slack periods might seek full-time work elsewhere. Private label contract work also allows the manufacturer the opportunity to develop new business by getting his foot in the door.

The private label business encompasses a complex situation. For example, a national brand manufacturer can contract for private label work. Sometimes he may contract out his own brand to a private label manufacturer who makes the product to the national brand specifications. The secret ingredients or formula of the national brand manufacturer often is chemically analyzed and duplicated for private label use.

National brand competitors copy an innovative new brand product as much or more than do private label manufacturers.

Sometimes a manufacturer will offer a so-called controlled brand or a packer label for testing consumer acceptance of a product. If the retailer finds that item to be a good seller, he may pick it up under his private label, dropping the packer label eventually.

Often a broker will work as liaison between manufacturer (the principal) and retailer/wholesaler (the customer). The broker, for example, can be especially helpful in organizing a private label program. A veteran broker, who specializes in private label and generics, explains:

> Today's broker is no longer a coupon clipper, who just sells a product and sits back. The business has changed: it now requires full service from the broker: He must provide retail support for stocking items and production rotation. He must look closely at the quality of products. He must find suppliers who can ship on time and deliver products with the specifications agreed upon. The broker who specializes in private label must concentrate on getting that product near to the branded item in terms of quality and similarity in feel, smell, touch, and effectiveness. He must also insure that private label's pricing is set 20–30% below the national brand.

The broker also must keep informed of market developments and trends through field work and by following SAMI data closely. Sometimes a broker also will work creatively in developing new private label products or in breaking into a new product category for private label.

While there lately has been some innovative packaging in private label, it is rare that private label is innovative in products. One exception is low-sodium canned vegetables, where private label has pioneered in developing the category ahead of national brands. Another "first" for private label is time-release vitamins. Retailers/wholesalers or private label manufacturers budgets for research and development, however, usually fall far short of the national brand manufacturers.

Some retailer/wholesalers prefer to deal direct with manufacturers. They believe the broker automatically picks up his fee with a minimum amount of work. But the private label broker who specializes in that category usually lets his presence be felt in serving two masters, the principal and the customer.

In some cases, the retailer may not only do his own private label manufacturing but also own equity in different manufacturing operations. Sears, for example, maintains some 11,300 U.S. suppliers, many of them long-time relationships. Some 28% of the merchandise purchases in dollar amounts comes from sources in which Sears holds an equity investment.

Private labels require hard work and a long-term commitment by the owner of those labels. His buyers do not merely buy, stock, and sell products under those labels. They must work to develop a sound program: research the market need, establish quality standards, locate the right supplier, negotiate for pricing, insure support (deals, on-time deliveries, etc.) create packaging and label design, adopt merchandising techniques, set safeguards for consistent quality, plan advertising and promotional campaigns, and continually update different product lines while weeding out poor sellers.

These store-spun products become the owner's responsibility, because he often puts his own store's name on the label. The consumer who complains about a national brand will automatically blame the national brand manufacturer first. But when that reject product is under private label, the retailer shoulders all the blame. An emotional consumer might generalize, saying that all the products under that label are not worth buying. In many cases, the one bad item can affect the image of all the products under that family of labels. So the key to success in many private label programs is the ability of the retailer to establish value—a price–quality relationship with the consumer, backed by a money-back guarantee, if not completely satisfied. When customers feel they are getting their money's worth, they become captive customers to private label and loyal to the retailer carrying that label.

Years ago, Woolworth's outlined its feelings about the importance of private label in a pamphlet for its buyers. Some of its comments are worth repeating, because they still epitomize the attitude of most dedicated private label merchandisers:

> Producing private label merchandise generates tremendous buying power . . . . We can order for over 2000 stores, gaining extra advantages in terms of cost.
>
> Manufacturers like to work for a company producing its own brands, because they know that we can guarantee a certain number of sales.
>
> Because our own brands are made and packaged to our specifications, every item is of known quality goods from reliable suppliers . . . and there are fewer return problems than on other merchandise.
>
> Our private brands have earned Woolworth the respect and loyalty of many customers . . . as expressed in continuous repeat sales.

Woolworth's in the same pamphlet also explained how its private brands could be offered as top quality merchandise at less cost than the brand names:

> In developing our own brands, we are able to cut production and promotion costs by working directly with the manufacturer . . . by mass production of large quantities, purchased at lower cost to us . . . doing our own warehousing and distributing. . . by handling our own national advertising, designing, packaging, and labeling . . . .This makes it possible for us to sell our brands at competitive retail prices and still make a higher mark-up on merchandise which is, in every respect, equal or better value than competitive items.

TO GO OR NOT TO GO INTO PRIVATE LABEL

The larger, well-established chains, which have built manufacturing capability into their business, find private label an attractive hedge, a good profit- and image-builder, and a guaranteed source of supply. Other non-manufacturing chains, also well-established, have built a strong buying activity around private label for much the same reasons. The smaller chains, while they also may be attracted to private labels for their profitability, do not always have the wherewithal to build a strong buying program. They tend to cater to their customer needs, staying more with national brands. These retailers get wide selection and consistently high quality merchandise from national brands. The result is fast turnover with little capital investment involved. Also, these retailers are wooed by national brand manufacturers with irresistable deals—$2.50 off a case of food product purchased in national brand versus only 50 cents off a deal on private label. Yet, smaller retailers are becoming more aware of the benefits of private label, especially as private labels come into their own in the marketplace. Consumers often trade down from the national brands during difficult economic times. Smaller retailers find a lower-priced private label line can serve as a draw for more customer traffic.

When a retailer adopts private labels, his name goes out to the customer as a form of advertising; that image on every package is carried into the consumer's home. Private labels give the retailer flexibility and full control in pricing and promotions. He can offer a product category in private label that may not be available in national brand. Private label offers him higher profit margins on many items (up to 60%-plus margin on some product categories) versus much tighter margins in national brands. When the retailer buys national brands, he can be cost-effective by also ordering private label, producing a larger quantity purchased for greater savings.

Perhaps one of the best reasons for adopting private labels is the growth and spread of this type of product. Consumers are more aware of private labels today, and manufacturers are capitalizing on consumer interest by introducing private label into more product categories.

There are product categories in private label that dominate a retailer's shelves. In frozen vegetables and frozen orange juice concentrate, private label facings extend down the aisle. A retailer's vitamin selection often will feature mostly private label in the alphabet and time-release vitamins. Paint is another strong private label category. Other strong private label categories include women's hosiery, paper products (towels, tissue, etc.), soft drinks, snack foods, plastic bags and wraps, dog food, and canned vegetables and fruits.

In past consumer studies, both the consumers and the researchers have been confused about what products actually are private label rather than a brand owned by a manufacturer. Market share information usually comes from the private label manufacturers or retailers who consult SAMI data in the grocery business. Whatever the category, private label share is steadily climbing. For example, a major manufacturer of private label first-aid products notes that private label market share has climbed from about 5% to nearly 9% of total market sales from 1969 to 1979.

In recent years, the trend has been toward introduction of more private label health and beauty aids and general merchandise, plus new household chemical items. Frost & Sullivan, Inc., New York, a market research firm, estimated that the private label health and beauty aids market could more than double in factory sales from 1977 to 1987. F&S also surveyed retail buyers who predicted a fivefold increase in private label sales in this category.

Personal products such as feminine napkins, adult diapers, and douches are now being sold under private label. Pizza, which has captured the American palate in recent years, also has risen to star status in private label—not only plain, but also cheese, hamburger, pepperoni, sausage, and combinations.

Traditionally, there have been some product categories where national brand preference is impregnable. Items like cold cereal, baby food, coffee, cigarettes, beer, liquor, and cosmetics have represented tough categories for private label penetration. In some cases, however, generics have pierced the barrier successfully. Cigarettes, beer, and liquors are cases in point. In some areas, consumers regard generics as the "in" product, not as something "cheap," but a "fun" item. Hollywood stars, for example, sometimes stock their bars with generic liquor and wines. In Denver, generics are regarded as more than a fad; they are a way of life.

Brand consciousness is difficult to crack in soft goods, especially fashion items. Retailers often opt for brand lines, then follow up with private label selections, based on the same quality, workmanship, and styling as the brands. Mass merchandisers will use their own store name for basic goods, like underwear and hosiery, and a unique private label name for fashion goods.

In the clothing category, private label has now begun to make inroads. *Vogue Magazine* (June 1981) reported in its "Newest Shopping Options" about private labels offering "more choices, more fashion at stores across the country. Often, at very good prices."

Vogue noted that private labels offer the retailer an opportunity to project its store image, while customers are offered reasonably priced unique merchandise, according to the article. Previously, private label items developed from proven best sellers. Customer reception has been so good that stores are now expanding their private label lines for a more complete fashion "look," *Vogue* stated, adding that there are recently introduced lines at Neiman-Marcus (N-M Club separates and western-styled Red River sportswear) and at Lord & Taylor (Claire McCardell's 'American Look'). Efforts also are underway at Bergdorf Goodman to expand its Jo Collection, at I. Magnin to concentrate more on Today's Agenda career wear, and at Saks to continue its full line of store labels.

The article also quotes Ellin Saltzman, vice-president and corporate fashion director of Saks Fifth Avenue: "Private labels guarantee a signature look to a store. They allow us to offer our customer something special."

We leave it to *Vogue* to spot a fashion trend.

The T. Eaton Company Limited in Toronto recently reinforced that store's signature by putting its store name, Eaton, on all its own marketing names: Vanity Fair pantyhose became Eaton Vanity Fair, Raphael shoes became Eaton Raphael, and so on.

At G. C. Murphy Co., McKeesport, Pennsylvania, a manager in charge of private label gave a breakdown of its top private label category sellers (Table 3).

Table 3

$ Ranking	Product category	Private label share (%)
1	Men's wear	40
2	Hosiery	65
3	Infant's wear	32
4	Notions	36
5	Paint	60
6	Boy's wear	49
7	Seasonal goods	14
8	Intimate apparel	19
9	Health & beauty aids*	5.4
10	Housewear	18

* Prior to the introduction of 15 new private label health and beauty aids products. Also, the chain was developing a new private label category in household chemicals.

Private labels can no longer be stereotyped as second class, bargain brands. There is change and excitement in today's retail environment. Merchants are becoming more aggressive, more creative in the handling of their own brands. It is not a cataclysmic change, but more of an evolution where parts of the past are recaptured and adapted to today's market. It is helpful to study the history of these labels in order to understand how they are successful today.

REFERENCES

Batten, W. M. 1967. The Penney Idea: Foundation for the Continuing Growth of the J. C. Penney Company. The Newcomen Society in North America, New York, pp. 13–14, 16.

Business Week. 1981. No Frills Food, New Power for the Supermarkets. March 23, p. 80.

SAMI. 1981. Private Label Trends. Selling Areas-Marketing Inc., New York.

Weir, J. (editor). 1981. Newest Shopping Options. *Vogue*, June, p. 136.

Woolworth's. The Growing Importance of Woolworth's Private Brands (8-page brochure). New York.

2

History of Private Labels

THE PIONEERS

Throughout its history, private label has been mislabeled or misrepresented as being cheap in quality. Most private label products suffer this stigma because they are priced lower than the competition. Bargain pricing is part of their identity. The idea of private label frequently is born out of a competitive reaction to high-priced merchandise. Customers assume or are told by the competition that something priced lower represents lower quality. This is far from the truth.

In the nineteenth century, merchants dealing in the mail order and/or retail–wholesale business recognized the need for lower-priced merchandise, but of a high quality. They cut the cost of goods by eliminating the middleman—an importer, jobber, or distributor, for example—ordering directly from a manufacturer or manufacturing products themselves. Other cost efficiencies were introduced, such as buying for cash (for better terms), buying in greater quantities, buying at the right time (for plentiful supplies), and buying with expertise in domestic and international trade conditions. "Satisfaction guaranteed or your money refunded" became the slogan backing private label quality.

Market conditions at the time were not favorable for the consumer. The merchant's responsibilities often ended at the time of a sale. *Caveat emptor* was the watchword for customers. Peddlers of different wares often charged high markups on everything they sold, sometimes exorbitant prices such as a 600% price hike for pepper, blaming it on a cut-off of import supplies or some other excuse. The customer had no way of checking the story. (Scull 1967, p. 31).

It was the beginning of specialization, where the merchant, once a Jack-of-all-trades—jobber, wholesaler, retailer, commission agent, distributor, trader, broker, and importer—was concentrating on one or two areas (Scull 1967, p. 72). For example, the merchant might operate a retail store and/or mail order house.

First Private Label?

One of the oldest private labels is perhaps that developed by Henry Sands Brooks, who opened his first shop under his own name in 1818 in New York City. In advertisements later, he claimed to be the first clothier to sell ready-made garments. Over the years, his shop came to be called Brooks Brothers, carrying a label that became synonymous with the conservative, well-dressed gentleman of the day. Brooks' operating credo was "To make and deal only in merchandise of the best quality, to sell it at a fair profit only and to deal only with people who seek and are capable of appreciating such merchandise" (Mahoney and Sloane 1974, p. 39).

Brooks Brothers adopted a Golden Fleece trademark, a sheep suspended in a ribbon, taken from the symbol of British woolen merchants dating back to the fifteenth century. Many fashion trends were established with that private label. In fact, Brooks Brothers set the pace in men's fashions, borrowing ideas from the Continent: silk Foulard ties, buttondown ("polo collar") shirts, Shetland sweaters, polo coats, and Harris tweed jackets.

Some of its fashion innovations in this century include:

lightweight summer suits with seersucker and cotton cords
solid pink shirts
Dacron/cotton blended shirts
Argyll panel support hose
Brooksflannel lightweight sports shirts.

> Its Famous No. 1 Sack Suit, three-buttoned and single-breasted with natural shoulders and straight hang, has been for about five decades the "uniform" that stamps a man as being correctly dressed.
>
> Brooks was also the first in modern times to sponsor linen crush, Shantung silk cotton cord and other cooler summer suits for men, jackets with odd trousers, and many styles in boys' clothing. It has introduced such items as the Norfolk jacket, the Tattersall vest and the deerstalker cap, and was in great measure responsible for the once overwhelming vogue of the box-cloth spat. More recently it launched a new man-made material and was the first in the world to offer shirts made of Dacron-and-

cotton Oxford cloth, called Brooksweave, and Dacron-and-cotton broadcloth, copyrighted as Brookscloth (Mahoney and Sloane 1974, pp. 36–37).

Today, Brooks Brothers, a chain of more than 20 stores, operates its own clothing and neckwear and shirt plants, which supply most of the merchandise in its outlets. The products are made to strict specifications before they are labeled "own-made."

Some old-time private labels have not endured or at least have diminished in importance. Burried with them are some interesting facts.

For example, it is very likely that one of the earliest private label customers was Abraham Lincoln. Early in his career, while in the village of New Salem, Illinois, Lincoln was a partner in a grocery store that failed, placing him in debt. Then he took up law, becoming an attorney in 1836. Soon afterward, he moved to nearby Springfield, Illinois.

One of his first clients was Jacob Bunn, who had opened his first grocery store, J. W. Bunn & Co., in Springfield in 1840. This operation specialized in retail and wholesale trade, selling many bulk items out of barrels, sacks, casks, kegs, and so on. Patrons could purchase all types of merchandise: sugar, coffee, soaps, rifle powder, nails, brandy, tobacco, paint, etc. Bunn called on Lincoln, a former grocer, to represent the business as its first attorney.

Their friendship grew to a point where later Lincoln called on Bunn to be his campaign manager. In a way, Bunn reciprocated by naming some of his coffee products after his friends: Lincoln coffee and Mary Todd coffee. Bunn also carried other private brand coffees, including Wishbone, Recipe, Golden Age, Cap, Old Timer, and Bunny (after himself). Of all those names, only two, Bunny and Golden Age, have survived as private labels. All the others have disappeared, except for Wishbone, which was sold to Manhattan Coffee Co. and the trademark eventually taken over by Lipton Tea, which now markets Wishbone dressing as a national brand.

J. W. Bunn & Co. evolved into a wholesale grocer first and then in the 1950s moved more into institutional business with its Golden Age, Bunny and other labels. Subsequently, the business converted 100% to food-service distribution as Capitol-Bunn Co. In 1982, the firm assigned its private labels to a major buying-merchandising co-op, F.A.B., Inc. Norcross, Georgia.

Early Pricing Strategies

Early in the nineteenth century, A. T. Stewart began selling Irish laces in New York City. Out of that business, he established a wholesale and retail dry-goods operation, which by 1862 became the six-story Stewart's Cast Iron Palace—considered by some to be the largest department store in the United States, if not the world. Stewart is credited with revolutionizing the practice of pricing, by establishing a one-price policy and putting a price tag on all his goods. As Scull (1967, pp. 79–80) explains:

> For all practical purposes there was no systematic method of pricing when Stewart opened his business; prices were established by the primitive method of prolonged haggling. Manufacturers and importers bargained for the highest amounts they could get from wholesalers and jobbers. Wholesalers and jobbers put the squeeze on retailers for the last possible dime, and retailers in turn charged their customers as much as they felt the traffic would bear. A prosperous customer was quoted one price—subject, of course, to considerable negotiation—while a less affluent customer was quoted a lower price, also subject to adjustment if the customer had the time and stamina to negotiate. Price lists, if they existed at all, were mere scraps of paper. Customers who were interested in saving money made it a point to wear old coats with frayed sleeves and dilapidated hats when they went shopping.

Another dry-goods merchant in New York City, Rowland Hussey Macy, adopted a one-price policy and also introduced a cash-only policy. Merchants previously had allowed customers the option to buy on easy credit terms. Macy believed that he could cut his profit margin with cash trading and thus sell his goods more cheaply (Scull 1967, pp. 81–82).

In 1858, R. H. Macy & Company started in New York as a fancy dry-goods store. Two years later, the store placed what probably represents its first private label advertisement: Macy's hoopskirts. About this same time, Macy debuted its general trademark, a five-pointed red star. The retailer's basic strategy was low prices (20–50% below the competition) along with heavy advertising, offering customers quality merchandise. To achieve that end, Macy began manufacturing clothing from day one—dresses, shirts, linen handkerchiefs, velvet wraps, linen collars, etc. He also contracted with outside suppliers for some of his private label merchandise, such as Red Star silk or velveteen, and La Forge kid gloves (Hower 1943, p. 164).

By the early 1870s, Macy's operation grossed in excess of $1 million; at the turn of the century, that volume pushed past $10 million. Meanwhile, Macy was diversifying his product line and in the process manufacturing more of his goods with brand names that indicated Macy's production (Ferry 1960, pp. 59–60).

Around the 1890s, Macy's private brands included clothing under the Macy's label and various household preparations under the Red Star label—perfumes, extracts, toilet preparations, tonics and remedies, ammonia, benzine, turpentine, etc. The Red Star logo also appeared on items such as wrapping paper, stationery, tea and coffee, kitchen laundry soap, etc. A sampling of private labels about this time shows these items: Our Own Soap, Star sewing machines, Red Star tea, Straus cut glass, Lily White canned goods, Webster collars, La Forge or Valentine watches, etc. (Hower 1943, pp. 250–251).

In the following century, Macy's private label selection eventually grew to some 4500 different articles sold under the various Macy brands (Hower 1943, p. 402).

A strategy quite different, yet similar, was adopted by Lord & Taylor, founded in 1826 by Samuel Lord. Late in that century, Lord catered exclusively to the "carriage trade" in New York City, with his Lord & Taylor label representing the finest quality. Lower-priced competitors did not change Lord's pricing position.

Private labels started off with a brand identity, pretty much on the same footing as so-called national brands. As entrepreneurs and companies developed products with different names, protected by trademarks, under a national brand franchise, so did some merchants as they developed their own private label lines. A merchant who put his own name on a product obviously had pride in that item.

In 1861, John Wanamaker opened a small men's and boys' clothing store in Philadelphia, selling ready-to-wear clothing at a low price. Over the next decade, as business prospered, Wanamaker was able to begin making demands on manufacturers. Before that, he had to settle for a "seedy quality," which carried no label at all. Wanamaker's buying power was weak; but with larger orders, he began to set his own terms and standards of quality, putting his label on every garment. With that label, he placed the warranty that "the quality of goods is as represented on the printed labels" and "the full amount of cash paid will be refunded, if customers find the articles unsatisfactory, and return them unworn and unimpaired within ten days" (Scull 1967, p. 84).

Society in North America during the nineteenth century was mostly rural. The department store catered to the growing cities, but most trading occurred in the farmlands. Rural regions became the market for mail-order houses, which were started, for example, by A&P, Sears, and Montgomery Ward in the United States and by T. Eaton Co., Ltd., in Canada. Timothy Eaton actually began as a retailer in Toronto in 1883, distributing his first mail-order catalog in 1884, featuring private label merchandise. Eaton established a cash only, no extended credit policy. In that position, he had to offer customers something different to entice them to pay cash, when they could buy on credit elsewhere. Private label merchandise, priced under the national brands but of the same quality, became an important part of this merchandising mix.

Brands Take Root

Inventions and innovations introduced during this time formed the basis for modern retailing techniques. The branded products that first appeared opened new product categories for all retailers.

There was very little brand identity in the late eighteenth and early nineteenth centuries. During the U.S. Civil War (1861–1865), branded soap, cleaning powder, and patent medicine became popular. Soldiers were supplied with Procter & Gamble's Star Candles as well as Procter & Gamble soap. P&G, which was founded about 1837, was really launched as a national brand company when Harley Procter dreamed up an ad slogan for Ivory Soap about 1876: "It floats."

The Colgate-Palmolive Company, New York, which had started into business as a producer of soap, starch, and candles in 1806, got its break in 1877 with the debut of Colgate toothpaste.

Packaged soap powder first appeared in 1845, when Benjamin Talbert Babbitt introduced soap shavings in one- and two-pound pokes. Twenty years later, Babbitt started to package soap individually.

Many different brands catered to gastronomic disorders—pills or powders, for example. Coca-Cola was introduced in 1886 as an exotic medicinal product in the patent medicine field.

In 1847, Smith Brothers Cough Drops appeared at James Smith's restaurant in Poughkeepsie, New York. Smith offered his patrons cough drops to relieve their colds, while his sons, William and Andrew, peddled the product outside. That soon attracted what might be called one of the first "knock-off" products in modern history. Imitators used similar names to confuse the customer. One competitor used the same name, Smith Brothers; another adopted the name Smith & Bros.; and someone introduced Smythe Sisters. As a result, the Smith brothers designed a trademark of themselves with the words "Trade" under William's picture and "Mark" under Andrew's picture. To protect against drugstores putting imitators' brands in glass jars on counter spaces, calling the product Smith Brothers, the brothers in 1872 packaged their product in paper boxes, which perhaps was the first "factory-filled" package introduced by a company. These efforts made the Smith brothers among the first manufacturers to recognize the value of a brand name and modern packaging (Scull 1967, pp. 42–43).

In the late nineteenth century, more branded food products started to appear including Salada Tea, Pillsbury Best Flour, Gold Medal Flour, Ralston Purina animal feed, Kellogg Corn Flakes, Post Grape Nuts Flakes, and Maxwell House Coffee. In 1870, Charles E. Hires developed Hires root beer, which came to national attention at the 1876 Philadelphia Centennial. Hires reportedly became the first soft drink to achieve national popularity through aggressive advertising and promotions.

Young America was catching up with England's industrial revolution. The social and economic structure of society was changing as technology advanced right into this century.

William Underwood of Boston started this country's first food canning operation in 1819.

Jacob Perkins invented modern refrigeration in 1834.

James J. Ritty developed the cash register in 1879.

A patent on the first paper bag and paper bag-making machine was awarded to Luther Childs Crowell in 1867.

Clarence Birdseye developed the basic multi-place quick-freezing process in the 1920s; a new company, General Foods, took over by marketing frozen products in grocery stores under the Birds-Eye label in the 1930s.

Farrington Manufacturing Co., Needham Heights, Massachusetts, introduced "Charga-Plate," a system of credit buying in the late 1920s, first tested in William Filene's department store in Boston.

Wallace H. Carothers of duPont engineered the first nylon stockings about 1940.

Rural America was turning toward the cities; the coming of the railroads and then the invention of the automobile and the airplane changed everyone's life-style. The impact of advertising, evolving from newspapers to magazines to radio to television, molded consumer buying habits. This impact began with the pioneering efforts of N. W. Ayer & Son of Philadelphia, an advertising agency, on behalf of such early clients as Hires root beer, Procter & Gamble soaps, Burpee seeds, and Montgomery Ward. National Biscuit Co. literally took crackers out of the cracker barrel and packaged them in boxes. Ayer's print campaign for National Biscuit Co. in 1899 turned its Uneeda biscuits into a household name.

Early in the twentieth century, the Cream of Wheat Co. began to illustrate its product box fronts, which served as effective point-of-purchase advertising.

Some brands actually debuted as private labels. A beverage chemist, Robert S. Lazenby, introduced Dr Pepper at his Old Corner Drug Store in Waco, Texas, in 1885. The same beginning can be traced with another popular national brand soft drink.

When pharmacist Caleb D. Bradham concocted a pleasing cola drink to relieve dyspepsia (stomach upset) and peptic ulcer, patrons at his drug store in New Bern, North Carolina, dubbed it "Brad's Drink" in 1898. For a short time afterward, it carried that private label until Bradham renamed it Pepsi-Cola and began distribution outside his drug store.

Claude A. Hatcher, owner of Hatcher Grocery Co., Columbus, Georgia, first developed a wholesale grocery trade in 1901. As business grew and spread, Hatcher wanted his local bottler, who supplied bottled drinks, to pay something to Hatcher for handling the products. In 1905, an argument erupted, causing Hatcher to pull away from the bottler and begin producing and bottling drinks under his company's own labels. The first private label for a soda water was called Royal Crown and the first cola drink Chero-cola. In 1959, this operation came to be called Royal Crown Cola Co., taking its name from the company's first private label.

Interestingly, the Rexall name followed an opposite course: private label to national brand. Louis K. Liggett introduced that name through a series of newspaper ads, starting with the letter "R," then "RE," then "REX," and so on. Liggett with that introduction opened his drug store in 1902, selling cod liver extract preparation under the name Vinol, as well as other products. The following year, he organized 40 druggists into sharing the costs of a limited franchise plan, whereby the top drug outlet in each area could receive the full benefits from the co-op advertising money. Each drug dealer, as a shareholder, shared in the profits, both as a manufacturer and as a retailer. From that beginning, Liggett formed the United Drug Co. in Boston where Rexall products were introduced. He began with packaged medicines and a few toiletries, manufacturing the Rexall line from the best materials available, every item sold on a money-back guarantee.

As Liggett's cooperative company idea spread, more members were added and the Rexall product line grew: stationery in 1911, rubber goods in 1912, brushes in 1913, pharmaceuticals in 1914. A Puretest line as well as hospital goods were introduced in 1919. By 1920, Rexall stores were full-fledged drugstores.

The product diversification at Rexall covered some interesting areas: Pearl Tooth Powder, Puretest Skunk Oil, Elkay's Wire-cut Liniment for horses and cattle, and Rexall Itch Ointment for Scabies.

Over the years, Liggett developed many different sales promotions, the first big one centered on Saturday Candy, which was advertised all week but sold only on Saturday. The cost to produce the candy was 40–45 cents a box, and it was sold at retail for 22 cents—a loss leader, but a powerful traffic builder.

Rexall's famous one-cent sales started about 1914, when Liggett, facing stiff competition, looked for a unique selling technique. In Detroit, he introduced a "2 for 1 Sale," offering two items of the same kind for the price of one. This idea—premature then, but effective today—fizzled until he changed his ads to read: "See what one cent will buy!" Customers were charged a penny more for a second item. That savings registered; police were called to control the crowds during one of these sales. Some 60 years later (1974), Rexall changed its one-cent sale to the Two-For Sale.

The Rexall operation eventually came to be called Rexall Drug Company; but when the company was sold to private investors, the new owners eliminated the store franchise program in order to expand distribution of Rexall products. So in 1977, Rexall shed its exclusive ties with Rexall franchise stores, going the route of a national brand.

Of course, many private labels could be called "national brands," even though they have followed a private course, that is, have been and continue to be sold exclusively by a store or group of stores. An outstanding example is A&P, which could be called the granddaddy of the private label business.

A&P's impact on this industry has been profound. Its experience did raise important questions. What percentage of private label should be included in the product mix with national brands? If A&P had been allowed to grow without opposition from national brands and the government, would the consumer be better off today with a dominant chain that undercut all its competitors, offering low-priced, high-quality private label products? Is a dominant chain dangerous to competition, being too powerful in the marketplace? These questions are now academic, because A&P was prevented from becoming the largest private label concern in the United States.

A&P's history started in 1863 as a mail-order house called The Great Atlantic Tea Company, based in New York. Soon afterward, the company diversified into retailing, developing The Great Atlantic & Pacific Tea Company. As news of its success spread, other grocery merchants adopted the "Tea" into their identities—The Grand Union Tea Co. (1872); the Great Western Tea Co. (1883), which was later changed to the Kroger Grocery and Baking Co.; Acme Tea Co. (1894); the Jewel Tea Co. (1899); and so on. These merchants began private label programs by selling their own tea and grinding coffee in their stores.

Even entrepreneur Frank Woolworth was influenced by A&P's success. He picked up the A&P red store front, adding a special golf-leaf gilding in the lettering and the molding. Woolworth also added his own "Diamond W" trademark on the outside of the stores, which in effect became his first private label. Merchandise inside was displayed in bulk without the benefit of labeling or packaging.

A&P's empire was built on a simple premise: low price, low profit margin, high turnover. When George Gilman and George Huntington Hartford ventured into the tea trade, they sold that commodity at wholesale prices or "marked at two cents per pound above costs." As expert importers and wholesalers, they were able to bypass the importer, who collected nearly 100% profit on teas. The partners first established four private brands: Cargo (72–78 cents a pound), High Cargo (80–85 cents per pound), Fine (87–90 cents per pound), and Finest (92–95 cents per pound). Hartford also developed the first economy brand of private label, called Thea Nectar. This was a black tea, made of a mixture of leftovers. At first, the product was not advertised as a tea, but as a tea product. "The product was cheap to make, profitable to sell, and it had the added advantage of using what was formerly wasted. It was an immediate success" (Hoyt 1969, p. 36).

As competitors copied this format in the mail order business, the partners launched the Great Atlantic and Pacific Tea Company to tap the retail trade. Tea again was their mainstay product, but soon other items were added, such as butter, sugar, and coffee. In 1882, as public taste for coffee grew, Hartford, then in full charge of the firm, gave coffee its brand name, Eight O'Clock Breakfast Coffee, packaged in a red bag, representing A&P. The business continued to grow to the point where A&P referred to itself as "the largest importer and retailer in the world," around the 1880s. At that time, the company started to manufacture its own baking powder and baking soda.

Opposition existed from day one. First the tea merchants were up in arms, and then local grocers cried "unfair competition" from the chains—from A&P and, to a lesser extent, from Grand Union. In 1900, A&P's sales climbed to $5.6 million.

"While another tea company might have figured a 50–100% markup on costs, the secret of the growing volume of A&P's sales was indeed the maintenance of low profit and high volume" (Hoyt 1969, p. 92).

The A&P slogan of the day was "Where economy rules." Its variety of goods was increasing: spices, soups, canned goods, soaps, and packaged products appeared on the shelves by 1904.

Because the housewife of the day was not considered price-conscious, A&P relied on premiums and trading stamps as traffic-builders. But times were changing.

John Hartford, son of George, tested what could be called the first no-frills box store. He opened a small store around the corner from a typical A&P. The test store opened without fanfare, using $1000 in cash for its opening stock of goods, $1000 cash for buying and emergencies, and the same amount for equipment. A manager-clerk ran the operation. "The cash-and-carry store made no deliveries and gave not one cent in credit. . . . It did not even have a name or a sign. It was just a store whose windows were loaded with groceries at cheap prices. And in six months, the little store around the corner from the big A&P put the larger store out of business" (Hoyt 1969, p. 102).

That success helped launch A&P Economy Stores, chopping away the frills of the premium stores. The company was opening stores at a rate of three a day or up to 1600 stores in two years.

Its policy of price cutting got A&P into trouble with the Cream of Wheat Co., when the latter insisted on setting its prices: Wholesalers were asked to charge $4.50 per case to retailers, who would charge its customers (the consumer) 12 cents a package. When the branded manufacturer cut off supplies, A&P continued to pick up product from jobbers at the wholesale price but found it was losing money by selling packages at 12 cents each. The retailer then sued the supplier under the Clayton Antitrust Act, charging restraint of trade and monopoly. But A&P lost the case; the result was that other brand manufacturers—Campbell Soup, Bon Ami, and others—established their own prices to be held at retail. (Hoyt 1969, p. 106–107).

Hartford's solution was to adopt a store brand in those essential products and push that private label. This offensive strategy moved A&P more into manufacturing bread and groceries. The Cream of Wheat case occurred about 1913; soon afterward, A&P established the Quaker Maid Company to can salmon and evaporated milk and to produce jams, preserves, cereals, and bread. Another subsidiary, the American Coffee Corp., was organized in 1919. Also, A&P added meat markets to its stores.

The idea of manufacturing products led many merchants into the private label business. Bernard H. Kroger began the Great Western Tea Co. in 1883, stocking goods but also packaging coffee and tea in the store's back room. Kroger also carried sauerkraut and pickles made by his mother. He is credited with being the first retailer to operate bakeries, selling a loaf of bread at 2 1/2 cents—a bargain with the quality guaranteed. He also was the first to introduce meat departments into his grocery stores in 1904.

Kroger incorporated his operation as the Kroger Grocery & Baking Co. in 1902. By then, he had begun expanding into other private label items, secured from outside suppliers. Some of the private brand names he adopted included variations on his name as well as the names of different parts of Cincinnati, where he based his operation. For example, "Avondale" became a brand named after a suburb and "Country Club" came from the Cincinnati Country Club. Eventually, Kroger's manufacturing effort helped to make his operation today the fifth largest retailing firm in the United States and the second largest supermarket chain, operating more than 25 processing facilities, out of which two-thirds of its more than 4000 private labels are produced.

There is an interesting case where a manufacturer was led into retailing, which ultimately resulted in a parting of the ways between its national brand and private label line.

Washburn Crosby Co., a grain miller, began operations in 1880 with the debut of its premium Gold Medal flour. The firm also became involved in a chain of provisional grocery stores early in this century. Its operation, St. Anthony and Dakota Elevator Company, charged with buying grain from farmers, also sold a few groceries, as well as lumber and "Red Owl" coal. Its first grocery food store, under the Red Owl name, opened in Rochester, Minnesota in 1922. That led to the development of a chain of stores, copying the success of eastern chain stores. Later in the 1920s, there were nearly 200 Red Owl food stores in business.

But in 1928, Washburn Crosby and other millers decided to form the conglomerate General Mills; and FTC rules required that Crosby spin off the Red Owl grocery business.

In subsequent years, Red Owl Stores, Hopkins, Minnesota, has grown into a network of more than 360 stores in six states, including both company-owned and independently operated units, all using the Red Owl name and its private label stock of more than 2000 items. Red Owl also continues as a manufacturer, operating its own processing and manufacturing facilities, involving such areas as baking, coffee roasting, prepared foods, candy and snacks, and meats.

Ward/Sears Quality Standards

Pioneers like George Hartford and Barney Kroger in the grocery business and Rowland Macy and John Wanamaker in department stores set high standards for their own labels. They were ridiculed by their competition. How could anyone sell quality merchandise at a lower price? The same reaction was faced by Aaron Montgomery Ward and Richard Sears in the development of their strong private label lines, first in the mail-order business and then eventually in retailing.

When Ward entered the business in 1872, his idea—offering customers honest treatment and quality general merchandise at wholesale prices—was labeled "outlandish." Ward overcame farmers' skepticism about sending their money for merchandise advertised through the mail by offering them a money-back guarantee.

In Ward's Centennial report, written by Frank B. Latham, an account is given of Ward's sewing machine, "The New Home," costing $26 by mail order, compared to $50 when sold by the competition at retail. The Singer Sewing Machine was perhaps the first household appliance that met with sales success in the United States. But local agents of sewing machine makers, seeing the Ward advertisement in its catalog, accused Ward of selling "cheap, second-hand machines." Ward answered them:

> Our machines are all new and have the latest improvements. . . . Our New York Singer Sewing Machines are exactly like those made by the Singer Manufacturing Co., excepting for trademarks; hence it is obvious they are just as good, and we can sell them cheaper. . . . It has long been the practice of most sewing machine manufacturers to sell their machines through local agents only, thus forcing the purchaser to pay the retail price. We have worked against this monoply for years and have furnished thousands of machines at 25 to 50 percent less than the retail prices. (Ward 1972, p. 20).

Richard Warren Sears started the R. W. Sears Watch Co. in Minneapolis in 1886, then moved to Chicago (Ward's home base), joining partner Alvah Curtis Roebuck to build a similar mail-order business, bargaining with suppliers for the lowest price with the promise of volume purchases, passing the savings onto the farmer. In the beginning, most items sold by Sears, Roebuck and Co. were Sears' own products; but very few store brand names were used.

As Sears and Wards developed their businesses, resentment from local merchants for a time forced both mail-order houses to send out their catalogs and goods in unmarked packages to protect customers. In its 1902 catalog, Sears explained:

> For the benefit of merchants, manufacturers, tradesmen and others, who, knowing they can buy from us at much lower prices than they can buy elsewhere . . . we have decided to leave our name and address off from every article we sell, so that even though the illustration may show the imprint of our name and address, it will not appear on the goods you get . . . . Remember our price to the storekeeper is exactly the same as to the consumer, and the same whether you order one article or one thousand, our aim being to protect every buyer and furnish merchandise of the highest standard of quality at much lower prices than it can be had from any other house. (Sears 1902).

About 1900, Sears began to outpace Wards, with sales topping $10 million, almost $2 million ahead of Wards. There is really no documentation on how Sears began its program of private brands. In its 1896 catalog, some items were listed generically or with brand names (the Western Star Washer, Schmuck's mop wringer) or with a manufacturer's name (Cline's Improved Steam Washer, manufactured by Seever Co., St. Louis, for example). In the 1902 catalog, some national brand items were included, such as Cracker Jacks, C. Rogers & Bros. silverware, and Colt firearms, but the majority of items belonged to the Sears family of labels.

In the 1902 catalog, a number of private brand lines started to appear. For example, Acme was a trademark used for at least 15 different product categories, including violins, clocks, buggies, carpenter tools, ranges, forges, and parlor heaters. In the descriptive copy, Sears talked about its Kenwood name, famous since 1890 for grade wheels: "An imitation of this registered name plate of the celebrated Kenwood Wheel is intended to deceive." The copy also explained how Sears took over the output of the Kenwood factory and became sole selling agents for the Kenwood bicycle as well as the wheel, which formerly was sold only through specially appointed agents and "always at the highest price." Sears also plugged the Kenwood name into its lines of cameras, plows, windmills, and hay loaders. Filled with folksy dialogue, describing each item, the catalog contained more than 1160 pages, which would convince any reader of the truth of Sears' slogan: "We Sell Everything." The catalog called Sears, Roebuck and Co. the "Cheapest Supply House on Earth, " adding the phrase, "The Great Price Maker," followed with a punch line, "the real value of this book is plainly shown in every price quotation."

This "Cheapest Supply House" offered little that could be considered cheap in quality. For example, the catalog listed gold-filled watches with a 20-year guarantee, "strictly high-grade" cameras, pianos, and organs with a 25-year guarantee, and the like. All merchandise was sold with a money-back guarantee.

Sears' prices were "cheap." The prices were listed as "beyond compare." Sears explained how this pricing was achieved with, for example, the Long Range Winner, a $3.98 rifle, reduced from $5.50. The copy explained: "How we make the price $3.98. We own the factory in which these guns are made and control the entire output. The cost to us is gotten down to merely the cost of the raw material and labor, and to this we add our one small percent of profit."

Shirts in the catalog carried the "S-R & Co." label in illustrations. In sewing machines, models were sold under a number of store brands: Minnesota, Howard, Burdick, New Queen, Edgemere, and Seroco. The last brand, Seroco, also appeared on refrigerators. Another private label used was Gem, appearing on organs and Gramophones.

In its drug department, Sears included a few questionable items. Under the "Sure Cure" label, there were cures for the tobacco habit and for drunkenness. Also, the 1902 catalog listed items like Dr. Rose's obesity cure, a cure for opium and morphine addiction, and a remedy for sleeplessness. There also was a 20-minute cold cure that "never fails." For the ladies, Sears offered a Bust Cream "unrivalled for enlargement of the bust."

Montgomery Ward, as the first mail-order house, took a leadership role in setting up a testing lab to assure that its customers got what they paid for. Ward's lab was established late in the nineteenth century at a time when controls over foods and other products were not that effective. About 1905, Sears Laboratories was in its embryonic stage when the company began cracking down on quality control. The first lab, opened in 1911, came to be called the "watchdog of the catalog," suggesting minimum standards for some merchandise, spot-testing mail order merchandise, testing Sears products against the competition, and helping to develop new products.

In Canada, T. Eaton Company Limited established its Product Research Bureau in 1917, which began by developing standard sizing systems for clothing. Its research work predated the efforts of the consumer movement in working to improve performance standards of consumer goods.

QUALITY DILUTED

The concept of private labels, as conceived by pioneering giants in the retailing field, was founded on the principles of quality at a lower price, representing value for the customer. Generally speaking, in the first half of the twentieth century that concept was weakened to a low price image only. In recent decades, the old concept—low price plus quality—has

Product by the sackful is ready to be loaded on this horse-drawn wagon from an A&P store in New York City. The store front advertises its name and product selection.

This interior look at a turn-of-the-century A&P store shows a full wall of dishware, lamps, bowls, etc. Attractive wall pictures of horseback riding appear on the right along with limited displays of coffees, teas, and baking powder. In the store rear, a banner advertises Fancy A&P Elgin Creamery Butter.

When A&P was involved in the retail and wholesale trade, during its formative years, it was not uncommon to see crates, sacks, and barrels of its staple products—teas and coffees—piled up in front of the store. Note the Victorian touches of gaslights and elaborate chandeliers. Colorful posters out front advertise the far-off countries where the coffees and teas are purchased.

Early in its development, A&P used a "T" logo to identify its major product offering—teas. Gentlemen of the day pose out front. Shipping carts are from the S.S. Bengloe.

National brands appear to dominate shelfing in this Piggly Wiggly grocery store around 1925. The retailer innovated with patented swinging price tags on each shelf.

Two old private labels, sold by Bunn Capitol Grocery Co., Springfield, Illinois, have since bitten the dust. The Wish Bone brand actually was sold to another company and eventually became a national brand.

A 1966 newspaper ad, placed by A&P in the New York Daily News, defines private label not as a price brand, but one of quality and value. This same message was picked up late in the 1970s by other retailers and wholesalers for their private labels.

what is the definition of a private brand?

To some people, it is a retailer's own brand
created with selling price first in importance
and quality second.

To us at A&P, it's the opposite.
Quality comes first.
Value...the best for the least
is the rule for our private brands.

If this wasn't true,
how foolish we'd be
to invest, as we have,
literally millions of dollars
in processing plants and testing laboratories.

If all we wanted were products
we could sell cheaply
without quality control,
anybody could produce them for us.

The idea of quality private brands
isn't new at A&P.
As a matter of fact,
it's one of our oldest policies–
and by golly, we're proud of it.

Are A&P Private Brands a good reason
for shopping A&P?
They're one of many.

COPYRIGHT © 1966, THE GREAT ATLANTIC & PACIFIC TEA CO., INC.

This apparatus found in the old Eaton Lab served to test abrasion effects on different products, measured by the impact of falling sand.

In this 1927 advertisement, J.C. Penney stresses value and quality in its selection of work clothes under such labels as Pay Day, Big Mac and Nation-Wide.

"where savings are greatest"

WORLD'S LARGEST CHAIN DEPARTMENT STORE ORGANIZATION

J.C. Penney Co. INC.

A NATION-WIDE INSTITUTION

DEPARTMENT STORES

RELIABLE QUALITY GOODS ALWAYS AT LOWER PRICES

618 and 620 Kihekah. Pawhuska, Oklahoma.

Men's Socks
"Automatic" Brand

Well made and very durable, in black and cordovan, no seams in heel and toe.

Women who buy for men know what a good value these socks are at the low price of—

15c

H. C. S.
Fine Gingham

"Honor! Confidence! Service!" This exclusive gingham measures up to these standards. You will find here are the wanted colors and all the newest patterns.

Priced Low!

You will come back for more of this eminently satisfactory gingham! The 32-inch width is priced, the yard,

18c.

When In Doubt—
Linen Finish Fabric for

New Cretonnes
For Many Uses

19c to 69c Yd.

Values Speak Louder Than Words
The Proof Found In Our Store!

This New Marathon Hat
Has the Concealed Welt Edge

"The Radium," as pictured, has grace of line and balance of design found only in hats of character and individuality.

The Radium finish gives lustre; also there is the concealed welt edge brim so new and attractive.

Richly satin lined. Shown in the season's newest colors—nut, pearl, steel. A feature value at—

$3.98

"Let Us Be Your Hatter"

Leather Belts
For Men and Boys

49c to 89c

"Honor" Is Fine Muslin!
Our Exclusive Brand

For Supreme Quality, You Want "Honor"

16c

18c

"Valet" Auto Strop Razor
With Blade, Case and Strop

A Safety Razor that makes possible an exceptionally fast shave; that is clean, sanitary and above all else can be stropped to a keen edge very quickly. Complete for—

25c

For Razor, Blade, Case and Strop

Men's Sturdy Work Shirts
At An Unusually Low Price

All Sizes 14½ to 17

49c

Well-made, standard-size, of Indigo-Blue Chambray, with full-length sleeves, one pocket and four-button front.

Made by skilled, well-paid workmen free as the air of America. One of the best Work Shirt Values we have ever offered at such a low price.

Notions
For the Family

A well-equipped Notion Dept. with the many well-known little things of every-day necessity, needed in every home.

Uniformly high quality and prices just a little less than you are accustomed to pay. Note especially our many useful notions at—

4c. and 8c.

Suits That Win
With Co-Getters

$24.75

Full Cut English Pants
For Young Men

Wide, full-cut, but not extreme. They have wide belt loops and back buckle straps. In cassimeres and flannels in newest plain shades and striped effects.

$4.98 to $7.90

English Corduroy Pants

$3.98 to $4.98

Odd Dress Pants

$3.98 to $5.90

School
For the
Everything Comp
This Feature Low

Here's Our Offering

See Our W

$1.98 to $4.98

Men's Union
Suits for Fall

$1.49

Men's "4-for-1" Hose
If You Want Value—Here It Is!

An extra fine quality heavy-weight, full mercerized lisle sock with extra heavy heel, toe and double sole.

Carefully made according to our high standards. A most exceptional value in spite of the low price—

4 Pr. $1.00

Gladio Percale
Variety of Patterns

15c

Young Men's Top Coats

A loose, easy box coat for cooler days with the tang of Autumn in the air. An unusually good value at—

$22.50

Supreme Shoe Savings
For Men, Women and Children

Our Obligations to You and to Others

The saying, "goods well bought are half sold," tells only a part of this Store's story.

Our obligation to our customers does not end with the actual purchase and sale of goods.

Every purchase you make from us must be the best from the standpoint of quality and price. Large volume buying for our hundreds of Stores assures greater values than are ordinarily to be had.

Each sale in this Store must carry with it absolute satisfaction to the customer. Our responsibility does not end until you are finally pleased.

J. C. Penney Co.

"Pay Day" Overalls Win!
Big Value! Union Made!

$1.39

Union Label on all "Pay-Day" Overalls

Boys' Sweaters
Shaker and Jumbo Knit

$1.49 to $4.98

Majestic Garters
For Men

25c to 49c

With the Tang of Autumn
Come the New Waverly Caps

Caps that have the style built-in with lines of a thoroughbred, as dependable in quality as an eight-cylinder motor.

$1.49

"Let Us Be Your Hatter"

"Big Mac" Wor
Real Shirts for Real

.C. Penney store in Pawhuska, Oklahoma, advertises some old-time private labels, h as Pay Day, Big Mac, Honor, Valet, and Automatic. The guarantee of value acked with this statement: "Every purchase you make from us must be the best from standpoint of quality and price. Large volume buying for our hundreds of stores ures greater values than are ordinarily to be had."

In its formative years, Walgreen produced many different products in its laboratory, almost every item carrying a different label. This display shows names such as Po-Do talc and brushless shave, Saybrooks yeast and iron tablets, K.X. salts, Kel-Dent dental powder, Orlis mouth wash, Keller wine tonic and cough syrup, Hillrose K lotion, etc. Only one product, aspirin tablets, carries the Walgreen's name. Today, the reverse is true: most Walgreen products carry the store name.

In 1917, the T. Eaton Company, Limited, of Toronto established a Research Bureau with its own laboratory equipped with the latest scientific equipment—a far cry from today's lab devices, such as infrared atomic absorption, gas chromatography and spectrophotometric apparatus, as well as sophisticated mechanical and electronic instruments. This early mechanical device tested snags in knitted fabrics using a spiked metal ball.

Old labels under the Ecco label show how Stop & Shop's private label packaging developed. Note the new label (top left) that advertises "no sugar added."

In Sears' first retail stores, opened in 1925, shoppers could examine the company's private label stock first hand without depending solely on the Sears catalog.

been reinstated. Of course, not all retailers can be accused of dropping their quality standards in favor of a price image.

In the competitive struggle against national brands, which emerged as category leaders, many private labels began to shed their emphasis on quality. At least, quality was perceived to be not as important as price. With strong advertising support, the national brands convinced consumers that brands offered the best quality. Private labels, without the advertising clout, had to fall back on a lower price sell. Also, national brands often conducted price wars in different market segments, forcing retailers to adopt more private label merchandise to recoup eroding profit margins. Overall, private labels were left with primarily a price image and as a result assumed second-class status in the marketplace. A follow-the-leader strategy evolved, whereby private brands were forced to skim off sales from the bargain shopper.

Private labels began to copy the national brand leaders in different product categories, which in some cases did not always represent the top quality advertised in the media.

Why was quality ignored so early? Stanley Marcus, former chairman of Neiman-Marcus, a quality private label retailer, offers some interesting theories in his recent book, "Quest for the Best" (Marcus 1979).

Marcus argues that as a business grows, management's personal involvement is diverted from "vital areas" such as product quality and service into administrative, financial, legal matters. The entrepreneur, who puts his name on the product, has pride in that product; the chairman of a corporation has pride in bottom line profits. Pride in a quality standard can make the independent businessman temporarily settle for lower profits; but the corporation executive does not think that way.

Marcus further argues that as small companies have grown or been absorbed by public firms, "proprietor ownership" has been replaced by professional managers who know management and finance, but have little specialized expertise in their industry (Marcus 1979, pp. 12–15).

The private label industry is crisscrossed with different attitudes or philosophies about how to position and market private brands. As such, retailers' attitudes and understanding about quality vary from operator to operator. No two programs are the same.

BUYING CO-OPS

There is no question that the pioneering merchants were getting bigger; their success attracted others to the growing retail business. Smaller merchants, to stay competitive against the more successful, lower priced chains, banded together into buying co-ops for greater purchasing power.

As early as 1897 in Canada, a Toronto department store conducted a "cut-rate" sale of nationally advertised drug products. Retailers there had begun using the loss leader technique to draw in customers. Local pharmacies to protect themselves formed a buying club and in 1904 incorporated that firm under the name Drug Trading Company Ltd., selling all drug lines at manufacturers' list prices. Since their efforts did not stop outsiders from gaining market share in the drug business, the independents formed an Independent Druggist Alliance in 1933 to inform the public through promotions about their competitive pricing. It became necessary to underscore the savings with their own private label line under the I.D.A. label, featuring drug products produced by their newly acquired Druggist Corporation Ltd.

From a modest beginning in 1901, Charles R. Walgreen, Sr., R. PH., started a drugstore in Chicago. Some nine years later, Walgreen began manufacturing his own line of drug products. This move allowed him to insure high quality, while offering his customers a lower price than asked for comparable merchandise sold elsewhere. Evenutally, Walgreen expanded production into his own brand of ice cream, a richer product with a higher percentage of straight cream.

Walgreen was not oblivious to the success of chain stores. In the Seventy Fifth Anniversary Report of the company (Gamm 1976), an account is given of its founder joining with 15 other noncompeting druggists in Chicago's South Side to launch the Velvet Buying Club (1911–1912), velvet connoting a profit. Their group was named the Federated Drug Co. in 1914 and, two years later, the seven-store Walgreen chain was incorporated. Its anniversary report also notes: "Where we once made a handful of drug store products with siphons, funnels and cooking pots, we now operate two modern manufacturing laboratories annually producing 275,000 gallons of bubble bath, 180,000 dozen bottles of shampoo, a half million cans of shaving cream, and over a billion vitamin tablets. More than 500 different Walgreen products were manufactured in our labs last year (1975)."

Walgreen's 1975 private label sales from manufacturing topped $40 million (at estimated retail), up 50% since 1970. Today, its private label program features 400-plus items sold in about 740 stores, covering high-quality health items, beauty aids, and household products. Walgreen claims to be one of the largest private label manufacturers in the world.

Independent grocers also were outpaced by the chains. The small mom-and-pop stores often were tied to a wholesaler, paying middleman costs, while the chains purchased directly from manufacturers and processors or produced their own products. As a result, the chains could pass their savings on to the customer with lower prices, prices that the local retailer could not meet. Chains became an attractive vehicle for growth.

The chains developed on their own power (A&P, Kroger, Grand Union) or through mergers (the American Stores Co., Safeway Stores, Inc., Lucky Stores).

In 1917, the merger of five independent retailers, collectively representing 1223 stores, formed the American Stores Co., Philadelphia. Together, the Acme Tea Co., James Bell Co., George M. Dunlap Co., Robinson & Crawford, and S. C. Childs Co. had sales approaching $50 million yearly. The partners, who traced their origins back to the last century, carried their own private labels, some of which were retained, while new brands were developed under the ASCO label, an acronoym of the company. In 1922, the company purchased a cannery, putting canned goods under that label, too. Over the years, its private label program developed into new product categories. An outstanding example was its Louella Butter, named after a town in Pennsylvania, which became the first sweet cream butter to be packed and widely distributed in the United States.

Safeway Stores, Inc., Oakland, California, traces its founding back to when Marion Barton Skaggs started into the retail business in 1915 in American Falls, Idaho. Ten years later, Skaggs operated his own wholesale operation in the Pacific Northwest. But it really was in 1926 that Safeway's history began. That year marked the merger of Skaggs' 428 retail stores with Sam Seelig's 322 stores, based in Southern Califronia. (Seelig a year earlier had renamed his operation Safeway Stores.) Their merged company had total sales of $50 million, serving 10 northwestern states eastward to Nebraska.

Another group of six independent grocers banded together in 1931 to form the Peninsular Stores, Ltd., San Francisco. Four years later they launched their first Lucky Store, which formed the basis for the Lucky Store chain.

Against these emerging giant chains—not to mention A&P, which in 1926 commanded a sales volume of $547 million from nearly 15,000 stores—it's not surprising to see that independent grocers grouped together for survival. One of the first retailer-owned wholesale buying groups was formed by 15 independents in Pasadena, California, in 1922, called Certified Grocers of California, Ltd. Through direct buying, these grocers could share in wholesaling profits. They merged with another grocers co-op in 1928 and the following year purchased Walker Grocery Co., pushing their volume to about $2.7 million. Over the decades, Certified has developed into a strong wholesale grocery distributor with an equally strong private label program. Its Springfield label was launched about 1955, and since then its program has expanded to include the Gingham, Special Value, Prize, and generic labels, together accounting for more than 1500 items.

The largest voluntary food co-op in the United States, IGA, Inc., of Chicago, a wholesale organization now serving more than 3300 IGA food stores, was organized in 1926 as a reaction to the chains. J. Frank Grimes, an accountant involved with wholesale grocery accounts, met with some 69 retailers in Poughkeepsie, New York (home base of W. T. Reynold & Co., wholesale grocers) to form an Independent Grocers' Alliance (IGA). United, they could centralize their purchasing and price their products competitively against the chains. These retailers initially adopted the "Acorn" trademark, which was soon dropped for the IGA logo. Their first IGA labels covered items like cake flour, nut margarine, coffee, tea, and canned goods. Recently, IGA stores' combined sales place that group as the fourth leading food retailer in the United States. The IGA private label line has literally become a national brand with some 2500 items, covering more than 40 product categories.

Mr. Grimes' success with IGA took him to Canada, where he worked with another group, representing 50 independent druggust in the Ontario Province. In 1932, these druggists, belonging to the Drug Trading Company buying group, developed a merchandising and advertising plan called the Independent Druggist Alliance (IDA), a voluntary organization of Drug Trading members. Their objective was to gain public awareness through newspaper advertising and circulars and through and IDA private label program. Today, the group covers 475 drug stores, offering some 150 IDA items, which represent about 10% of store sales.

Manufacturing and distribution strengths helped make some of the co-ops and many more of the chains powerful. These strengths are a key factor in Safeway's success, pushing its 1926 $50 million volume up nearly 300% to $15 billion today, making it the leading supermarket chain in the country. A&P's 1926 sales volume was 10 times that of Safeway; yet today, A&P's volume is barely half of Safeway's volume. What happened to make A&P lose its position to Safeway (and to Kroger)?

There are a number of reasons that A&P lost position, but one of the primary reasons is its policy on private labels. A&P was premature in merchandising and marketing its own brands both offensively and defensively, at the expense of national brands. The chain met resistance at all levels: the competition, the brand manufacturers, and even the government.

Initially, A&P operated on the policy of a small profit—a 2.5% margin—and a large turnover of goods. When A&P lost its case against the Cream of Wheat Co. in establishing prices at retail without a price cut, A&P retaliated by introducing its own brands and pushing them aggressively.

That led to more manufacturing activity: the Quaker Maid Co., the American Coffee Corp., etc.

In the 1930s, after the Depression, A&P, which was then decentralized into six divisions, found itself working on higher profit margins and lower sales. Its buying power was too much for the independents, who were forced to organize into buying groups. In 1934, the Federal Trade Commission, at the request of the National Association of Retail Grocers and other trade groups, began investigating chain stores. The independent merchants, supported by Representative Wright Patman of Texas, looked upon A&P (and other growing chains) as manufacturers, producers, wholesalers, and retailers—an unbeatable combination against the small retailer. In 1936, Congress legislated against price differentials with the Robinson-Patman Act, "which forbade manufacturers or producers to give discounts, commissions, advertising allowances, brokerage fees, and more favorable ('discriminatory') prices unless these could be justified by savings to the manufacturer or producer in his own costs."

The upshot of this ruling was that A&P could no longer get national brand allowances, forcing A&P to mark up its merchandise. A&P reacted by continuing to stock the national brand but positioning its A&P brands right next to it. The American housewife was given a choice, in which the private brand was several cents cheaper than the national brand.

"So A&P's advertising changed. Soon the plan was to feature Ann Page salad dressing, instead of Best Foods or Kraft Miracle Whip. It was Nectar Tea (modern successor to Thea Nectar) instead of Lipton's; Rajah mustard; Ann Page catsup; Iona pork and beans; A&P bread; and Sunnyfield chickens. When products other than A&P's own were advertised, they were usually listed simply as pure lard, cane sugar, pink salmon, and salt" (Hoyt 1969, p. 169). These first ads appeared in September 1936 with A&P's own coffees and bread featured. The chain also began publishing a new monthly magazine, *Woman's Day*, expressly for its private brand advertising. Of course, A&P suppliers could also advertise their brands at a page rate of $1125.

At one time, John Hartford also considered selling out the A&P retail stores, staying in just the manufacturing and wholesale businesses. This move would have converted all its private brands—Ann Page, Jane Parker, Sultana, Iona, Sunnyfield, and so on—into national brands (Hoyt 1969, p. 169).

It was aggressive private label merchandising, an idea whose time had not yet come. In 1930, Hartford was quoted: "We do not attempt to push our own brands. We leave it to our customer to buy what they want. Of all the food products we handle, only 10 percent comprise private brands, which may be regarded as strictly competitive with national labels" (Hoyt 1969).

In the new advertising strategy, introduced in 1936, one of the first price-comparison ads of private label was introduced: "The A&P stores in New Orleans listed in parallel columns fifteen nationally known brands of food products against fifteen similar products manufactured under A&P lables. The prices of the national brands added up to $2.40; the prices of the A&P brands added up to $1.70. 'Compare! Save 29 percent! shouted the handbill" (Hoyt 1969, p. 178).

The president of the Associated Grocery Manufacturers of America was furious over the ad, charging A&P with unfair competition. John Hartford actually was forced to admit to a "regrettable" mistake (Hoyt 1969).

(Some 45 years later, retailers began using this "innovative" ad strategy, comparing their private label brands against the national brand prices.)

Nevertheless, A&P continued to build customer loyalty around its own brands. By 1940, its volume passed the $1 billion mark, with private label sales climbing from 15 to 20% (in 1936) up to 25%. Since A&P realized high profit returns from its manufacturing operations, its stores were encouraged to promote private brands.

"These private brands were sold at a considerable profit in every case, and still they were cheaper than comparable national brands, as the comparison in Table 4 submitted by the A&P Central Division showed (Hoyt 1969, p. 180).

Table 4

A&P Brand	Standard Brand
Ann Page salad dressing—23 cents	Miracle Whip—32 cents
Sparkle gelatin dessert—3 for 10 cents	Jello—3 for 14 cents
White House milk—4 for 25 cents	Carnation milk—4 for 27 cents
Ann Page ketchup—2 for 25 cents	Heinz ketchup—16 cents
Dexo shortening—14 cents	Spry shortening—16 cents
Ann Page beans—5 cents	Campbell's beans—3 for 20 cents

In 1940–1941, the Antitrust Division of the Department of Justice took A&P to court, charging that "A&P had used its power over the years to coerce competitors and suppliers into cutting prices and giving the big company special price treatments. By trade restraint, unfair competition, and other monopolistic practices, the company had grown to be the behemoth of the food business. Without these illegal practices, said the Government, A&P could never have attained its position" (Hoyt 1969). (Justice also moved against Safeway and Kroger on similar grounds.) As a result, A&P was forced to pay fines.

The case continued until 1946, when A&P was finally accused of "conspiring to monopolize a substantial part of America's food business . . .

> The crux of the Government's case was that the huge mixture of operations shored one another up. Quaker Maid Company, the manufacturing subsidiary, accounted for 13 percent of A&P' profits. The coffee corporations accounted for 12 percent. White House Milk added 6 percent. The Government case ignored the A&P principle that these manufacturing companies were entitled to make profits on their sales, even if they sold only to A&P (Hoyt 1969).

It is also interesting that all focus was placed on the industry with little or no attention paid to the consumer, who benefited from the lower priced private labels.

When a new Administration moved into Washington during the 1950s, government interest in antitrust-law enforcement abated. Nevertheless, the legal fees and the cost of campaign publicity to fight the suit cost A&P plenty.

For some 20 years, A&P published *Woman's Day*. In 1957 the company was forced to sell that property when a court case claimed that the magazine's national brand ads constituted illegal rebates for A&P. The chain was vindicated in the case, but it made for strained relations with potential manufacturers–advertisers.

Many factors weakened A&P's position in the marketplace. Its image as primarily a private label store—emphasizing its brands through promotions, preferential aisle positioning, greater number of item facings on shelves, and advertising—hurt the company competitively, especially with the brand-oriented shopper. The population shift to the West, where A&P was ill-represented, also contributed to its weakened position. The chain carried a lot of dead weight in its smaller stores, especially with the increased interest in larger supermarkets and/or super stores.

In recent years, A&P has trimmed back and repositioned itself with more emphasis on national brand promotions. Ironically, A&P's competitors have had as much private label coverage, yet did not carry the private label stereotyped image of A&P.

For the retailer, private label can prove to be a two-edged sword. Safeway began handling that "weapon" first with six bakeries at the time of its 1926 merger. In the firm's 50th Anniversary Report, it is noted that "those bakeries represented the first important ventures by Safeway predecessors into 'making our own.' The idea originally was as much to have an assured supply as it was to reduce costs and lower prices for the customer.

> By the mid-1930s, Safeway had 21 bakeries, six creameries, six coffee roasting plants, three meat distributing plants, a milk condensery, a candy and syrup factory, and a mayonnaise plant. We were also well into field purchasing of fresh fruits and vegetables with our old Triway Produce Company.

The secret to effective private label merchandising is not to flaunt it as A&P did early in this century. Safeway and Kroger learned this lesson early. Others also have applied the strategy of not positioning private label in a more favorable manner than national brands.

A good example is Wakefern Food Corporation, Elizabeth, New Jersey. This wholesaler co-op of some 200-plus ShopRite stores, started in the 1950s, has a private label mix approaching 40% of sales. Yet the co-op maintains a strict policy. A company representative says: "We're proud of our private label, but we don't protect it in a way where it's given an edge over the brands. We give consumers value—special deals with private label as well as with national brands."

GENERAL MERCHANDISE MANUFACTURING

Like the giants in the grocery segment, entrepreneurs in the general merchandise segment also became directly involved in manufacturing operations for their private label supply. James Cash Penney, an exception, avoided any manufacturing tie-in. His first dry goods store, the Golden Rule, was opened in Kemmerer, Wyoming, in 1902. Some 16 years later, Penney launched his own brands, beginning with Pay Day work clothes, then developing other lines: Foremost for refrigerators, Gaymode for women's hosiery, Towncraft for men's suits, Penncrest for electronics, and Penncraft for tools and hardware.

Penney protected his quality standards by setting up a research and testing lab in 1930, which eventually became one of the largest and best equipped facilities in the country for consumer end-use testing of textiles.

Montgomery Ward was one of the first merchants to set up a testing lab for consumer goods. The company had to protect its trademark, a black diamond, which first appeared on alpaca goods in the 1870s. As early as Ward's 1875–1876 catalog, the company began to offer shoppers a choice: "Our design in this issue has been to offer several grades in each class of goods, thereby giving a range of prices and qualities to meet the requirements of every purse." This idea later served as the basis for Ward's "Good-Better-Best" tier of product categories. (Sears also picked up on this quality distinction, but eventually kept only its "Sears Best" label.)

In 1901, Ward built its first vehicle factory in Chicago Heights, which eventually helped construct perhaps this country's first private label automobile, called "an Assembled Car." Besides Ward, there were 15 other suppliers involved in the project. An auto manufacturer assembled the final product. This five-passenger, four-cylinder vehicle, subsequently named Modoc, sold for $1800 in 1912. Ward failed to make its mark with Modoc. Unfortunately, the mail-order house could sell the cars, but not service them. No Modoc dealerships had been set up. Modoc was dropped in 1914 (Latham 1972, pp. 59–60).

When World War I struck, Ward first moved by advancing funds to its important suppliers so that they could purchase raw materials before prices shot upward. Ward also moved forcefully into manufacturing itself, purchasing a plant in Springfield, Illinois, for the production of implements, gasoline engines, cream separators, brooders, incubators, and hardware specialties. A few years later, the company added a gas engine plant and foundry in Springfield. Other factories also were established to produce steel beds, wallpaper, clothing, knitwear, sporting goods, window shades, and other items. The Ward catalog soon began carrying Wardway Paints, produced in the firm's Chicago Heights plant (Latham 1972, p. 60).

During the Depression years, Ward changed its strategy somewhat, offering merchandise as Supreme Quality and Standard Quality with the products repackaged, bearing the "MW" monogram instead of the manufacturer's brand name previously used for its merchandise. The firm eventually went back to its Good-Better-Best selection in private label, which proved successful in subsequent decades.

Very early in its history, Sears began courting suppliers, investing chunks of money into their production, sometimes with a 100% commitment. Indications of this involvement appear in the 1901 catalog, where Sears admitted to taking "practically all" the paint from "one of the largest makers of ready mixed paint," of establishing a "modernized gun factory," of starting its own drug department backed by "a competent chemist and registered pharmacist," of operating its own foundry for ranges, of running its own vehicle factories for surries and buggies, and the like.

Sears has secured stock in a number of manufacturing companies that supplied goods to Sears, including such names as Whirlpool Corp. (refrigerators, home laundry appliances, freezers, and vacuum cleaners), Sanyo Electric Co. (TV sets), Armstrong Rubber (Allstate tires), and Globe-Union (Die-Hard batteries). Sears went so far as to sponsor the merger of Kellwood Co. (wearing apparel, home furnishings, and camping equipment), bringing together 15 smaller companies that had been giving Sears 90% of its requirements in their line (Weil 1977, pp. 138–139).

Reporting on the history of its origins, Sears in its 1978 booklet, "Merchant to the Millions" indicates that

> fanciful catalog writing started by Sears became less fanciful. A testing laboratory was set up to find out just how good Sears and its competitors' products were. What's more, buyers began looking beyond price tags to the quality of the goods they were buying.
>
> The change in the catalog from the flamboyant to the factual appears to have started by the turn of the century. . . . Not only did copy improve, but some of the products such as patent medicines were dropped. . . . As early as 1905, the company began insisting not only on accurate catalog descriptions, but also on quality merchandise.

Sears backed its quality claims with a laboratory, opened in 1911.

When Sears attempted to enter the high fashion world with the Lady Duff-Gordon line of women's clothing in 1916—before the company operated retail stores—the fashion as illustrated in the catalog did not strike the rural housewife's fancy. But Sears did succeed in the clothing area with its Perma-Prest finishes, developed by its laboratory and carrying the Sears trademark registered for no-iron merchandise (Weil 1977, p. 68).

In the many brands that Sears has launched, the names have derived mostly from its buying department. There are exceptions, of course. In 1926, for example, Sears ran a contest, looking for a new name to replace its Justice tires. Hans Simonson, a draftsman from Bismarck, North Dakota, came up with the winning name, Allstate, which today is still part of the Sears family of brands, covering automotive equipment and insurance (Weil 1977, pp. 152–153).

Sears reminisced about its trademarks in a 1972 press release, stating that file cabinets in its headquarters contain names that date back to 1902. One is on file for "J. C. Higgins," a name attached to sporting goods for many years. John Higgins was in charge of the Sears bookkeeping department when someone suggested his name for the sporting goods line. Sears liked it and, although John Higgins retired in 1930, his name carried on for years afterward.

"Some of the names suggest a product function or attribute," Sears notes in its release, "such as 'Coldspot' for refrigerators and 'Silvertone' for phonographs.

"But no one knows where the name 'Kenmore' came from. It was registered with the U.S. Patent Office in 1933, and some believe the name was inspired by a hotel across from the Boston Catalog Order Plant. Others say it was named after a street in Chicago."

Sears notes that its staff investigates up to 150 names each month. Its catalog has more than tripled in size from the 1958 edition of 532 pages. The more recent catalogues list more than 79,000 items, with some 12,000 suppliers in the United States filling the Sears pipelines.

The T. Eaton Company Limited, Toronto, at one time probably the second largest mail order catalog house (next to Sears), started its private label lines (2 and 3 cent wool gloves, etc.) in its first catalog in 1884; by 1904, the company had formally adopted its first trademark Eatonia for shoes. That name became so famous that a town in Saskatchewan was named after it. Over the years, other names were added: Birkdale, Canterbury, Haddon Hall, etc., many with a "British Isles orientation" because the founder, Timothy Eaton, had come from Ireland. Early in this century, entrepreneur Eaton established his own product research lab (1917). He also started his own factories for furniture, soft goods, stoves, and refrigerators. Eventually, these operations were sold when they became too expensive to maintain. The trademark library meanwhile built up to a point where at one time there were 129 names in the store.

Since 1976, Eaton's entire catalog business has been discontinued, with the private label business actually doubling to more than 5000 items. The trademarks have been cut back to about 29 names, all of them now being married with the Eaton name: Eaton Viking, for example.

Another pioneering giant, Frank Woolworth, avoided the manufacturing route in developing the world's first successful "5 and 10 Cent Store." Woolworth expanded his product selection into wider varieties by dealing directly with manufacturers, ordering mass quantities at a low price, bypassing the jobbers. At the beginning, he was snubbed as an "upstate [New York] upstart," but as business grew so did respect from both the jobber and the manufacturer.

When World War I hit, some of Woolworth's biggest-selling items disappeared from the store counters because of shortages in labor and raw materials. That led to the introduction of perhaps one of Woolworth's first private labels, Woolco (an acronym for the company). Before the war, Woolworth sold great quantities of imported crochet cotton at 10 cents. With a cut-off of imports, the company talked a U.S. mill into producing a product of equal quality, guaranteeing the spinner against any loss. That launched Woolco quality crochet cotton. (In 1962, the Woolco name was affixed to Woolworth's new discount chain of low-margin, high quality mass merchandising stores with department store service.)

Woolworth's wartime strategy paid off for other merchandise as well. As other 5-and-10-cent companies boosted their prices, because not enough merchandise could be sold profitably at a low cost, Woolworth held to a fixed cash price of a nickel or a dime. This was achieved because of the company's

> flexibility and expertise . . . the skill of its master buyers, the strength of its manufacturer relations, and the buying and selling might of its network. . . .
>
> Woolworth had already standardized its leading lines of merchandise. Its buying experts now concentrated not only upon ferreting out substitutes for goods gone to war but also, as production consultants, upon helping American manufacturers to fabricate goods profitably that had exclusively been imported before World War I. Woolworth's guarantee against loss, and the extent of its volume buying, were persuasive inducements (Nichols 1973, p. 105).

As with other merchants, Woolworth really had no orientation to private brands or a private label program at the beginning. The retailer's own brands were just competing brands, not regarded as a separate category. Some of the earliest private label names adopted by Woolworth appeared in the 1920s. In its 1929 "Home Shopping Guide," published to commemorate its 50th Anniversary, the Woolworth name was carried on many of the 250 items listed. Some of the oldest private brands included Woolco paste and glue, Lorraine hair nets, Herald Square stationery, and Fifth Avenue linen writing paper with matching envelopes. Since Woolworth's headquarters were established in New York City, the company drew inspiration for its name from the area: Fifth Avenue, Herald Square.

COMPETITIVE PRESSURES

The retailer's attitude about private label really determines its success or failure. When the retailer makes a commitment to *own* brands, he must assume responsibility over those brands.

As manufacturers' labels evolved into nationally advertised brands, many retailers who once commanded the trust of the consumer began to reassign that trust to outside suppliers. The retailer's role as arbiter in setting product standards fell to the outside manufacturer. Those retailers who fought against national brands, using private labels offensively or defensively, found themselves no longer selling a competitive brand. Instead, it had become a lower priced buying alternative: thanks to advertising, consumers did not perceive private labels to be on the same level as the national brands. No matter what an aggressive private label merchandiser might do at the store level, its impact was not as great as national brand advertising. That advertising built familiarity and trust. To maintain their lower price and higher markup, private labels were not advertised. The manufacturers' brands, through advertising, were positioned as top quality products said to offer the customer the best value for their money. Without the benefit of that support (not to mention more sophisticated packaging), private labels were sold mostly on the basis of price and through the efforts of store salespeople. Many retailers, who had become order-takers for the national brands, left the selling of those products up to advertising. When self-service took hold in supermarkets during the Depression years, customers, influenced by advertising, were more likely to choose the familiar national brand over the lesser known private brand. Low-margin supermarkets allowed national brands also to be priced competitively against grocery chains with private label lines.

The marketplace was constantly changing at an accelerated pace. Competition kept intensifying, often turning to cut-throat tactics as a matter of survival. The retailing field was evolving.

- The giant mail-order houses, Sears and Montgomery Ward, moved into the retail market in the 1920s.
- Advertising increased first with radio in the 1920s and 1930s, then TV beginning in the 1940s.

- Marketing research, which began first with the government providing statistics, developed in the publishing field, then evolved with new polling and attitude research techniques introduced by Crossley in 1926, then Roper and Gallup in the 1930s.
- National brands, packer labels, and private labels proliferated through the marketplace in all sizes and shapes—literally thousands of different labels.
- Independent grocers fought chain dominance with retailer-owned wholesale and voluntary co-op buying groups.
- Independents also adopted the chain's strategy of cost-effective mass distribution with the emergence of supermarkets, which marked the beginning of mass merchandising.
- National brand price wars erupted among many merchants, especially department store retailers, who turned to private label merchandise to maintain their margins.
- Cut-rate drug stores emerged.
- Discount department stores debuted in the late 1940s when Korvettes introduced a low-margin, low-service, high-turnover store in New York City.

As early as 1914, Alpha Beta, a grocery retailer in Pomona, California, began innovating with an idea of allowing shoppers to "serve themselves and save the difference." The merchandise for a short time was advertised and arranged alphabetically—antipasto next to ant paste, for example. It was one of the first retail stores to adopt self-service.

Clarence Saunders started the Piggly Wiggly stores in Memphis, Tennessee, using self-selection, turnstiles, and checkout counters.

Fred Meyer, Inc., Portland, Oregon, credits its founder, Fred G. Meyer, with opening the world's first self-service drugstore in 1930. In that decade, the supermarket came into its own as a limited assortment, self-service store, first with King Kullen stores, started by Michael J. Cullen in Jamaica, New York, in 1930. This 20- by 80-foot store featured only dry groceries (all national brands) with a new merchandising technique, described by Cullen in his ads: "I opened my little store on a shoe string and sold everything I could lay my hands on for cost or slightly above cost." Cullen farmed out different concessions in other stores he opened, to a baker, a shoemaker, etc. Eventually, he took over the concessions because of the poor name they projected through their management.

A couple of years later, Robert M. Otis and Roy O. Dawson teamed up with a wholesaler, the American House Grocers, to take over an auto plant in Elizabeth, New Jersey, and converted it into a supermarket for food and household goods. Big Bear literally bear-hugged the industry, and it has never been the same since.

In its 50th Annual Report, Certified Grocers of California (1972) gives an interesting account of the supermarket, called "the dawn of modern retailing. . . . "

> Compared to other retail outlets, early supermarkets were enormously large and crude. They occupied converted warehouses, automobile garages and even roller skating rinks, and some of the bigger ones had over 50,000 square feet of space. Supermarkets further capitalized on mass distribution—the concept chain stores developed so effectively in the 1920s. Other retailers, both chains and independents alike, considered supermarkets a passing fad. They nicknamed them "cheapies," not only because of their low prices, but also because of their unorthodox merchandising approach.
>
> Inside, the supermarket was a world unto itself. Boxes and barrels of merchandise, displayed in self-service fashion, were strewn everywhere. Dangling banners and posters announced sensational bargains. Aisles were placed so shoppers passed all merchandise before reaching the checkout counter, where cash registers briskly rang up an endless stream of sales.
>
> Each supermarket carried a different selection of merchandise, but most featured groceries, meat, bakery goods, fruits and vegetables, dairy products, tobacco, paint, hardware and automobile accessories.
>
> Although retailers were slow to see the supermarket's advantages, consumers were not as shortsighted. They liked the larger stores. Shoppers enjoyed browsing at their own pace, filling baskets and carts with items of their own choosing. They appreciated easy access to products without a clerk's interference and were loudly voicing their opinion in favor of lower prices.
>
> The United States had sunk into the Great Depression of the 1930s, and consumers eagerly welcomed a way to stretch their shopping dollars. With an economic climate threatening to get worse, supermarkets shot up almost overnight. By decade's end, it was obvious that supermarkets were here to stay.

In a couple of books about the supermarket business, author M. M. Zimmerman outlines these formative years. "Like King Kullen and Big Bear, these early supermarkets laid emphasis on price, self-service, and mass displays of nationally known brands. No thought whatever was given to appearance. Fixtures were of the crudest type. The buildings were mostly vacant factories, garages, etc. As a matter of fact, the cruder the building, the greater was its appeal to the public, since it suggested economy to the customer" (Zimmerman 1965, p. 55).

The move to supermarkets obviously was an attack on the grocery chains, which had strong private label programs. Supermarkets naturally followed the national brand route. Zimmerman in an earlier book describes how one wholesaler operated a supermarket with 40 brands of peas for greater selection—three times that offered by the chains. Zimmerman quotes this wholesaler's attitude: "We find that private labels in supermarket merchandising are about as productive as fishing in the Dead Sea—except, of course, when they are manufactured items to which you can give some kind of trade name. A packer's label of unknown value is as bad except when it is standard merchandise priced under the advertised brand to appeal to a certain type of consumer who must acutally economize" (Zimmerman 1937, p. 99–100).

The battle lines appeared to have been drawn. Zimmerman, who was editor and publisher of Super Market Merchandising Magazine, quotes from its October 1937 issue, in which W. H. Albers, president of Albers Super Markets, Inc., talked about the "increasing trend of consumer alertness against private brand substitutions."Albers also notes that the growth of supermarkets caused chains to close thousands of neighborhood stores, creating opportunity for the small retailer to take over: "The small merchants will see the advantages of carrying only nationally advertised brands of food, keeping down their inventory and making better profits on their investment. The real competition will be between two systems of distribution: national brands through supermarkets and independents versus chains with private brands."

Albers noted: "The issue is clear enough. Private brand people can only emphasize price. The national food advertisers must manifestly and necessarily depend on value."

The chains, of course, followed the independents into the supermarket business, taking their private brands with them. Also, independents eventually adopted their own private labels for supermarket trading. The determining factor became not type of operation but product availability.

At the beginning, canners of fruits and vegetables actively developed their own packer labels for the grocery trade, establishing several grades of product—fancy, choice, and standard. At the beginning of this century, Minnesota Valley Canning, Le Seurr, Minnesota, developed two labels, Artesian and Minnesota Valley cream-style corn. In 1907, that canner began packing peas for the grocery trade under packer labels and in the 1920s introduced its Green Giant packer label. In finding a winner, that canner began supporting mostly that label, which developed into its national brand.

Canners proliferated in the Midwest. In the 1930s and 1940s, there were more than 100 companies with canning plants in every county in the state of Wisconsin. Each canner had two or three of their own packer labels, sold mostly to the wholesale grocers and to some chains. They also provided private labels to the chains. About 150 labels of canned peas were sold in the state at one time, each with less than 1% market share. Some canners expanded into regional and national brands with their packer labels, others stayed with packer labels and private labels only.

Meantime, the frozen food business was expanding. Birds-Eye's entry into the retail business in the 1930s drew other distributors and packers into the picture. In the 1940s, Penn Fruit Co., Philadelphia, became one of the first chains to start a private label frozen food line, marketing 12-oz cellophane bags of vegetables under its "Green Valley" label. Later, fruits were added (Williams 1963, pp. 28, 69).

Topco, a Midwest buying co-op, then called Food Products Cooperative, started to experiment with frozen foods under its label in the 1940s. Not until early in the 1950s did Safeway Stores launch its private label frozen food program with Bel-air Peas.

In the 1930s and 1940s, Safeway started to build its private label program. Perhaps from the proliferation of labels or from the pressures exerted by the government on the chains (i.e., A&P's plight with an antitrust suit) or whatever the reason, Safeway adopted a strategy of adopting numerous labels, private labels that were disguised as packer labels. The chain established a family of more than 100 different names that, Safeway admits, really got out of hand. In the firm's house organ, Safeway News, August/September 1980, this situation is described:

> Once upon a time, Safeway had more names attached to its products than anyone ever bothered to count. A budget-conscious shopper, probably unaware the items were Safeway's, could load up a baskart with Beverly peanut butter, Montrose butter, Dutch Mill processed cheese, Farm Fresh eggs, Prairie Schooner Bread, Jan Arden cookies, Tea Timer crackers, Suzanna pancake mix, Golden Heart flour, Mayday salad oil, Show Boat rice, Pennant tea, Wakefield coffee, Fair Winds tuna, Sundown fruit cocktail, Country Home corn, Anthem peas, Moneca plums, Destino tomato paste, Cascade salad dressing, Old Mill vinegar, Hy-Pro bleach, El Rapido soap, Sno-White salt, and Snow Cola soft drinks.
>
> And that baskart would contain only a smattering of the names once used to designate Safeway products.
>
> No one really seems to know exactly what led to such an unwieldy profusion of names. But many did know that the proliferation of names led to a lot of confusion, shared by customers and employees alike.
>
> Aside from the confusion, observed senior vice president/supply Lorenzo Hoopes, "we were limited in the amount of promotion that could be directed at good-quality items because of the many different names."
>
> The effort to reduce the variety of names, based on these facts, began. "S" Brands got first priority.

The chain worked toward unification of its private labels, ending up with about a dozen names under the S Brands umbrella—Lucern dairy products, Bel-air frozen items, Cragmont soft drinks, White Magic household items, and so on.

The suppliers also followed that pattern toward consolidation. In canning, for example, 180 plants were operating in Wisconsin in the 1950s; today, some 80 plants are operating at five to ten times the volume.

For retailers, it became a matter of building equity around certain brand names they owned. A&P, for example, in about 1960 operated some 23 manufacturing and processing plants, which produced 498 grocery flavors and varieties plus 500 dairy and fish items, 12% of that total volume concentrated in the Ann Page and Jane Parker labels.

In the 1960s, Montgomery Ward's private label volume had leaped ahead from 40 to 95% of total sales, while national brands were reduced from 168 to 16. The firm had built equity into such brands as Signature, Airline, Riverside, Garden Mark, Brent, and Power-Kraft.

Woolworth's report, "The Growing Importance of Woolworth's Private Brands," indicated that "just 12 of our brand names presently account for 85% of total private label sales"—not including the "Woolworth" label. The dozen were Audition for radios, musical instruments, record players, and accessories; Fifth Avenue stationery where "papers are never made from reprocessed paper or mill seconds; but only of the finest quality vellum, rich in quality to see and to touch"; Happy Home furnishing lines, contributing about 32% of private label sales in items like rugs, curtains, towels, picture frames, included hardware and rubberware, electrical devices, and home appliances with "heavy gauge aluminumware the same quality as nationally advertised lines, giving us the same gross markup but selling for 25% less"; Herald Square office and school supplies; Home Cote paints and brush accessories" equal in quality to nationally advertised brands and always better values"; Lorraine hair goods; Pata Cake infants' wear and accessories; Petite Belle budget hosiery for women and girls; Primrose nylon hosiery and tights which "go through more than 15 tests and inspections during manufacturing to insure best quality. . . [and] have even earned the famous Good Housekeeping Seal"; Primstyle fashions for dresses, sleepwear, and other clothing; Sunny Lane candies, nuts, and novelties; and TopsAll men's and boys' dress and sport shirts "made of quality fabrics by famous manufacturers, tailored to exact specifications with top quality features and the latest styling details."

Lower priced merchandise—whether national brand or private label—has always caught the eye of the consumer. In the 1930s, fair trade prices were established by manufacturers to protect retailers against competition under pricing merchandise; nevertheless, resale prices kept edging upward. That opened up a market for the supermarkets, selling at a discount price with self-service and taking lower margins.

In the late 1940s, the same effect hit the department store business. Eugene Ferkauf started a discount department store featuring luggage and appliances sold at less than the list price. Ferkauf took a low margin (under 10% markup), provided little service in his stores, and realized a high turnover of goods. He started Korvettes in 1948 in New York; six years later, his operation developed into the country's first full-line discount store. But even Korvettes fell victim to the markup fever. Its prices started to creep upward into the 30%-plus markup area. That opened up the door to lower-priced private labels.

Korvettes' "own controlled brands" grew to some 65 registered names. Kerkauf started the program with tiers of quality similar to Wards, but he eventually went to only top quality merchandise, comparable to or better than the national brands. The chain used its Korvettes name on drugs, vitamins, hardware, personal care, and certain soft goods. At any one time, only 15 other brand names were kept active. Some of the brands included Ann Robin, Young-Mate, and Carina on soft goods; XAM for radios and major appliances; and Power King for sporting goods. Private label, ironically, carried more than twice the markup of the branded merchandise, 60 to 65%. The chain maintained a strong, viable private label program, representing about 15% of its total sales (roughly $90 million-plus).

Korvettes, however, make the mistake of changing its discount image to that of a fashion center. Other mistakes in management and funding led to the company filing for bankruptcy in 1981.

The discount store concept did not die. After World War II, discount stores began to spread; more and more appeared during the 1950s, drawing in participants from the department store, variety store, food, and drugstore segments.

In the variety store segment, Woolworth opened its first Woolco discount department store in 1962 with an emphasis placed on branded merchandise sold at competitive prices. The Woolworth strategy was to stay primarily with nationally advertised goods, thinking cusotmers would identify the merchandise more easily.

But the real success story in discount general merchandising was experienced by S. S. Kresge Co., Troy, Michigan, one of the country's oldest retailers. The company was founded by Sebastian Spering Kresge, who started into business for himself opening dimestores, similar to the Woolworth concept, in 1900. When shortages hit during World War I, Kresge added green storefronts (to his red ones) and upped the prices to $1. Subsequently, a private label program was added to the stores.

Competition from the discounters (Korvettes and others) hurt Kresge's profits, forcing the chain to launch its K mart concept in 1962. That move literally catapulted Kresge into a new identity and leadership in its market segment. The success of K mart and its smaller discount store version, Jupiter, eventually took over the variety store image of Kresge. Since 1971, the company has not added one Kresge store; in fact, its Kresge stores were dropped or converted to the K mart concept. That became the principal business, so much so that in 1977 the company changed its name to K mart.

K mart positions itself as a mass merchandise chain within the department store category. Its strategy continues to be discount pricing. The growing chain added product categories not usually included in a conventional department store, such as tires, batteries, accessories, prescription drugs, building materials and home improvement goods, plants, and garden supplies. Its success was built on the effort "to offer the consumer goods of high quality and durability at prices substantially lower than the competition was generally offering—discount pricing." Its motto has become "satisfaction always." Private label has continued to be an integral part of that strategy and motto. The firm's buyers worked closely with manufacturers, setting standards of quality. When its business grew rapidly, efforts were intensified "to supplement the existing assortment (of national brands) with private lable merchandise where K mart could control production and merchandise flow to meet high demands."

In the 1977 Annual Report, K mart noted:

> K mart is the major retailer of national brand merchandise in the United States. A national brand, by definition, implies good quality. However, a store that carries the breadth of merchandise of a K mart must sell more than just nationally-branded products. K mart assures consumers that all merchandise on K mart shelves, regardless of the name on the label, is of high quality by utilizing a knowledgeable buying organization, a broad quality control program, and systematic on-site inspection programs.
>
> Ultimately, what consumers seek in their purchase is value. Value is a function of both price and quality of the merchandise. K mart is unquestionably the price leader in the industry. That however is not the reason for our success—it is the combination of our price and our quality which results in high value to the consumer that has made us the successful retailer we are today.

Today, K mart's private label selection amounts to some 1600 items, which vary according to the season. Its philosophy about what makes the chain successful—the combination of price and quality—in effect recaptures what had been lost in the past. Price and quality—not just a price identity—that combination once again made private label a competitive brand.

The message is brought home forcefully by Marcus

> . . . but many have been the requests for a new Neiman-Marcus label to replace one that has become frayed or soiled. I've known of black-market operations in Neiman-Marcus labels with prices as high as $10 for coat labels (Marcus 1979).

K mart understands only too well the importance of that identification or image inherent in a private label. Its chairman, Robert E. Dewar, speaking at a 1979 stockholders meeting, said:

> The name "K mart" has become a household word. It is a generic term standing preeminently for low price. . . . K mart's philosophy is to give the customer good-

> quality merchandise at highly competitive prices. We expect to run the most competitive and highly promotional low-margin store in any area in which we operate. . . . Our buyers, supervised by merchandise managers, recognize the need to be alert to the changing needs of the modern-day consumer. We have often stated we do not intend to be a fashion leader, but will be very quick to follow. In our low-margin business, we cannot afford the markdowns necessary to be a real leader in fashions. But our current network of over 26,000 vendors, and the advance work we do with these vendors, enables us to follow promptly on fashion trends.

It is a case of the "follower" becoming a leader—not only with a store name, but also with an image reflected in its store-labeled merchandise.

REFERENCES

Ferry, J. W. 1960. A History of the Department Store. Macmillan Co., New York.

Gamm, I. 1976. Seventy-five Years of Walgreen Progress, *Walgreen World.* Vol. 43, No. 5. September-October. Walgreen., Deerfield, Illinois.

Hower, R. M. 1943. History of Macy's of New York, 1858–1919. Harvard University Press, Cambridge, Massachusetts.

Hoyt, E. P. 1969. That Wonderful A&P. Hawthorn Properties (Elsevier-Dutton Publishing Co., Inc), New York.

Latham, F. B. 1972. 1872–1972. A Century of Serving Consumers: The Story of Montgomery Ward. Montgomery Ward, Chicago, Illinois.

Mahoney, J. T., and Sloane, L. 1974. The Great Merchants. Harper & Roe, Publishers, Inc., New York. Copyright 1947, 1949, 1950, 1951, 1955 by John Thomas Mahoney. Copyright 1966, 1974 by John Thomas Mahoney and Leonard Sloane. By permission of Harper & Roe, Inc.

Marcus, S. 1979. Quest for the Best. Viking Press, New York.

Nichols, J. P. 1973. Skyline Queen and the Merchant Prince: The Woolworth Story. Pocket Book, New York.

Sears. 1902. Sears, Roebuck and Co. Catalog. Sears, Roebuck and Co., Chicago, Illinois.

Scull, P. 1967. From Peddlers to Merchant Princes: A History of Selling in America. Follett, Chicago and New York.

Weil, G. L. 1977. Sears, Roebuck U.S.A.: The Great American Catalog Store and How It Grew. Stein and Day, New York.

Williams, E. W. 1963. Frozen Foods: Biography of an Industry. Cahners Publishing Co., Boston.

Zimmerman, M. M. 1937. Super Market: Spectacular Exponent of Mass Distribution. Super Market Publishing Co., New York.

Zimmerman, M. M. 1955. The Super Market: A Revolution in Distribution. McGraw-Hill Book Co., New York.

3

Trends in the Industry

The retail marketplace is experiencing a private label renaissance, recharged recently in the food store segment by the emergence of generics (no-frills merchandise), in the drugstore segment by the expansion of private label lines and generic prescription drugs, and in the mass merchandise store segment by the renewed interest in private label as a reaction to the proliferation of designer label merchandise.

Food chains, independents, and wholesalers, who have steadily increased their private label stock-keeping units (skus), now are scrambling offensively or defensively to add generics in response to consumer demands. Drugstores with larger store areas, with more diversified operations (including vitamin and health and beauty aids manufacturing), and through mergers with other drug chains and a tie-in with grocery drug operations have steadily deepened their commitment to private label. As patents expire on national brand drugs, generic knock-off drugs also are gaining strength. To establish or reinforce their own identities, mass merchandise discounters, specialty shops, and variety chains are moving more into private label. Even home improvement centers are beginning to broaden their mix to include private label household chemical items and other merchandise.

The basis for most of the recent private label growth can be traced to a tightening of the economy. It began to grow taut in the late 1960s (as reflected in consumer boycotts), then was drawn near the breaking point through the 1970s and into the early 1980s (first with mounting inflation and unemployment, followed by deepening recession). As a result, today's customer has become more sophisticated or less gullible as a matter of economic survival. Shoppers no longer automatically buy the advertised image of national brands without first thinking about value for their dollar. There is much more trading off from national brands to private labels and/or generics. In recent studies of brand preferences and consumer analysis, the percentage of respondents who usually answer "no preference" has increased appreciably, up from about 3% in 1976 to around 11% in 1981.

There is a growing enlightenment on the part of retailers and wholesalers about private label's higher profit potential, its greater control over pricing (insulation against national brand price competition), its capability of offering products and labels unique to a particular store or chain, and its inherent feature of building customer loyalty.

Retailers no longer regard themselves as merchandisers of national brands only. Part of their emphasis has switched to private label, as more retailers develop marketing and merchandising strategies for their own brands. For some retailers, the problem of switching their loyalty from national brands is related to management's reluctance to change. Top managers who came up from the ranks learned to run only with national brand ads. Today's retailer's marketing philosophy is changing: They give the customer what he or she wants.

In the marketplace, generalities are misleading. Too many factors come into play in a highly competitive environment. For every action, there is some reaction. There are no clearly defined battle lines. Some merchants aggressively promote private labels, some demean them, and some play both strategies in different retail operations. Woolworths, for example, recently introduced a specialty store concept called J. Brannam, an acronym for Just Brand Names, where only branded apparel, footwear, and domestics are sold at 20–60% below department and other specialty stores.

Not all private labels are necessarily equal to or better than national brands, just as not all national brands measure up to so-called national brand quality and value.

More manufacturer involvement in private label has taken place in the past decade. In the United States, many small suppliers have entered the business; lately, they have been joined competitively by larger manufacturers, including national brand suppliers, many of them beginning to supply generic products, too. Interestingly, in Canada, the national brand manufacturers represent the major source of supply for private label and generic products. But smaller firms are beginning to tap the potential, particularly in generics.

A market for private label export also is beginning to open, especially for those retailers who have developed manufacturing facilities for their private label lines. Conversely, mass merchandisers have begun to look more to imports, where they find better quality merchandise at a lower price.

Once many different brands from many different sources filled the pipelines. In recent decades, however, there has been a cutback and a consolidation of brands and, within companies through acquisition and merger, a greater concentration of market share. In other words, conglomerates are beginning to rule the marketplace.

As part of this evolution, distinctive major categories of products are forming—national brands versus private labels versus generics. Regional brands or secondary brands and packer labels are fading away. (Packer labels, however, have gained new life in the form of black-and-white generics.) In this process, the smaller manufacturer not supplying one or more of the major categories is being squeezed out of the market. With shelf space at a premium, there is no place for weak sellers. Also, the small manufacturer, who now supplies private label and/or generics, is being threatened by large national brand suppliers, who are beginning to tap those categories in the United States.

The costs of consumer products keep mounting with higher ingredient costs, more expensive advertising budgets, the continual upgrading of packaging, increasing distribution costs, and so on. Fixed retail prices are becoming a thing of the past; there is more flexible pricing today, especially with the discount concept having the greatest impact across all market segments. Early in the game, today's market leaders—K mart, Safeway, and Revco Drug Stores—began tapping the discount concept, selling quality merchandise at a discount price with an emphasis on private label quality.

In spending millions of dollars to research and develop new products, then millions more to advertise and promote them, national brands have been forced to raise their prices proportionally. Private labels, unable to keep pace with the same budget support, traditionally follow the market leaders, setting similar quality specifications, upgrading that quality, and knocking off their packaging, advertising, and merchandising techniques wherever possible.

Private label's market strategy is by no means unique in the marketplace. For years, manufacturers have copied their competitors' innovative product ideas; it is part and parcel of the free enterprise system. Nevertheless, private label's blatant copycat pursuit has earned it a second-class status, tagged as the price brand. Recently, consumers have begun to perceive private label not only as a price brand but also as a brand offering greater value, with quality products sold at a savings. Perceptions have changed through their direct buying experience, from the greater availabilty of private labels, from the move by merchants to upgrade and tighten their quality standards for store brands, and from more awareness of private label value in the press and by consumer groups.

Also, retailers have developed either a single, top quality private label line or a tier of quality levels, selling a flagship brand as their best quality, backed up by a secondary good quality alternative offered for less money, and sometimes a third level of acceptable quality. Since 1977, generics have filled that third and some of the second tier, replacing the private label or packer labels at those quality levels.

Additionally, retailers have sharpened up their private label programs by hiring or assigning people exclusively to private label. In the past, this buying function often was incidental or an afterthought. A buyer usually devoted a fraction of his time to private label sourcing. In truth, it was easier to be an order-taker of national brands versus working to develop a strong private label line.

Now, private label departments or buying offices are being organized. Expertise in sourcing with backup in quality control and quality assurance—either internally through an in-house lab or through outside testing labs—has become commonplace. Efforts are underway to concentrate on one or two private label lines: a top quality brand and a secondary quality and/or generics.

Retailers are responding quicker to new product entries, following up with a private label counterpart. Today's test markets for new national brands are no longer kept secret very long. Within weeks or days, a merchant can have a private label response to a new product idea. A national chain like Safeway, for example, through its divisions, keeps tabs on every market across the country.

PRIVATE LABEL VERSUS NATIONAL BRANDS

In recent years, national brands have lost more market share to private label and generics. Recently released nationally projected sales data by SAMI (Selling-Areas Marketing, Inc., New York) showed that for the 12-week period ending 13 November 1981, regular private label increased 0.5%, generics climbed 1%, and all other brands declined by 1.5%. That brought regular private label to an 18.9% market share, generics to a 2.5% share (total private label 21.4%), and other brands to a 78.6% share in the grocery market category (SAMI 1982).

National brands by no means have given up their competitive struggle; their assault comes on all fronts, particularly against generics.

National brands advertise against private label, labeling it the "price brand." Lately, the attack has been directed against the "no-name brand" or "bargain brand." Procter & Gamble, the biggest advertiser in the country, has compared its Joy liquid detergent against the bargain brand, showing the performance difference. P&G's Tide also has openly challenged the bargain brands on TV.

A TV commercial with Tetley Tea spokesman Tony Randall shows him singing the Tetley jingle when he discovers a woman who has spilled her groceries in an apartment corridor. Randall, seeing the generic tea box, advises her that Tetley tastes better than her tea, which doesn't even have a name. (Ironically, both P&G and Tetley now own private label manufacturing firms.)

Hefty garbage bags match their strength against the bargain bags in TV commercials. A recent newspaper ad announced a "Hefty price cut! Without cutting quality, prices immediately reduced up to 20%" on Hefty trash and garbage bags.

Proctor and Gamble took another offensive stand recently with the introduction of its Summit brand of paper towels and bathroom tissues, debuting in June 1981. This so-called unadvertised brand, priced 25% below P&G's Bounty and Charmin brands, is targeted at customers who judge value by price. Summit represents lower quality but performs better than the low-priced competition, according to P&G.

The long-term trend in national brands is toward development of "super brands." To avoid the costs involved in the start-up of a new brand name, brand suppliers are using their well-known names as an umbrella for line extensions, i.e, Lipton Tea to Lipton Soup, Life Saver candy to Life Saver gum, Minute Maid orange juice to Minute Maid apple juice, Gerber baby food to Gerber baby shirts, and Fruit of the Loom underwear to Fruit of the Loom bath towels. This product line extension or product diversification, sometimes with another name leaning on the national brand name works like the private label strategy: creation of a family of products under a single identity. Some observers feel that effort dilutes the brand image, creating confusion with the customer. A retailer's brand names are strongest in his stores, where customers can recognize the relationship: a family of products under one roof. A brand manufacturer's family of products, sold everywhere, do not carry the same relationship. Yet efforts are underway to have national brand suppliers talk about tradition in their family of brands. These well-known and respected products have built up loyalty and trust with the buying public. The key to their success has been consistent quality, which the company is dedicated to.

National brand suppliers also now attempt to convince the consumer that their brand name itself signifies unsurpassed quality. In effect, their brand is not just another national brand but of itself, and no other brand can measure up to its quality. Some brands overqualify themselves with "new, improved" formulas to maintain that distinction. In some cases, the improvements work only to enhance their image as a distinctive product. The older formula works just as well.

A retailer's response to these maneuvers: "Today's shopper is not so easily fooled."

In recent years, retailers and wholesalers have put new emphasis on achieving the same quality and consistency in their private label manufactured products as is found in national brands. Their goal is to create a national brand image with their private labels. Many of these labels already have established a leadership role, setting their own high quality standards, not necessarily following the national brands. Through more aggressive marketing and merchandising efforts, merchants are working to position their brands as top sellers, offering customers value equal to the best that national brands can provide, no matter what hype is put into the brand image. Private labels seek not to usurp the national brands necessarily but to offer the customer an alternative.

If national brands or conglomerates controlling certain market segments are allowed free reign to command the marketplace, it is inevitable that greed crop into their objectives, affecting the consumer. Private labels afford the consumer a buying hedge, an alternative choice that is mostly less expensive, but not necessarily less in quality. Caveat emptor still applies in today's market; the smart shopper has only to be more wary about being influenced by creative selling techniques.

CUTTING THE FRILLS

Much can be learned from history; private label's past certainly is prologue to today's retailing business. In the 1930s, early supermarkets debuted with all the frills cut out of the operation in order to achieve discount pricing. Today, food merchants are opening no-frills stores again, now called limited assortment, box, and warehouse stores.

The no-frills approach captured Grand Union's fancy in September 1979, when this Elmwood Park, New Jersey-based chain introduced its Basics Food Warehouse in Sunrise, Florida. The store was a high-volume, low priced warehouse outlet carrying some 3300 different items in grocery, meat, produce, and general merchandise. Its success led to a chain of 22 Basic stores in six states and also inspired Grand Union to introduce a Basics generic line into its traditional supermarkets, the first new product name introduced by the chain in several decades. The line now includes more than 100 items.

The no-frills store craze began in 1976, when Aldi GmBh of West Germany acquired the 24-store Benner Tea Co., Burlington, Iowa, converting those units to the Aldi format of low gross margins and high-volume sales. Aldi began with national brands, offered on special deals, but soon developed a mix of 85–95% packer labels, all carrying different names, all identified as distributed by Aldi–Benner. Aldi's approach was really a private label store, but without any claim to consistent quality.

In August 1979, A&P launched its Plus Discount Foods limited assortment store, stocking these outlets with 90%-plus private labels, all under the new "Plus" label. The Plus store is a replay of the cash-and-carry store that A&P tested early in this century as a precursor to its Economy Stores.

Looking backward again to the 1930s, A&P did the unforgivable thing of comparing its private label prices against national brand prices. Today, retailers are beginning to employ this tactic, carrying it a step further with ingredient comparisons in health and beauty aids, for example. A recent convert to this strategy is an oldtimer, Montgomery Ward. For the first time ever, Ward in its 1981 fall–winter general catalog is using a comparison shopping program, where "direct feature-by-feature comparisons of the Ward item (are made) with well-known brand name items" allowing "the catalog shopper to judge quality versus price on 15 pages of fashion merchandise to a degree not previously possible in the catalog." Ward's catalog merchandise manager Sidney N. Doolittle explains: "In order to duplicate the brand name items as exactly as possible, and not to be lower-quality imitations, we established stringent requirements for their development and manufacture. Stitch for stitch, button for button, this merchandise duplicates their more expensive counterparts in every way we were legally able." Doolittle adds that this program has been underway for more than two years, encompassing "painstaking tests" by both Ward's own test lab and an outside agency to assure validity of duplication.

In his book, "Quest for the Best," Stanley Marcus attacks the designer labels as "security blankets" for the professional managers who have "a limited qualitative knowledge of merchandise" Marcus argues that these managers now adopt the designer names because it's easier than attempting to improve their own stocks (Marcus 1979, p. 34).

Once only specialty shops carried these lines; now they are available everywhere, including discount chains at a discount price. Designers often license their names to diverse lines of products. And this product line extension, where the designer collects a royalty fee, pushes the retail price up 10–20% more than if the item carried the store's own label (Marcus 1979).

But the designer label fad has now backfired. This proliferation of designer labels has convinced the specialty stores to look to private labels made exclusively for their stores. By so doing, they gain an exclusive "brand" image with unique merchandise (their own lines) priced attractively for their customers. Private label also offers the clothes manufacturer better control with overhead, knowing that a particular store will order merchandise versus just throwing their goods out to the general market.

Steven Somers, president of I. Magnin, was quoted early in 1982 in the *Wall Street Journal*, saying that I. Magnin's private label sales have climbed from 5% in 1980 to 15% currently. He expected them to increase to 25%.

Donald V. Seibert, chairman of the board of J. C. Penney Co., told stockholders at the firm's 1981 annual meeting (Seibert 1981):

> A prime growth opportunity for J. C. Penney is the development of quality basic fashion items under our own private labels. In recognition of the fact that the vast majority of American consumers shop for price and quality as well as fashion, traditional department stores are now beginning to emphasize their own private labels. Penney's private labels have made extremely healthy gains over the past few years. Two good examples are "Plain Pocket" jeans and our "Fox" shirt, both of which started in the men's division and were subsequently extended to both the children's and women's division.
>
> In the home furnishings area, our bed and bath accessories and decorative items have a look and quality of department store designer brands and, like all our private labels, offer a substantial price edge. Our established Penney fashion labels are an important element in helping to position the company to serve profitably a growing base of consumers in the years ahead" (Seibert 1981).

DRUG CHAINS' INTEREST

In the past decade, there has been phenomenal growth of private label in the food and the drug chains, which individually now report yearly sales gains of from 10 to 40% or more in their private label lines. The penetration of private label climbed from 20 to 30% of total sales in major food chains, while drug chains are just now beginning to edge upward from 5 to 10% or more of sales.

Private label in the food retail segment evolved first in the canned food category, then in frozen foods, followed by household chemicals and paper supplies. More recently, there has been strong growth in health and beauty aids (including vitamins—now breaking into a category by itself) and general merchandise. The increasing consumer awareness of private label value coupled with its improved quality have earned the trust of shoppers. It is now possible for manufacturers to market private label feminine napkins and disposable douches. Manufacturers are now looking closely at the cosmetic area for possible private label penetration. With new product categories opening for private label, areas familiar to the drugstore segment, it is not surprising to see drug chains take more interest.

In the drug segment, private labels started out strong through the efforts of Rexall and Walgreen, both having developed franchise programs with a uniform advertising support. Retail druggists supported fair trade laws (resale prices) on drugs and cosmetics to stay competitive and not be preyed on by competition's price cutting. When these laws were weakened in the late 1950s, private label in the drug chains suffered. Drugstore competition began offering discount prices on national brands, drawing customers away from the chains. In some cases, drugstore private label items were priced higher than comparable national brands.

Walgreen moved to develop self-service in 1949. Mail-order firms and discount food stores began to move into the prescription business, the lifeblood of drugstores. In reaction to this, Walgreen began to stress low-priced prescriptions in the 1960s.

The trend obviously was toward discount operations. Revco Drug Stores, Winesburg, Ohio, began business in 1956 as a discount drug chain, pioneering the low-overhead discount concept in the drug field. As part of its low-priced image, the chain introduced private label under its Revco label in 1960, primarily to build up customer loyalty which, in the drug business, is marginal at best. Its first stores averaged about 3200 square feet; today, they are closer to 8450 square feet, permitting room for more Revco-branded items. The company reports that in 1970 there were less than 100 private labels in its program. That number has shot upward to more than 400 different items today. In five years, 1974 to 1979, private label sales at Revco leaped by 300%. Now the company reports that 7% of its total $1 billion-plus sales are in private label.

Revco has strengthened its manufacturing capability through acquisition. In 1971, the chain purchased Private Formulations to guarantee an adequate supply of vitamins and food supplements and to tap the potential for additional business. (Today, the company operates a similar facility, Winning Labs in Santa Ana, California.) Another important acquisition came in 1977: Barre–National, the country's leading producer of liquid generic drugs. Says Revco:

> Generic prescription sales are increasing at an annual rate of over 15%. It has been estimated that by 1985, the market for generics will have increased to over $3 billion. . . . Changes in state anti-substitution laws, new laws allowing advertising directly to the consumer, the expansion of third party plans and their insistence on low cost but high quality pharmaceuticals, physician acceptance—all have the potential to contribute directly to the growth of the generic manufacturing business.

Revco also recently has diversified with the addition of Carter–Clogan Labs, manufacturer of human and veterinary injectibles.

Rite Aid Corp., Shiremanstown, Pennsylvania, which started as a discount drug chain in 1962, started into private label modestly, at around 2–3% of sales. Its private label sales now exceed 10% of total sales. Up until 1979, Rite Aid had not once changed its logo shield; but then a complete modernization program was enforced, affecting all aspects of its business including private label packaging. Three to four years ago, its private label sales were about 6%; they now represent 11% of front-end volume, accounting for about $750 million, with more than 1000 items in the program.

Well-established drug chains also are waking up to the potential in private label. Gray Drug Stores, Cleveland, which began its operations in 1912, over the years has expanded regionally through acquisition. In the 1960s, Gray reacted to the discount competition by acquiring Rink's Discount Department Stores, a six-store chain. A few years later, Gray purchased the Bargain City Discount Department Store chain. All this while, Gray's private label program was asleep, amounting to no more than 120–130 items. Not until 1979, when new management came in aware of private label's potential, was Gray's program jarred awake and boosted to more than 500 private label items.

In the drugstore segment, private label has been helped by greater consumer awareness of generic prescription drugs. Under patent laws, a brand name manufacturer has exclusive rights to make a drug for 17 years, giving them enough time to recover their costs and profit from the introduction. When the patent expires, the drug can then be manufactured under its generic name, selling for less because there is no cost involved in research and development. According to Walgreen in its house organ, "Walgreen World":

> A generic drug is a pharmaceutical product manufactured and sold under the compound's generic name, usually a contraction of the compound's complex chemical name. All drugs have a generic name. . . . The main difference between generic and name brand drugs is not inside the bottle, but outside—the name on the label. But there is another important difference: Generic drugs are often significantly lower-priced than name brands, sometimes as much as 50% or more. . . .
>
> The tremendous current interest in generics is due to the fact that many of the brand name patents are expiring, paving the way for increased availability of lower priced generic equivalents. By 1983, 70% of the 200 most frequently prescribed drugs are expected to be off patent.
>
> Thirty-nine states and the District of Columbia currently have laws permitting pharmacists to substitute lower priced generics for brand name prescription drugs, although the details of each law vary from state to state (Walgreen's 1979).

In the past, physicians have prescribed brand-name drugs because they are more familiar with them and, like the consumer, feel more confident with the familiar. Also, drug manufacturers' detailmen and trade advertising have had their effects. Lately, more public awareness of the benefits of generic drugs has come from TV, magazine, and newspaper reports, explaining just what generic drugs are all about.

Private labels in the drug store environment also have benefited by the increase in store selling space, either as in a single larger store or in combination with a food or a home improvement store. Combination stores can be as much as 60,000–to 80,000 square feet.

The move toward larger supermarkets, combining general merchandise with food and drug items, is another European influence—the hypermarche concept, or one-stop shopping store, which can include up to 100 checkout lanes, massive displays of a wide selection of merchandise, low pricing, and a warehouse look. This concept has had its impact on FedMart, San Diego, California, which now offers about 40,000 different items in its "general store" concept. FedMart's stores range in size from 20,000 to 208,000 square feet. The company, which developed into predominantly a private label discount chain, has lately begun to expand its selection of low-priced branded marchandise. FedMart also has adopted a generics program.

Jewel Companies, Chicago, which takes credit for introducing combination food and drug stores to the United States embraced the hypermarche idea, calling it the "Grand Bazaar." Now Jewel is switching away from discount department stores to concentrate only on drug–food operations. Interestingly, Jewel, which owns Jewel Food Stores and Osco Drug Stores, among other properties, has found that its Jewel generic program has not been successful in the health and beauty aids category. Jewel Food Stores were selling both generic and private label health and beauty aid items without any distinction in quality. Customers soon found out the only difference was price, so they naturally bought the less expensive generic items. To recapture its private label program in that category, Jewel has called upon Osco Drug to provide its Osco brand of health and beauty aids along with Osco film and its Velvetouch brand of hosiery for sale in Jewel outlets.

In keeping up with current trends, Jewel Food Stores in April 1981 introduced 10 private label fruit and vegetable items without salt or sugar added in response to growing consumer dietary needs and concerns. The cost savings with these new items are estimated at from 7.5 to 52%, according to the company. A refinement like this in private label products has been unheard of before. It is a case where private label pioneers a trend. Other regional food chains also are developing this trend with private label canned goods. Major national chains lately have started similar lines with their private labels.

CONSOLIDATING

Private labels are continually changing to meet customer demands. Retailers also are affected by the trend toward multibillion-dollar chains and buying co-ops. These merchants, however, never lose sight of the importance of private label in their product mix. The tendency has been toward fewer names. Not too many years ago, Fleming Companies, Inc., Oklahoma City, Oklahoma, operated its wholesale business with close to

30 different private labels. Recently, that number has been reduced to three major labels, True Value, Good Value, and Montco, to better position its brands as well as realize savings in printing costs. This food distributor also handles private labels for Piggly Wiggly, IGA and other independent retailers.

Safeway began its label consolidation by marrying all its quality brands under the "S" Brand, then switched attention to its "good quality" items. The company had narrowed its choice to eight names, such as Penny Worth, Scotch Treat, and Scotch Buy, deciding on the last because it suggested thrift, economy, and good buys. This strategy was being worked out months before Jewel Food Stores, Chicago, launched its first test of generic products in April 1977 and before the impact was felt throughout the industry. Safeway was divided on whether to adopt a generic approach, too, but decided against it. Instead, the company continued its housecleaning of a proliferation of low-end standard grade labels—Highway, Ovenjoy, Pack Train, Par, and so on. Safeway adopted the Scotch Buy label, calling its line a "second generation of generics."

In its house organ, "Safeway News," August/September 1978, the company explained its thinking. "The reasoning behind the decision boils down to a simple vote of confidence for a tried-and-true way of doing business at Safeway. Too many employees have worked too long and too hard building Safeway's reputation for quality to risk tarnishing it by adding a line of unbranded merchandise of uncertain quality." Sterling Smith, manager of the chain's Brands Buying Division, noted: "If we gave in to pressures to lower quality, our entire 'good quality' label program would suffer. With Scotch Buy, we will continue to maintain the quality levels previously enjoyed by these products, and will not suffer from a 'junk' image which may well become associated with 'generics.' "

Safeway would not adopt generics, but the chain has picked up on all the merchandising and advertising strategies, calling Scotch Buy a no-frills line, merchandising the line in mass displays like generics, and offensively attacking generics with the Scotch Buy label.

In effect, Safeway has established two categories of private label, the S Brands, representing top quality (Bel-air, Captain's Choice, Crown Colony, Cragmont, Lucerne, Town House, White Magic, and so on); and the Scotch Buy label, representing good quality. Over 40 secondary labels from different Safeway divisions have since been reintroduced under the Scotch Buy label, which now encompasses some 400 items, including all sizes, colors, and varieties.

The merger between Pic-N-Pay Supermarkets, Maple Heights, Ohio, and First National Stores, Somerville, Massachusetts, married two well-established private labels: Pick-N-Pay's Edwards label dates back to 1853, while First National, formed in 1925, has for years sold store brands under such labels as Finast, Richmond, Yor Garden, and Brookside Farms. The merger created a new label, the Edwards– Finast label, a marriage of trademarks, retaining both famous names.

At one time, Lucky Stores, Buena Park, California, carried its store name on a private label line. But in recent years, Lucky has diversified into general merchandise discount stores, auto centers, family department stores, and apparel stores. Within its food division, the company operates Lucky stores, Gemco Food Departments, Memco Food Departments, Food Basket, Eagle Stores, and Kash N' Karry stores. To overcome problems in inventory, warehousing, labeling, and chain identity, Lucky opted to develop the Lady Lee label as its top quality private label and Harvest Day as its secondary line, which now are carried in the different operations. The labels, printed with the line "distributed by Markets, Inc.," in effect creates a corporate private label not sold exclusively in Lucky Stores, but available in different operations within the company. In 1980 Lucky studied development of a yellow-and-black label generic program, which the following year was rolled out throughout its divisions. The company also centralized its corporate private labels in Dublin, California, identifying all its brands as "distributed by LKS Products."

Loblaw Companies Limited, Toronto, one of the largest food distribution firms in North America (1980 sales of $5 billion-plus), since 1975 has organized its private label programs for its various retail and wholesale operations under a buying and merchandising service called Intersave. All private label activity is coordinated through this group. Certain private labels, belonging to retailer in the Loblaw group of companies, have become corporate private labels for use by all Loblaw companies. For example, Loblaws Ontario's private label Pride of Arabia coffee is now available to all the companies. Intersave also has marketed its No Name generic program the same way. In effect, Intersave is creating national brands within its universe of companies. In 1980, a similar group, Intersave USA, was formed to develop a national brand network within Loblaw Companies' U.S. operations—National Tea Co., Peter J. Schmitt Co., and Western Grocers. A generic program and other corporate labels owned by Loblaw are being distributed under the Sunfresh identity to create the same type of network.

Today, American Stores, Salt Lake City, Utah, is the amalgamation of three separate companies, each carrying a rich private label history. In 1961, there was a marriage of Alpha Beta, La Habre, California, into Acme Markets, Philadelphia. Their combined operation recently merged with Skaggs Companies, Inc., Salt Lake City, thus bringing together the Acme, Alpha Beta, and Skaggs labels under one roof. The surviving company, American Stores, has set up the American Stores Buying Co., San Mateo, California, to handle all private label programs such as item sourcing, quality control, and packaging. There already has been some consolidation of brands plus the creation of new brands. Alpha Beta's Econ Buy generic line, for example, has been introduced into Acme markets. The company feels the time is premature to discuss its marketing strategies.

Whatever labels evolve out of this activity, they will have a solid background, dating back to the last century, when the five predecessor chains of American Stores Co. were started: Acme Tea Co. (433 stores), S. C. Childs Co. (268 stores), James Bell Co. (214 stores) Robinson & Crawford (186 stores), and George M. Dunlap Co. (122 stores). The newly created 1223-store chain early in the 1920s developed a private label program under the ASCO label, an acronym for American Stores Co., starting with canned goods. The company also retained private labels taken from the founding companies. In 1937, the company entered the supermarket business, adopting the Acme name for private labels in that type of operation, as distinguished from the ASCO label found in its grocery and combination stores. Through another acquisition Mutual Grocery Stores in 1941, the company adopted that chain's private label name, Ideal, for its first line of canned goods plus other choice grade foods.

The 1961 merger with Alpha Beta brought in another company with a rich private label history, starting early in the 1900s. Alpha Beta's first store brand appeared under the "Big 7" label, representing the seven stores in the chain. During the Depression years, Alpha Beta added the Sunrich label for standard quality products sold at reduced prices, primarily on canned fruits and vegetables plus general food products.

In one of the most impressive books published about a grocery chain, "The Alpha Beta Story," these and other tidbits about private label development are found (Cramer 1973).

During World War II, Alpha Beta was helpful in forming the Food Products Cooperative, Inc., which in 1948 came to be called Topco Associates, Inc. (Skokie, Illinois) a national co-op buying group that packed quality merchandise under the Food Club label for select food chains. Since supply sources were low during the war, Alpha Beta's private label program didn't pick up until the late 1940s.

When the chain merged with American Stores, the Topco line was discontinued as Alpha Beta picked up with products under the ASCO, Ideal (canned and frozen foods), Louella (dairy), Lancaster (meats), Virginia Lee (bakery), and Acme labels (Cramer 1973 p. 183).

The Alpha Beta label, used almost since the chain started, was reemphasized in the 1960s as the chain developed manufacturing capability in the bakery, creamery and meat packing areas.

Both Acme and Alpha Beta, since their merger, have diversified into the drug field: Alpha Beta picking up Hy-Lo Drug stores in 1961 and Acme adding Rea and Derick in 1964. Their commitment to the drug business multiplied in July 1979 with the merger into Skaggs Companies, a chain of drug and grocery stores.

Skaggs, formed in 1934, during the 1970s had a partnership with Albertsons Stores for the operation of combination food and drug stores; but that deal ended in 1977 when both chains divided up the stores.

Over the years, Skaggs has developed its private labels under a variety of names, primarily the Skaggs identity. Roughly 6–7% of its sales are in private label.

This review shows the complexity or involvement associated with retail chains and their private labels. The trend is toward a close relationship between food and drug chains with private labels carrying over from one chain to the other. Today's drug chain often carries many items once found exclusively in food or department stores. The product categories no longer differentiate between market segments such as food, drug, and mass merchandising.

The trend toward consolidation of brands has been influenced in part by the grading system of standards issued by the U.S. Department of Agriculture.

IGA, for example, over the years has developed two controlled brands, IGA and Happy Host, both top quality that duplicate the national brands. In 1979, IGA instituted a three-tier labeling program, keeping IGA as the top grade while introducing Royal Guest as an extra standard grade line and Much-More as the standard grade (IGA's answer to generics). That same year, the buying co-op introduced some 500 new private labels, including many items under the new labels. Usually, IGA introduced no more than 75 private label items a year. (In 1981, IGA dropped its procurement function, serving its membership only as a franchise operation.)

In the mid-1930s, another buying co-op of independent retailers formed as the National Retailers Grocers, headquartered in Chicago. But when differences in philosophy as to how private label should be handled erupted in different regions of the country, the group broke into three geographic sections: West Coast, East Coast, and Central states. The latter section developed in 1948 as Shurfine Central, eventually becoming one of the largest distributors of controlled labels in the country. Some 1756 items are sold to its membership of warehouse operators. This retailer-owned co-op developed as a nonprofit middleman, supplying its members with some 10 to 15 different brands, items like Soflin paper products, Embassy appliances and gloves, Energy charcoal, MC^2 detergents, Viktor aluminum foil and plastic bags, Sheerfine pantyhose, Shurfine food items, Shurfresh perishable items, and Food King standard quality products. For better merchandising control, these labels have been consolidated into Shurfine, Shurfresh, and Thrift King (the latter representing standard grade items in response to generics).

Shurfine Central started its private label program basically with staple items—canned fruits and vegetables, shortening, salt, margarine, and flour. The group then expanded into frozen foods and health and beauty aids. In the past 5 years, the line has been extended into manufactured packaged foods: macaroni an cheese, dry-frozen items, and so on. The group provides such services as buying, quality assurance, package design, package procurement, shipping, promotions, and computerized data services.

In 1948, another group, Topco Associates, was organized on a cooperative basis by supermarket chains and grocery wholesalers. They wanted centralized services to handle purchasing, product development, quality standards, packaging, and distribution (from production to end user–member warehouses). Its controlled label program centered around first quality goods under the Top Frost label for frozen foods, Food Club for dairy and processed foods, Topco for household products and health and beauty aids, Top Crest for general merchandise, and Top Fresh for produce. Topco also developed the Gaylor and Valu Time brands for lower quality goods, as well as brands like Dog Club for pet foods, Top Spread for margarine, and Beacon for beauty aids. A subsidiary, Kingston Marketing, introduced the Kingston label for first quality items and Dartmouth for lower quality items.

Today, Topco lists more than 2000 private label items. It has become one of the largest distributors of generic products under the Valu Time label. Two Topco member chains are out front in terms of generic skus: King Sooper in Denver with 550-plus items and Smith Food King, Salt Lake City, with more than 350 items. Other labels have become less important than the Topco and Valu Time lines.

In recent years, A&P has consolidated its private labels into three tiers, A&P brand being top fancy grade, Ann Page a secondary or extra standard grade, and Marvel the standard grade. When generics made their impact, A&P introduced a no-brand, black-and-white label into what it calls an Economy Shop section in its stores. That line more recently has been relabeled with a "P&Q" identity, replacing the Marvel label.

The move toward consolidation has affected other market segments with well-established private label lines. As early as the 1960s, Montgomery Ward cut back its family of trademarks from 168 to 16. The firm had been dealing with some 15,000 suppliers. That number was trimmed to 7000 with about 50% of the merchandise coming from just 300 manufacturers, thus creating more efficient control.

About 1965, G. C. Murphy Co., McKeesport, Pennsylvania, a general merchandise retailer, carried some 26 different store brand names, a name for nearly every product category. The firm's discount chain, Murphy's Mart, started in 1970, has literally wiped away the memory of

Carole Joanne, Carolina Moon, Patti Jo, etc. The company has retained just three private labels: Pelham for male clothing, Big Murph for work and play clothes, and the Murphy's Mart label for everything else. The last named may soon take over the other two holdouts.

At one time, the T. Eaton Company Limited, Toronto, carried 129 private label names in its store. But in 1976, this department store chain underwent major surgery, dropping its huge catalog operations (started in 1884) and decentralizing its buying operations. Eaton had to begin from scratch, restructuring its private label program and in the process cut back its trademark count to 29 names. The company also brought all its labels home, so to speak, by adding the Eaton name to each trademark identity. Viking appliances became Eaton Viking, Vanity Fair pantyhose became Eaton Vanity Fair, and so on. Where a name was weak, it was dropped, replaced by just the Eaton name. The company was careful not to discard a trademark that had built up a following. It was also cautious about packaging changes with its new logo identity and stronger tie-in with the Eaton name. Its labels now cover nearly every product category—clothing, major appliances, home entertainment, sporting goods, toys, carpeting, sheets, blankets, and pillows.

THE GENERICS SHAKEUP

What pioneering retailers did in the late 1800s, what the supermarket did in the 1930s, what the discount store did in the 1950s, generics is doing in the 1980s. The common thread: Give customers a price break plus value for their dollar. Generics were introduced to the United States market by Jewel Food Stores, Chicago, in 1977.

As with other trends, generics started as a reaction. Its roots trace to Europe, where retailers in the mid 1970s reacted to national brands by adopting their own brands, using different label styles. In 1976, Carrefour, a chain of hypermarche stores, introduced 50 "brand free products as good as the best, but less expensive." The advertising talked about "no amount of fancy wrappings and free offers will make it taste any better. . . . Simple packs. No giveaways. No sendaways. That is why they can afford to be as good as any of your favorite brands." Produits Libre, which was really a private label line, had simple packaging: a red-and-blue band with the Carrefour symbol against a white background along with just the generic name of the product on the label.

Jewel, which already had a private label line of top quality products, picked up on the "brand free" concept as its reaction to the debut of Aldi–Benner's no-frills, limited assortment store. A few months after Aldi opened its operations, Jewel began testing "generic label products," packaged in a plain white label with a green-and-black stripe in some 13 stores during February 1977. Jewel also covered itself by quietly launching a no-frills store, Jewel T Discount Grocery, in Florida, aimed at the price-oriented food shopper. By the end of 1977, there were 11 Jewel T stores; 1978 ended with 29 stores; 1979 with 100 stores; and 1981 is projected to close with more than 190 Jewel T units, making this concept Jewel's fastest growing chain.

The generics program at Jewel has had similar success. Started as a small selection of basic items, the line now numbers 350-plus items, making it one of the largest generic selections in the country. Jewel introduced this line as a price brand. In a brochure, headlined "Jewel is peeling away the frills to get down to brand new savings! Basic bargains are here—the 'no brand name' alternative," Jane Armstrong, Jewel's vice-president of consumer affairs, identified them as "our generic (no brand name) private label family of basic bargains.

"These products represent real savings," Armstrong continued. "When applicable, they are of standard grades as opposed to Grade 'A' or the 'top' qualities. On items that are nutritionally labeled, you can see for yourself that they are the same, or very close to the nutritional values of comparable brand name items."

Jewel explained in that brochure that generics may not have eye appeal, but they did work well in casseroles and stews; in household products, they get the job done.

This introduction marked the beginning of generics in the United States; and Jewel's strategy pretty much set the pattern for other retailers and wholesalers. The key elements in a generics program became standard or acceptable quality, plain packaging, one size—usually the best seller in a product category, no extensive advertising or promotions, constant low pricing, and a special generics section set up in the store with some generic items cut into other sections of the store.

Since Jewel Food Stores operates only in a few Midwestern states, its generics test was not considered significant until others began their own generic programs. Supermarket chains jumped on the generics bandwagon early in 1978. But the most significant newcomer to the generics fold was Topco, which had more national penetration through its membership. Topco debuted its Valu Time generics line, a black-and-white label, in February 1978. As it happened, one of Topco's members, King Soopers Discount, a chain based in Denver—(the city where late in 1966 consumers began a series of supermarket picketing efforts to protest the rise in food prices) had a good working relationship with Star Markets in Boston. The latter chain, a division of Jewel Companies, had already picked up on Jewel's generics program. Learning about how successful generics were, King Soopers worked with Topco to develop a similar program. King Soopers also shares data with three noncompetitive chains: Pathmark, Woodbridge New Jersey; Schnucks, Bridgeton, Missouri; and Ralph's Grocery, Los Angeles. Almost immediately, Pathmark and Ralph's followed King Soopers lead into generics, each picking up a slight color design to distinguish their otherwise black-and-white labels. Ralph's identified its line "Plain Wrap" off the label but within its merchandising and marketing effort, while Pathmark called its line "No Frills" on the label as well as in promotion and advertising efforts. Schnucks, also a member of Topco, started its generics Valu Time program in April 1978. They all have pretty much developed a "store within a store" selling concept, which features a wide selection of generic items. At last count in January 1982, King Sooper took the lead with some 550-plus items—the largest count of generic products in the country.

As generics developed, the reception elsewhere was at best lukewarm to icy cold. At the May 1979 Food Marketing Institute Convention, a special generics session (the first of its kind for FMI) featured prominent speakers who almost unanimously pronounced generics dead. They said that generics was only a fad, which eventually would go away. One speaker, broker Marsh Blackburn, president of Sales Force Companies, Shiller Park, Illinois, contradicted his fellow panelists saying that generics would not go away because the customers wanted them. Blackburn went on to say: "Generics does present a challenge to retailers that hasn't been met by many . . . the consensus is most retailers concentrate on 'buying best' and 'selling cheap'! Generics requires marketing ability, since it can be positioned as both an offensive or defensive merchandising concept. Defensively, the line can be placed as a counter to price competition, and only promoted when threatened by a price leader. Offensively, generics provide the opportunity to present a low price image through advertising and promotion, as well as floor displays." He added that customers believe in generics and perceive them as a price/value item.

Most retailers who adopted a program did it more as a defensive strategy to stay competitive. The giant supermarket chains dug in for a fight, Safeway merchandising its secondary line of Scotch Buy items with a generics sell and Kroger pushing hard with its secondary line, Avondale.

A&P, however, was quick to spot the trend and added generics in the spring of 1978. Its move was defensive in response to strong programs being developed by Pathmark on the East Coast and Jewel in the Midwest. When Pathmark introduced a No Frills generic line, its market competitors, retailer Acme Markets and wholesaler Wakefern Food Corp (Shop-Rite Supermarkets) declared war on generics. Acme brandished its own brands in advertisements, saying "the price is the same. Acme quality at a generic brand price." Shop-Rite lumped all its packer labels together under the banner headline "Money Saving Brands," saying its stores are proud of these little known local and regional brands that save customers the same as generics—"the anonymous alternative."

Since then, Acme Markets has joined the generic camp with its Econo Buy line. Recent reports say the chain plans to increase the count from 60 up to 200 items, replacing several secondary private labels, such as Farmdale and Glenside items.

Shop-Rite, also has rolled out a generics program defensively under the M$B (Money $aving Brands) label, quietly introduced and cut into its regular aisle space. The company in August 1981 for the first time devoted a full page ad to M$B with copy lines such as "The Plain and Simple Way to Save," "Variety Plus Value," "Goodness Without Fanciness," "M$B products have the same money-back guarantee as any Shop Rite product." The ad included 42 generic items with prices quoted and the frequent use of "Why Pay More," appearing 21 times in different product mentions. This wholesaler co-op now carries more than 200 generic items.

In 1978, retailers approached generics cautiously. Jewel ended the year with no more than 90 generic items. Pathmark opened its program with 27 generic grocery products. A&P started with about 14 grocery items. Stop & Shop's generic debut began with about 25 items under its "Economy" label. H. E. Butt Grocery Co., Corpus Christie, Texas, a regional chain of 150 stores, introduced 25 generic items, calling them No Frills and No Name. In Canada, Loblaws Ontario introduced the No Name yellow label line with 16 items; its competitor, Dominion, launched its White Label line with 25 products; while Steinberg started its generics entry with 30-plus products.

As generics have become more acceptable, retailers have grown bolder in entering this competition. Most retailers have adopted lines of 100 to 200 generic items.

The opposition to generics has not subsidied. It began early in 1978 and continues today.

Kroger in its 1978 annual report lashed out at generics:

> We are giving customers the same lower prices with known Kroger brands, consistent supply, guaranteed quality, and a full assortment of products and sizes. Since Kroger shoppers can get the price advantage of no-name products along with the benefits of Kroger brand products, we have no present plans to market this type product. Much has been made of the plain label, but it costs just about the same as a regular label—and could even cost more for a smaller printing run. (A label costs less than one-half cent per can.) As most companies offering these products have pointed out, the major savings comes from the fact that they are buying lower-grade products (e.g., Standard grade versus Choice or Fancy for the national brand products to which they are compared).

In expanding its private label selection, G.C. Murphy Company, McKeesport, Pennsylvania, has introduced a number of new health and beauty aids items, including these first aid products—all under the Murphy's Mart label.

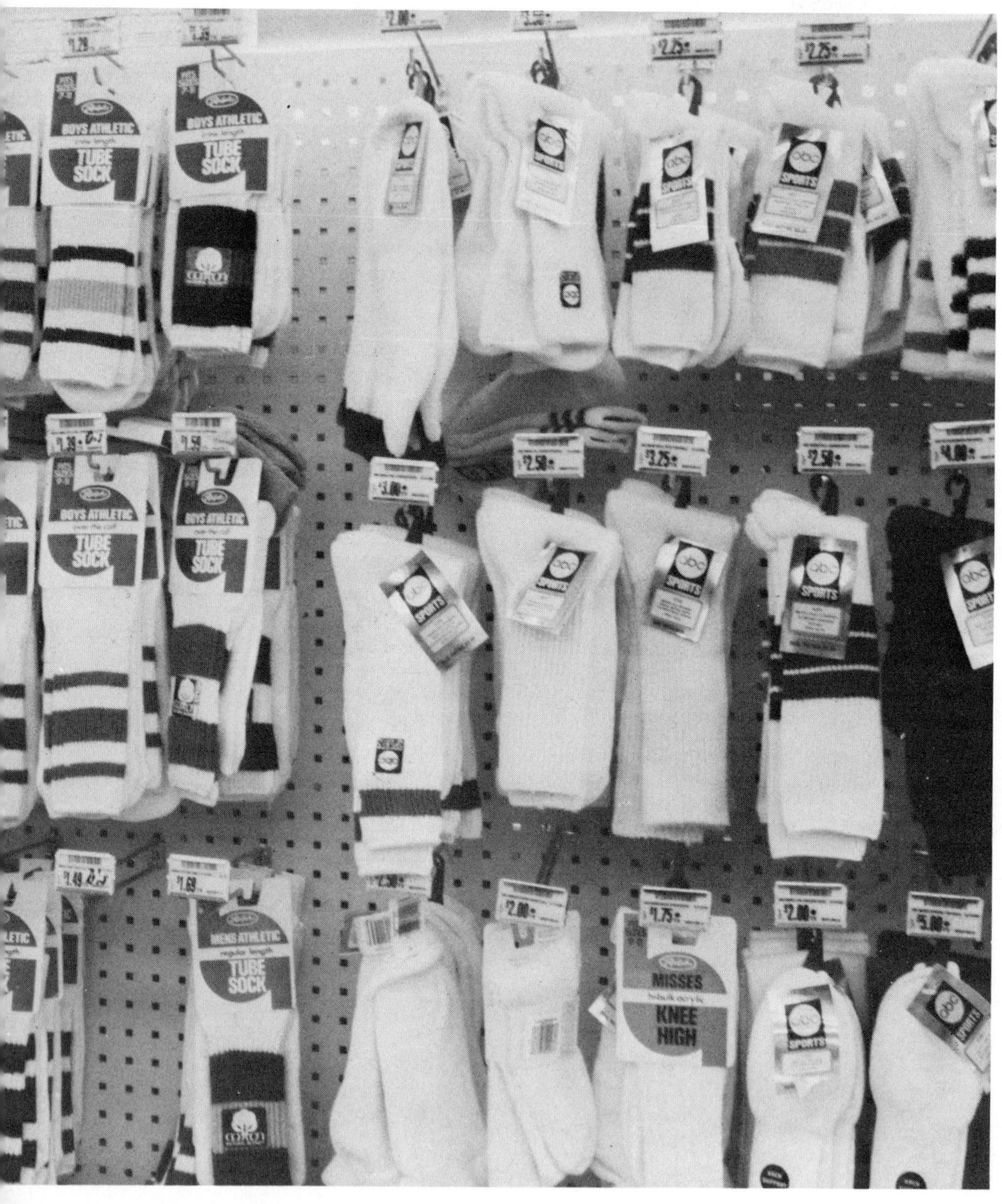

Food retailers, like Ralph's Grocery in Los Angeles, have expanded into private label general merchandise. This pegboard display shows a wide selection of socks under the Ralph's label.

Jewel Companies, Inc., Melrose Park, Illinois, was one of the first retailers to pioneer low-sodium products under its private label canned vegetables. Both its Cherry Valley and Mary Dunbar labels also feature low-sugar content.

Jack Eckerd Corp., the country's leading drug chain in terms of sales, has embarked on an aggressive private label program. Here, some new items are promoted in-store including a comparison with the national brand: Eckerd 16-ounce cocoa butter at $1.69 versus Ponds 12-ounce version at $2.89.

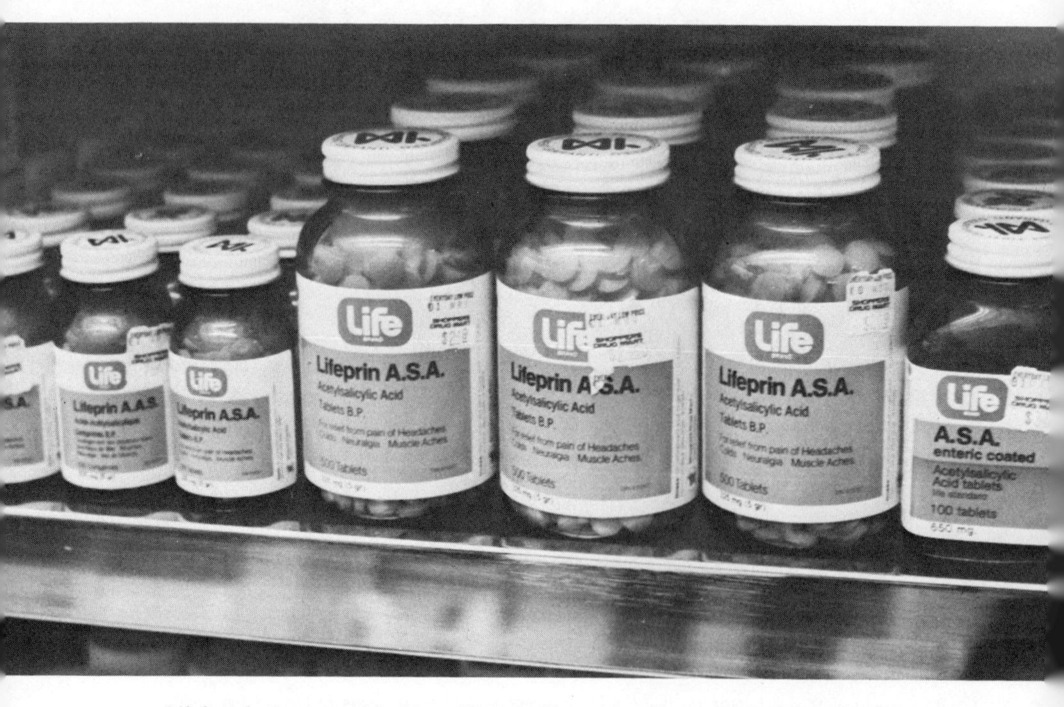

Life brand vitamins and health and beauty aids are treated as a national brand by Shoppers Drug Mart, Canada's leading drug chain. The company nevertheless sells the Life lines only in its outlets. Also, a separate private label program is maintained under the Shoppers Drug Mart label for such items as stationery, bagged candy, paper products, nuts, hosiery, and so on.

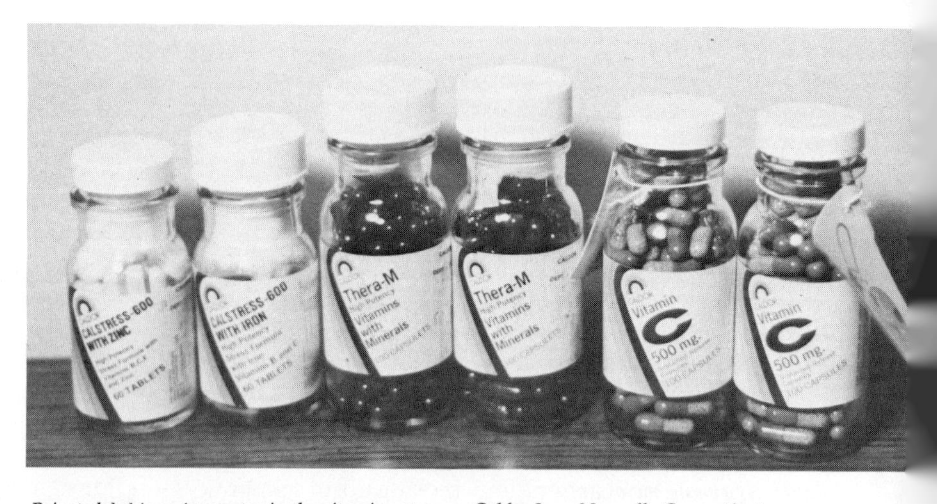

Private label is an innovator in the vitamin category. Caldor Inc., Norwalk, Connecticut, offers complex formulas—Calstress-600 with zinc or iron and Thera-M high potency vitamins with minerals—plus time-release vitamin C in a higher dosage (500 mg). The clear plastic bottles also feature consumer information attachments.

In March 1981, Kroger began rolling out its economy label, Cost-Cutter. Previously, the company had used Cost Cutter as a merchandising slogan for all its brands. The Cost Cutter count now exceeds 100 items and is beginning to cut into Kroger's secondary labels Avondale, Embassy, Kandy, etc. Unconsolidated, these labels do not carry the impact of a generics line. The new label was adopted as a private label generic line, much like Safeway's strategy with Scotch Buy and A&P's latest strategy with the P&Q label.

In September 1981, A&P introduced P&Q, the letters in white against a green logo shape similar to A&P's logo identity, along with the letters representing price and quality.

Richard Beazer, vice-president of national procurement at A&P, noted recently at a Private Label Manufacturers Association (PLMA) meeting that after evaluating its generics program "we recognized that consumers wanted this quality level product and wanted to save money, but they also had some doubts about what they could expect from the generic products in various categories. We felt that if this was to be a long-range program, we had to identify this product and the quality levels with the consumer and A&P together. We then began to develop the P&Q label. This is A&P's generic price and consistent quality product. We feel that anything that sells strictly on price is a short-lived product. Consumers are looking for a real value, the trade-off between price and quality. The quality of the product must be consistent; the consumer will be more confident in a product or program if she knows that the store will stand behind it. By putting our identity on the product, we feel that this is our way of telling the consumer that we will stand behind our claims" (Beazer 1981).

Shortly after P&Q's debut, Winn-Dixie Stores, Jacksonville, Florida, introduces its version of a plain generic line with the label Price Breaker—identified in red letters against a white background contained in a star-shaped setting. Most of the label, however, is yellow, including four-color graphics of the product. It is really a private label, positioned against competitor's generics. The company says that its products will not be standard grade, but extra standard or fancy, depending on supply. Price Breaker replaces the chain's packer labels, which were becoming too difficult to merchandise.

In fact, during 1981, the country's second, third, fourth and fifth largest food chains—Kroger (Cost Cutter), A&P (P&Q), American Stores (Econo Buy), and Winn-Dixie (Price Breaker)—have followed Safeway's lead with a private label generic line, picking up on economic-sounding names.

Wholesalers have been more reluctant about adopting generics. Yet, they have relented. In a generics survey of its membership, the National-

American Wholesale Grocers' Association, New York, found that most of its members waited until 1980 before taking on generic programs. Its 1980 report showed 76% of the wholesale food distributors carried generics, while 40% of that number had introduced it in 1980. The wholesalers added generics mainly because their customers demanded it and because it added new sales volume to their stores.

At the same PLMA meeting where A&P's Beazer spoke, Art Grundberg, principal at Arthur J. Grundberg Inc., Arlington Heights, Illinois, also addressed generics. Grundberg cited one buying group for 36 wholesalers in 30 states offered 50 generic items to only three wholesalers in the group during 1980. But in January 1981, 20 wholesalers carried generics out of 250 items offered, averaging 50 items per wholesaler. Nine months later, 28 wholesalers were committed, while generic case movement multiplied tenfold from June 1980 to June 1981. He added that only 12 wholesalers in the group really promote generics and do very little to merchandise them.

When focusing on specific markets or in specific chains, generics usually rank as the top seller among the top three "brands" in a product category. A 1981 Denver Post Consumer Analysis study, sampling 2482 people in the Denver ABC city zone, showed generics ranked near the top in 82 product categories. In 28 of those categories, generics ranked among the top three in consumer preferences.

Retailers in that market report that in three years many generics shot up to the top three positions in a product category, with no mortality in sight. The popularity of generics has virtually allowed that grouping of products to serve as a launching pad for many new products that achieve their potential almost immediately. Generics also are creating new consumption habits, bringing back products that were almost dead in the national brand or private label categories. Preserves and jellies, for example, suffered poor sales in one chain, until introduced as generics.

The profit margins on generics range anywhere from 15 to 30%, but can climb higher in health and beauty aids. In Denver, which is considered one of the hottest generic markets in the United States, it is estimated that generics take an estimated 10% of grocery sales.

Some say that the publicity that generics has received through the press has really made generics successful. The bargain prices—30–50% lower than the national brands—have made good copy especially in an economic situation that has eaten into everyone's budget.

The press helped generics appreciably in Canada, where the leading retail food chains, Dominion, Loblaws, and Steinberg, all adopted generics early in 1978. Loblaw Companies has been an exceptional leader in promoting generics, thanks to the efforts of David A. Nichol, president of the Loblaws Ontario chain, developing his No Name program differently. Instead of positioning generics as a price brand only, using standard grade product or acceptable quality, Nichol went after what he calls a "differentiated marketing approach." He searched for value first, "making the generic quality sometimes better than the national brands, sometimes the same quality, sometimes different, but in all cases always representing a better value." The potential generic products were consumer tested for their quality; attempts were made to create top quality by looking to other means to cut costs—packaging with less expensive materials, standardizing the packaging molds, changing distribution methods. A distinctive yellow label was developed, contrasting sharply with the traditional black-and-white label that sometimes featured a color stripe. Recently a number of U.S. retailers have adopted a similar yellow label for their generics programs: FedMart's Bright Yellow Wrap, Handy Andy's Smart Yellow Wrap, Lucky Stores yellow label and Twin County Grocers' Budget Line. Western Grocers and other U.S. companies belonging to Loblaw Companies are also adopting the yellow label through efforts of Loblaw's new division, Intersave USA.

Loblaws Ontario and David Nichol in particular have become outstanding representatives of generics. At a generics conference held in Toronto in May 1979, Nichol announced: "The time has come for No Name products and No Frills merchandising. These two ideas in their various manifestations will revolutionize your way of life in the 1980s." He also drew a distinction between generics and private labels:

> The answer is that they are derived from two different product development philosophies, pricing policies, and profit objectives.
>
> Private labels are "me-too" brands that begin with the question, "How can I exactly replicate this national brand and still offer the consumer adequate savings to switch loyalties while still preserving the same cents profit per unit?
>
> No Name product development starts with the question, "How do I change this product to produce savings which will make it the best overall value in this market while still preserving my category percentage gross margin?

Since then, Loblaws Ontario has increased its generic count to more than 350 items, representing close to 20% of warehouse shipments. Loblaws' private label program (items carrying the Loblaws name) has taken a back seat as the company has promoted No Name almost exclusively in its advertising. The generics program at Loblaws has grown so large that the company no longer mass-displays the items, but cuts them in with its regular product selections. This allows customers to make price comparisons and often reaches customers who normally would skip the generics aisle. Also, the attractive yellow packaging stands up well against more sophisticated national brand packaging.

At that Toronto generic conference, Nichol also predicted that the "me-too" national brand products will be rejected by consumers as "unjustifiably wasteful." He went on to explain:

> Lack of meaningful product differentiation is the key problem facing nationally advertised product manufacturers in Canada and the consumer knows it.
>
> A recent study of new products introduced to supermarkets over the past five years indicates that of every 500 products introduced, only two survive. Why? Because of lack of meaningful product differential.
>
> North American product managers are caught up in a line extension mentality. They're spending their time on the hype instead of the product—the sizzle instead of the steak. After all, it's easier to change a package, an ad campaign, or add a holiday contest than it is to develop a meaningfully differentiated product that is difficult or impossible to duplicate as a No Name product (Nichol 1979).

These "undifferentiated products" on grocery shelves will be eliminated. One proof Nichol pointed to is the development of no-frills stores carrying some 500 items. He added that "secondary brands that just take up shelf space will have to go and national brands that can't justify their price differential to the consumer will find a great deal of competition for shelf space from faster moving, better value private label and No Name products."

One other Nichol prediction made in 1979: Within five years, 25% of all grocery sales would be in generic products. (In the spring of 1981, Nichol reported that "17% of Loblaw's grocery sales are generic and they would exceed 20% if Canada manufacturers could make Loblaw's No Name fast enough.")

IMPACT OF GENERICS

What started as a private label line and then evolved, copycat-fashion, has now turned into a revolution. Generics developed as a natural extension of private labels, but now are bumping hard against the national brands, eliminating packer labels and secondary quality private labels, and creating shock waves throughout the marketplace. Generics began within a chain's parameters, identified with a distinguishable label; today part of their strength comes from their identification as a so-called no-name brand sweeping across all retail stores, almost like a national brand, but with a price differential that national brands find tough to beat. Generics are no longer perceived as exclusive store brands, but as a national trend in the marketplace. Generics, while still developed as a private label program, are considered more a part of the public domain, where all retailers and wholesalers draw from the category. Major retailers are fighting this trend with identifiable labels (mostly economic names) that they can control with respect to quality and consistency. Different strategies with generics—packer label (black and white), one-color identity, private label economic-sounding names—are still being tested.

Many brand manufacturers are passing up advertising in favor of in-store promotions and coupon deals to compete on the same price level as generics. More frequent and deeper case allowances on brands are being offered to retailers as part of a price-cutting fad. Some national brand manufacturers are coming out with secondary price brands without any advertising—Proctor & Gamble's Summit, for example,—to compete with generics. There also is more interest on the part of national brand suppliers in producing generic products, often through a subsidiary that is difficult to trace back to the parent firm. A number of major firms that would not have considered producing generic products are now actively bidding for business with retailers.

Generics are revitalizing the private label category, virtually carrying it along as an alternative value for the customer. The battle lines are being clearly drawn in most retail outlets: national brands, versus private labels, versus generics.

Many other benefits are built into generics. The category, for example, is picking up flat sellers—items that were being phased out in private label or national brand categories. Generics are helping the retailer sharpen his image as a discounter, offering the customer a constant low price. Sometimes generics pull a manufacturer out of the red, especially when a commodity is affected by price increases. Generics, sold at a lower price, can double the volume of sales. Without generics, customers would resist the higher priced brands; with generics, they get some pricing relief. Generics also are helping retailers build store traffic and increase their sales volume.

Not all generics are standard grade products. Some items (especially manufactured goods) equal private label or national brands in quality. When supplies glut the market, packers will put choice and fancy grade into the plain label packages. There is danger here, because customers who try these products and come to expect that quality in a particular commodity may be disappointed later when the supply dries up, leaving only standard grade in generic. Perhaps the consumer has learned to expect inconsistencies in generic quality. Perhaps not.

Generics have already covered the basic grocery categories and are now penetrating the other categories—health and beauty aids, frozen foods, meats, general merchandise—almost to a point of being ridiculous, with items like generic potting soil or generic apples, and the like.

In the product mix, generics have caused many retailers to expand their no-frills item selection at the expense of general merchandise line. Also, the secondary brands or those brands that do not sell well are being weeded out to create room for generics. Additionally, retailers are reappraising the variety and size selection of national brands. Of course, generics do not necessarily succeed in all product categories. In fact, some areas are tough to crack, such as coffee and cereal. Generics are usually perceived as a lower quality product. When that quality is the same as private label, some retailers balk at offering the generic at a lower price. On the other hand, some manufacturers refuse to reduce the quality of their products in order to offer a generics counterpart. They react by providing the same quality for both generics and private label.

Overall, generics are being marketed in one size (the best seller) at a constant low price. The generics program now gets frequent advertising support, sometimes aggressive support, from retailers. Side-by-side price comparisons between generics and national brands are not uncommon in newspaper ads. Two-page spreads, once a rarity for private label, are commonplace in newspapers now. While private label gets some of this billing, generics get the greater portion. The generic products are frequently positioned in special aisles and sometimes get double exposure by being integrated into the regular product mix as well. A passive supporter of generics will usually cut in the black-and-white label or no frills products into regular shelf space by product category, hoping they will go away eventually. Generics are not high-profit items when compared to private label or national brands.

The story is still being written on the generics phenomenon. The trend appears to be a development of no-name generics (black-and-white or yellow-and-black labels) and private label generics (the retailer/wholesalers' own brand identity or color design). The no-name lines can be positioned as packer label generics (each plain label identified with different manufacturers as the source) or as a no-name generics (identified as distributed by a retailer/wholesaler or its manufacturing subsidiary). The private label generic lines are often no frills labels with a simple, plain design distinctly linked to the retailer/wholesaler; sometimes, however, the packaging can be four-color with effective graphics, almost like the private label lines. The difference between private label generics and regular private labels is that the former are marketed and merchandised like generics, positioned as an economy brand.

NEWCOMERS

There are many other developments that point to significant changes in the market.

Private labels, which have been around for decades, have been strongest in the food and mass merchandise market segments. In recent years, more drug chains have either started or boosted their private label programs, particularly in the health and beauty aids area. While no single drug chain now accounts for more than $2 billion in sales, the drug operations through horizontal (chain mergers) and vertical (manufacturing acquisition) growth are paying more attention to private label and generic prescription drug programs. One of the largest drug chains in the country, Jack Eckered Corp., Clearwater, Florida, has started to expand its interest in private labels, which at best was a mere token effort in the past. A company representative recently confided: "We're just learning to walk with private labels."

Jack Eckered is located primarily in the South, which traditionally has been a weak market for private label development. Perhaps private label has not had the impact there as in other parts of the country, because of its physical and demographic characteristics: The South is still fairly rural; most of the Black population in this country live in the South. Consumer studies have shown that the poor, uneducated consumer is more likely to buy national brands than private label, because of the status recognition built into brands. TV advertising also plays an important part of their buying decision.

But these factors are changing. And the South is waking up to private label, and generics. A number of retailers and wholesalers based there are now launching or expanding their programs.

Winn-Dixie Stores, Inc. for the past 25 years has carried private labels. Its brands include Thrifty Maid in canned goods and commodities, Arrow in household supplies, Sunbelt in paper products, Crackin' Good in snacks and desserts, Tropical in jellies and preserves, and Astor in various grocery items. The chain also carries bakery and dairy items under its label. As mentioned previously, Winn-Dixie has recently consolidated more than 15 of its packer labels under the new economy label, Price Breaker, as a response to the growth of generics in its marketing areas.

Piggly Wiggly Corp., claims to be the first in the food business to feature a full line of nationally advertised brands. All the stores that operate under the Piggly Wiggly name are licensed by the corporation. The system is made up of members of any size, from one- and two-store operations up to chains of 50 or more stores. The members are voluntary groups of Piggly Wiggly operators who share a common buying source or cooperative groups that own their own warehouses. Their private label program under the Piggly Wiggly brand really did not get started until 1970. The corporation began cautiously putting its name on products only when they measured up to expectations. It was difficult to get the right quality, a company spokesman notes. Eventually, the program expanded from canned goods into health and beauty aids and then processed foods. Today, there are some 650 private label items in the line.

Alterman Foods, Atlanta, until the mid-1970s had only a few private label products. Its marketing thrust had always been toward national brands, because the company believed that the famous brand names offered at a low price served as a better customer draw. The brands also provided co-op advertising allowances, special trade deals, and promotional support. Why change?

Change did come when Alterman's competition began expansion of their private label lines, chains like Kroger, Winn-Dixie, Colonia, and Tenneco. When Del Haize, a grocery giant based in Brussels, Belgium, took over Alterman Foods in 1980, the new corporate thinking became: Convey a low price image in the marketplace.

Alterman's new pro-private label strategy is now based on the belief that more private label products help (Martin 1981):

- To convey a low-price image to the customer.
- To ensure continuity of product, general quality and price with a label that is uniquely Alterman's.
- To produce a slightly better profit margin than national brands.
- To serve as a rein on national brands, preventing them from overpricing especially in areas where a single brand is dominant.
- To give Alterman's control over the quality and nature of the products.

Alterman's Big Apple stores have all been converted to the Food Giant label.

Associated Grocers of Florida, Inc., Miami, a retail-owned co-op (member of Shurfine-Central, Northlake, Illinois and its controlled label program), sees a greater demand for lower-priced products in the past couple of years. Its Thrift King economy line reportedly has increased by 50% in the past two years in terms of warehouse shipments.

CATEGORY PENETRATIONS

The newcomer making the most noise in the private label business is generics. As an extension of private label, generics since 1978 (while Jewel was testing the concept) have been popping up everywhere in the food segment: Topco's Valu Time, Pathmark's No Frills, Ralph's Plain Wrap, Stop & Shop's Economy Line, Fedmark's Bright Yellow wrap, Dominion's White label, Loblaws No Name, Von's Slim Price, and First National's Good 'N Plain. Generic labels also are evolving with more color. Handy Andy, which started in 1977 with a white label identified with a brown stripe, lately has adopted a Smart Yellow Label identity.

Most of the newcomers to the private label business have been in new products and new product categories.

Private label women's hosiery got its biggest boost in 1970, when Hanes introduced L'eggs with a multimillion national advertising campaign. Its marketing efforts pioneered the use of promotions and incentives for hosiery in supermarkets. Its unique package, the plastic egg, and its boutique display sparked attention from the consumer; and private label took advantage of the hoopla by positioning its lines right next to the L'eggs display. When Kayser Roth introduced its No Nonsense hosiery in a pouch early in the 1970s, the effect hurt private label temporarily. Since then, private label hosiery has improved in quality and packaging, adopting many of the merchandising techniques of the national brands.

Food markets recently began diversifying into general merchandise products—batteries, socks, motor oil—until generics developed, causing some of them to pull back on that selection. Nevertheless, general merchandise still represents an important new area for private label development. In 1978, for example, Safeway, added some 300 new private label items, many of them in the general merchandise category: two new private label categories—automotive supplies (air filter, oil filter, and motor oil) and footwear (jogging shoes)—plus expansion of existing categories with some 69 items, including: kitchen and bath textiles (sponge, furniture polish and air fresheners), aluminum foilware pans, health and beauty aids (toothbrushes, petroleum jelly, cotton swabs, aspirin, vitamins, and minerals), and camera film (added in 1979).

A Safeway spokesman recently noted: "Used to be Bayer Aspirin had it all, now we have a good share of that. We didn't think we could ever stock film against Kodak."

New private label items continually appear in the marketplace, such as room and carpet fresheners, baby towelettes, and feminine napkins. Private label is beginning to crack into some of the toughest product categories, such as douches. Some new products do not always succeed under private label. Liquid soap, introduced a couple of years ago, has failed somewhat in private label due primarily to stiff national brand competition and interest in this developing category. It is still also difficult for private label to find its share of business in baby food, cold cereals, cosmetics, beer, and cigarettes, but generics has had a strong impact on the last two categories.

At one time, drugstores served as the only important source for vitamins. Today, health food stores, supermarkets, and mass merchandisers are taking their share of the business, particularly with private label lines in the alphabet vitamin segment. Private label vitamins C and E command the market. The national brands go after the multiple, B-complex, children's chewable, and iron tonic formulas. More and more retailers now realize the high profit margins—up to 60% or more—found in private label vitamin sales. Generics also are making an impact in the vitamin areas. Retailers recently have begun testing vitamin or nutrition centers in their stores as a reaction to the health food store craze.

Private label quality and consistency are keys to its success. Consumer awareness of that quality is increasing through their own trial-and-error buying and through more publicity in the press.

In a TV news report, "Cosmetics, The Big Put-On," WCBS-TV New York reporter John Stossel investigated how a private label cosmetics manufacturer in New Jersey produces cosmetics for all the prestige companies: Payot, Orlane, Charles of the Ritz, Germaine Monteil, Diane Von Furstenberg, and Lancôme, producting items like lipstick, mascara, cream rouge, liquid make-up, face powder, and eye shadow from the raw material to a final product.

Using undercover buyers, Stossel was able to compare two lipsticks, one a $3 item sold in discount stores, the other a $7.50 Lancôme lipstick, both with the same purple shade and the same ingredient label. The case for the lower-priced lipstick cost 40 cents versus Lancôme's container at 45 cents.

When Stossel confronted Lancôme Cosmetic, asking why there was a $4 difference in price, a company spokesman explained: "The expense in the product sometimes goes into the development of the product."

Stossel asked: "But is Lancôme better than, say, Wilson cosmetics or the cheaper imitations? Is there a difference?"

The Lancôme spokesman answered: "We feel it is. We feel we have the best quality control in the business."

Stossel went on to explain that the product came from the same plant in New Jersey using the same stock shades.

The Lancôme man argued that the formula was made under Lancôme's specifications and belonged to the company. Later, he admitted that the formula belonged to the New Jersey cosmetic manufacturer, but still insisted that the Lancôme lipstick was different.

When Stossel interviewed a cosmetic chemist, asking if the cost was worth it and whether the ingredients were higher quality in the Lancôme product, the chemist commented "bologna." Chemist Herman Heinrich said the products contain the same ingredients. Sometimes a company will add an exotic ingredient to its formula, but that only helps in the advertisement to convince the customer that she is getting something different.

Stossel concluded his report by saying, "[the] consumer doesn't get the facts. You got them from us only because we went under cover and because one retired chemist would talk."

The facts are simple: When private label maintains its quality, the product line can be as good as or better than the advertised brand.

The "me too" strategy of private labels is slowly changing in today's market as retailers develop stronger programs. They set their own specifications, not always exactly like the national brands, but of top quality. Their reputation is on the line, carried on every product that goes under the store labels.

TRADE MAGAZINE ESTABLISHED

The growth and evolution of private label signaled the need for a publication to cover this activity. In the trade, private label received no more than spotty coverage or just a mention in passing. Private label was mostly regarded as a second-class citizen in the marketplace. Trade associations ignored it completely in their educational conferences, while exhibitors at a trade show sold private label under the table.

That has all changed with the launch of *Private Label* magazine, which first appeared with the April–May 1979 issue. In its first editorial, E. W. Williams, president of *Private Label,* said: "*Private Label* will act as a rallying point for the furtherance of store brands across the whole spectrum of retailing: in supermarkets, drug chains; discount, variety stores and other mass merchandisers; department stores, home centers—every facet of retailing where private labels are a logical force to profitability promote store brand loyalty and profit."

In October 1979, Williams and Ralph Selitzer, editor and publisher, helped to organize the Private Label Manufacturers Association at a meeting in New York, where 20 private label manufacturers from different product categories agreed "to communicate the idea of promoting and furthering private labels to retailers and ultimately to consumers." Since that meeting, PLMA has grown to a membership of some 300 companies. The association has held major conventions in St. Louis, Chicago, and New Orleans. Its first trade show, held in Chicago in 1980, featured 58 private label exhibitors. The 1982 trade show, also staged in Chicago, attracted 230 exhibitors.

The most significant proof that private label has come into its own comes from consumers. Recent studies indicate that today's shopper is better educated and more sophisticated. And it is that type of shopper who is the best customer for private label, according to a 1979 consumer study released by Simmons Market Research Bureau, Inc., New York. The study, commissioned by *Private Label* showed the typical private label buyer as a person who earns more than $25,000 a year, is a college graduate and a professional or manager at work, and lives in a large metropolitan area. The report, extracted from data in Simmon's 1979 study of Media and Markets, covering 15,000 adults, found private label user share strongest in 30 product categories, each holding 10% or more in total category usage. The strongest private label penetrations were in interior wall paint (43.7%), car batteries (42.6%), frozen orange juice (41.4%), exterior house paint (41.1%), and vitamin tablets (39.8%) (Simmons 1979).

The 1979–1980 National Study of Supermarket Shoppers by Burgoyne, Inc., Cincinnati, showed 62.8% of consumers rate private labels "equal to or better than the national brands." They had a similar attitude about generics. Of the 37.8% of respondents who purchased generics overall rated their quality as the same as national brands. More than half of that sample felt generic paper products were somewhat lower or much lower in quality than national brands and about the same as private label products. Burgoyne found that nearly 61% of the respondents pointed to the elimination of advertising costs as the reason that private labels are priced lower than national brands. Only 31% indicated that it was because the quality was not as good or consistent (Burgoyne, 1980).

In its 1981 Food Marketing Industry Speaks/Trends, Food Marketing Institute, Washington, reported "the most popular methods shoppers use to economize are stocking up on bargains, using more price-off coupons, buying store or lower priced bands, and buying specials." Besides the traditional methods of economizing, FMI indicated that a number of people recently have begun economizing: "About one in five shoppers have only recently started buying fewer luxury or snack items and less meat, buying more store or lower price brands, and using price-off coupons." FMI also indicated that a majority of shoppers reacted favorably to supermarkets offering more generic goods (FMI, 1981).

Bon Appetit, New York, in its Trendsetter Tracking Study Wave II in the fall of 1980, prepared by Audits & Surveys, while finding data correlating closely from 1979 to 1980 in national brand and store brand familiarity, also discovered that no-frills brands are increasingly significant: 6% of respondents were not aware of generics, 32% were aware but did not try them, and 62% tried them in 1980, versus 12%, 39%, and 49% respectively in 1979. Interestingly, while no-frills brands rated low on such criteria as taste, price, dependability, and nutrition, they did much better on value: 31% for generics versus 45% for store brands and 51% for national brands (*Bon Appetit* 1980).

A few years ago, retailers were not optimistic about the future of generics; but that has all changed now, according to the results of a recent survey by Kline (1981). This report states that health and beauty aids in plain packaging represents up to 5% of total sales in that category in stores that carry generics. In polling supermarket executives, 75% of them indicated they had plans to expand their generic health and beauty aid lines.

Kline also reported that these store representatives pointed to generics as a viable alternative to higher priced national brands. They represent substantial savings to customers: priced 25–40% below the national brands and 5–20% under private label brands. These differentials, Kline continued, will likely result in reaction by national brands toward more frequent promotions in order to: "Emphasize the quality image of national brands, and decrease the price differences through coupons or special offers."

Truly phenomenal growth has been reported in generic health and beauty aids, according to Towne-Oller & Associates, Inc., New York, which began tracking private label/no name warehouse withdrawals to food stores in 1980. Percentagewise in selected product categories, no name sales and unit volume has soared dramatically from 1980 to 1981.

The growth of generics has prompted the former medical director at Warner-Lambert Co.'s Parke-Davis operation, Dr. Arthur D. Flanagan, to resign his post in order to start the Institute for Generic Drugs. The branded drugs have a back-up service at the manufacturing facility, where doctors and druggist can ask for information about unusual side effect or questions they may have about the drug. Dr. Flanagan expects the Institute to provide that same service for major generic drug producers, which he estimates at about 40 firms. National brand manufacturers, who also make generic drugs, will be invited to subscribe to this activity, too.

PRIVATE LABEL IN FOODSERVICE

Brand loyalties are crumbling not only in the retail store business, but in the foodservice industry as well. A number of foodservice operators are looking to private label products, under their own name—instead of the national brands—to expose that name before their customers. The operators feel that it re-enforces the store identity, established on the store facade as well as through advertising and promotions.

In a special report, *Institutional Distribution* Magazine (1981) found brand loyalty weak among foodservice operators, particularly in canned and frozen fruits and vegetables. In 20 product group categories, the study listed only four—shortenings and oils; frozen cakes and pies; soups; and frozen toppings—where more than 50% of respondents "always" purchased by brands. More than 30% of respondents in each category indicated they "sometimes" purchase by brands; while a significant percentage (30%-plus) in two categories, frozen coffee whiteners and frozen fruit, said they "never" buy by brand. (See Appendix 4.)

Foodservice distribution is a relatively new phenomenon. Its roots were established in the 1920s through the 1950s. Distributors, acting as middlemen between manufacturer and retailer and/or foodservice operator, began shipping goods in the retail trade with only a token effort in foodservice. As the foodservice industry began flourishing—and retail chains took up their own distribution—distributors efforts were focused more on serving restaurants, fast food chains, schools, hospitals, and other institutional markets. The trend also developed where distributors moved from dealing only in specialized goods—fish, meat, produce, or paper—into full-line distribution, supplying all the needs of their customers, the foodservice operator: food, paper products, chemical cleaning materials, tabletop items, restaurant equipment, etc.

One of the oldest private labels in foodservice is Pocahontas, started by the 107-year-old brokerage firm, Taylor & Sledd, Inc., Richmond, Virginia. The Pocahontas label was available to the retail trade back nearly to the beginning of this century. In the 1930s, Taylor & Sledd teamed up with Monarch Institutional Food Service to help the latter expand its product line beyond produce into other foods, thus making Monarch the first foodservice distributor of the Pocahontas label. Pocahontas Foods USA sold that label to retail whoesalers and chain operators as a controlled label or private label, in some cases allowing it to serve as the springboard for a retailer or wholesaler to develop labels under their own name.

Today, Pocahontas operates as a foodservice sales and merchandising group, providing purchasing and marketing services to independent foodservice distributors, who are members of the group. The Pocahontas label in this activity is considered a controlled label available only to the members. They can buy products under the Pocahontas fancy quality label, the Mount Stirling extra standard label, and Wigwam standard quality label, as well as under national brand labels. Pocahontas Foods USA supplies over 80 independent foodservice distributors nationally, handling a total volume of some $800 million in product sales, which encompasses more than 12,000 items in all product categories. The Pocahontas label is positioned in the marketplace as a national brand with advertising and marketing support provided by the group. But the label is still privately held by the group and made available only to its membership. (Other foodservice groups, formed in later decades, have followed a similar strategy, offering three grades of quality under their controlled labels.)

In 1954, seven independent foodservice distributors, all specializing in frozen foods (a relatively new product idea at the time) organized the Frozen Food Forum, introducing the Frosty Acres private label brand. Eventually, that group changed its name to the brand itself, Frosty Acres Brand, Inc., Atlanta, which today serves more than 90 foodservice distributors with more than 5000 foodservice items, not only in frozen foods, but in all other areas.

In 1957, a group of independent foodservice distributors organized a group in Chicago called the United Institutional Distributors, which was destined to become the largest foodservice distributor marketing/buying group in the country under the name North American Foodservice Companies, Inc. Its 20-plus distributor members now ring up sales of $2.5 billion-plus, all of them carrying their own private label lines in addition to the controlled label (common or corporate label) supplied by the group under the Host Favorite top quality, Host Delight extra standard, and Host Pak standard quality. In recent years, this group has witnessed more growth toward the corporate Host labels, because of increasing costs in freight and inventory, experienced by the members. Today, there are about 1000 Host-controlled label items, while distributors in the group carry over 6000 items under their own labels.

The third largest foodservice group in the country (after North American Foodservice Companies and Frosty Acres Brands), Nifda, was started in 1958 when 33 distributors joined to form the National Institutional Food Distributor Associates, Inc., Atlanta. Today, more than 6000 items are now packed under the Nifda label, representing fancy quality. The group also supplies Chef-Pac extra standards, and Econo-Pac standard quality lines.

During the 1950s and 1960s, other foodservice groups were also formed, often drawing in foodservice distributors with long histories of serving the industry. In 1922, for example, Ritter Food Corp., Pittsburgh, Pennsylvania, began operations as a dairy distributor, serving both the retail and foodservice markets. Its interests eventually centered on foodservice, leading that firm in 1966 to join with four other foodservice distributors to form a buying group called CODE (Continental Organization of Distributor Enterprises) a co-op venture in purchasing, merchandising, and marketing. Today, more than 70 distributors make up the membership, the five largest also carrying their own private labels. All of these distributors also subscribe to the CODE controlled label program (color coded in quality tiers—red for fancy, blue for extra standard, and green for standard), covering more than 8000 items.

Nugget Distributors, Inc., Stockton, California, began as a purchasing co-op also in 1966; today, its group serves some 137 independent distributors, almost 100% of them carrying the Nugget label with just some fill-in with national brands.

All Kitchens, Inc., Lyndhurst, Ohio, began operations in 1969, developing a controlled label program around its All Kitchens brand, which now covers about 5000 items. Some 96 independent foodservice distributors subscribe to the program. In recent years, this group also has inaugurated an "associate member" program, allowing independent distributors to carry their own private label, which the group agrees to manage. But the group sees more movement toward a corporate controlled label.

Of course, things do not always follow the same pattern. There are variations in the scheme of anything. In other words, there are distributors who deal in both the retail and foodservice area. Plee-zing Inc., Glenview, Illinois, which started in 1955 as a private label broker for foodservice accounts soon afterward also began serving retail accounts. Today, this foodservice group, serving some 100 foodservice distributors, counts 70% of its volume in this area. The Plee-zing label plus some other labels are made available to its accounts.

Fleming Companies, Inc., Oklahoma City, Oklahoma, the country's second largest wholesale food distributor, has expanded into foodservice with distribution centers in Texas and Florida.

Federated Foods, Inc., Park Ridge, Illinois, a private label retail distributor, also franchises its Red & White, Parade, and Lead Way labels to independent foodservice distributors, serving them pretty much in the role of a foodservice group.

It does not necessarily take more than one distributor to start a group controlled label program. Embassy Grocery Corp., Maspeth, New York, which began in business in 1927, in recent years has been 100% foodservice. Within the past couple of years, Embassy has begun franchising its labels—Lucky Boy fancy grade, Three Castles extra standard, and EMBCO standard grade—to other foodservice distributors. So far, some 14 distributors have signed up for the label program, which includes close to 1800 items, mostly dry groceries. Following the lead of other foodservice distributors, Embassy is pushing strong into frozen foods for its labels.

Under the definition of private label, when a manufacturer owns the label, it is not considered private label. Yet, there are cases in foodservice where the manufacturer develops a controlled label program, serving as the distributor. Beatrice Foods Co., Chicago, owns John Sexton & Co., a food distribution and warehousing operation, which sells product under the Sexton label: some 10,000 items. Not all of these items are manufactured by Sexton or its parent company. In fact, the firm makes only a few foods and chemical products—soups, detergents, coffee, tea, etc. Yet the firm provides full-line distribution capability. Sexton positions itself as a national wholesale grocer, serving the institutional and commercial foodservice markets.

There are cases where the foodservice distributor limits his product capability. The group, ABC Affiliated Distributors, Inc., Chicago, for example, deals only in nonfood merchandise, helping its members buy and merchandise foodservice equipment, tabletop items, and related supplies. The general nonfoods foodservice distributor, Edward Don & Co., North Riverside, Illinois, specializes in equipment, janitorial supplies, and cleaning materials with a minimum effort put into foods.

An interesting tie-in lately has been Don's move to put its name on certain product lines along with the national brand manufacturer. Don now sells Silverstone fry pans, identified as "Don by Vollrath" and china and ovenware items called "Don Stack Ups by Hall." Private label tie-ins with a brand manufacturer are uncommon, but they do occur. It is a case where the manufacturer, contracted to make the product, is identified on the packaging or product along with the private label distributor. The latter sees benefit in using the brand name, because of the "good name" or reputation of a manufacturer for certain quality. (In the retail segment, Woolworth has identified its store brand flash cubes as manufactured by General Electric on the packaging. K mart in a recent TV commercial for its Performer paint identifies the manufacturer, adding the line "Quality by Dutch Boy, the Price by K mart.")

Foodservice distributors usually require a large sales volume ($25 million plus) to support a private label line. The independent distributors usually pick up on a group's controlled label program not only for purchasing and warehousing economies, but also for its national advertising and merchandising support. They, in effect, buy a "national brand," owned and controlled by the group.

Foodservice operators can buy direct or through distributors. In many cases, the foodservice operator in the commercial segment, particularly chain restaurant operations, will develop his own private label identity. The chain operator often prefers a private label—his chain's name or trademark names—over national brands, because, as one chain operator (now planning to add to his private label stock) puts it: "Once the customer believes in your quality and the fact that you maintain rigid specifications, private label speaks well for that effort. The product is positioned to your standards and not perceived as just an off-the-shelf product. Private labels say this is our specification, our quality, and we police that."

As a distributor explains, the restaurant chains like continuity of label, which translates to continuity of quality. Private label provides that insurance plus offers the advantage of projecting the chain's image to the consumer.

Sometimes the foodservice operator will allow his private label to break away as a so-called national or regional brand. Nathan's Famous Inc., New York, whose famous frankfurters were first sold from a stand in Coney Island in 1916, early in 1979 licensed John Morrell & Co., a division of United Brands Co., New York, to manufacture and distribute Nathan's Famous packaged frankfurters and other beef products for sale to supermarkets and retail food stores.

Until 1982, United Brands also owned A&W Restaurants, a chain of family restaurants that traces its founding back to 1919 when the first A&W Root Beer stand opened in Lodi, California. In 1971, a year after United Brands took control of A&W Restaurants, its principal product, A&W Root Beer was introduced to the retail trade—supermarkets, food stores, and vending machines—in cans and bottles. Since then, the A&W brand has grown to become a leader in soft drink root beer sales with national distribution. Meanwhile, A&W Restaurants continue with their private label program, which includes A&W Root Beer.

Like his counterpart in the retail market, the foodservice operator also can become involved in manufacturing and distributing product under his own label. Some operators also sell that merchandise outside their chains to other operators in both retail and foodservice. Collins Foods International, Los Angeles, operator of Sizzler Family Steak Houses and Kentucky Fried Chicken stores, also runs a wholesale distribution business, Collins Foodservice Division, which distributes grocery products, chicken, meat, and other perishable foods plus paper and supplies both to its retail operations and to stores and restaurants owned by outside firms.

Denny's Inc., La Mirada, California, one of the largest foodservice companies in the world, operator of Denny's Restaurants and Winchell's Donut Houses, also owns Proficient Food Co., a corporate subsidiary involved in foodservice distribution, drawing on stock from six regional warehouses. With the 1980 deregulation of motor carriers, this operation with its 100-plus trucks is becoming more aggressive in developing new customers. Another subsidiary, Portion-Trol Foods, started in 1974 with a meat plant in Texas, now supplies Denny's Restaurants with beef products as well as a number of specialty meat items and recently the addition of frozen soups.

Morrison Inc., Mobile, Alabama, operator of cafeterias, buffets, and a contract foodservice business, also oversees the Morco Industries Group, which through its operations can purchase, warehouse, process and manufacture foods (salad dressings and coffee), transport food and supplies, make chemicals and foodservice equipment, etc. In 1981, salad dressings under the Morrison label were introduced to supermarkets in the Southeast.

Many observers view the 1970s as the decade that truly launched private labels. The 1980s are evolving into the decade of generic products and corporate labels. There also is a stronger movement by national brand manufacturers into the private label business, through the start-up of manufacturing operations or through acquisition of firms specializing in these products. The story continues to unfold; whatever the outcome, the private label renaissance, started in the 1970s, is by no means over.

REFERENCES

Beazer, R. 1981. The Pros and Cons of Generics: Issue of Quality Aired. *Private Label* Magazine, October-November, p. 16. E. W. Williams Publishing, New York.

Bon Appetit. 1980. Trendsetter Tracking Study, Wave II.

Burgoyne, Inc. 1980. National Study of Supermarket Shoppers 1979–1980. Burgoyne, Inc., Cincinnati. (*Private Label* Magazine, August-September 1980, p. 45.)

Cramer, E. R. 1973. The Alpha Beta Story. Anderson, Ritchie & Simon, Los Angeles.

FMI. 1981 Food Marketing Industry Speaks/Trends. Food Marketing Institute, Washington, DC.

Institutional Distribution. 1981. ID Survey: How and Why Operators Buy. Institutional Distribution, April, p. 74. Restaurant Business Inc., New York.

Kline, C. H. (1981). Cosmetics and Toiletries report, 6th Edition, Charles H. Kline and Co., Inc., Fairfield, New Jersey.

Marcus, S. 1979. Quest for the Best. Viking Press, New York.

Martin, S. 1981. Altermans, Powerful Brand Supporter Has Become Private Label Leader. *Private Label* Magazine, August September, pp. 30–32, 34. E. W. Williams Publishing, New York.

Nichol. 1979. No Name, No Frills, Generic Merchandise: The Revolution is now. Speech delivered at Toronto Generics Seminar sponsored by the University of Toronto's Faculty of Management Studies, Toronto, Ontario, Canada.

SAMI. 1982. Private Label Trends. Selling Areas-Marketing, Inc., New York.

Seibert, D. V. 1981. Interim & Annual Meeting Report: Chairman's Address to Stockholders. J. C. Penney Co., New York.

Simmons. 1979. New Consumer Study Profiles: The Private Label User. *Private Label* Magazine, April-May 1980. E. W. Williams Publishing, New York.

Stossel, J. 1981. Cosmetics—The Big Put-on. May 18–21 WCBS-TV, Channel 2, New York. CBS Inc., New York.

Walgreen. 1979. Generic Drugs: Good News for the Consumer. *Walgreen World*, Vol. 46, No. 2 (March-April). Walgreen Co., Deerfield, Illinois.

Part II

The Private Label Program

4

Organizing a Private Label Program

How do you start a private label program? For many retailers and wholesalers, private labels have been in existence for years. These labels could have been inherited from a merger, acquisition, or spinoff; they could have evolved first as packer labels taken over and sometimes renamed by the store; or they could have been started by the store as a private brand to fill a particular level of product quality, a product category, or a line of products. Although private label "programs" have existed for decades, it is only within the past 5–10 years that an organized effort has been undertaken to consolidate, control, and expand these programs, insuring that standards of quality are consistently kept high, that packaging is updated and refined, and that more aggressive marketing and merchandising techniques are employed.

Theoretically, a private label program can develop around one product, but the impact of one or a few items would be lost in most stores. A smaller chain of stores is at a disadvantage with private labels because it does not have enough built-in controls (manpower or capability) to insure a successful program; also, the smaller operation cannot take advantage of full truckloads of product to effect greater cost savings. A token effort in private label does not work.

A chain that is ready for a private label program is one that can adopt a large selection of products in different categories plus a representative variety of products (sizes, weights, types) in order to reinforce the store's image as a vendor of top quality store brand merchandise sold at a low price. In the food store, for example, a wholesaler recommends at least 300 private label products to get a program started. With slightly more than double that number of items, the retailer/wholesaler has a complete program. Of course, the commitment does not cut off at a certain amount. Aggressive merchants can carry 3000-plus private label items in their program.

A generics selection can be much smaller—about 100 items—because these products are usually introduced only in one size or type. Additionally, generics are often mass-displayed, reinforcing their impact in a store, while private label traditionally is cut in or integrated into all aisles, according to the product category and its location in the store. Since a grocery store can be more than triple the size of a drug outlet, it is possible for the latter business to choose fewer private label items. In a smaller product mix, limited private label facings can still carry an impact. Overall, a significant presence of private label in the merchandising mix gives the store its particular identity, its signature, or its "personality." If the store carries only national brands, it becomes like any other retailer in a market segment.

When considering a private label program, some basic guidelines do apply—not totally, but appreciably. In an interview in *Private Label*, William A. Robinson, vice-president, private label sales at A&P, spelled out some of these ideas:

> Basically, the most effective way to sell private label is as a percent of the total (category) and not at the expense of the total within a commodity. There are natural share market levels that items drift to, whether you have a program or not. . . .
>
> When private label's share of market gets out of proportion, the total category volume generally suffers in the long run. Which means that private label isn't going anywhere. It just gets its share of market by default. . . .
>
> In measuring private label's success, you cannot use the same standard across the board. You have to look at it by commodity, by subgroups. There also are seasonal shifts in share of market, mainly because of the seasonality of the business. Minor brands do better in season, major brands do better year round. . . . Private label is very similar to national brands, the points of difference being: its value, its profitability to the retailer, its variety of choice (it's not really a proliferation or unnecessary duplication), and its low media costs. Many times, private label's packaging size, configuration, package quality, graphics, etc., can be superior let alone equal to national brands. If it's less, then it's generally targeted to be less. Generics (an extension of private label) is a good example of this. . . .
>
> If you start looking at the total financial picture, it must be on the basis of cost of handling, cost of storage, cost to the store with everything loaded in, the amount of labor it takes to handle the product in and out of the store, the potential for breakage and other losses, what kind of total system do I have in terms of how fast that product

turns through the customer, how am I tying up capital, the case pack size (items packed 12 to a case offer a better return than 24 to the case, because the base allocation takes less space, the amount of residual stock is less, the freshness aspect is enhanced since product moves at a faster rate), etc. You must also consider the disadvantages of a smaller case pack, which cost more, requires more rotation labor, etc. On the bottom line, it can become a more profitable product, even though you may take a lesser gross on it. A direct delivery product doesn't need as high a gross rate on it to get the same net profit as one that goes through your own distribution system. . . .

We plan to increase private label's market share only where it expands the total commodity. We first analyze whether it expands the commodity or gains share of market at the expense of the commodity. If there's room to grow in share of market, we will expand. . . .

If you do everything else right as a merchant, private label is a positive; but if you're not doing the other things right, then private label can be an anchor, that is, it will keep you from going anywhere. You must run the store right by satisfying the customer first. Then you can go into the priority of other various merchandising techniques. Private label rarely shows up as the reason why a store is shopped most. In fact, I look upon private label as a dangerous item, if that's all the customer really likes about the store. I think private label is important only as one of the reasons for shopping there. There are so many other competitive factors that you must appeal to the customer with before you get to private label. . . .

As a rule of thumb in retailing, whether it's in private label or anything else, the merchant should never get greedy. If there's a fair share that's affordable to get, then the retailer is entitled to it. The day he starts to get greedy, tries to get it too fast, or too much of it, it will cost him more than he gains. A&P was greedy probably by default. A&P was forced into a private label image, while the rest of the pack ran faster.

The retail business is not like a checkers game, where everyone follows the same moves. Its participants play more of a chess game, where the players make different moves—some powerful and aggressive, others edging forward little by little. Their philosophies about private label vary considerably, because people plan the strategies and implement the tactics. There has been no book written about how to organize a private label program effectively. It is like trying to match up a hockey player, who hits a puck across the ice into a net, against a tennis player, who hits a ball over a net on a clay court.

A private label rules book cannot be written. Private label programs are run according to the type of store operation. Retail store operations are structurally different. One person's title at one company may be the same as that of a person at another company, but their responsibilities can be poles apart. Some chains operate with divisions that must adapt to their own marketing needs. A private label product launched at headquarters may succeed in the Northeast but fail miserably in the Sunbelt region. One type of store can generate the same sales as another, but realize three times the profit margin, because of its location, demographic profile, or competitive situation. A wholesaler, often dealing with independents who do what they please, must appoint someone to call on those retailers to convince them to become involved in and actively support a private label program. They may fully commit to, remain apathetic to, or even oppose the introduction of private label into their stores. Accordingly, the following steps and procedures are offered as suggestions of what a program could entail.

SETTING A POLICY

Usually, the retailer/wholesaler will set policies for a program at the executive level. Policies and procedures really should be decided and delegated by top management for better coordination, control, and consistency. Management sets the program purpose. What does the retailer/wholesaler want to achieve with private label? What does the company expect from its private label program? Goals are established with respect to sales volume to warrant stocking particular private label item and to profits necessary to make the effort worthwhile.

The private label program involves much more than merely ordering products from manufacturers and slapping on store labels. Private label buying and selling covers the full product cycle, from sourcing of product right to final sale to the consumer. The retailer/wholesaler should establish a private label policy for his buyers and store management and personnel. Details of the program can be presented in an operations manual. Of course, an organization can be highly structured with many different departments involved in the program, including a person appointed as private label coordinator or manager. Basically, a private label program should first be organized with the following:

- Sales and profit objectives (working with dollars)
- Staff designation and responsibilities
- Product procurement procedures
- Quality control procedures
- Logistics regarding in-house versus outside support in manufacturing, sourcing, quality control, quality assurance, packaging, and advertising
- Tiers of quality established with appropriate identifying names
- Product turnover rate determined at the store level
- Update review for necessary additions or deletions
- Warehouse space allocations
- Delivery system established with checks for on-time deliveries
- Spot-checking routines

The private label program is a very creative effort, one that requires hard work, total commitment, and a conviction that the program will succeed. This effort falls mostly into the lap of the buyer, who must literally spend hundreds of hours putting together a program. He also must be extremely patient: Private label will not necessarily be an overnight success. Sometimes it takes years before a private label program gets off the ground.

The buyer can work alone, in concert with company departments, through a private label manager, or reporting directly to an executive who oversees the program. Whatever the structure, there must be input from the field and from research on a product category. Usually, a buyer is familiar with certain products, an expert in his area. Sometimes the private label buyer must cover many different product categories. This requires research, study, field work, tracking trends, spotting developments, attending trade shows, talking with noncompetitive retailers, and reading publications, In other words, the buyer should be knowledgeable about the marketplace, particularly about what the competition is doing. Also, a buyer should expand his horizon, looking beyond his market segment into other retail markets and even into other industries, related or unrelated. Good ideas can develop from these exploratory efforts.

The buyer does not take direction as much as he assumes it. He must directly participate in a number of activities:

- Locating the right manufacturers
- Setting the quality standards with the manufacturer
- Sizing the product against the leading national brand
- Packaging and designing the trade dress
- Checking quality standards with a testing lab
- Positioning the product on store shelves and in special aisle or end-aisle displays
- Setting the price differentials between his label and the national brand
- Marketing and promoting the product
- Insuring consistent product quality that's equal to or better than the national brand standards (if this is a goal of his company's program)
- Reviewing private label sales and turnover progress with appropriate additions or deletions
- Clearing the legal implications for compliance with Federal and state laws
- Checking on store level support for the private label program

(Subsequent chapters in this book cover these areas in more detail.)

Of course, the buyer does not necessarily handle every one of these assignments. A good part of the job could be assigned to a broker who specializes in private label. The company structure dictates how its program is executed. A single commodity buyer may handle all private label buying as an incidental activity, or a buyer may specialize exclusively in all private label buying. Alternatively the president or a top executive could handle the private label program. A committee of executives and/or buyers can oversee the private label program, or private label buying can be divided up among the buyers.

One of the most important elements in an effective private label program is communications between and among all participants. Decision-making at headquarters should be carried out at the top management level, delegated through the merchandiser and buyers, and implemented at the store level by store management and personnel. Lack of support anywhere along this chain can weaken the program.

One large retail organization has appointed a planning board, composed of executives from key areas in the company such as merchandising, marketing, and operations, to oversee the program. The company's buyers in different product categories select new product candidates for private label, planning the marketing and merchandising strategy, maintaining the quality standards, and monitoring the product performance. This company also has set up a private label coordinator, who acts as liaison between the planning board and the buyers. A private label manual covers responsibilities and objectives in the program. The manual includes a guide for store management showing the company's private label objectives, its private label philosophy, how the program is structured, how products should be merchandised, how to position products in a planogram, and different marketing strategies. The manual also updates progress in the private label program.

A PRIVATE LABEL "PHILOSOPHY"

The guiding principles of this firm's private label program are outlined in the manual, which reads in part:

> The need for consistency in dealing with private label products has resulted in the adoption of a set of guiding principles to direct management decisions in this important and growing category. Called the private label philosophy, it contains six elements, which are considered vital in the successful analysis and marketing of private label products. The following is a complete outline of these principles.
>
> 1. *Product quality.* High quality and good value should be primary characteristics inherent in all private label merchandise. Product specifications for each item will be developed by the appropriate buyer and approved for consistency by the planning board. Where possible, product characteristics exhibited by established national brands will serve as the basis for comparative analysis. In categories where standards have not been clearly established, our minimum quality standard will be determined by a concern for providing our customers with high quality products which represent a good value.
>
> 2. *Quality Control.* Strict adherence to quality control procedures will ensure the consistent offering of high quality private label products to our customers. All poten-

tial additions to the program, therefore, must be accompanied by product specifications against which the quality of incoming merchandise can be measured. Specifications will be established by the appropriate buyer and any product source that fails to meet them will be rejected.

3. *Product pricing*. Retail prices on private label products will be set meaningfully at levels below those of competing national brands. The dollar or percentage differential which constitutes a meaningful level may vary between commodity goods and even among items within a grouping. Buyers responsible for a given category of products will establish and monitor each item's retail. Pricing guidelines will be set by the planning board to ensure consistency with formulated marketing strategies.

4. *Product selection*. Our company will merchandise approved private label items in addition but not to the exclusion of national brand products. This guideline may be waived for items of a generic nature where brand identification is an insignificant consideration. For example, rubbing alcohol. Buyers will be responsible for the selection and analysis of candidates for the private label program and will present them to the planning board for advisory and approval action. No item or group of items shall be placed in any store without specific prior approval of the board.

5. *Brand name and packaging*. The naming and packaging of all private label merchandise will be subject to approval by the planning board which will proceed after considering the following:

a. A review of the industry and interorganizational norms for naming or packaging the type of product in question.

b. The proposed positioning statement and marketing strategy.

c. A determination of which operating division or divisions will carry the private label to ensure that the product's name and package will be consistent with their overall marketing and image objectives.

d. Legal requirements based on the given type.

6. *Product suppliers*. The selection of suppliers for private label merchandise will be the responsibility of the appropriate buyer in each category and will be subject to review by the private label planning board. Potential suppliers must exhibit good financial stability, carry adequate product liability coverage, to ensure that our company will not suffer financial loss from consumer litigation.

While there are no startling revelations in this outline, it is significant that the principles have been organized and recorded for reference. Not too long ago, retailers did not even think in terms of private label. An organized program was never considered. Today, it is becoming standard operating procedure for most retailers.

Not all product categories lend themselves to being copied by private label. For example, the Coca-Cola formula is still a carefully guarded secret. Retailers are said to be better equipped to aim for a Pepsi Cola or an RC Cola taste. It is also impossible to duplicate Welch's Grape Jelly, according to one private label manager. Yet, chemical houses claim they can analytically break down and duplicate any formula.

Traditionally, some product categories have been very difficult to penetrate with private label because of the advertising dollars spent by the national brands to sell consumers on the brand image. For example, private label has an uphill fight in such areas as cereal, cigarettes, liquor, wine, beer, light bulbs, candy bars, and baby food.

One private label buyer offers this opinion: "I suspect that private label has never really penetrated the baby food market because mothers will just not risk harming their baby. They *trust* Gerbers and Beechnut, etc. The same applies to personal products, such as shampoo and toothpaste, but not to as great a degree. On the other hand, who can be harmed by toilet paper or paper towels? The consumer will readily try these products in private label."

The recent growth and consumer acceptance of generics has cracked this barrier somewhat. Generics have successfully penetrated some of these categories, perhaps because these products are sold not on an equal quality level (as with private label) but more on a price sell. Consumers today are willing to compromise on quality, if the price is low enough.

A wholesaler in Denver reports that one of its top generic sellers is the 2 lb grape jelly jar; after less than five months with generic cigarettes, that no-name brand climbed to the thirty-fifth best seller out of about 220 cigarette items. (Recently, a Denver retail chain reported its generic cigarettes were the number two seller, second only to Marlboro.) In the coffee category, however, this wholesaler observes continued brand resistance: "The brand loyalty is still there, beating generics as well as private label. We've merchandised them, advertised them right, priced them right, but we're having a difficult time selling them."

The buyer usually has the best input on what new private label products to add to a program. When a program is started, the selection of prducts should be targeted toward the top brand in each product category. Private label can sometimes make its mark best in a category where not one dominant national brand but two or more brands are competing for dominance. Customers who find just one dominant brand in a product category may be less likely to switch to private label. That national brand can almost be synonymous with the category identity. In fact, it can be a generic trap, where the identity falls into common usage. When several brands vie for the number one position in a category, customers may more readily switch, and that switch can include a move to private label.

In one of the early issues of *Private Label* Magazine, brokers Stan Pavlak, Greg Phillips, and Dan Scher of the firm Gregory Marketing Corp., Fairfield, New Jersey, offered some interesting comments on new private label entries. Excerpts of that interview follow:

> Pavlak: "If the product category is not big enough, there should only be one private label commitment. In a giant category, like corn, you can have 15 sources of supply and still not saturate the market. But there are certain categories, such as private label tabasco sauce, where the demand is small. . . ."
>
> Phillips: "The greatest chance for success in private label comes when you have two strong national brands in competition. When women shoppers periodically switch brands, you can reasonably assume that they will try private label as well. . . ."

Scher: "A dominant brand can so dominate the market, that customers think in terms of its name. When they think in terms of a category, then private label is almost unequivocally going to be successful. But when one brand is the only one people think of, then you have a problem in getting them to try something else.

"We had that experience once up against a unique national brand product. At the request of a customer (a retailer), we helped develop a fine knock-off product. Even the national brand acknowledged its quality. However, the national brand advertising and the name of the product itself were so strong that our item never reached a fraction of what its potential normally would have been in the private label game. The product has been with our customer some four to five years and is just starting to come along.

"Normally, a private label item that knocks off a branded item selling 1,000 cases a week can expect to do 400 to 500 cases a week within six months. But it's taken us five years to reach that point and in some other chains we're still not there yet with this particular item."

Pavlak: "In certain categories, private label dominates. In a strong private label chain, private label can be as high as 30% of total volume in a category like vegetables. But in other areas, it can be very small, almost in its infancy.

"We like to consider ourselves as the private label cereal experts. We got into that category, because there was a need. Kelloggs and General Mills and Quaker Oats dominated the market with 99.5% of total sales. We saw the potential for private label. Today, those three branded companies dominate the market with 95% market share. But we've got about 5% going through this house in private label and the potential is there for growth of another 10%. . . .When we sell private label cereal to a chain without the store brand in that category, we tell them that they don't own that aisle. Quaker, General Mills, and Kellogg own the aisle. We say the retailer doesn't control the pricing, the setup, etc. It's run by the branded companies. We ask them if they want to have some say in the matter."

In the selection of private label products, the key question is "Does the item have long-range potential?" It is not always easy to forecast this, because of fast-changing trends in the marketplace. Private label buyers today plug into new national brand products—sometimes fresh out of the test market—almost concurrent with their introduction into an expanded market or in their roll-out phase.

A 1979 interview with Richard Beazer, A&P's director of private label procurement, contained some interesting points on A&P's strategy in expanding its private label commitment:

In this area (motor oil and the car care market), the merchandising department gets involved, as does the private label sales department, our executive vice-presidents of purchasing and merchandising, plus warehousing distribution. We initiate new private label areas through research of categories, watching SAMI trends, market trends of particular categories, and try to spot prospective private label items. Then we do some leg work to determine whether or not they will sell. If it's an area that we think we should be in, then we do some preliminary artwork and decide what label to adopt: A&P or Ann Page, what it should sell for, and what we can gross on it, what benefit it offers to the consumer, can it be purchased at less cost than the national brand and still have the same quality in order to be of value to the customer. After these considerations, we submit a request for approval. The buyers carry out most of this work."

Once approval is secured, the company starts its process of procurement and distribution, getting the product out to the stores. Beazer's department then insures that the A&P divisions "maintain programs to support that private label item and built its sales and growth:"

> We usually don't limit ourselves to one supplier. We will go out for bids. We come up with the kind of specs that we want to meet. If we're developing a heavy-duty liquid detergent, for example, we'll get specs on Wisk and Era, measuring what those products do and what they're composed of, then design a product that will match their quality. We ask different suppliers for their best effort to meet what we're targeting against—Wisk or Era. Suppliers come back with a product and a pricing and service program. We'll work with up to a dozen suppliers—anyone interested; we want their input. We'll tell them what program we want and ask if they can support it. Then we select two or three suppliers, based on our geographic locations. One supplier isn't sufficient, because of the freight involved. Suppliers usually give only partial coverage of our marketing areas. In paper, we deal with three or four different suppliers.

A successful private label program does not sleep. It has been a sleeper for too many years, and activities must hum in this area. Product cuttings should be scheduled regularly. Frequent planning meeting should be scheduled. Buyers not familiar with their manufacturers' plant facilities should plan one or more visits. Promotions must be planned far in advance. Incentive programs should be inaugurated to help drum up support at the store level—a sales contest for private label, for example.

Wayne Redfern, a broker based in Los Angeles, notes that "private label is sold differently from advertised brands. It's a program sell. Most retailers know a little about a product category, but they don't understand the full implications of a marketing program, private label pricing, promotions, procurement of product, specifications, packaging, artwork, etc. . . . Private label has always been a me-too business, and it will continue to be so. But there are new activities to consider: cents-off labeling, cross-couponing, floor shippers, merchandising in mass displays, bonus packages, etc."

At a recent FMI seminar on private label conducted by *Private Label* Magazine, Glenn Fischer, director of grocery procurement, Wetterau, Inc., Hazelwood, Missouri (a wholesaler), suggested this philosophy statement for a private label program:

> Our private label will be of equal or better quality than the best selling national or regional brands within our marketing area. We will return our customers, the retailer, a profit greater than the brands, and we will offer the consumer a recognizable value which will reinforce our identity. Our generic items will be of acceptable quality at the lowest price possible.
>
> After acceptance of a philosophy such as this, you then must gain a commitment from every department within your organization and their objectives must be set to achieve these goals.
>
> Your procurement or buying department should constantly be aware of the quality which you have available under your private label as continuity of quality is important,

because once a consumer is convinced to buy your private label, changes in quality are not readily accepted or appreciated.

Packaging graphics should be modern and appealing.

UPC symbols are an absolute must.

Generics simply need to be black and white.

While quality of generics is not as important as it is in your private label, the quality under generics must be acceptable.

Private label suppliers must be urged to develop long-range promotional schedules, not from the standpoint that an exact per-case allowance be made know, but that awareness of promotional activity on particular items will exist on a preplanned schedule. Your procurement department must work in close coordination with your advertising department to guarantee and develop opportunities for private label products.

Your advertising department must support private label on a regular basis within the advertising media which you normally use. Again, advertising and procurement must work together to develop these opportunities.

The nationally accepted standard of approximately 80-20 percent brand-to-private label works well in our ads and, in addition, once per quarter we tell our private label story by reversing these percentages: 20% branded items and 80% private label items.

Our merchandising department must be aware of the comparison of prices at retail between the brands and private label, and private label must be lower, while considering the return to our retailers.

Shelf placement must be considered with planograms for all major private label entries available to properly present private label at retail.

It is a matter of planning, coordination, communications, spot-checking, and continual monitoring of the program.

REFERENCES

Beazer, R. 1979. Troubled A&P Chain Gets Private Label Face Lifting-Par II, A&P's Expansion Plans and Procurement Policies. *Private Label* Magazine, June-July, p. 46. E.W. Williams Publishing, New York.

Fischer, G. 1981. Getting the Most Out of Your Private Label (and Generics) Program. *Private Label* Magazine, June-July, pp.56–57. E.W. Williams Publishing, New York.

Pavlak, S., Phillips, G., and Scher, D. I. 1979. The Nuts and Bolts of a Private Label Broker. *Private Label* Magazine, October-November, p. 28. E.W. Williams Publishing, New York.

Robinson, W. A. 1979. Troubled A&P Chain Gets Private Label Face Lifting-Part I. *Private Label* Magazine, April-May, p. 15. E.W. Williams Publishing, New York.

5

Sourcing of Private Labels

By definition, a private label product is private. The manufacturer who produces it does not necessarily have to be identified as its source. On national brand labels, the manufacturer's name and address appear; but on private labels, only the distributor's name—the owner of the label—appears. Questions arise. Who makes the private label product for the distributor? Why not put that manufacturer's name on the label, too?

If a manufacturer's name were put on a private label, it would become that manufacturer's brand and not be exclusively owned by the retailer/wholesaler. The source of private label is any manufacturer who can meet the product specifications set by the label owner. The source of private label products can be anyone from the small manufacturer who is 100% dependent on his contract sales to private label retailers/wholesalers, up to a Procter & Gamble, which recently took over its first private label company.

The fabric of industry is interwoven is such a way that what appears to be black or white is, in fact, murky gray. There is such an interchange of manufacturing that distinctions between who makes national brands and who makes private labels can be confusing. A large national brand manufacturer will sometimes provide its ingredients and labels to a contract packer, who will produce the national brand. Private label retailers/wholesalers do the same thing. Work is often contracted out. To put it more bluntly, the manufacturer who produces national brands can be the source for private labels and vice-versa. If there is business out there—potential sales and profits—the manufacturer, no matter what his identity, very likely will embrace it. Private label and generic business is growing rapidly; and all manufacturers have not lost sight of this fact.

The question of who makes private label is easier to answer today than a few years ago. Before private labels were consolidated and upgraded, with greater emphasis placed on quality, the private label manufacturer had good reason to stay under cover. There was no guaranteed consistency, except by a few retailers and wholesalers. Private label programs were not that well organized. Private labels had only a price image working in their favor (or to their detriment). Today, private labels also carry a quality image—quality with lower price, which translates into value for the consumer. Because private labels have become more respectable, private label sources are coming out of the woodwork.

Manufacturers are not as shy about broadcasting their capability in producing private label. Lists go out to prospective retail buyers. Advertisements now appear in the trade press, where traditionally only the brands would appear. The debut of *Private Label* magazine in April 1979 brought out scores of manufacturers who had never advertised before.

Like debutantes, they strutted out onto the magazine's ad pages, showing off their latest trade dress at different chains. In fact, some retailers got a little bit upset over being shown with their competitors, all of them drawing from the same manufacturing source in a particular product category. In some cases, the new private label advertisers had no ad agency, no way of producing ads. The work had to be farmed out. It was a bit amateurish at the beginning; but soon the magazine started printing four-color ads more frequently. A new sourcing point was established.

Private Label magazine also worked to help form the Private Label Manufacturers Association, a group of private label manufacturers seeking to promote private labels to the retailer/wholesaler and ultimately to the consumer. PLMA conducted its first trade exhibition in Chicago in October 1980, drawing 58 private label exhibitors. The 1981 exhibition featured 120 exhibitor booths, an unprecedented showing of private label and generic products. In 1982, booths nearly doubled to 230.

At other industry trade shows, which are dominated by national brand manufacturers, private label has received a fraction of the attention, if any. Usually, private label and generic products are hidden in catalogs or under booth counters. Lately, however, there has been an increase in private label exposure at these shows.

The key to sourcing is held by the buyer. If he cannot open the right doors, then one of the major prerequisites for a solid private label program—a viable source of supply that provides consistent top quality, a good price, and on-time delivery—is weakened. Unfortunately, not all buyers know what this "key" looks like, let alone how to turn it for profits.

In an early report on the developing generics phenomenon, Burck (1979, p.72) talked about developing a generics program, indicating that "to do the job properly requires sophistication, determination, and a willingness to break with customary buying practices. Most retailers are passive customers—manufacturers' salesmen come to them and they choose among the competing offerings. Indeed, the manufacturers' representatives, like drug-company detailmen, serve as informal but skilled consultants to store buyers and managers, advising them about promotional strategies, shelf arrangements, and other operational details."

The article also referred to Topco Associates, Inc., Skokie, Illinois, a cooperative owned by supermarket chains and grocery wholesalers, quoting its president, Marcel Lussier, who explained how Topco's generics program was started: "We contracted the work out to sixty to seventy production facilities. We've been at it a little over a year now, and it's been a lot of work. It's taken some very senior people to make these decisions. Your quality control is critical. . . . If a low-quality product falls below standards, the customer will never pick that label again. So you need more control with generics—without it, you could just kill the business."

Today, Topco handles distribution for what is perhaps the largest generics program in the country, approaching 500 items in some chains. The company's strategy regarding sourcing is outlined somewhat in a pamphlet, which describes its buying program (Topco 1979):

> Topco maintains product quality through its own specifications and testing techniques. Topco buyers and technologists spend much of their time in the field working with sources of supply, first to develop the desired products and then to insure their consistent quality. A constant flow of samples both from the producers and the retailers are subjected to tests both in Topco labs and, where required, in outside laboratories.
>
> Topco, like other strong distributors of their own brand products, is an important ally and outlet to its many sources of supply. Some of these sources are large enough to produce and market products successfully under their own brands. In many cases, however, they are small and medium size producers who do not have the financial strength or organization to market their own brand products effectively in competition with giant competitors. Topco's staff works with these smaller sources to develop, produce and package products which do compete successfully in the marketplace.

It is a strong, symbiotic relationship, in which the private label distributor works *with* the private label manufacturer and not independently. Often, this relationship carries on for years.

J. C. Penney's marketing research department began studies in 1977 on an untapped customer segment—women who wear large-size clothing.

With its findings, the retailer "took a leadership position in guiding our suppliers toward silhouettes and styling which would satisfy both the younger and older age segments of the large-size range" (J. C. Penney 1980). (The company sources its merchandise through about 10,000 domestic and foreign suppliers, most of them associated with the company for years.)

This association with the manufacturer boils down to a positive attitude: both parties stand to gain from the relationship. Daniel J. Turcott, director of quality assurance at Woolworth's Quality Assurance Laboratory, New York, relates how an open dialogue is maintained among the company's buyers, its manufacturers and the Lab:

> We keep our buyers up to date on new government regulations as well as on trends in the industry. It's important that they know about safety regulations, so they can discuss them with manufacturers or potential manufacturers. Many times, the manufacturers are the last people to know about new regulations.
>
> With manufacturers, sometimes the word laboratory is a stigma. They feel that when they give a product to us, we're going to find something wrong with it. I would say that in a majority of cases, it's not true. If we do anything at all, we put the manufacturers at ease. After our first dealings with them, they want to resubmit right away. They know that we are helping them, not hurting them; and most of them appreciate this.
>
> But it's really the buyer who we work through. If he or she isn't interested in the product, we're wasting our time. We act as a service organization for the buyer. If they are interested in a product or potential product, we then discuss it with the manufacturer, including any improvements that can be made in it. The buyer gets a copy of our report, his director also gets a copy, and we keep copies on file. We make these reports as simple as possible, avoiding too much technical language and keeping them as short as possible so the buyer's time isn't wasted with extra paperwork. In the first paragraph, we get right to the point: this is wrong or there is nothing wrong with the product, offering any suggestions for corrections of the first page (Turcott 1979).

Sometimes the manufacturer can plant the seed. Zodys, a regional discount department store chain operated by Hartfield-Zody, Inc., Los Angeles, met with a health and beauty aids supplier to plan a private label program, based on national brand knock-offs, packaging the private label items to look like national brands for a quick visual identification by customers. Zodys, at the suggestion of the supplier, went a step further, also knocking off the national brands in terms of ingredients. Frank Newman, Zodys divisional merchandise manager, explains:

> We previously had bought a cheap product, put it in a cheap package, and undersold the national brand. Now we are talking about a product that we could really be proud of and say with confidence to our customers that it's every bit as good as the nationally advertised brand that they would pay more for. This gave us something we thought we could really go to town with, because we could absolutely have full confidence in the product (Newman 1980).

Zodys has taken its commitment one step further. It started with knock-off packaging, then went to knock-off ingredients; now the chain is copying marketing techniques of the national brands, offering cents-off labels, trial sizes, and in-store demonstrations for its private label merchandise. This aggressiveness is an outgrowth of its communications with suppliers, working closely with them to make its private label program work.

In 1980, the company's commitment deepened with plans for the launch of a private label diaper program. Newman explains: "For us, it's a major change, because it represents a lot of dollars. We went through an extensive comparison between the three principal suppliers of private label diapers, spending about six months going into their factories, analyzing their product, and seeing what differences exist. Just within the past month, we finalized the source" (Newman 1981).

Just as the suppliers have cooperated with the chain in giving it special packaging and labeling, this diaper manufacturer also has agreed to provide in-store demonstrators to help Zodys launch this program.

It is give and take; sometimes the giver is more sophisticated or better equipped than the recipient; sometimes vice-versa. There are really no easy answers in sourcing products for a private label program.

One of the beauties of such a program is the fact that it is homespun, so to speak. Many different concepts are at work producing the variety of product programs that now operate in the industry.

In a candid interview, a private label grocery buyer of a relatively large chain, who preferred to remain anonymous (Private Label 1979) offered some insight into his techniques for buying merchandise. "I'm responsible for all the private label grocery items in the chain. I don't believe in a buying committee, where four or five people make decisions about something that should or should not be added to our line of goods. We operate on the principle that one person decides what items will carry our store label."

This buyer has the distinct advantage of experience, which has allowed him to spread his buying responsibilities over different categories: canned goods, paper items, aluminum foil, plastic bags, and so on. Other chains usually appoint buyers to a specialized category area.

"I base my choice on years of experience plus something that people may laugh at—gut feeling. . . . It has nothing to do with my personal taste for a particular product. . . . But I can tell the difference between a good and bad product. . . . You learn (this) by using your eyes and ears. It's not something that can be passed along to someone else. You might say it's an old-fashioned approach; but it's also an objective one."

He also is highly critical of the private retailing business in general. "Private label buyers compromise on price or on lack of supply. They settle for second best. They can't always get the grade they want, so rather than do without it, they buy the next best thing. I do without it. If that means I must be out of stock for four or five months, then so be it."

In his home "laboratory," he and his wife test products where it counts most for the consumer—in the kitchen. "I don't open my can of peas against a national brand; but I may eat my store brand on Tuesday and the national brand on Friday."

For the salesmen who visit him with prospective products to be fitted into his private label program, the buyer has this criticism:

> One thing really disturbs me. It's the fact that the food manufacturer and canner are very poorly represented. The people who call on the private label buyer today simply are not qualified; and no one is teaching them. For example, a man recently walked in to sell me private label plums. He put the can down in front of me. I picked it up and asked him the most basic thing: "Where are they from?" He looked at me, saying "What do you mean, they're plums." I said: "Well now, are they Northwest plums, or California plums, or are they from Idaho, Michigan, or New York state? Those varieties are all different, you know." He answered: "I don't know. They told me it was a very good price and this is the price. Besides, it's cheaper than anyone else."

This represents a perfect example of the old price sell for private label clashing against today's attitude of top quality private label.

The buyer also explained that his chain's program is very selective, not always picking up on new items. The chain moves cautiously:

> Our strategy is to watch a new product out on the market to see if it will endure and really stick. . . . There has got to be good sales of the national brand first. It has something to do with personal preferences, too—feel, touch, experience, all contributing to the decision to go into private label. Another consideration is warehouse space. Then there is need: Do we really need another private label on the shelf? Sure, we make more money; but do we really need it. You can have a smaller demand on a particular product line than someone else.

An important consideration that the manufacturer should make is follow-through. This buyer points out that the manufacturer "may think that once he produces a product and sells it to the retailer, it becomes the latter's responsibility to sell it. The manufacturer forgets that if he doesn't particularly care about the product, neither will the retailer care; and it's the manufacturer's merchandise that suffers by not selling.

> Once, the practice was: Give the retailer a rock-bottom price and that's it; let the retailer do the merchandising. Well, that's all changing now. Some of the more progressive manufacturers understand that they have to promote their private label the same way as national brands. From time to time, manufacturers and private label packers will run promotions on their products, featuring them two or three times a year. . . .

> Our chain has had a lot to do with this change in attitude. When I go out looking for a private label manufacturer, I ask: "This is your price, but do you have any promotional programs? Will you contribute, if the product's sales lag, or do something to help move the product?" Years ago, everyone would have said: "No. This is the price and that's it." Today, it's a different ballgame. . . .
>
> The job of finding the right private label supplier is sometimes difficult. So when we locate such a source, we usually make him our only supplier for particular products. Most chains want two or three different suppliers. I believe in trust between myself and a supplier. If it's someone I trust, he comes to me and says: "We have to get a half dollar more, whatever the circumstances are. I don't care if this makes me noncompetitive." If I know that man is honest, he gets his half buck. Other people would not do this, they think by having several suppliers, they have a hedge. I'd rather have one supplier to be the most important guy, rather than three half-important suppliers.

While there may be more private label suppliers available, that one "important guy" is sometimes a rare find. At the first Private Label Manufacturers Association meeting in St. Louis in 1980, a panel on quality control underscored this weakness. Duane Vogelsburg, president, Walgreen Labs, Deerfield, Illinois, discussed the industry's state of the art: "Seventy percent of health and beauty aids manufacturers should be shut down. There's a lot to be desired in their ability and knowledge." Likewise, the retail buyer falls short: "I haven't met a retail buyer who knows the real guts of manufacturing specs. They're like freshmen in high school, talking about pH and solid content. They like percentages. Not one of them really questions the manufacturer's specs. I laugh at the specs they submit." Vogelsburg added that he has yet to meet "the buyer who insists on stringent quality controls. Buyers should pick a product and follow through, examining the nitty gritty of manufacturing and not just rely on a cotton test."

In the audience, a grocery retailer agreed with this assessment of "ignorance on the part of the buyers. We don't know what we're talking about. A mystique still exists in health and beauty aids. We want our products to be identical with national brands, but haven't looked at the labels" (*Private Label* 1980).

EXCEPTIONS TO THE RULE

Of course, there are exceptions—many of them. Examples of an outstanding supplier and a retailer/wholesaler follow to illustrate just what is considered in a sourcing situation.

Witco Chemical, Ultra Division, Paterson, New Jersey, presented its position as "a totally committed private label detergent manufacturer" in a sales brochure "How to improve profits from your detergent aisle" that listed 11 points for the private label buyer to consider when choosing a product supplier:

1. Profit margins—a high-quality, low-cost product that offers a better margin than nationally advertised brands.
2. Homogeneous product—product uniformity with all its detergents made by the spray-drying process.
3. Quality control—all quality monitored by computer; the firm, vertically integrated, makes its own surfactant, the most important element of any detergent.
4. Product choice—wide selection—phosphate, nonphosphate, all-temperature, cold-water, blue or white, or customized to customer's needs.
5. Package sizes—complete line of standard sizes: 20-ounce regular, 49-ounce giant, 84-ounce king, and 10 pound, 11 ounce family size.
6. Promotional support—regular, strong support to help the customer merchandise the product with marketing specialists to help plan and execute promotions.
7. Packaging design—carton designed around customer's established graphics or made from scratch.
8. Product labeling—all labeling requirements met, since supplier is knowledgeable and current on all legal, legislative, and environmental matters related to its product.
9. Technical service—customer service specialists and complete laboratory facilities available to resolve customer's concerns about the product supplied.
10. Product performance—fulfillment of performance and value, backed by firm's 25 years of experience.
11. Multiple plants—product can be manufactured at different locations to realize maximum flexibility in deliveries and reduction in freight costs.

Loblaws Ltd., Toronto, Ontario, literally puts potential private label and generic products through a gauntlet of testing. Through Intersave Canada, the company's buying and merchandising service, the Loblaws Ontario chain gets customized service. Says Rogert G. Chenaux, vice-president of Company Brands, Intersave, "we do everything: we identify what private label products are needed, we go out and source them, we develop the label, and we do all the testing. Our responsibility is to deliver on a consistent basis products to the Loblaws warehouses at a quality level based on our specifications and at a competitive price" (Chenaux 1981).

At a generics seminar in Chicago, David Nichol, president of Loblaws Ontario, talked about Loblaws No Name generic program and specifically about Intersave's work:

> Sourcing No Name products is too difficult and too important to be a part-time job. If a proposed product promises to be the best value and provide an adequate return to Loblaws, it must then pass the second and most demanding hurdle: It must be tested for value. Loblaws Companies owns Diversified Laboratories in Toronto, which is equipped with the most up-to-date food quality control laboratory in North America. It employs over 75 technicians and one of its major functions is to insure that no No Name products get on the shelf of Loblaws unless its tests are the best value in Ontario. Nonfood products are tested against leading national brands on the very latest testing equipment. And every proposed No Name is tested by a professional taste panel against the leading national brand. After the taste test, the panel is given the proposed pricing compared to that of the national brand. If the panel doesn't select the proposed No Name as the best value, it doesn't get on Loblaws shelf. Before a product wins final approval, quality control personnel must visit the manufacturing plant to ensure that the plant is capable of maintaining product specification and the final step of Loblaw's No Name quality assurance program involves testing samples of selected finished product at Loblaws warehouse prior to shipment to the stores.

Loblaw also innovates with packaging and distribution to effect cost savings. Its generic quality is positioned to represent "the best value in the marketplace. . . . What you perceive as quality, I may not perceive as quality," says Chenaux, "so we rely strictly on consumer testing. With items that we can analyze chemically, the quality can be changed." This change, Chenaux indicates, can encompass a change in formulation that does not make the product less efficient, just less costly.

There are some fundamental steps involved in locating a supplier. The buyer must first research the market, finding out who produces the product and whether or not they are close by. The buyer then asks for product information and price lists. He looks for customers of suppliers now using these products. The buyer gets firsthand information by taking samples and testing them. He also may investigate the manufacturer, through various financial reporting services. That manufacturer's market position—a dominant factor, a secondary brand, a small operator with excess capacity—can determine its bargaining position. Factors also considered are the supplier's dependability in quality performance and in delivery.

A MARRIAGE OF SORTS

Once the source is approved, "it's like a marriage situation; we have to be compatible," says Allen Kallach, merchandise manager, health and beauty aids, Gray Drug Stores, Cleveland, Ohio. At PLMA's second major meeting, held in Chicago in October 1980, Kallach told his audience (Kallach 1980) at a workshop on sourcing how his chain jumped from 180 up to 425 skus in the first nine months of 1980. The steps taken in locating supply sources included:

First, you have to determine a need for a particular product in a particular category. Then you look for a vendor. We check out possible vendors in five ways:

1. I have sales contracts: people who have called on me and indicated their line and its capability.
2. We're totally committed to using an independent testing lab. I use them to find out about all the manufacturers they know about.
3. I consult with my noncompetitive peers in the industry, getting their ideas on who they use, who they suggest, who is in my price range, who is in my area, etc.
4. My past history with current vendors: what they can do and what their capabilities are.
5. In the past year, checking with both the Private Label Manufacturers Association and *Private Label* magazine, which lists vendors in its issues.

Kallach explained how he narrows the selection from eight to 10 different vendors, weighing such factors as distance, history of quality, delivery performance, manufacturer's integrity ("Do they produce what they say? Do they mean what they say? Do they stand behind their products?"), and most important of all, cost structure. The three to four finalists are then reviewed. "I obtain from each of them a price schedule and product specs; then I require samples that I send out to our testing lab to see if they match our specs and national brand comparability. Also, I try to get an idea of their potential delivery schedule." The final two choices are scrutinized: "Now we get down to the cost structure: costing, analysis of history, their pricing schedule, their delivery schedule. One manufacturer could be totally out of the program because of the cost structure."

"The final test of any of the vendors we deal with is a trip to their plant. I go with the buyer and the technical consultant from our lab to check the manufacturer over for government compliance of regulations (Good Manufacturing Practices), quality of plant personnel, and finally the physical plant and equipment. Can they do the job we want?"

Kallach then explained the follow-up procedures, once the vendor is selected: "When the product is produced and the first order comes in, it's guaranteed briefly. Samples are sent from our warehouse out to the testing lab and within a few days, I have a report back about whether the vendor had delivered what we asked for. . . . Also, we spot check on a periodic basis taking products out of the warehouse and out of our stores to be sent out for testing."

Kenton A. Gast, director of grocery procurement, Kroger Brands, The Kroger Co., Cincinnati, Ohio, warned that same audience (Gast 1980) at the workshop that "it takes a lot of digging and patience to develop a dependable, qualified supplier. The most important source (for locating suppliers) is our regular industry contacts and our general knowledge of the industry" . . . . Gast also referred to printed information as well as his chain's various brokers.

In the sequence of selecting a supplier, he noted that an interview must be set up to review product needs, the quantity, quality levels, cost range, financial stability, and so on.

> The supplier submits samples. If possible, we will pick up actual retail samples of his merchandise produced for another retailer. Then we have a series of product cuttings and consumer panels to approve the product for our use. Sometimes, we will work with a particular supplier to refine and improve their product and maybe change it a little bit, so that we can certify it for use in our private label program. Last of all, our buyer, accompanied by a person from the general office quality assurance department, must make a visit to that supplier's plant. This way, we're assured that the supplier is a good operator and has the capabilities of meeting our requirements, both as to quality and volume. This has the added advantage of giving the buyer a more intimate knowledge and working relationship with that supplier.

As a follow-up to this, Kroger also conducts annual audits with product samples taken from all its suppliers. Gast adds: "Depending on the product category, we also have production sampling, quarterly audits, and a number of other quality assurance procedures, which are designed to meet the audit needs of a particular commodity or product."

How about the new supplier who might offer a better price on the same quality merchandise? If the retailer establishes long-term ties with his vendors, is there room for new suppliers? Gast responded to those questions by saying: "You depend on the category and whether there's elbow room in there for another supplier. The new supplier can feel he's done a lot of work for nothing. But put the shoe on the other foot: you are the current supplier; for some time you too would like to have some consideration. It's kind of like belonging to a fraternity, once you're in, you're in. It's easier to get them in than to get them out."

The retailer's preference: a specialty manufacturer or a full-line manufacturer? Kallach answered: "I'm not as much interested in a one or two item situation as I am in an entire program. I'm not only talking about the vendor with 200 items, but looking at a line extension of eight or 10 different shampoos or 20 different vitamins. We need the specialty items because they definitely satisfy a need. Many of our specialty items are the bread and butter in our profit mix."

As Gast (1980) noted during this workshop, "there really is no magic answer in locating a qualified supplier." If quality is the primary goal in a private label program, then the buyer must not stumble at this critical beginning stage of finding the right source. A weak source can doom the program.

Some retailers may have a guaranteed source—manufacturing capability within their operation—but not all products can be secured within the organization. The buyer, therefore, must look outside. One important consideration should be not only to establish long-term relations with a reliable source but also to keep the doors open to new manufacturing sources. It pays to test products from time to time. Almost like testing a new product, the testing of a new source can prove to be better than an existing relation.

REFERENCES

Burck, C. G. 1979. Plain Labels Challenge the Supermarket Establishment. *Fortune* Magazine, March, pp. 70–76. Copyright 1979 Time Inc., New York. All rights reserved.

Chenaux, R. G. 1981. Loblaw's Buying/Merchandising Muscle: Intersave. *Private Label* Magazine, August-September, pp. 71, 74. E. W. Williams Publishing, New York.

Gast, K. A. 1980. PLMA Fall Meeting: Retailers Tell How They Locate Private Label Suppliers. *Private Label* Magazine, October-November, pp. 45–50. E. W. Williams Publishing, New York.

Kallach, A. 1980. PLMA Fall Meeting: Retailers Tell How They Locate Private Label Suppliers. *Private Label* Magazine, October-November, pp. 45–50. E. W. Williams Publishing, New York.

Newman, F. 1980. Zodys Rejuvenates Its Private Labels. *Private Label* Magazine, February-March, pp. 26–27. E. W. Williams Publishing, New York.

Nichol, D. 1980. Experts Critique Generics Impact. *Private Label* Magazine, June-July, p. 44. E. W. Williams Publishing, New York.

J. C. Penney. 1980. Annual Report. J. C. Penney Co., New York.

Private Label. 1979. A "Home-Spun" Philosophy About Private Label Buying. *Private Label* Magazine, August-September, pp. 42–47. E. W. Williams Publishing, New York.

Private Label. 1980. PLMA Convention: Mystique Surrounds H&BA Quality Control. *Private Label* Magazine, April-May, p. 86. E. W. Williams Publishing, New York.

Topco. This is TOPCO. Topco Associates, Inc., Skokie, Illinois.

Turcott, D. J. 1979. A Built-In Insurance Policy: Woolworth's Quality Assurance Lab. *Private Label* Magazine, June-July, p. 40. E. W. Williams Publishing, New York.

6

Setting Up a Quality Control and Quality Assurance Program

In national brand advertising, there sometimes is mention of the term "bargain brand," which refers to private label products. The word bargain, of course, connotes merchandise that is cheaper, not only in price but in quality. It suggests that a bargain is a "second," or something irregular, or that something is wrong with it. The ad message is clear: bargain brands do not measure up to national brand quality. This strategy could be called a counterattack on private label's claim, "as good as or better than the national brand." The brand manufacturer's label's offensive reply is "bargain brands are not as good as, but worse than national brands."

While this may be true with some bargain brands (especially generics), it is not true of all private labels; just as it is not true that all private labels are as good as or better than national brands. There are no qualifications offered in any of the national brand advertisements.

It would be refreshing to see one of the so-called bargain brands step forward and challenge the national brand attack. That bargain brand would have to be one of the private labels from a retailer/wholesaler who backs his claim with a strong quality control and quality assurance program.

The trend in the private label industry recently has been the shedding of a price-only image for one of quality. Yes private labels continue to be bargain brands, but not with the advertised meaning of second best. Private labels that come from the right supply source and are produced in accordance with proper specifications can be on the same footing as the nationally advertised brands; private labels just do not spend the same marketing dollars, which allows them to sell at a lower price.

Private labels fight the national brands on the same ground when it comes to quality. But on the issue of price, private label is positioned mostly below national brand. This gives private label a decisive edge in today's market. Quality and price combine to give the customer value. Real value consists of a trade-off between price and quality. A buyer can pay dearly for quality and not neccessarily receive value. In these inflationary times, products are not always worth what they sell for. Relief comes in a bargain price. For private label, there can be no compromise on quality, however; it must be of a quality and consumer perception comparable the the national brand or it deserves its old image of being just a price brand or the newer identity of bargain brand, generics, with all the shortcomings attached to those terms.

Private label retailer/wholesalers achieve the highest level of continuing quality through a quality control and quality assurance program. The quality backup can be farmed out to a supply source or a testing lab, but it also can and should be operated partly in-house, particularly if the retailer/wholesaler runs its own manufacturing facilities. Quality assurance—the safeguards built into a private label program once products are received for retail sale—must be run by the retailer/wholesaler. This activity can include sampling products, checking specifications, and periodic audits.

QUALITY CONTROL

What is quality? Dr. Herbert V. Shuster (1979) founder and chief executive officer of Herbert V. Shuster, Quincy, Massachusetts, a technical consulting firm, defined quality as a philosophy:

> The major chains, and these include those that give more emphasis to private label, have adopted the "national brand concept." Not only do they want the appearance of the private label to be a reproduction of the national brand, but the odor, flavor, nutritional quality—even the ingredient statement—have to be in line. They feel that

> they can then sell their private label products to the consumer with a high level of confidence, that they can promote their products without fear, that they will build up consumer loyalty to their store and, above all, that they won't stand the risk of losing a customer, either for the private label brand or for the store itself. Price is not the sole criterion.
>
> On the other hand, there are those who buy a quality level that has been adjusted to meet their guidelines for cost, mark-up, and retail selling price (Shuster 1979, p.48).

What the retailer wants is not always what the manufacturer can provide. When the retail buyer follows the national brand concept, Dr. Shuster notes:

> The subjectivity of the buyer is all but eliminated and this makes the manufacturers' products easier to sell. . . . [It's] a highly subjective thing—more relative than absolute. In the case of canned and frozen fruits and vegetables, both buyer and seller have a big helper in the form of the United States Department of Agriculture. The USDA has established Standards for Grade, which are sometimes used as guidelines and in many cases where the plant is operating under continuous USDA inspection, serve as an "official" quality stamp. Many buyers insist that a USDA Standard for Grade Certificate accompany every private label shipment. Some buyers, who purchase strictly to grade, indicate continuous USDA inspection and the actual grade on the principal display panel of the label.
>
> With many food products there exist what the U.S. Food and Drug Administration terms "Standards of Identity" which specify what a particular product must contain, both qualitatively and frequently quantitatively. It also indicates the optional ingredients that may be used in order to call a product by a particular name.
>
> The Food and Drug Administration is also issuing on a continuous basis an ever-expanding series of publications they call Monographs, which relate to over-the-counter drugs and which serve the same purpose as the "Standards of Identity" referred to above.
>
> Now, let's think about the broad spectrum of manufactured food products not covered by a Standard of Identity, about proprietary OTC drugs not covered by a Monograph, about household chemicals, about paints, about pantyhose, etc. Here the plot thickens. What is good and what is bad? Even more difficult, what is good, better or best? Here's where the adoption of the national brand concept makes life a lot easier, with certain provisions. The supplier must possess the technology to "duplicate" the reference brand in every respect and the buyer must be able to assure the duplication claim by being able to evaluate it in a thorough, scientifically sound manner. The discharging of this joint obligation puts a significant onus on both the buyer and the seller and, in fact, separates the men from the boys. It requires a sincere dedication by both parties to effectively close the circle (Shuster 1979, pp.48–49).

There is no common denominator for quality. Levels of quality vary across the board, depending on the type of product, the judgement of the buyer, the capability of the supplier, the standards of government agencies, and the performance established by national brands.

What is common, what is important, is consistent quality. In a panel discussion on private label quality control held by the PLMA in Chicago in October 1980, Lon Lonker, president of Certified Chemicals Inc., Cinnaminson, New Jersey, emphasized this point: "The customer has got to feel confident in buying anything, from hammer and nails to cosmetics. Every time the customer purchases that product, there's a certain degree of consistency that the customer has grown to expect from the chain. Once the chain has determined that they are going to maintain a level of consistency, then that filters down to their suppliers. They demand that of their suppliers."

What is quality? It is the standard of excellence set by the retailer/wholesaler. As one grocery buyer put it recently, "it's an attitude not to accept anything but quality that we can be proud of." That buyer once approached the company's bakery plant manager, asking why no more whole raisins were being put into the raisin bread. The manager said that the raisins are now ground to spread raisin flavor throughout the bread slice. The buyer said customers would rather find whole raisins in the bread. The manager argued that a better flavor was produced when the raisins were ground into the bread formula. The buyer, however, insisted on having whole raisins—a scoop in every loaf. The manager said that the price per loaf would have to be raised by seven cents. Results: This retailer now sells raisin bread at $1.33 per loaf versus $1.25 for the competition; but the retailer also sells more raisin bread than anyone else. The product contains both ground raisins for enhanced flavor and whole raisins for the customer's pleasure.

One of the oldest drug chains in the country, Walgreens, prides itself on its quality control program: "Private label buyers have not always stressed quality," according to Duane Vogelsburg, president of Walgreens Labs, "About 10 years ago, buyers in the industry talked strictly price. We've been extremely careful with internal analytical checks on our products, running tests continually from once a month to two years or longer."

Walgreens operates one of the largest private label manufacturing facilities in the country in its lab. This facility was featured in the firm's house organ, "Walgreen World" (October 1972), offering an interesting glimpse into the workings of this "company within a company, which does its own marketing, engineering, maintenance, and purchasing. . . . Raw materials pour in from around the world, including karaya gum from India, cinnamon from Ceylon, gum arabic from the Sudan, flower essences from southern France, cloves from Zanzibar, vanilla beans from Madagascar, menthol from Brazil."

The lab supports Walgreen products with chemical research and testing, quality control, and modern production equipment. In analyzing "starting materials" for a batch of Walgreens' Super Aytinal vitamins, the chains' best seller, the report explains how quality control chemists "perform 42 separate chemical assays to verify the material's purity and strength. They will use a variety of specialized equipment—everything from 29 cent test tubes to a $20,000 infrared spectrophotometer—much of it custom-designed for the Walgreen Lab.

"Later, during product manufacturing and packaging, the quality control staff will carry out another 17 chemical tests. To make sure the product is properly perepared and processed, they will weigh 280 individual tablets, make continuous 'on-the-line' checks of packaging procedures, and hand-inspect all 1,388,889 tablets."

This special report also gave a short review of how a product was developed in the lab.

> Fine beauty products don't just happen. They require a lot of time and work.
>
> In July 1971, our marketing department requested the development of a Walgreen label "balsam" hair conditioner.
>
> Research and development chemist Debbie Fry was given the assignment.
>
> Calling on her experience both as a chemist and a former Walgreen beauty consultant,Debbie carried out six months of extensive research.
>
> She evaluated the leading brands, then experimented with a variety of ingredients, before developing just the right formula. This formula then underwent rigorous product testing.
>
> Stability test results: Positive.
>
> Marketing Test Panel verdict: Excellent.
>
> Pilot batch production run: Flawless.
>
> So in June 1972, the first shipment of Formula 20 Balsam Plus Protein Instant Hair conditioner was delivered to our stores. And early reports show that it's selling extremely well.

One effective means of quality control comes through the retailer's move toward vertical integration. Revco D. S., Inc., Twinsburg, Ohio, for example, has acquired a manufacturer of vitamins and food supplements, a supplier of liquid generic drugs, and a producer of injectables. This production muscle allows the retailer to fill all its private label vitamin and aspirin needs plus many other items. Revco realizes a healthy profit return from manufacturing as well as from retail sales of private labels. (Decades ago, A&P was penalized for this strategy, an idea too innovative at the time).

Quality control actually works hand-in-glove with quality assurance. In its fiscal 1980 report, Stop & Shop Companies, Inc., Boston, Mass., noted:

> Quality control begins with a commitment to excellence. But it doesn't stop there. Our commitment is translated into specific, quantative standards, backed by tightly monitored methods and procedures and carried out by a skilled staff of experienced professionals.
>
> In our manufacturing operations, quality control means constant checking every step of the way—from inspection of incoming materials, through processing and shipment, to frequent in-store testing. We rely on sophisticated chemical and micro-

> biological analyses, as well as visual inspections and expert taste testing. Our emphasis on this critical part of our business was highlighted this year by our decision to expand our USDA-approved corporate laboratory in Readville, Mass. . . .
>
> Before any private label product or imported merchandise reaches the shelves of our Bradlees and Medi Mart stores, our quality control experts have subjected it to repeated and rigorous tests. Through our Playsafer Program initiated by Bradlees, samples of every toy sold in any of our stores are fully tested for safety, durability and performance. Such attention to quality control has built the high degree of consumer trust which continues to be a major asset in this rapidly growing segment of our business.
>
> By emphasizing quality control in all our operations and at every level of the company, we seek to guarantee the consistency of value in all our products. And it is this consistent value that is our greatest assurance of consumer satisfaction, upon which our future growth and prosperity are ultimately based.

The retailer/wholesaler can dictate quality and in fact call the shots, sometimes creatively improving the product. This strategy not only guarantees desired quality, but also helps guard against liability.

Korvettes, Inc., New York, which unfortunately traded itself up from a discount to a fashion department store, causing the company to go under, nevertheless operated one of the sharpest Product Development and Quality Assurance Departments in the business. Dick Niedz, director of the department, spelled out the thinking that goes into quality control:

> When a product goes through our lab, it is thoroughly specified as to what its components are, its performance characteristics, the thickness of various elements, its stitches per inch, fabric weight, and much much more. When you lack controls or checks in a private label program, you are totally exposed. Without the laboratory and inspection controls, you could very easily put an inferior product out on the market. In private label, customer dissatisfaction and a loss in repeat sales is your exposure . . . . When a vendor wishes to make certain claims, we look at them both as a consumer and as a Federal regulatory agency. If the vendor makes certain claims, he must be prepared to indemnify us from liability in the event he cannot substantiate the claims. This way, we see truth in advertising very quickly. All of a sudden, certain claims are rearranged. Only when we feel confident that claims can be substantiated, will we put our name on the product (Niedz 1979).

QUALITY ASSURANCE

Shuster (1982, pp.24–27) discusses the three primary elements in a "basic quality assurance program."

1. Specifications

The product specs are supplied by the manufacturer, including formulation, ingredient statement, nutritional labeling, and selected data on chemical, physical, or microbiological constants. Shuster advises the chain to have personnel on their permanent or consulting staff, who have intimate knowledge of the product, its composition, its manufacturing operations, the cost of key ingredients, and most of all how these ingredients affect the value of the product both from an elemental cost standpoint but, more important, from a consumer perception standpoint. To accept the so-called specifications of any supplier is sheer madness.

Prior to establishing quality criteria . . . the retailer must establish exactly how he wants this product to be perceived by the consumer. Where can he cut corners, which performance elements are important and which are unimportant, which are noticeable by the consumer and which are not, which products have a level of consumer expectation such that a viable generic product is unobtainable without lowering the overall corporate standard of value? During this entire process, the national brand must be used as a continuing yardstick for comparison.

The specification development is the most critical element in the quality assurance program. It is the true foundation and without it the program superstructure cannot exist on any permanent basis. Be aware of those products for which Standards of Identity exist and where latitude for value development is limited by the very restrictions of such Standards of Identity.

2. Comparative Evaluations

The retailer compares the supplier's submission against preestablished specifications. Shuster's advice:

> Don't lose sight of the national brand. Above all, be flexible in your thinking, which requires an expertise to know where you can and where you cannot be flexible. Establish the deficiencies, if any, in the prospective products. Communicate with the supplier(s) and try to establish how such deficiencies can be corrected, hopefully without escalating costs beyond practical limits. Reevaluate and reevaluate again, if necessary, to ensure that the product is what you would like it to be.

3. Routine Testing

The retailer insures that the purchased product conforms to specifications, consistently meeting the quality established. Shuster notes: "The routine testing aspect may consist of testing every shipment of the item in depth, testing every shipment of the item in a cursory way, testing the item on a cyclical basis be it monthly or two, three or four times a year. Above all and irrespective of the frequency, testing it 'routinely' is a must. Problem products will merit closer monitoring."

One of the most important activities that a private label buyer can engage in is the plant visit. A firsthand inspection of the supplier's facilities not only serves to protect the image established for a private label program but also assures the buyer that his "product is being made under the best possible conditions so that his customers will receive top quality, uniform, stable, clean, safe and cosmetically attractive products." That is the advice of Dr. Shuster and his associate, Stanley

Skelskie, vice-president of Herbert V. Shuster, Inc. In an article about vitamins, they co-authored an interesting summary (Shuster and Skelskie 1979, p.24) of how the buyer should prepare for a plant GMP (Good Manufacturing Practices) audit:

> Obtain from the FDA Freedom of Information Office* (FOI), copies of the plant's "Establishment Inspection Report" (EIR); FD 483's, "Inspection Observations"; "Regulatory Letters"; "Quality Assurance Profiles"; and company responses for the past two years. The EIR is the complete report of the inspector. The 483 is the list of observations the inspector leaves with management. Regulatory letters list critical problems and advise management to correct the problems within a short period of time or be subject to regulatory action. Quality Assurance Profiles are digests of FDA activities relating to the establishment; company responses are written responses from management.
>
> Do not be swayed by an occasional problem. All plants have problems from time to time. The repetitive problem that does not get corrected signals "danger." Also through FOI, obtain copies of the current GMP for drug establishments and the current and proposed GMP for food establishments. *Read them carefully!*. . .
>
> What should the buyer look for at the proposed vendor's plant during a GMP audit?
>
> Start at the receiving of ingredients and follow the processes and controls all the way to the finished product shipping area.
>
> - Look for orderliness in the warehouses, overall plant cleanliness and "spit and polish."
> - Are screens provided for open windows and open doors?
> - Check that label control is organized to prevent mix-up.
> - Do they have the production capabilities to handle your work?
> - Speak with the production and quality control supervisors; do they seem to have the training and experience to do their jobs?
> - Ask management about their FDA inspections. If you have read in the FOI information that the plant has had many repetitive problems and management says everything is wonderful and there are no problems . . . be alert! FDA inspectors are well-trained and typically highly motivated. Seldom, if ever, does the FDA send out inspectors without training.
> - Ask to see their product stability studies in the final package. Many manufacturers can provide a minimum expiration dating of three years.
> - Question management to see if they are knowledgeable of formula changes in the national reference brands.
> - Does the plant laboratory check the microbiological levels of incoming natural products, water used, and finished products?
> - Does the plant laboratory assay all finished product lots to determine if all vitamins and minerals declared on the label meet not only their declared potency but the formulated overages?
> - Does the plant laboratory assay all incoming ingredients or do they receive a certificate of assay from the ingredient manufacturer and do they perform an identification test?
> - Does the laboratory have specifications for all ingredients, finished products and packaging materials?
> - Do they have Standard Operating Procedures which describe all phases of their operations including cleaning and sanitizing?

* Freedom of Information Staff, HFI-35, Food & Drug Administration, Room 12A08, 5600 Fishers Lane, Rockville, MD 20857.

It is not uncommon for retailers to conduct seminars and workshops, where private labels products can be cut open for inspection and taste comparison tests. Here, FedMart, San Diego, California, invited its suppliers to show products to FedMart employees to orient them to the quality standards of the company's private label lines.

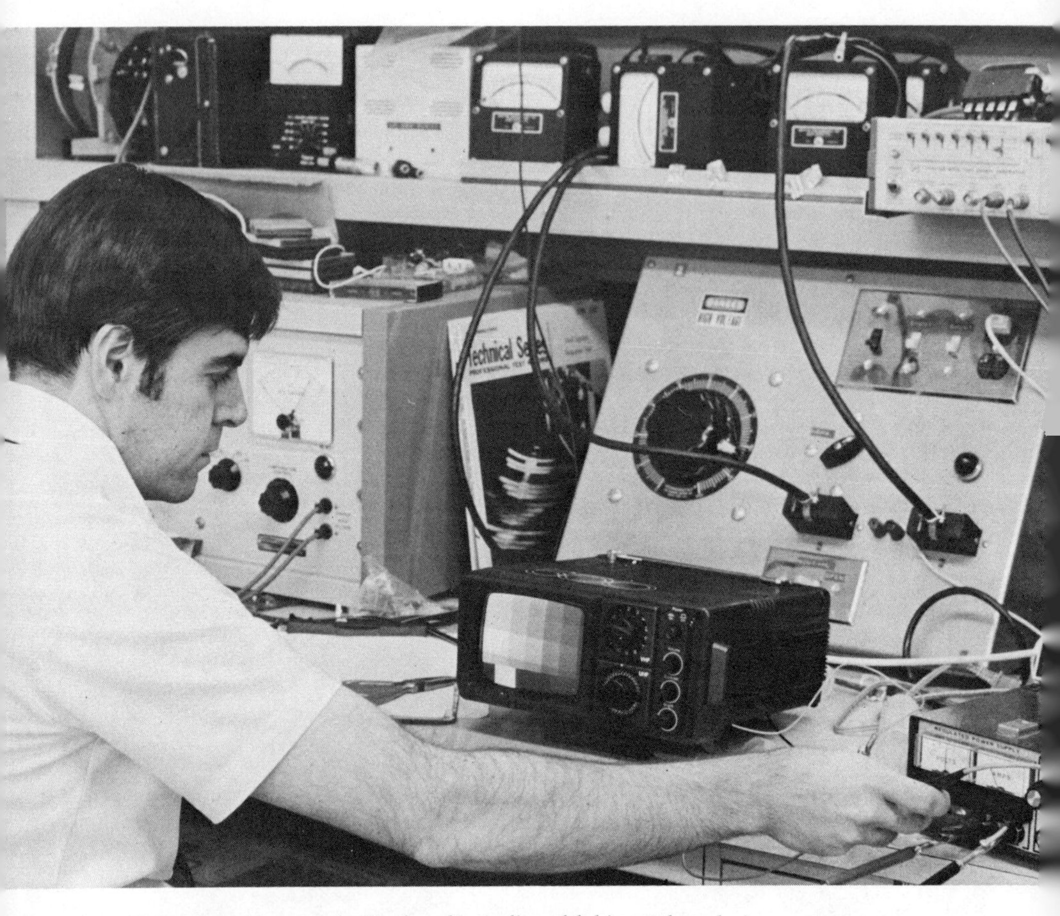

Electronic equipment under Woolworth's Auditron label is put through rigorous testing at the company's Quality Assurance Laboratory. Much of the testing is similar to the Underwriters Laboratories as a double check on safety and performance.

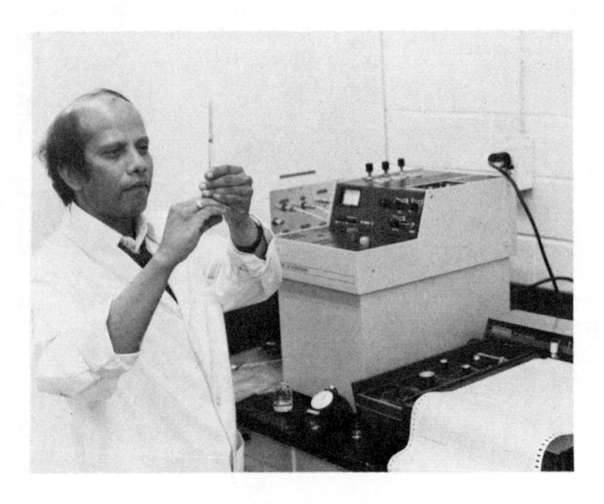

In Canada, Eaton's Product Research Bure is charged with quality control over the retailer's controlled brands, subjecting the to rigid quality specifications and testing. Lab personnel use the latest scientific equipment, including microbiology lab checks on foods and drugs.

A lab technician at Woolworth's Quality Assurance Laboratory studies fiber content in different materials in this chemical test.

ShopRite encourages in-store product testing of its private label products. Customers sample the store brand; if they like the quality, they will purchase the product.

One of five quality assurance mobile labs, which ShopRite dispatches to its member retailers' stores to conduct on-site testing of products taken from the stores.

- In the warehousing area, see whether first-in-first-out procedures are followed for ingredients and finished products.
- Ask to see their recall manual which should specify in detail how a recall would be handled.
- Ask to see the customer complaint file.

While this checklist is geared to vitamin buying, many of the tips apply as well to other product manufacturing. The authors indicate that the buyer can distinguish between a good and a not-so-good plant through experience and the ability to compare: "Visit many plants, ask questions and learn from what you see and hear! Utilize a prepared checklist of critical plant factors that you want to check. Record your observations and compare plant to plant" (Shuster and Skelski 1979, p.24).

The leaders in each market segment recognize the importance of quality assurance. In 1976, Safeway Stores opened its quality assurance center in Walnut Creek, California, which handles most of the research and development and product testing. The company already maintained product testing facilities at each of its manufacturing and processing plants. Safeway states categorically that it does not compromise on its standards, which meet or exceed government grading requirements. For assurance, the company employs "a highly trained staff of food technologists, chemists, engineers, and other specialists. In addition to quality control and product formulation, their efforts are devoted to developing better manufacturing and packaging methods" (Safeway 1977).

In the following year Safeway (1978) stated: "A good value image is important to the success of a private label program; the key elements are price, quality, and reliability. Every Safeway Brand is backed by an unconditional, money-back guarantee as our assurance that the quality equals or exceeds that of competitive brands. We believe this combination is unmatched by any other program in the industry."

Under the K mart trademark, there appears a phrase, "Satisfaction Always." That represents the motto of one of the strongest merchandising chains in the country. It stands for K mart's strategy of offering consumer goods of high quality and durability at prices substantially lower than its competition. The motto also serves to motivate its buyers to seek out new merchandise, suppliers, and merchandising ideas. More than words, satisfaction always for K mart means delivery of quality to customers. The company, in a rare discussion about its buying strategy, revealed how this is accomplished (K mart 1977). Excerpts of that report follow:

> Styling is the number one factor in gaining customer interest in apparel. Buyers extensively shop fashion markets worldwide reviewing manufacturers' lines before deciding on the look with the strongest appeal.
>
> K mart's buying staff, however, must go beyond eye appeal to insure fit, durability and the lowest possible price. The quality control process begins with technically

knowledgeable buyers who can evaluate all the variables—fabrics, cut, trim, stitching, seaming—that determine the quality and the cost of the product. By constantly researching the fabric market and competitive manufacturers, buyers are able to offer fashion at discount prices.

Before K mart places an apparel order, the vendor has to submit an approved sample which is modeled for fit and size specifications. The sample then goes to our own quality control laboratories where tests for shrinkage, color fastness and durability are performed. As garments are manufactured, production line samples are tested. Reorders of the same merchandise receive frequent and thorough review. Warehouse inspection teams continually check shipments and prepare vendor analysis reports on all their inspections. In addition, store department managers provide their evaluations on merchandise received in their departments and on ticketing and packaging . . . .

One outstanding K mart Focal product is film which was developed [in 1970] by K mart to give consumers a high quality film at a true discount price that would still generate a reasonable net profit for the company. Buyers worked with two manufacturers to develop a film exclusively for our stores. A prominent American film manufacturer was selected to produce our product.

K mart stocks Focal film in its own distribution centers in controlled quantities to insure its freshness. Quality is also maintained by constant laboratory testing of sample packages. . . .

[In home improvement departments] immediate emphasis [upon taking over a license in 1969] was placed on developing an exclusive paint line so K mart could more effectively control quality and color selectivity, and offer nationwide discount prices and warranties that would reflect K mart's satisfaction always policy.

In this line, K mart recognized the need to have its own top-of-the-line exterior latex house paint, if the company were to compete for its share of the market.

K mart surveyed name brand manufacturers to determine the most desirable qualities of a top-of-the-line exterior house paint. From the manufacturers' information and from K mart's own analysis of competitors' quality products, the buyers determined that, in an exterior house paint, do-it-yourselfers wanted: durability, non-yellowing, one coat coverage, gloss retention, and resistance to mildewing, chalking and blistering.

K mart then asked several manufacturers to formulate such a product and submit it to K mart along with quantity cost bids. These samples were thoroughly tested by the manufacturers and selected testing laboratories. After K mart chose the quality product it wanted, a label was designed to emphasize the quality of the paint. . . .

[In automotive accessories] typical of the quality products that evolved are K mart's KM tires which are manufactured for the company by two of the world's leading tire and rubber manufacturers.

This association enables K mart to utilize the manufacturers' extensive research and quality control facilities. K mart's best quality tire—the KM 40 (radial)—was subjected to 18 months of research and testing before it was offered for sale.

Programs for quality assurance include preproduction evaluation of new tire designs and construction, laboratory analysis of tires as they come off the lines, and road evaluation on test links. KM tires undergo endurance, mileage, and high speed performance tests, strain and bead unseating tests, dimensional checks, and X-ray analysis. . . .

Seven years ago (1970) K mart added to these national brands [in fishing tackle] by directly importing some key merchandise items. Shortly therafter, it became apparent that K mart's rapid growth was making it essential to supplement the existing assortment with private label merchandise where K mart could control production and merchandise flow to meet high demands.

> K mart buyers work with manufacturers for extended periods of time on each private brand item to build in quality before the product is introduced on the market. For example, K mart's popular skirted spool spinning reel was under development for two years and a combined rod and reel that made its debut last year (1976), the K mart "Mini-Max," was researched for more than two years. . . .
>
> [The company looked to increase jean sales as] K mart's buyers purchased samples of all the leading name brand quality jeans. A laboratory analysis of fabric content, construction, workmanship and fit was conducted on all the samples. The decision was that a tri-blend, piece dyed jean would give the consumer the greatest value in durability, fit, appearance, and price. The first jean introduced—under the K mart "Our Best" label—is the top seller in K mart's boys' jean assortment although four other "Our Best" numbers have been introduced since 1974. Ninety percent of K mart's jeans are manufactured domestically.
>
> Every three to four months, K mart "Our Best" jeans are laboratory tested to insure strict adherence to K mart specifications. Competitive jeans are also analyzed to make sure our quality is as good as or better than other leading quality jeans.
>
> The sales results from this program have resulted in the introduction of a K mart "Our Best" jeans line in K mart's girls and women's apparel departments.
>
> K mart is the major retailer of national brand merchandise in the United States. A national brand, by definition, implies good quality. However, a store that carries the breadth of merchandise (today more than 60,000 items) of a K mart must sell more than just nationally-branded products. K mart assures consumers that all merchandise on K mart shelves, regardless of the name of the label, is of high quality by utilizing a knowledgeable buying organization, a broad quality control program, and systematic on-site inspection programs.
>
> Ultimately, what consumers seek in their purchases is value. Value is a function of both price and quality of the merchandise (K mart 1977, p.6–12).

This rather lengthy quote is included here to illustrate that K mart's quality assurance does not stop at just a few items. This retailer's attention to quality does not end with a policy statement or a copycat approach to following national brand trends. K mart buyers literally roll up their sleeves, working shoulder-to-shoulder with manufacturers (sometimes several manufacturers at one time) in developing products at a quality level that K mart guarantees for its customers. The retailer often calls in testing labs to verify its tests with manufacturers.

K mart is a leading retailer. When its store name or its trademarks appear on a product—no matter what the category—standards of excellence back that item. The quality matches or exceeds the best that national brands achieve. It is a policy that K mart can rightfully boast about. It is a policy that has made K mart a leader in its market segment.

In the firm's 1981 annual report, quality standards that support the chain's private label wearing apparel were outlined. Its quality control personnel perform some 30 apparel tests, including thread count, yarn number, fiber content, washability, and color fastness.

In some cases, there is no difference in the source of material or even the material itself, i.e., private label versus national brand. Challenger jeans by K mart is an example. In comparing a manufacturer's infant's snowsuit with the K mart version, the only difference is in the method of sizing: K mart snowsuits are based on age, the manufacturer's brand based on height and weight. Yet, K mart's article retails at $4.02 less than the brand sold at another merchant's outlet.

K mart also notes in its recent report that it is not uncommon for the company to take clothing samples and literally tear them apart inside out, working to come up with different seam construction and finished garment dimension recommendations. Other retailers also take painstaking effort to ensure the quality of their private label lines.

In its $1 million Quality Assurance Laboratory, Woolworth's continually looks for "good buys," testing thousands of items yearly. Lab personnel track government regulations, develop use-and-care data for products and packaging, field consumer inquiries and complaints and test merchandise for quality and value. Says Daniel Turcott (1979), director of quality assurance:

> Roughly, there are more than 100,000 items in our store, everything from crayons to bathrobes and towels, etc. We cannot test everything. If a buyer has been dealing with a given manufacturer, say in men's underwear, for years; and there have been no complaints, we let that go. If there is a complaint, then we get involved. We try to make a round robin, covering just about everything. If the manufacturer is new, we spot check his merchandise.
>
> We use sophisticated electronic military equipment for testing; some of the testing devices have been fabricated by us. Also, there are pieces taken from industry testing labs. Most of the electronic equipment falls into this category.
>
> We follow different industry standards and sometimes grade up to protect ourselves, such as in flammability testing. If an industry is very vague about what is right or wrong, we sometimes use military specifications.
>
> Our lab is staffed with people who are not necessarily specialists. They are trained personnel who are able to handle several testing areas. This is an advantage, because we can send people off to industry meetings and back them up while they're away. We hire people with some schooling in an area and also accept industry experience. There are different levels of technicians, some at lower levels, willing to learn and grow.
>
> When we have a problem with a product, we know that the buyer has spent a lot of time with a given manufacturer. He likes what he sees on the surface. He very likely has generated a certain line (say clothing) with the manufacturer. This fact alone is important: the buyer's time spent. If we reject the item and ask him to look to another source, that can cost us money. Time is money. What we like to do is sit down with the buyer and manufacturer and, if possible, work out the problems., This is probably the biggest satisfaction we get, receiving the product we want, while the manufacturer ends up with our business. Problems sometimes can be very complicated and costly; for example, a manufacturer of jeans, offering a full size range and different styles—all with the same problem.

Many retailers shoot for excellence in quality and value; Marks & Spencer, one of England's largest retailers, has an aim that is deadly. All of its merchandise—clothes that are "classic and well styled" and food that "tastes good"—is sold under private label, the St Michael brand.

Its insistence on "Marks & Spencer standards," guarded by nearly 200 technologists in fabric, garment, and food ("Our technologists are not back-room boffins, but experienced practical people working closely with our buying departments and suppliers.") is demonstrated in the following nit-picking list:

- In food—the choicest of ingredients: "We're so fanatical about freshness, we put 'best before' dates on just about everything."
- Tags on everything: "We guarantee all our garments' washability/cleanability and wearability."
- For fabrics, "we select all our own dye-stuffs . . . compatible with each fabric used . . . for consistency in colour."
- Trouser pockets made of woven fabrics, never knitted: "They're more durable. Very comfortable. And they won't pull out with your hand."
- In shirts, if the pockets aren't even and the stitching is puckered, the sample is rejected.
- Sweater sleeves are never woven, but all knitted binding tapes are used: "Seams stretch evenly, bounce back nicely, resist shredding. So sweater lasts longer."
- Jeans stitching must meet, otherwise the fit is poor, the feel uncomfortable.
- Handy and thoughtful touches such as hanger tapes on skirts, a touch usually reserved for more costly clothes.
- Belt-loops a shade darker than the rest of the pants.
- Exact color match of zipper to rest of fabric for "hidden" effect.
- Extra button on shirt, blouse, dress, etc.
- Prime grade-A beef, aged right for tenderness, trim yields 95% lean meat.
- Polyfilament thread always specified because a monofilament thread used to hem coats, pants, and skirts is weaker.
- A shirt gripper put all the way around the trouser waistband to keep it neat.
- Use of top-fuse collars with fusing matched to the shirt fabric to keep collars crisp after repeated machine washings.
- In specifying zipper heft, the type of garment and need for strength is considered.
- All fabrics are tested for color-fastness.

This meticulous attention to detail, touching fine points that even the most discerning shopper might overlook or be ignorant about, has made Marks & Spencer the largest clothing retailer in the United Kingdom. It is a tradition that traces back to 1884, when Michael Marks set up Mark's

Penny Bazaar in Leeds, England, selling household goods, haberdashery, and other items for a penny. The St Michael label debuted in 1926. Since then, this label has appeared on clothing, housewares and accessories, and food items, all representing the best quality available in more than 30 countries where the goods are sold. Marks & Spencer's 450 stores are located mostly in the United Kingdom and Canada, while merchandise also is exported to other countries with a few stores located in Europe.

A good retailer's quality control program can begin with product packed by major national brand companies. The retailer follows up with its own product specifications, periodically sampling and testing items from warehouses or in stores to insure that specifications are maintained.

Wakefern Food Corp., Elizabeth, New Jersey, maintains a staff of some 40 people working in quality assurance, through three lab facilities. Nearly 95% of this wholesaler's product testing is conducted in-house. Food technologists, all registered sanitarians, charged with checking products for viscosity, torque strength, color shading, sweetness, and so on, depending on the product classification.

Myron A. Schmutzer, vice-president of quality assurance at Wakefern, notes his department is charged with three major functions: lab testing, regulation compliance, and retail certification. "Our efforts," Schmutzer adds, "are directed not as a replacement to the vendor's quality control, but as another tier for better quality control. We're geared to catch problems further away from the warehouse, especially at packer plants when it involves large volume commodities. We're not content with just warehouse inspections. We have six inspectors who spend their time on the road, inspecting meat plants. Our inspectors also are on hand for inbound inspections at dockside; they oversee inspections for frozen products, dairy-deli products, and so on."

Wakefern also operates five mobile lab vans that check product and store shelfing at the store level.

Of course, not all private label retailers/wholesalers have their own testing facilities for quality assurance. The option open to them is the independent commercial laboratory, which provides such services as quality assurance, food labeling review, safety testing, and performance testing. At the fall 1980 PLMA meeting, Bill Gilman, assistant vice-president, Chemistry Division, U. S. Testing Co., Hoboken, New Jersey, outlined eight ways in which the laboratory can assist a private label program:

It's utilized by all parties along the chain from raw materials to complete consumer product for simple and routine substantiation of laboratory data evaluation.

As a third party, the lab independently establishes the validity of data from a second source, such as a manufacturer.

> It provides a service of substantiation of advertised claims, establishing the basis for making performance and ingredient claims for the product, including the critical consumer acceptance factors.
>
> The lab is frequently involved in thoroughly examining products and evaluating and suggesting new uses for them as well as developing new products and concepts for the marketing of products.
>
> These labs are used for the evaluation of basic materials to determine which one is appropriate, has the greatest performance potential, and could conceivably be of sufficient quality to be marketed on a large scale.
>
> The lab is called upon to develop new test methods or techniques to evaluate raw materials for products. This is especially true where a company may not have a specific expertise or facilities and require some outside assistance.
>
> Labs are used occasionally with time constraints or when the client's lab requires another backup.
>
> Finally, the outside lab may be used more economically to supply testing data for a specific requirement (Gilman 1980).

The national brand manufacturers put the highest priorities on the quality of their products. It behooves the private label retailer/wholesaler to "knock-off" that strategy well before they copy packaging configurations. After all, what is inside the package is what counts.

REFERENCES

Gilman, B. 1980. PLMA Fall Meeting: Retailers Tell How They Locate Private Label Suppliers. *Private Label* Magazine, October-November, pp. 48–50. E.W. Williams Publishing, New York.

K mart. 1977. Annual Report, Troy Michigan.

K mart. 1981. Annual Report, Troy Michigan.

Lonker, L. 1980. PLMA Fall Meeting: The Importance of Product Consistency. *Private Label* Magazine, October-November, p. 58. E.W. Williams Publishing, New York.

Marks & Spencer Limited. What Simon said. . . A no-nonsense look at the Marks & Spencer phenomenon. Marks & Spencer, London, England.

Niedz, D. 1979. Taming Private Label Liability at Korvettes. *Private Label* Magazine, August-September, pp. 50–51. E.W. Williams Publishing, New York.

Safeway Stores Inc. 1977. Annual Report, Oakland, California.

Safeway Stores Inc. 1978. Annual Report, Oakland, California.

Shuster, H. V. 1979. The Technical ABCs of Private Label. *Private Label* Magazine, April-May, pp. 48–49. E.W. Williams Publishing, New York.

Shuster, H. V. 1980. Quality Assurance: The Prerequisite for Private Label Success. *Private Label* Magazine, August-September, pp. 24–27. E.W. Williams Publishing, New York.

Shuster, H. V., and Skelskie, S. 1979. What Every Buyer Should Know About Private Label Vitamins. *Private Label* Magazine, August-September, p. 24. E.W. Williams Publishing, New York.

Stop & Shop Companies. 1980. Annual Report, Boston, Massachusetts.

Turcott, D. 1979. A Built-In Insurance Policy: Woolworth's Quality Assurance Lab. *Private Label* Magazine, June-July, p. 41. E.W. Williams Publishing, New York.

Vogelsburg, D. 1979. Looking Behind the "100% Guaranteed" Walgreens Label. *Private Label* Magazine, June-July, p. 27. E.W. Williams Publishing, New York.

Walgreen. 1972. Behind Each Label is THE Lab. *Walgreen World,* Special Issue. Vol. 39. No. 9. October. Inside front cover. p. 1. Walgreen Co., Deerfield, Illinois.

Walgreen. 1972. Case Study In Quality. *Walgreen World,* Special Issue. Vol. 39. No. 9. October. Back cover. Walgreen Co., Deerfield, Illinois.

7

Legal Aspects of Private Label

In legal affairs, the private label retailer/wholesaler, manufacturer, supplier, and broker can face litigation in the normal course of business, especially in such matters as violation of the antitrust laws related to price fixing, product liability if a product is ruled dangerous or defective, and trade dress infringement on someone else's protected copyright, patent, or trademark. While there are many other forms of litigation, these three—price fixing, product liability, and trade dress—correlate with the private label business. A discussion of each topic follows.

ANTITRUST/PRICE FIXING

The retailer in his stores can legally discriminate in pricing products. He can sell brands and private labels at whatever price he wishes. Of course, a competitor's pricing strategy can influence his pricing differentials. However, the manufacturer or the wholesaler selling to a retailer *cannot* practice price discrimination under the 1936 Robinson–Patman Act. This law covers unfair price discrimination and inequitable quantity discounts, brokerage payments, and promotional payments.

In part, the act states that it is unlawful "to discriminate in price between different purchasers of commodities of like grade and quality. . .

where the effect of such discrimination may be substantially to lessen competition or tend to create a monopoly in any line of commerce, or to injure, destroy, or prevent competition with any person who either grants or knowingly receives the benefit of such discrimination."

In an interpretation of this act, Robert F. Hartley, professor at the George Washington University, writes:

> The inclusion of the phrase "to injure, destroy, or prevent competition" meant that the FTC no longer had to prove that competition was *substantially* lessened, but only that it was *injured*. This was soon interpreted to mean "injury to competitors," and greatly increased the ease of prosecution. . . .
>
> A firm charged with price discrimination has two available defenses: a cost defense, and a good-faith defense.
>
> If a seller can prove that specific cost savings result in the "manufacture, sale or delivery resulting from differing methods or quantities," price differences may be permitted. This primarily refers to quantity discounts, but even such discounts still could be limited if large firms are given an undue advantage, since the Federal Trade Commission is empowered to fix and establish quantity limits.
>
> The cost defense has been quite difficult to use, since most firms do not have such cost data to begin with. If the cost evidence is prepared after the discrimination has occurred, instead of before, there are problems concerning the intent. Some firms do not want to bare their confidential cost figures, and there is always the risk that the cost information or the method of computing it may not be acceptable to the FTC and the courts.
>
> In the good-faith defense, a seller attempts to prove that a price was lowered in good faith to meet competition. While this had been a permissible defense if it occurred as a defensive rather than an aggressive action, a more recent Supreme Court decision makes this more murky. A small firm, the Utah Pie Company, entered an established market with a low-price appeal. This led to price cutting, including sales below cost by the larger national companies. The defense of the national manufacturers that they were meeting competition was disallowed since it involved "persistent sales below cost." ('Court Raps Price Cuts,' *Business Week*, April 29, 1967, p. 50; and 'Utah Pie Co. v. Continental Baking Co. et al.,' *Journal of Marketing*, October 1967, p. 74.)
>
> Besides price differentials, the Robinson–Patman Act outlaws brokerage payments to buyers unless they actually perform the function of a broker. The major chains had been claiming such discounts due to their large purchasing volume, but were consequently denied this. The Act also requires that advertising allowances or any special services must be provided on "proportionately equal terms" to all buyers. Therefore, the providing of demonstrators, advertising allowances, display material, and so forth, cannot be offered to some customers and not to others. Proof of injury to competition is not even necessary for prosecution of such cases (Hartley 1972).

As to the law's impact, enforcement has varied from weak to strong; the situation, Hartley continues,

> is still unclear, and many court decisions are made on narrow votes.
>
> The result has been that many cost savings are not passed along. Fear of possible legal action causes price rigidity, so that competition is on a nonprice basis, rather than price. The Robinson–Patman Act may even be seen as a direct contradiction to the Sherman Act. The Sherman Act prohibits collusion or agreement on prices, and therefore encourages hard competition on a price basis. The Robinson–Patman Act, by limiting quantity discounts, even when justified on the basis of cost savings, and by

frowning on the use of price as a competitive tool, infers that you cannot compete too hard without fear of FTC intervention.

LANDMARK CASE

The Supreme Court in a landmark court case upheld an FTC ruling (Federal Trade Commission v. Borden Co., 383 U.S. 637 (1966) that found the Borden Company guilty of price discrimination in selling its private label evaporated milk at a lower cost than its branded version, when both, in fact, are "physically and chemically identical." Earlier, the Court of Appeals for the Fifth Circuit Court set aside that FTC ruling on the grounds that "the customer label milk was not the same grade and quality as the milk sold under the Borden brand." The Appeals Court considered both products to be "commercially" different and as such representing different grade even though physically identical and of equal quality. The Appeals Court decided that consumer preferences for one brand over the other was sufficient grounds to differentiate chemically identical products and thus place a price differential on them.

The Supreme Court sided with the FTC decision that labels do not differentiate products for the purpose of determining grade or quality, even though one might have more appeal than the other and command a higher price.

The Supreme Court decision was not unanimous. Two justices dissented, arguing that "consumer preferences can and do create significant commercial distinction between otherwise similar products . . . . The product purchased by a consumer includes not only the chemical components that any competent laboratory can itemize, but also a host of commercial intangibles that distinguish the product in the marketplace."

Those "commercial intangibles" were spelled out in the justices' letter in a footnote, citing Chamberlain (1962).

> A general class of products is differentiated if any significant basis exists for distinguishing the goods (or services) of one seller from those of another. Such a basis may be real or fancied, so long as it is of any importance whatever to buyers, and leads to a preference for one variety of the product over another. Where such differentiation exists, even though it be slight, buyers will be paired with sellers, not by chance and at random (as under pure competition), but according to their preferences.
>
> Differentiation may be based upon certain characteristics of the product itself, such as exclusive patented features; trade-marks; trade names; peculiarities of the package or container, if any; or singularity in quality, design, color, or style . . . . In so far as these and other intangible factors vary from seller to seller, the "product" in each case is different, for buyers take them into account, more or less, and may be regarded as purchasing them along with the commodity itself.

This was followed by another reference, to Brown (1948):

> The buyer of an advertised good buys more than a parcel of food or fabric; he buys the pause that refreshes, the hand that has never lost its skill, the priceless ingredient

> that is the reputation of its maker. All these may be illusions, but they cost money to create, and if the creators can recoup their outlay, who is the poorer? Among the many illusions which advertising can fashion are those of lavishness, refinement, security, and romance.

The justices further argued: "The record also indicates that retail purchasers who bought the premium brand did so with the specific expectation of acquiring a product of premium quality. . . . Borden took extensive precautions to insure that a flawed product did not reach the consumer." Footnotes supporting this argument followed:

> Borden's Food Products Division maintained a staff of field representatives who inspected code-datings on cans of Borden brand milk in retail stores, in order to insure that older milk was sold first off the retailer's shelves. . . . Borden dispatched its milk to wholesalers and retailers under a first-packed, first-shipped rotation plan that occasionally involved high-cost shipments from distant plants or warehouses. In addition, before shipment from a cold storage warehouse, Borden "tempered" its premium brand milk in order to prevent condensation on the cans, which might have resulted in rust to the cans and damage to the labels.
>
> As counsel for the respondent candidly stated on oral argument to the Court, "The difference as to the private label brand packed by Borden is that, as to that product, the Borden Company washed its hands of it at the factory door."

The justices concluded, after numerous other arguments, with a warning about creating price uniformity and rigidity, noting: "In the guise of protecting producers and purchasers from discriminatory price competition, the Court ignores legitimate market preferences and endows the Federal Trade Commission with authority to disrupt price relationships between products whose identity has been measured in the laboratory but rejected in the market place."

In 1967, the Supreme Court sent the case back to the Court of Appeals, which found no evidence of injury to competition since the pricing differential between brand and private label did not go beyond the "recognized consumer appeal of the Borden label."

In retailing there is an unwritten law that states the customer is always right. If customers wish to satisfy their fancy, to be influenced by illusions, they should be allowed that choice. Private label, a more practical buying alternative, may not always carry the romance of advertised brands, but it should always guarantee a happy ending: customer satisfaction or your money refunded.

PRODUCT LIABILITY

Product liability is intrinsically part of a private label quality control and quality assurance program (see Chapter 6). Responsibility rests with everyone involved in the product's chain of distribution, from supplier of raw materials to the retailer. Ralph Behr, member of the New York and Oregon bars and vice-president of Food Oils corp., Carlstadt, New Jersey, offered some interesting observations on this subject:

> Product liability is not, as some would believe, a carte blanche to corporate coffers. Understanding its scope and its limitations is useful and helpful in conducting your business.
>
> It is well established that a manufacturer, or a seller, is *not* liable for a product related injury without proof that the product was defective or dangerous when it was in his control. Underscore in your mind the words *defective, dangerous,* and *control.* Unless the product is proven such, there will be no recovery by our injured consumer.
>
> There must be something wrong with the product, in its design or manufacture; or a failure to warn of a forseeable but unreasonably dangerous use. A knife is not unreasonably dangerous merely because it can cut a finger. The knife would be useless if it could not cut.
>
> Swift & Company had the honor, in 1936, of finding the rule, and Sears, Roebuck & Company in 1961 of restating the rule, that one who labels a product with his own name, or otherwise represents it to be his own, is to be treated on the same basis as if he had manufactured the product.
>
> The rule, as stated above, can be quite harsh, but it is generally enforced in all states. The private label seller is liable, as is the manufacturer, for injury or damage caused by a dangerous or defective product bearing his name. Courts have reasoned, like it or not, that you have, in effect, vouched for the product.
>
> When I put my name on a product, such as "Ralph Behr's Fancy Pitted Prunes" and Farrah Fawcett Majors breaks one of her famous front teeth on a pit, her lawyer will name me and my negligent supplier as a defendant. When I put my name on a product I am asking the consumer to associate my image of quality with the product: I have in effect adopted it.
>
> When my product is defective or dangerous, the consumer can look to me for the negligence of my supplier and the courts will make it hold. I am not, however, stuck, because I will in turn sue my private label supplier and hopefully escape liability.
>
> To avoid this exposure, I should ask my supplier to make sure he has sufficient product liability insurance to cover such a claim. Both your liability and responsibility should be discussed with your company's counsel if you are concerned.
>
> In summary, we can state a general rule: The law of strict liability for a product which is dangerous or defective applies to the manufacturer of the product as well as the one who puts his name on the product. Except in a very small number of states, this general rule applies to a wholesale dealer as well as a retailer. . . .
>
> We purchase product liability insurance, or require it of our suppliers so that our exposure is limited to the deductible in our insurance policy. Business and consumers benefit from this in that the risk is spread through insurance, the cost of which is built into the shelf price.
>
> Perhaps you may feel that product liability is not bad for business, but is it too expensive?
>
> In 1977, the Federal Interagency Task Force on Product Liability, created by the White House, issued its briefing report. Among other things, it found that the cost of product liability, spread throughout a product category, is above 1% of the cost of the product as reflected in the consumer's cost. In some high risk categories, such as pharmaceuticals and products with potentially dangerous moving parts, it can run as high as 10%.

> Few will dispute that the cost is high, and that it has prevented many useful drugs and products from reaching the consumer because potential product liability exposure is too great to be borne in the product price, by the manufacturer, or in some cases by the insurance carrier itself. The costs are high and should be reduced.
>
> The reduction of costs will come about when we either limit the responsibility of manufacturers by statute, or require more accountability and balance from the courts in awarding damages to injured users (Behr 1979A).

TRADE DRESS

Many private labels are dressed in packaging that looks like the leading national brands. Formulations also are often carbon copies of the national brand. This activity has led to an overreaction by some observers, who believe that private label knock-offs threaten the future of national brands. Some pretty reputable people have been concerned.

In a full-page ad, *Good Housekeeping*, the magazine of the famous seal, asked, "National Brand or Private Label. . . . Who's going to 'own' the grocery business in the years ahead?" The ad copy read in part:

> There is no doubt in our mind that in the development of grocery products, in the perfecting of new techniques, the creation and testing of new convenience foods, it is the manufacturer who takes the initiative, makes the tremendous investment and has the great capacity.
>
> And if these innovations, these basic contributions to better nutrition and more varied diet, are to be properly recognized and made easily available to the public, we think each should have its *own* name, the *same* name, everywhere. That means national brands. And that, in turn, means imaginative, effective, convincing advertising . . . the establishment of strong brand names in which women do have confidence.

The United States Trademark Association, took issue with what it called private label's "piracy of trade dress" (USTA 1973). USTA discussed how a private label owner designs his label to "simulate" national brand packaging, minus only the brand name, then merchandises that copycat on retail shelves next to the brand. The outcome: Some customers are "fooled into buying its privately labeled counterpart." When the brand manufacturer fails to respond, he stands to lose sales and even the ability to protect his trade dress, according to USTA.

The Lanham Act, USTA argued, does not allow for class action suits under such activity, because trade dress features are frequently not protected by trademark or copyright. A suit would require proof of consumer confusion along with people testifying in court to that fact.

USTA also noted that "the biggest impediment" to a class action suit is the fact that private label owners are customers of the brand manufacturers. USTA concluded that when customers buy private label, thinking it is a brand or from a brand manufacturer, the private label is taking "unfair advantage and the competition (is) unfair competition."

There is, of course, a line that must be drawn when private label copies the national brand trade dress. The private label should not confuse the customer; but private label also must duplicate some of the brand's trade dress features, because customers recognize the brand's packaging from advertising. Private label does not carry the same advertising impact and so must relate to the brand—not only with equal formulations, but also in a comparable trade dress. This tells the customer there is an alternative choice, where he or she can realize a savings.

Throughout the history of private label, there has been very little consideration given to the consumer; usually all trade attention is focused on the industry players—manufacturer, wholesaler, and retailer—especially on who is being cheated.

Despite what people say or think—and attitudes have not changed much since the 1970s—national brands are not the only quality choice. Private labels, imitative or not, give the consumer another choice. It is only because private labels are more exposed—honestly admitting they are like the national brands and blatantly copying their trade dress—that they are criticized and sometimes condemned for "ripping off" a manufacturer's brand. While that argument may be partly justified, it cannot be said that consumers are robbed (or fooled) when they are given the choice of a less expensive buying option.

There is nothing wrong with copycat products in a competitive environment. The United States Court of Appeals is on record saying: "Imitation is the lifeblood of competition" (American Safety Table Co. v. Schreiver, published at 269 F2d 255, 272—1961, the opinion of the Second Circuit Court of Appeals). In our free enterprise system, product knockoff activity is as common as a retail sale.

Every day, brands are replicated by competitive companies. It can be an innovative product like Ideal Toy Corp.'s Rubik's Cube, which has attracted copies like Challenge Puzzler, Magic Puzzler, Le Cube, and Perfect Puzzler.

It can be a specialized product like Miller's Lite Beer, picked up with a different spelling by Schlitz's Light and Michelob Light.

It can be a fad like designer clothes: Sassoon, Calvin Klein, Jordache, Cheryl Tiegs, etc.

It can be the auto parts aftermarket, where General Motors, Ford, Chrysler, and General Electric find their products duplicated by the so-called gypsy supplier in similar packages.

It can be prescription drugs that are chemically copied from the national brands by generic manufacturers.

It can be beautifully designed jewelry, fashions, cosmetics, all copied over and over again.

It can be the Japanese monster Godzilla recreated as Sears' Bagzilla, a much friendlier creature; or the Izod alligator reformed as the "Braggin Dragon," also by Sears, or as "The Fox" by J. C. Penney.

It can be a whole marketing program like Hanes L'eggs—unique egg package, boutique display, new market penetration (supermarkets and drug stores)—picked up by Kaser Roth in the No Nonsense pouch with its own boutique display and marketing strategy, followed by private label hosiery boutique displays.

As a copycat product, private label cannot be singled out as the exception.

Whenever any product duplicates the protected rights held by someone else, that product runs the risk of breaking what have been called federal law monopolies:

- Patent law covering technological innovations
- Copyright law covering literary or artistic works
- Trademark law covering commercial goodwill and avoiding consumer confusion

Legally, it is permissible to copy anyone's innovative ideas; but when the imitator produces an exact form of the trade dress so that the consumer is misled into believing the product to be the same as the original, it is unlawful.

Comparatively speaking, private labels can be as good as or better than the national brand, but they cannot be the brand itself. It is possible for a private label to infringe on the rights of a national brand through packaging, through labeling, through graphic design, through symbols, through any distinguishable form that identifies the branded product. The private label, therefore, can come as close as possible to the form taken by the national brands—the product category leader and therefore the consumer's first buying choice—but not to the point where the consumer is deceived into believing the private label is the national brand.

While many private label owners copy the national brands in order to tap a successful market, there are notable exceptions. Woolworth's, for example, innovates with its private label wherever possible. As H. Chazen, director of packaging, notes, however:

> in a few instances, where a product is so strongly defined with a certain type of package—size, color, shape, or whatever—it would be foolish to go in another direction, because our product then would not be recognizable as that type of product. Specifically, with something as simple as aspirin, if you put them in a little cardboard box or plastic bag, they wouldn't look familiar; and people would distrust them immediately.

> In the case of the consumer, there's a certain accepted image vis-á-vis a product; and that's the way it should look to make it acceptably believable in that product area. To fight that, especially in private label, is wrong. If someone were to come out with a new national brand and there were positive reasons for having it in a new package and there were millions of advertising dollars backing it, that's another story. Packages ride on images that have preexisted. You cannot go so far afield in packaging that you'd have trouble selling your product (Chazen 1979).

So even the exceptional innovator must sometimes follow the copycat rule in the private label business. That step can lead to problems with several federal laws that serve to protect a copyright, a patent, or a trademark. Whenever a private label owner adopts a name or design, he runs the risk of violating someone else's rights, especially when the private label is a knock-off product.

The Federal *copyright law* covers an original work of authorship, not only words, but music, fabric design, jewelry, and art work. This law applies also to a product label, including the written portion and its graphics. Copyright protection is established by putting the symbol © on a package. Once the material is published on a label, in a brochure, or in an advertisement, a copyright is established. Registration comes by filing that material with the Library of Congress. A copyright can remain in effect for the duration of the author's life plus 50 years.

Both the Federal *patent and trademark laws* fall under the jurisdiction of the U.S. Patent, Design, and Trademark Office. Patents are commonplace in the retail business. Infringement battles involve businesses from the giant corporations down to the single entrepreneur, seeking redress for an invention. Polaroid Corp., for example, is fighting Kodak in the courts over patents on the instant camera. Inventor Peter M. Roberts has charged Sears with infringement of a patent on a quick-release device on socket wrenches in a lawsuit pending in the courts.

Patents can cover new and nonobvious useful inventions, allowing the owner exclusive rights to make, use, or sell the patented invention for 17 years. This protection usually covers a product, process, or device that is novel and useful. Plans and a working model are supplied to the U.S. Patent Office. Once the patent expires, the public can use the invention freely.

There also are design patents that cover new, original, and ornamental designs for articles that are manufactured. This protection is issued for up to 14 years, only after a search is made to determine if the design is novel.

Some 140 of the 200 most frequently prescribed drugs are expected to be off their patents by 1983, after which other manufacturers can produce the same drugs under their generic names, selling them for less because development and research costs are not incurred. But the old tests are now being put aside in the courts as judges are making new assumptions not previously considered, according to William Boland, partner of the firm of Kenyon & Kenyon, New York, counsellors at law. Speaking at the spring 1981 PLMA meeting, Boland said: "The generic houses traditionally have followed the ethical houses in their products in color, shape, etc., when the patents for these drugs ran out. Until recently, it was felt that no one manufacturer had an absolute monopoly in color or shape of their drug product, because partly it was functional and partly people didn't identify the product by the color or shape, etc. This is beginning to change today." The ethical houses are bringing generic houses to court over matters where the latter produce products that "copy pill-for-pill or capsule-for capsule in coloration, size, etc." arguing "that the generic product was not the bioequivalent of their product for the same therapeutic purposes. The courts have become very upset, thinking that people are being subjected to drugs that might cause them harm or might have deleterious effects on people's health." Boland added:

> I think that the judges get emotionally involved in this situation. But it is the language in some of these cases that is terribly broad. And this can apply to private label products as well as to the drug field. Many manufacturers put out products that are ingested by people, or products that offer personal care, which might have a deleterious effect upon people, if they do not have the same effect as a product sold under a brand name. This would be one argument given in the courts. It could apply to food products in a supermarket. If the customer thinks he or she is getting product A, but gets product B, because somebody has put out B in a trade dress similar to A, then the judge might enjoin the manufacturer of product B from producing that product in that trade dress (Boland 1981).

A 1981 court case in New Jersey enjoined a generic house from producing its product in particular colors, with no appeal as yet set. Boland suggested that manufacturers can be "held liable for the damages which are suffered by the person who owns trade dress rights. That person also can get the profits for the products you've sold. The injunction can prevent you from shipping any other products, destroying what you have in your warehouse, including all labels and promotional pieces connected with that particular product."

Judges now no longer talk about irreparable damage, they assume it: if someone copies another's trade dress, irreparable damage will be caused. Boland continued:

> One of the conditions for being successful at trial is the likelihood of confusion. There are cases that say they will assume there will be likelihood of confusion if the trade dress is similar. One of the ways that you see if a person has rights in a particular trade dress is whether he has secondary meaning. That can only be shown by taking an extensive survey and having people associate that trademark and trade dress with a particular source. There are several cases which now say that the very fact that you as a defendant would copy proves that there is secondary meaning, otherwise you wouldn't copy. That, to me, seems that they're throwing away most people's defenses just by making assumptions that in the past have not been made (Boland 1981).

In packaging that is just as appealing, featuring delicious-looking slices of cake in four-color, Ralph's Grocery imitates Betty Crocker, positioning its Ralph's logo (coincidentally similar to the Betty Crocker logo) on the top left part of the package. The national brand logo, however, is in the form of a spoon, while Ralph's is an oval.

Sears' answer to the designer jeans fad is the trademark Cheryl Tiegs, carried over into a collection of clothes introduced during 1981. The famous model's name appears on sweaters, shirts, and other clothing items, all sold exclusively in Sears stores.

FedMart has adopted a distinctive graphic front panel on its dandruff control shampoo, picking up only on the Head & Shoulders wave symbol, but in a different wave pattern.

The more established Sears trademark, Craftsman, is used on numerous tools, representing top quality merchandise.

Giant Food "copies" the Quaker State motif only as far as its first letter "G" used to enclose the trademark name and generic identity, versus Quaker State enclosed in a "Q."

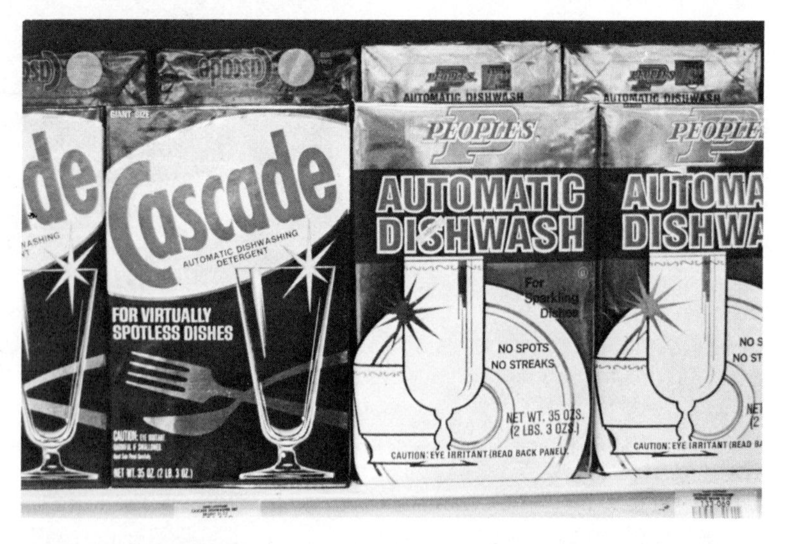

Displayed next to the leading national brand, Cascade, Peoples Drug has established its own distinctive trade dress for automatic dishwash detergent. Note that even the star symbol for a sparkle is positioned on a different part of the glass; Peoples has also taken care to represent a white glass in front of dishware, rather than a clear glass in front of a fork and spoon as in Cascade's front panel.

In this sensitive area, the ripoff argument comes into play. An article in *The New York Times* (May 9, 1981) discussed Biocraft Laboratories copying the brands Bactrim and Septra (infection-fighting drugs) on the market since 1973, at a cost of $350,000. With that savings, Biocraft is able to offer the knock-off generic drugs at half the price of the brands. Biocraft took advantage of a Food and Drug Administration (FDA) ruling that allows for smaller producers to draw information from pioneering research in order to circumvent duplication of costly research. The article stated that large pharmaceutical houses pay out $70 million average and spend upwards of 10 years of testing and research, after a patent is granted, to obtain FDA approval.

The *Times* also referred to data from the Pharmaceutical Manufacturers Association (PMA) which reported 12 new drugs approved by the FDA in 1980 versus 50 in 1960. Investment dollars also declined from 12.2% of total sales in 1965 down to 7.9% in 1979.

Irwin Lerner, president and chief executive of Hoffman–LaRoche Inc. and creator of Bactrim, was quoted: "We are being squeezed from loss of revenues taken by imitations at one end and a drought of new drug introductions at the other. It's a tough go."

In these inflationary times, relief for the consumer in the form of low-cost generic drugs appears to spell no relief for the brand manufacturers.

In a related incident, PMA lost a suit which it, together with a group of pharmacists brought against the 1977 generic drug law, which permits generic substitutions to be written by doctors, especially if it is less expensive than the branded version and the customer asks for it. The New York State Court of Appeals ruled unanimously in favor of the laws' constitutionality, arguing that it was a legal and safe way to reduce health care expenses. The court said that the law produced a "beneficial effect," in that it offered a patient a choice of needed medication.

That beneficial effect is inherent in all private labels, which offer the consumer an alternative product choice, often as good as the more expensive branded version.

In a significant trademark decision, the U.S. Supreme Court in June 1982 overturned a Federal appeals court (New York) ruling that charged three generic manufacturers with "contributory trademark infringement" of the branded drug, Cyclospasmol (for increasing blood flow) manufactured by Ives Laboratories, Inc., an operation of American Home Products Corp., New York. The argument, centering around the generic drug manufacturers' right to sell a generic equivalent in the same color, shape, and size as the blue-and-red capsule sold as a branded product, focused on pharmacists substituting the look-alike generic drug (cyclandelate) for Cyclospasmol, writing that brand on the label. The appeals court found the generic manufacturers guilty in supporting this practice;

but the Supreme Court said there was no proof that the manufacturers "intentionally induced the pharmacists to mislabel generic drugs or, in fact, continued to supply cyclandelate to pharmacists whom the petitioners (the manufacturers) knew were mislabeling generic drugs." The higher court, however, did not rule on the manufacturers' right to imitate the color, shape, and size of the branded drug, charging the appeals court (The U.S. Court of Appeals for the Second Circuit) to rule on that question (*The New York Times*, June 2, 1982).

Ives' patent on Cyclospasmol expired in 1972; yet, the manufacturers have argued that Ives wishes "to use the identification between the drug and the color of the capsule . . . to inhibit competition." The appeals court now must resolve the conflict between promoting competitive product imitation and using trade symbols to identify source or origin, as prescribed by the Federal trademark law, the Lanham Act.

Such arguments are by no means restricted to drugs. Nike Inc., Beaverton, Oregon, recently filed a $2 million suit against retailer Zayre Corp., Framingham, Massachusetts, charging the latter with trademark infringement and dilution, unfair competition, and deceptive trade practices over the use of Nike's "swoosh" trademark on running shoes. Nike has filed similar suits against other retailers and manufacturers with rulings that were favorable for Nike.

TRADEMARK INFRINGEMENT

The trademark is by far one of the most valuable assets that a company can own. It covers the words, names, symbols, and devices that identify and distinguish the owner's goods and services. The trademark is a reference to the source and the quality to be expected from that source. In private label, the retailer/wholesaler stands behind the trademark as the source, either directly manufacturing the product or contracting the work out to small or large manufacturers who pack the product to the trademark owner's rigid specifications. The value of a trademark truly cannot be measured; its worth increases with usage.

Obviously, trademarks are valued. In 1978, more than one million had been registered with the U.S Patent and Trademark Office. The count today is more than 1.1 million trademarks.

In a 1972 press release, Sears talked about hundreds of Sears trademarks, describing file drawers full of names:

> Some of the names in the company file date back to 1902. Early medicine men were the first to name their products—usually after themselves or mythical characters, and gradually companies began using names to identify their own products, Sears included. . . .

> Most company trademarks originate in the buying departments. But before they can be used on products, the Trade Practice Division of Dept. 733B must research and approve each one. Its staff, consisting of an attorney and assistant, investigate as many as 150 names monthly—three times the volume they had a few years ago. And they determine if similar names on similar items already exist.
>
> Many of the submitted trademarks can be eliminated after checking office records. Others which pass the first test, are sent to a professional search company for a detailed investigation. There, each name is checked with the 36,000 registered and pending trademarks in the U.S. Patent Office. . . .
>
> Trademarks which are then registered are usually slated for major advertising campaigns and long-term usage such as the "DieHard" battery. Registration forms for these trademarks are sent to the U.S. Patent Office, and after about a year of processing and review, the acceptable trademarks are published in the weekly Patent Office *Gazette*. Thirty days later, if no opposition has been made, Certificates of Registration are granted. And from this point on, each Sears trademark is followed by a ® proclaiming it the property of Sears Roebuck and Co.

Recently, the U.S. Court of Appeals for the Ninth Circuit dismissed trademark infringement and unfair competition charges brought against Sears by Toho Co., Ltd. of Japan, creators and owner of the "Godzilla" mark. Sears had developed a monster caricature, "Bagzilla," for its line of trash bags packaged in boxes featuring the monster and a slogan, "monstrously strong bags." In a May 18, 1981 decision, the circuit judge ruled there was no likelihood of confusion regarding the source or sponsorship of the product: Sears "means only to make a pun" and not to confuse consumers. Bagzilla is a humorous caricature and not an exact copy of Godzilla.

Trademarks, like copyrights, become effective once they are used. Registration, which helps in defending one's rights in court, can come later. The trademark protection lasts as long as the mark retains its identifying and distinguishing function.

A company can hold the rights to hundreds of trademark names. In the past, private label retailers have had uncountable numbers of names. Safeway still maintains about 250 registered names.

A&P years ago printed a consumer brochure, featuring a sampling of its trademarks: A&P, Sail, dexo, Yukon Club, Crestview, Jane Parker, Sunnybrook, Iona Brand, Tudor, Crescent City, Crestmont, Super Right, Excel, Our Own, Silverbrook, dexola, Allgood, Sunnyfield, Wildmere, ahoy pink, Cap'n John's, Coast to Coast, Encore, Warwick, Nutley, Ched-o-Bit, Mel-O-Bit, Marvel, Sultana, Look-fit, Eight O'Clock, Bokar, Red Circle, Daily, Cheeri Aid, Ann Page. Today, only a few of those names remain, since most chains have consolidated their trademarks for better control and handling. Yet, new names are adopted. If a careful search is not conducted, the company can run into some sticky litigation problems.

A&P has had that unfortunate experience recently when it launched the Plus Discount Foods concept, including the Plus private label. The company was served with a charge of trademark infringement and false designation of origin, and unfair competition under the Lanham Trade-Mark Act. (This 1946 law provides for trademark registration and protection, giving the FTC authority to prosecute in cases of fraud, deception, or antitrust violations.) The complaint, issued by Plus Products, alleges that that company has used the word Plus as a trademark on food supplements, food fortifiers, and health and beauty aids as well as in marketing activity for years. The case is now in discovery. A&P has denied all wrongdoing in this matter.

In the private label business, the retailer/wholesaler is forewarned to tread carefully in the imitation of national brands. Lawyer William Boland warned his PLMA audience that:

> trade dress can include the coloration or configuration of product and also a particular trademark, either in the word or symbol that appears somewhere on the product. The shape and coloration of a product can have trademark significance. Color per se is not protectable, but the way color is arranged on the product is protectable. The shape can be protected by a design patent on the aesthetics, but not on the function of the packaging.

[As an aside, Johnson & Johnson in April 1982 countersued I.C.D. Industries, King of Prussia, Pennsylvania, over its use of the colors blue and green, resembling those on the box of J&J's Stayfree external sanitary protective pads for women. I.C.D. initially had sued J&J to determine whether *it* could use those colors on private label protective pad boxes. I.C.D. argued that some product categories are color coded for easy identification by the consumer—disposable diapers, for example, follow this coloring scheme: purple for toddler, green for extra absorbent, red for daytime, blue for overnight, and light blue for new born babies. There are other product categories, where the national brand colors are picked up by private label manufacturers: dandruff shampoo, toothpaste, and so on. I.C.D. also argued that today's consumer was more sophisticated and able to distinguish package differences, especially when the private label package (carrying the same colors as Stayfree) also included a highly visible store logo on the front panel. But I.C.D., pressed by lawyer fees and wasted executive time in court, backed off, agreeing to change the blue to purple, but keep the pink and green that appear on Stayfree packages. I.C.D. also had the option to drop the green and pick up the blue, if it desired.]

> But you should feel that you can fairly compete with them, using standard shape containers. You can use colors that for years have been used with particular products; but you shouldn't use the same design or sequence of colors, and you should

make sure you do not give an overall impression that your product looks like their product.

It behooves you to be very careful when you make your choice as to what kind of packaging you're going to use with your products. If you find a product that you want to produce and there is no patent on that product, then you have every right to produce it. (The only exception is when you steal a trade secret, which can stop you.) Next you come to packages. It is justified that people do want to get as close to the national brand as possible. Customers are used to the national brand and like it. There is no reason why the national brand shouldn't be competed with under our national law, if it's done fairly. The question is: How do you do it fairly? You don't take their trademark and put it on your product. If you think that mark is descriptive, I suggest you investigate to see whether they're registered with the Patent Office. . . . You should also investigate and make sure there are no copyrights covering any of the graphic material that appears on containers or on the labeling being used by the national brands. Also, you should look into any patents that cover a container's configuration. Some household formulations are being patented; so you should keep that in mind when you decide to produce a product. You should be very careful in designing your own product to stay away from the proprietary rights of the national brand (Boland 1981).

In the business world, a familiar childhood taunt can be twisted slightly to read: "Sticks and stones will break your bones, but names will hurt you more." It is one of life's ironies: Private labels can be branded as "private label" with its inferior connotations up against brand names, especially through imitation. Can a copycat be as good as the original? There are terms used generically or descriptively, which are not exclusively owned by any one company. There also have been protected names that have lost their exclusivity.

Trial attorney Bernard J. Cantor of Cullen, Sloman, Cantor, Grauer, Scott & Rutherford, Detroit, writes:

In order to emphasize that the mark is a trademark and not merely a product name or a nondescript word, it is well to apply the descriptive word of the goods underneath or near the mark. For example, the word "IODENT" printed in bold letters above the word "TOOTHPASTE" tells the customer the identification of the origin and the generic word for the product. This avoids customers using the brand name as the generic name for the product.

If customers use the mark as the generic name or description of the goods, the trademark rights are forever lost. Many once popular trademarks were lost because customers used them as the descriptive or generic words of the goods. Examples of popular trademarks which were destroyed because consumers used them generically are cellophane, nylon, escalator, linoleum, milk of magnesia, mineral oil, shredded wheat, aspirin, and thermos. The exclusive, legal trademark rights in these words ended, because the customer stopped using the words to designate origin and instead used them as the identification of the goods.

[The latest fatality is "Super Glue," a trademark registration owned by Loctite Corp. The company was judged to have used that term in a "generic or alternatively at least descriptive" way—devoid of a secondary meaning. Loctite's problem was to properly identify the product. It should have been designated Super Glue cyanoacrylate adhesive. Instead, the company used only the word Super Glue, causing the name to lose its trademark significance.]

Each private brander is entitled to use the generic names for the goods. However, every other member of the public is equally entitled to use the generic names. Consequently, giving the consumer the generic name in addition to the trademark symbol is a technique used for preserving the trademark.

Another common technique, which is widely used to inform the consumer that the selected symbol is a trademark, is to specifically state so on the label. That is the word "brand" printed beneath the mark is widely used for that purpose. Likewise, the word "trademark" printed beneath the mark or the initials "T.M." next to the mark are used to inform customers of the nature of the symbol. An asterisk next to the mark and a footnote that the mark is a trademark, is another technique. . . .

Another common technique for indicating that the symbol is special, and not a word of conversation or descriptiveness, is to print the word in a special type, such as bold type. Printing it in a stylized form is better still, although not necessary. Where the word is used in advertising literature, or printed material, capitalizing it, or indicating it in quotation marks or any special way which makes it stand out, enhances customer recognition.

One purpose of a private brand is to help develop customer loyalty to the retailer who offers it. Since no other retailer offers the same private brand, a satisfied customer may come back for more and may buy other things at that store, provided that the customer remembers which store the goods came from. Consequently, when the store uses separate brand names for various lines of goods, a common merchandising technique is to prominently place the store's own name or logo on the goods in addition to the good's trademark. This dovetails with the trademark law requirements of use and consumer recognition to make the store's own name or logo a legal trademark. The result is two trademarks, namely, a "house" brand used on all goods, and separate goods trademarks. Obviously, that technique may not always be consistent with the store's particular merchandising programs. But, where it is feasible, including the store's name or logo conspicuously upon as many private brand goods as possible, strengthens it as a trademark.

Summarizing, a valuable, exclusive legal trademark right can be created if the mark selected is capable of designating origin. That right is maintained by using the mark in a manner which develops customer recognition of that mark as your designation of origin. As long as customers recognize the mark as your trademark, the legal rights are exclusively yours (Cantor 1979A).

LOOK-ALIKE GUIDELINES

In imitating national brands, Cantor offers these look-alike guidelines:

The first and best guideline for the private brander to follow to avoid consumer deception is to make the consumer well aware of the private brand name. Educating the consumer to recognize the private brand name not only avoids confusion or deception, but furthers a major goal of private branding: to develop consumer loyalty to the private brand and to the store in which it is carried.

Private brand goods ought to be plainly labeled, legibly and boldly, with the private brand itself. The private brand could be the store sign name of the retailer. It could be the logo used by the retailer or merchandiser. It could be some fanciful brand name selected for use throughout the store. . . .

A second guideline to avoid claims of deception or likelihood of confusion is to not use any nonfunctional, distinctive,unique design features of the corresponding national brand package. This refers only to any distinctive appearance features that the consumer recognizes, like a trademark, as designating the maker of a particular product. For example, a Coca-Cola bottle is probably recognized throughout the world by its distinctive, unique shape, even without the words Coca-Cola, as being a bottle of a particular brand of drink. That kind of consumer recognition is relatively rare and is legally called "secondary meaning." That is, where an arbitrary design or appearance feature has acquired a "secondary" trademark or brand name meaning to the consumer. Not using that particular feature obviously reduces the possibility of consumer deception.

It should be noted that there is no legal restriction against copying nonarbitrary functional features, regardless of their popularity or consumer recognition (Cantor 1979B).

In one situation, Food Oils Corp., a supplier of private label cooking oils, introduced a controlled brand under the Cornola label, which was targeted to compete with C.P.C.'s Mazola corn oil. The latter national brand company objected to the name Cornola, the shape and color of the bottle, and the colors and layout of the label. As Ralph Behr of Food Oils explains this case:

C.P.C. sought to protect its Mazola label and informed Food Oils Corp. that unless the Cornola label was voluntarily withdrawn from the market, C.P.C. would pursue its case in the courts. . . .

The resources of Food Oils Corp. were no match against C.P.C. International. A prolonged court battle, in all likelihood, would have resulted in a label battle won for Cornola but the economic war lost for Food Oils Corp.

Knowledge of the law combined with artful negotiation can spell the difference between preserving your brand and its identity, and pulling your product and your hopes off the shelf. After negotiations, certain changes were agreed upon. They principally involved the arrangement of the ear of corn, the colors in the "pure corn oil" flag, the bottle color, and other minor adjustments. . . .

Before you spend your dollars in court, however, check with an experienced trademark lawyer and save your dollars for marketing. The more you know about trademarks and trade names the better you can protect your rights (Behr 1979B).

The selection and handling of a trademark are expertly discussed by Joseph J. Joyce, trademark counsel for PepsiCo., Inc. Joyce's comments, while they apply primarily to advice for national brands, have important meaning for the private label trademark owner. It should be remembered that today private label is no longer merely a follower, but also an innovator. Private label has come into its own as a brand by itself.

A trademark is the maker's monogram, a marking which identifies a product as to source rather than kind or type. It also stands as a symbol of the quality which

> purchasers expect in products sold by the owner of the trademark. It is the trademark to which reputation, immediate recognition, and goodwill are attached. . . .
>
> A trademark should be considered a corporate asset because it initially denotes the source of the product and at the same time its nature and character. But it also is an important merchandising and marketing tool which increases in value as the years go on, if it is properly employed. The selection of a trademark, therefore, should be undertaken with the assistance of the advertising, marketing, design and art, research, sales, public relations, corporate management, and legal departments (Joyce 1977).

Joyce also offers these pointers in selecting a trademark:

- Determine a need over the long term; and "where a company has previously established a housemark or a family mark, there may be no need for an additional trademark."
- Consider what trademark type is appropriate: *arbitrary* where "there is no immediate relationship between the product and the trademark," i.e., Scotties for Black and White scotch, or *suggestive*, which is "related to certain attributes of the product, i.e., Lip Quencher lipstick, which was chosen to reinforce its moisturizing ingredients."

Joyce warns: "If a trademark is too descriptive, however, you might find yourself being sued by a competitor and having a court rule that your mark is not capable of exclusive ownership. . . . Whichever type of trademark you choose—arbitrary or suggestive—keep in mind it shouldn't be deceptive or misleading. For example, Eggso would be an unwise choice for a salad dressing containing no eggs."

- Establish a generic name for your product at the time it's selected: "unlike a trademark, a generic name consists of a word or words commonly used to identify a product as to kind or type. For example, the terms cola, sangria, and corn chips are generic names and anyone is free to use them. . . . That generic term should always accompany your mark but generally should not appear in the same logo style."

"In the process of selecting a trademark," Joyce continues:

> one must keep returning to the company's objectives. Is there a probability that the product line will be expanded? If so, will the trademark remain appropriate? Is there an intention to enter foreign markets? If so, precautions must be taken to choose a trademark which reads and sounds well in non-English languages. Certain trademarks may have an unfortunate connotation in certain foreign countries.
>
> Further terms which are registrable and capable of exclusive ownership in the United States may be considered merely descriptive or not capable of being distinctive in some foreign jurisdictions. This is particularly true with regard to numerals and laudatory terms.

Other tips:

- Don't select a geographically descriptive mark, especially one of a place known for that product.

- Avoid surnames, because others with that name can use it.
- Stay away from "confusingly similar" trademarks of similar products in the same geographic area.
- "Use a trademark as a capitalized proper adjective (Kleenex facial tissue); never use it as a common noun (generic term)."
- Be consistent in usage to familiarize the consumer with the mark.
- "Never use a trademark as a verb."
- Minor changes in a trademark may need only to be amended; major changes (type face, spelling, labeling), which are substantial, may require another trademark registration.

WHO IS RESPONSIBLE?

In the private label relationship between supplier (manufacturer) and user (retailer), there often develops a situation where the retailer will plan packaging graphics without manufacturer participation. At the PLMA meeting in the spring of 1981, lawyer William Boland tackled this problem. The major chains have their own graphics department: if that chain has a philosophy of duplicating as closely as possible national brand imagery, where does the manufacturer fit into the legal process? Does the manufacturer have the right to refuse to put the label on a retailer's packages? Are manufacturers obligated to tell the chains they are making a mistake? What is the alternative other than to say that the manufacturer refuses to pack under such circumstances?

Boland answered that the manufacturers could "ask for an indemnity from the chains. The manufacturer would be liable to the owner of the rights which are being enforced, even though your customer requested you to do this. But in many situations, you just can't get an indemnity or you wouldn't want to for one reason or another. You should bring your concerns to your customer and at least ask them to obtain some kind of opinion from counsel that what they are doing is legal and will not violate any enforceable right of another. In the end, you can say I won't do it" (Boland 1981).

That advice bears repeating: In any of these legal matters, seek expert counsel advice.

REFERENCES

Behr, R. 1979A. How to Deal with Defective or Dangerous Private Label Products. *Private Label* Magazine, October-November, pp. 52–53, 68. E.W. Williams Publishing, New York.

Behr, R. 1979B. David vs. Goliath Story: A Fight Over Trade Dress. *Private Label* Magazine, June-July, pp. 58–59. E.W. Williams Publishing, New York.

Boland, W. 1981. Trade Dress: Let the Manufacturer Beware. *Private Label* Magazine, April-May, pp. 75–80. E.W. Williams Publishing, New York.

Brown. 1948. Advertising and the Public Interest: Legal Protection of Trade Symbols. 57 Yale L. J. 1165, 1181.

Cantor, B. J. 1979A. Private Brands Can Be Legal Trademarks. *Private Label* Magazine, June-July, pp. 49–50. E.W. Williams Publishing, New York.

Cantor, B. J. 1979B. Private Brand Look-Alike Guidelines. *Private Label* Magazine, April-May, pp. 44–45. E.W. Williams Publishing, New York.

Chamberlain. 1962. The Theory of Monopolistic Competition.

Chazen, H. 1979. Packages Must Sell the Product. *Private Label* Magazine, June-July, p. 38. E.W. Williams Publishing, New York.

Hartley, R. F. 1972. Marketing: Management & Social Change, pp. 178–180. Harper & Roe, Publishers, Inc. (Intex publishing), New York. Intex Educational Publishing, Scranton, Pennsylvania.

Joyce, J. J. 1977. How to Select and Protect a Trademark. Product Marketing/Cosmetic & Fragrance Retailing, May, pp. 26–31. Charleson Publishing Co., New York.

Sears. 1972. Sears News Service. January 17. Sears, Roebuck and Co., Chicago.

USTA. 1973. Information Bulletin. Vol. 28, No. 34, September 24. United States Trademark Association, New York.

8

The Imagery of Packaging

Until recently, private label retailers/wholesalers have been oblivious to one of the most important marketing tools available: packaging. At best, they have addressed the more mundane functions of packaging—that it protects, contains, identifies, presents, and informs, besides being durable and convenient for handling—paying little if any attention to the more intangible but absolutely necessary function of product enhancement. Packaging serves to heighten a product almost as imagery serves poetry. This creative, aesthetic aspect, delving into mental images of memory, imagination, and fancy, works on consumers' perceptions of a product, intensifying and illuminating them in their eyes.

"Research indicates that over 80% of the information received by the human mind is transmitted through the eyes," according to the marketing/design firm, S&O Consultants, Inc., San Francisco. "In marketing terms, an average person is exposed to over 1,500 trademarks per day. And a supermarket package can generate in excess of one billion consumer impressions per year."

Package imagery deals with value perceptions, which include illusions, that is, something more, something else, or something that is not necessarily contained in the package. It is what a majority of the Supreme Court jurists did not consider valuable enough to charge extra for in the case of Borden's brand versus its private label evaporated milk (see Chapter 7). It is what the advertising, designing, and marketing community argue is of paramount commercial value. It is what the consumer wishes for: that extra something suggested by the packaging, which they feel or fancy is worth buying and worth paying more for.

Private label's image for years has been that of low price only. Recently, many retailers and wholesalers have upgraded their quality and, out of necessity, are now reflecting that image in their packaging. In their efforts to duplicate national brand quality, they have had to follow the brands' lead in packaging.

This awakening process, which began in the 1970s, is only now beginning to affect the industry. Many private labels are still decades behind the national brands in this critical marketing strategy.

There is no question about the leadership of national brands in different product categories. They have positioned themselves as leaders partly through the imagery of packaging. Early in their development, national brand manufacturers learned about market research and how to tap consumer response to their products.

In 1924, Procter & Gamble began its market research studies. Today, it is routine for that company to conduct surveys by telephone, questionnaires, group discussions, and home visitations, continually asking the customer what she wants in a product, what special features she would like to see, and what motivates her to pick up a certain package. P&G has technical centers that not only research new product formulations but also examine every aspect of product development from raw material to final usage and disposal by the consumer. Part of this research includes packaging evaluation studies to ensure that the company's products reach consumers at the peak of quality.

Consumer preferences are a top priority at P&G. Quality is not only "built in" but also wrapped around its products. Packaging is continually improved and changed to meet changing consumer tastes. In tracing a century of packaging Ivory soap, P&G states:

> The first Ivory wrapper design—an ornate affair of checkerboards and curlicues—was perfectly suited to a world of tasseled lamps, Edwardian mustaches and honeymoon scrapbooks of Niagara Falls. Black and white, it looked well on the shelves of kitchens untouched by the hand of the interior decorator, a partner to the scrubbing board, the pot-bellied stove and the kettle that was always boiling. And what was more, the checkerboard design admirably concealed the dust that settled on the soap while it waited, in the small, low-volume grocery stores, to be bought.
>
> That is quite a contrast to the familiar Ivory wrapper of today—a crisp white and blue design with a dash of red which conveys to modern eyes an idea of the fresh, white soap inside.
>
> Ivory's wrapper is its outward face and serves, just as the packaging for other P&G brands, to tell consumers that they can find a familiar, quality product inside. And because this outward appearance is so important in identifying the contents, change, when it comes, must be undertaken with skill and concern that the results will still be modern and up-to-date for years to come (Procter & Gamble 1979).

P&G admits that change does entail risk, a gamble with the goodwill established with consumers over the years: but change is mandated by competition, by changing shopping habits. Early in the Ivory soap wrapper history, the key function of the package was to protect the product from dust and dirt. Then a waxed paper wrapper was introduced to keep the product fresh. Finally, packaging was enhanced, that is "transformed into a lively blue and white modern design. Prim little wavelets were added, dancing along both top and bottom. The waves remain in today's design, but in a bolder form, underscoring the name of Ivory."

THE NAME IMAGE

This focus on the brand name is subtle, the result of years of careful evaluation. It illustrates an important packaging trend developing with the national brand and more recently with private label brands. S&O calls it a brand identity system:

> created by visually distilling the graphic personality of a brand into a cohesive but flexible entity. The use of this entity is then systematized by developing a complete set of usage guidelines that govern all major brand media.
>
> Anheuser-Busch's leadership in the beer category, for example, reflects the scope and depth of its marketing programs. The consistent and powerful images conveyed by its individual brand identity systems are one of its primary marketing strengths.
>
> These identity systems are used in a broad array of media; secondary packaging, selected advertising, correspondence and promotional materials, vehicles, and point of purchase/point of consumption items.
>
> Given the effectiveness of such systems, we believe that brand identity will become a major marketing tool in the 1980s for a broad spectrum of products and services . . . ranging from fast food restaurants to consumer products to financial services.

Michael F. Purvis, S&O vice-president, says: "In packaging, graphics must not only communicate brand names, product types, key benefits, etc. . . . they must project the product's positioning and establish the product's essential character with consumers."

It is this positioning or repositioning that concerns many private label retailers today. The greatest effort is being made in upgrading quality impressions through packaging.

In one national brand example, S&O cites its work with U.S. Borax's Borateem, which had lost market share to competition. Says S&O: "A visual audit in the marketplace helped pinpoint the brand's image communication problems: 1) Poor product quality impressions, primarily as a result of outdated graphics; 2) poor communication of product effectiveness, partly due to the use of the words 'bleach substitute'; and 3) poor shelf impact due to package design."

Many private labels still suffer this same weakness in their package imagery, but that is changing as retailers and wholesalers move into the

1980s with their own brand identity systems. They literally have jumped out of a packer label world into national brand identities. The impetus partly comes from their consolidation of brands. This positioning and reinforcement of a brand name is especially evident in large chains. Nowhere does the move toward national brand identity show up more than in private label packaging and store identity.

In 1974–1975, A&P adopted a new modern logo, highly visible: A&P in white letters against a bright red oval background, reinforced with crescent moon-shape shadings of orange and yellow on the right side. This effective logo replaces the familiar A&P red circle used for years. The new basic design has been worked into the top of the line A&P brand products with some color variations, depending on the color scheme of the package. Recently, A&P added the P&Q generic logo with the same basic design, but in shades of green with white lettering—a subtle extension of the A&P store identity carried into its generic category.

About 1975, Safeway began a redesign program of its store brands, because of its awareness that "packaging has a significant effect on consumer perception of product quality. A systematic, long-range plan was implemented to upgrade that image, working with a design firm. In 1976, newly designed labels began appearing to give our packaging a more consistent and attractive visual appeal. In conjunction with this, we also developed new graphic standards for certain design elements, such as the (S) symbol. This new insignia will eventually appear on nearly all 'S' Brands, to quickly and boldly identify them as our first line products that equal or exceed the quality of top national brands" (Safeway 1977).

More recently, everywhere you look, retailers and wholesalers are upgrading and modernizing their packaging, many of them moving toward a national brand identity.

In 1979, Grand Union Co., Elmwood Park, New Jersey, adopted a "Red Dot" marketing program, taken from its new corporate identification, which stands for "price competitiveness, service, customer information, and an appealing store design." The company also began redesigning its private label packages in line with this Red Dot philosophy: The attractive designs make our high-quality foods even more appealing, while also providing important nutrition information on a unique yellow band circling the label. Our objective is to develop a group of products which provide quality equal or superior to national brand leaders at much lower prices" (Grand Union 1980).

Since 1978, Rite Aid Corp., Shiremanstown, Pennsylvania, has undergone a complete store renovation, which included dumping its Rite Aid shield used as an identifying logo since the firm was formed in 1962. The new logo, developed by design consultants, is "more easily readable but, at the same time, conveys a contemporary feel while maintaining a continuity of identification with our long-established trademark" (Rite

Aid 1979). The new identity also appears on all its private label lines: a broken shield design with white lettering of "Rite" against a blue background and of "Aid" against a red background, which is also adapted to different packaging to blend with their color scheme.

Gray Drug Stores, Inc., Cleveland, up until 1979, had bland private label packaging—an older, "antiseptic" look completed with a microscope logo. A new promotional program, "We're For You," launched in 1979, touched every aspect of its business, including packaging. As Allen Kallach, merchandise manager, explains, the redesign involved two packaging strategies:

> Actually, there's two ways to go into a private label knock-off program. One is to identify 100% with the national brand. The other way is to go with a family program. We melded these two approaches together to establish a family identity with our new "G" logo and color-shaded bars throughout all the packaging to identify with the national brands. Where we have a so-called generic item, like rubbing alcohol (no national brand top seller), we adopt our company colors of orange and brown on the bars and as part of the background for the G logo. For the national brand, we adopt its colors. So we really have a combination of national brand identification with the color schematic; and we have our own family line, where all the products carry the bar scheme (Kallach 1981).

Retailers and wholesalers are learning that packaging appearances do count when they wish to project a quality image. Outdated packaging defeats that purpose. As one private label buyer puts it:

> We've learned that we can't put out a sloppy product. If we're going to produce the product to compete with national brands, we must also do it with packaging—the container, the label, the artwork, everything has got to be set to standards. The consumer just won't accept an outdated, second-rate package. There's just no eye appeal. Retailers are moving toward more sophisticated packaging. We pulled the label off our vitamin line because it looked hand-made. It served its purpose. Now we're going into a double-foil label, because that's what our competition is doing. It's costlier and it took us a year to develop this, but it keeps us competitive.

Super Food Services, Inc., Dayton, Ohio, one of the country's largest food wholesalers, after some 21 years of business, decided to repaint its image in 1978, adopting a new "SF" design to illustrate its "forward-moving, progressive results." The company, through its distribution arm, Fame Marketing Corp., described the purpose of its new package design:

> Fame's package design communicates a quality image that consumers buy. Fame knows how to create the visual impact needed to attract the shopper's eye in a split second. With hundreds of competitive products on the market, it is crucial to have visual shelf impact. Fame regards each of its packages an ad that must communicate quickly and effectively in order to sell.
>
> Fame's image stands for quality and "fame." The Fame Shield with its curved bottom is simple, clean and adaptable to the variety of packaging forms and sizes. The Fame logo type with the distinctive star "A" has become a recognizable symbol for

> quality. Every Fame package is designed with the competitor in mind. In many cases, Fame packages have more eye appeal that their heavily-advertised national brand competitors. Color combinations and type styles are carefully chosen. Legibility as well as character and product relatedness are important considerations.
>
> Fame is known for its consistency in packaging design throughout the product line. Each Fame product helps to build a strong cumulative Fame image in the consumer's mind.
>
> Fame goes beyond producing an attractive package, however. Fame realizes the need for nutritional information and provides a complete breakdown of nutrients on every product possible. Metric weight statements are also included along with the regular contents on nearly all Fame packages.
>
> If there is a need, Fame provides directions for the product, plus serving and storing information. Fame also prints the latest recipes and premium offers on many containers. Consumers do get extra special benefits on the Fame package.
>
> Above all, Fame package materials are selected for maximum protection of the product. The package is designed for trouble-free, cost-saving machinability . . . as well as consumer convenience. Wherever needed, Fame packages have barriers for oil, aroma, and moisture. The type and weight of all Fame packaging material are closely related to maximum product protection. Rigid specifications must be met and complete testing procedures must be passed by all Fame packages (Fame Marketing Corp. 1979).

Most of the packaging work at the buying co-op Shurfine-Central Corp., Northlake, Illinois, emanates from its packaging department. Says Ray Avischious, president and general manager:

> We have an excellent packaging department that maintains the rules, regulations, and registration of our brands. Our philosophy with packaging as well as with the design of packaging is to have top quality so that the consumer just by looking at it will know it's a quality brand. We never use any product cuts that can be used by someone else. All our illustrations are owned by Shurfine. We do most of the artwork and the photography work, working with a major studio in Chicago, under the direction of Carl Hirt, our design director. Tom Groark, our director of packaging, works with four other people in packaging.
>
> We attempt to evoke appetite and good-looking illustrations in our packaging, rather than our old 1890s logo. The new look is geared around the look presented by General Foods, General Mills, and other leading national brands (Avischious 1980).

POSITIONING STRATEGIES

Private label's public debut comes through its packaging. While the package design helps to attract customer attention, package positioning in the product mix helps customers identify a quality level, serves as a basis of comparison, and stimulates instant customer recognition. The basic strategies for positioning private label products include

1. A unified, single brand identity (usually the retailer's name) across all product categories—*the family look*, i.e., Revco label.

2. Multiple brand identities within and across product categories—the *diversified look,* i.e., A&P brand, Ann Page brand, P&Q brand, Eight O'Clock Coffee, Bokar Coffee, Red Circle Coffee.
3. The combination of a store name tied to multiple brand identities—the *relative look,* i.e., Sears DieHard, Sears Craftsman, Sears Best Kenmore.
4. Corporate brand identity that extends beyond one chain operation into other operations within a diversified company—*the corporate look,* i.e., Our Own label used by Stop & Shop Companies—Stop & Shop, Bradlees, and MediMart.
5. Creation of a new label to consolidate other names or to accommodate the merger of companies—the *new look,* i.e. Beaumark and Duramark used by the merged Hudson Bay Co. with Simpsons in Canada or Edwards–Finast used by the newly formed First National Supermarkets.
6. A non-private label image—the *regional* or *national brand look,* i.e., Bonnie Hubbard used by United Grocers Ltd.

Retailers can adopt one or more of these strategies, depending on their product mix and their structure of product quality tiers. Within each method there can also be different tactical maneuvering employed, such as innovative packaging, national brand knock-off packaging, and unique or different packaging.

Walter P. Margulies, president of Lippincott & Margulies, New York, one of the world's leading packaging authorities, recognizes the move by private label retailers away from their classic stance of competing on price alone and moving toward greater emphasis on package design, package positions, as well as the functional aspects of a container. The problem they face is how to handle many different brands owned by the store. Margulies (1979) discussed two of their positioning strategies. He cited the following reasons for adopting a single coordinated identity program:

1. Creating a strong level of customer awareness of the private label line by a unified product identity;
2. Greater efficiency in terms of advertising and promotion, when there is only one identity to communicate;
3. Less problems with printing production and ease of introducing new products into the private label system.

Creating a strong coordinated overall retail posture if the private label name is the same as the overall retail identification.

His list of advantages in a multiple identification strategy included

1. To differentiate different levels of private label product quality along with different prices;

2. To avoid an identification conflict among private label products that appear to be mutually exclusive, such as bread and bleach;
3. To create a distinctive product stance for a certain private label category that complements the unique features of that particular food or merchandise;
4. To avoid the negative identification rub off from one private label product to another, if the level of product quality is not up to standard.

Margulies continued: "One obvious drawback to this multiple system is that continuity of expression is lacking, both in nomenclature and design." In a unified approach, such as that adopted by Pathmark of Supermarkets General Corp., Woodbridge, New Jersey,

> labeling creates a visual and verbal flow through all products and lines in both food and nonfood categories. Identical in both nomenclature and feel of design, there is a continual exchange of equity, both in-store and out. Shopper recognition is immediate, an important plus on the highly charged selling floor where private labels must compete with national brands.
>
> The private label system that is fragmented by an abundance of identifiers, such as that of A&P, tends to confuse the shopper. It is often difficult for an involved merchant to realize that his familiarity with names and designs in his own private label program is not necessarily shared by the uninvolved consumer.
>
> At the same time, we recognize possible drawback to the systemized approach. For instance, one of the strengths of the program lies in the exchange of equities among products. When the exchange is, say, between a cake mix and a bleach, some areas of opinion believe there may be resulting connotations that are undesirable. . . . In the case of private labeling, however, it is not the maker of the product placing the guarantee, but the retailer. Thus the consumer does not have to be convinced of the brand claim to legitimacy, but must be convinced of the retailer's reputation . . . a poor reputation can adversely affect the entire line of private label products. Thus, tight quality control of products is essential to unified branding.

The unified branding approach, he noted, appears to outweigh the fragmented approach. Citing Pathmark's private label unified program, he continued: "Its flexibility adapts to a variety of package shapes, allowing it to endorse more than food. Red and blue, the posterlike quality of design is believable in terms food, gasoline, drugs, and other product categories. It has punch and recall through a step-down band. It identifies from all angles and directions by bands of color across the label. It lends itself to clean, uncluttered bulk displays, with extremely high visibility." Marketing strategies and need dictate the retailer's strategy, Margulies concluded.

The need to establish and reenforce store identity—in fact, to build an image not around a brand, but around the store itself—has grown in recent years, as retailers realize their unique position in the marketplace. The retailer as owner of his own brands can offer customers a unique product line, available nowhere else. It may be easier to adopt national brands into the product mix, but these brands also are sold in competi-

A selection of private labels distributed by Shurfine-Central. Each item measures up graphically with the best that national brands offer. The exception, of course, is generics, packaged in stark black and white; but this co-op also offers standard grade Thrift King in attractive packaging.

Some of the newest packages at Steinberg include this whip topping mix for desserts and mini chocolate chip cookies—a knock-off of McDonald's cookies.

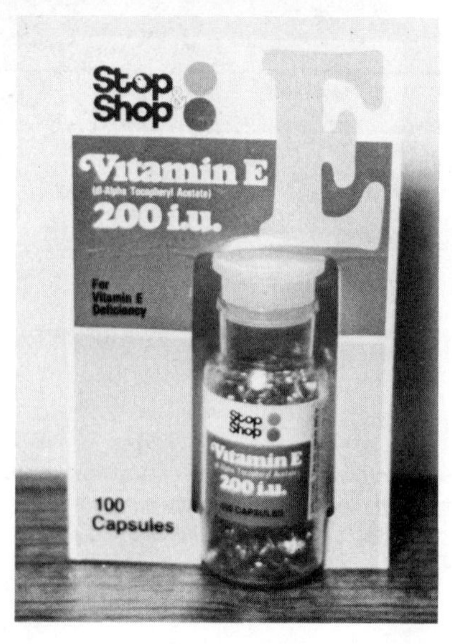

Stop & Shop takes the unusual step here of adopting secondary packaging—a blister pack with cardboard panel to help merchandise the item with a giant "E" that pops out at the consumer.

re is nothing dull about Woolworths private label packaging under its various trade nes: Garden Power, Happy Home, Big W. Product illustrations are key to the chandise sell in a self-service store.

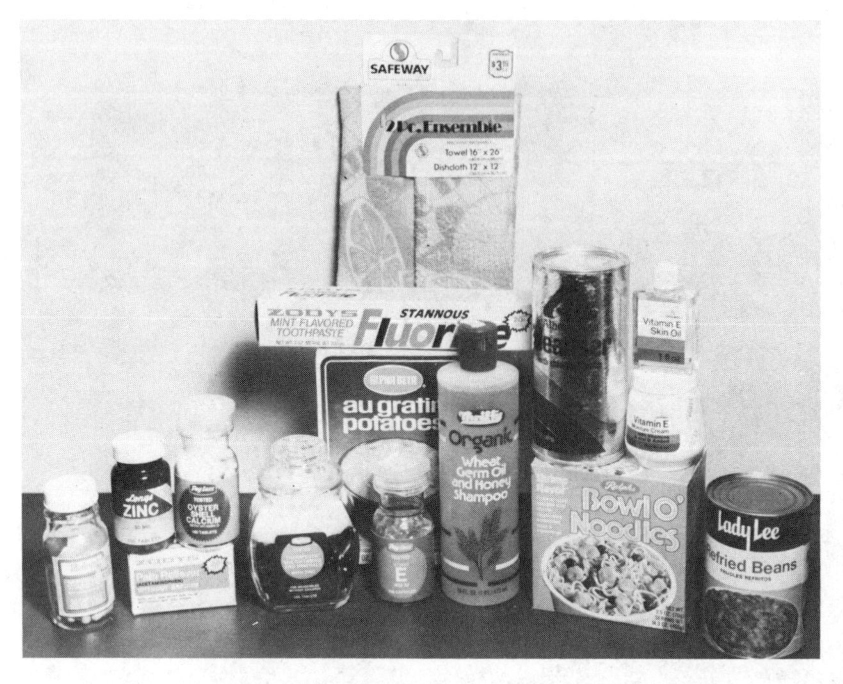

West Coast retailers package their private label lines in a variety of designs—all attractive to the consumer. This selection ranges from health and beauty aids to foods to household chemicals to general merchandise.

Steinberg uses the corporate label, "Our Own For You," on different health and beauty aids, borrowing the identity from Stop & Shop Companies.

Steinberg recently introduced these margarine products under its label, each merchandised with specific selling features: polyunsaturates, saturates, and (on one only) liquid corn oil percentage content. The packages rely on top quality photography and color.

Steinberg of Canada uses valuable packaging space to inform consumers that its product does not contain sugar and that the product is laboratory tested: a microscope logo indicates that this item has been "tested and approved by Steinberg's own laboratories." The "S" logo appears with a blue ribbon, indicating fancy grade, the peaches being packed "in grape juice from concentrate."

An example of how Woolworth's Woolco identity is tied to a national brand supplier, General Electric, also identified on the label. The innovative package introduced flashcubes on a blister card.

Eatons of Canada has recently changed its packaging design. The old graphics relied on an insignificant Eaton logo, while the newer packaging marries the Eaton name with a private label trademark that the retailer has established over the years—Viking.

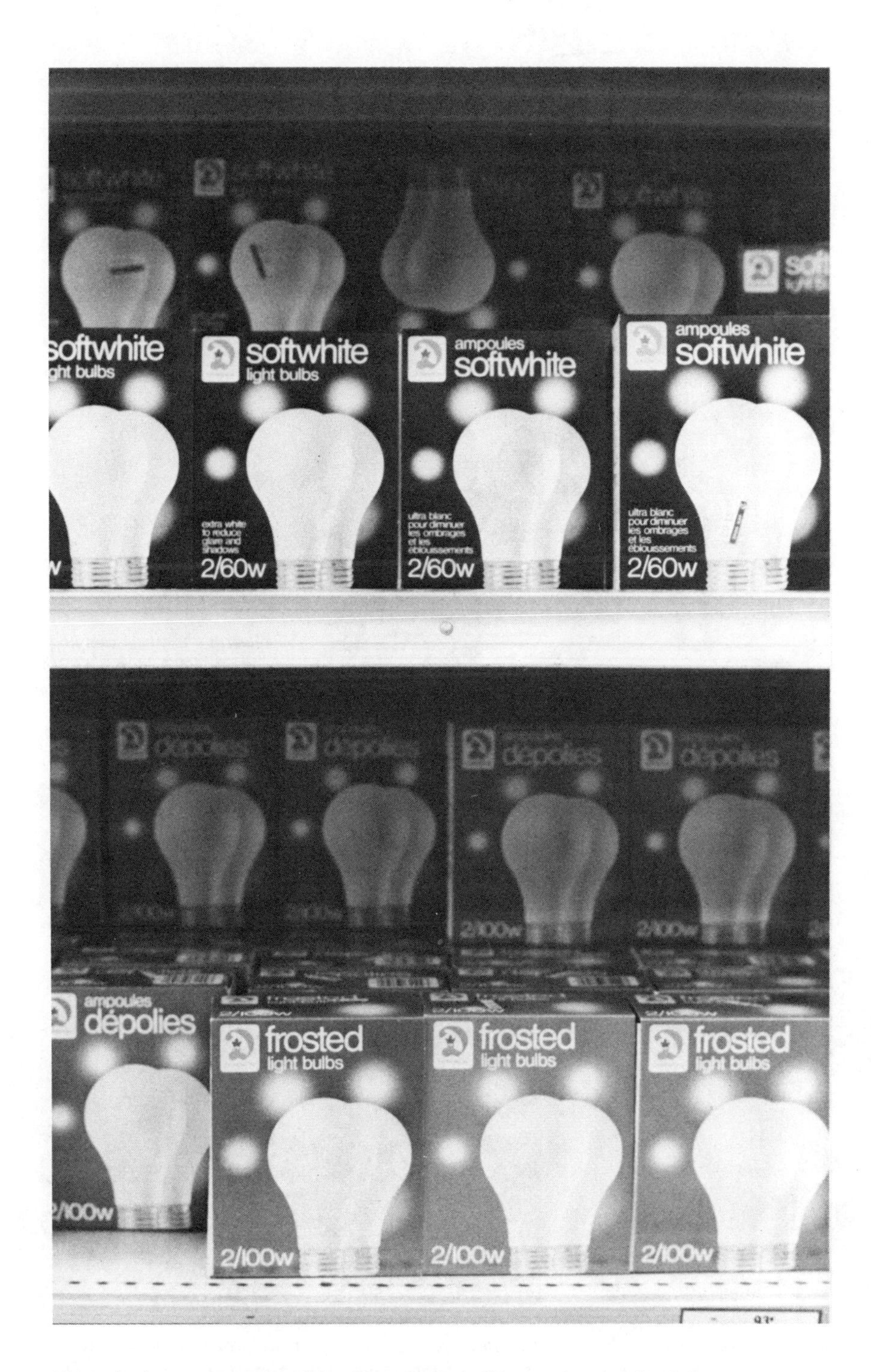

The packaging strategy at Dominion Stores Limited of Toronto is to equal or better the national brands. This display of light bulbs is as up-to-date and effective as anything the major brands merchandise.

Woolworth's Winfield camping equipment and Auditron electronic products also get full colorful graphic treatment in the packaging.

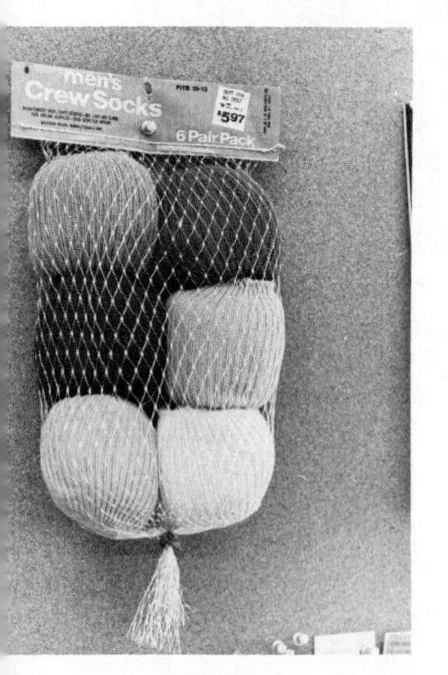

As an innovative packaging idea, Woolworth adapted a produce net mesh bag to hold crew socks, displayed in different colors and rolled up as people handle them after washing and drying them.

Certified Grocers, a wholesaler, features attractive four-color packaging for all grades of its private label lines. These canned items each illustrate the product for greater eye appeal.

tors' stores. Stronger store identification comes by controlling one's own exclusive brands.

This awareness came to the T. Eaton Company Limited, Toronto, when in 1978 it divested its catalog business and then began decentralizing its buying program across Canada. That meant possibly dropping its private label program. Buyers found it much easier to buy national brands; but the company quickly realized it had equity built into certain store brand names. Since the chain started in 1884, some 129 trademark names had been established. The new strategy called for trimming back that collection to 29 names.

Margaret Howard, controlled brands manager, explains an important change that began shaping Eaton's marketing philosophy:

> We decided to bring all our private labels home. Our marketing names weren't attached to Eatons at all. Our appliances are called Viking, women's shoes Raphael, lingerie and pantyhose Vanity Fair, and so on. People didn't associate those names with Eaton's, they just knew they could get them at Eaton's. . . .
>
> Before, the name Viking alone didn't bring the product home. By putting the Eaton name on, it does. This concept was a major insight for us. Suddenly, we weren't knocking our heads against brick walls trying to market a national brand or build an image as you would around a national brand. We started to build an image around ourselves.

For years, Lucky Stores, Buena Park, California, has followed a corporate brand identity strategy for its private label lines: Lady Lee premium products and Harvest Day secondary value products plus some other labels. Initially, Lucky Stores did carry the Lucky brand as a private label, but through growth and acquisitions—expanding into department stores (Gemco and Memco), other food chains (Eagle and Kash N' Karry), as well as automotive, sporting goods, and other stores—warehousing became a problem. Extra private label brands meant carrying more inventory in its central warehouse points.

Today, Lucky operates some 1500 stores in 33 states. Its own labels—Lady Lee for top of the line items, Harvest Day for edible items, Villa for nonedibles, High Class for pet food, and Gold Seal for top quality hard and distilled spirits—can be picked up in some of these different operations without the problem of being identified exclusively with one chain, i.e., Lucky stores. Lucky identifies these items as "distributed by Market Inc.," treating them just like any other brand carried in its stores. In developing a generic yellow label, Lucky recently appointed a corporate private label manager to oversee all Lucky's brands, now identified as "distributed by LKS Products, Dublin, California." This reflects its move toward consolidation and centralized control.

The Stop & Shop Companies, Boston, operating Stop & Shop supermarkets, Bradlees discount department stores, and MediMart drug stores, is now experimenting with a corporate label on bulky and high-volume items in general merchandise and health and beauty aids in order to minimize packaging costs and eliminate the need for large warehouse inventories, which would be required with separate labels in those product categories for each chain.

A new label strategy was developed when First National Stores Inc., Somerville, Massachusetts, merged with Pick-N-Pay Supermarkets, Inc., Maple Heights, Ohio, to form First National Supermarkets, a chain of more than 250 stores. Part of the merger called for combining the private label programs, taking the 125-year-old Pick-N-Pay "Edwards" label and merging it with First National's "Finast" label (established in the late 1920s or early 1930s). As the new label, Edwards–Finast, was being phased into different product categories, the company took the opportunity to upgrade and modernize its packaging with colorful graphics to help enhance the quality image. A bag stuffer, for example, proclaimed in part: "The labels are changing but our dedication to high quality remains intact."

The Hudson Bay Co. ("The Bay") traces its history back to fur trading in the seventeenth century. Recently, The Bay merged with the Simpsons Co., also of Canada, bringing two well-established firms together. The merger caused Simpsons to end its alliance with Sears, Roebuck, which included an agreement to sell Sears' Kenmore brand merchandise: major appliances, hardware, tools, sewing machines, vacuum cleaners, and household appliances. That left Simpson without a private label in these merchandise categories. The idea came to buy this type of merchandise for both The Bay and Simpson under new labels. The Bay had established one label, Lifestyler, for personal care appliances in this merchandising area. So the merged companies developed two new labels: Beaumark for major appliances (vacuum cleaners, sewing machines, etc.) and Duramark for hardware, power tools, outdoor garden supplies (lawnmowers, snow throwers, barbecue units) which could be sold in both chains. These new labels actually created a split in the company. The Bay people argued for the exclusivity of their brand, but Simpson said that bulk puchasing could effect cost economies in warehousing and distribution.

The repositioning of a private label can also be part of a new attitude by the retailer/wholesaler. That owner may no longer regard their controlled brand as an exclusively owned line. United Grocers, Ltd., Oakland, California, the largest wholesaler in northern California, wanted to revitalize its controlled label, Bonnie Hubbard, sold to most of the independent grocers in its market. The wholesaler worked with Landor Associates, San Francisco, which helped design a new regional brand image.

John Diefenbach, president of Landor, speaking before the 1980 Grocery Manufacturers of America Conference, noted: "The concept of Bonnie Hubbard that had been around for any number of years as a controlled label grew to regional status overnight. Landor's packaging was developed to bring a branding status to the product, and that became the long-term strategic plan. Strong emphasis was placed on design effectiveness and mass display. As the packaging developed, a search began for a new advertising agency. Utilizing Landor's research and packaging, the new agency came up with a perfect slogan ("Local Girl Makes Good") and a modern brand was born."

United Grocers now markets its Bonnie Hubbard line as a regional brand; the company no longer regards its brand as a controlled label or private label, because of its new packaging–advertising thrust.

It is really a matter of how products are perceived. Sears could be called a national brand, since it is advertised and sold nationally. But like United Grocers, Sears does not manufacture the product. One of the best-recognized brand names in American business history, Thom McAn, is in fact, basically a private label. Thom McAn shoes are sold through 1244 Thom McAn specialty shoe stores besides being distributed through 2400 authorized dealers.

PACKAGING MANEUVERABILITY

Packaging can be more important in some product categories than in others. For example, a frozen food dinner displayed without its wrapping would stimulate very few appetites. Likewise, a woman's dress hidden inside a beautifully wrapped package would not sell. Generally speaking, packaging's role varies from market to market or from product category to product category. It is critical in areas like dry groceries, frozen foods, cosmetics, or health and beauty aids. Sometimes a retailer/wholesaler may develop a family look for all of its product lines, but make an exception in the health and beauty aids area, where private labels copy the national brands' graphics is in order to create a more aesthetic look that appeals to the customer. But packaging has little aesthetic importance in the meat, deli, produce, or dairy sections of a supermarket. In a drug store, a major portion of space is reserved for the pharmacist to sell prescription drugs and medicine, where packaging is insignificant. In a discount mass merchandiser outlet or department store, most merchandise is displayed without packaging. Yet in each market segment, packaging serves an important role in identification, instruction, and recognition. The mass merchandiser, for example, gains considerable marketing strength by color-coding a line of women's hosiery or auto parts or hand tools. Health and beauty aids and vitamins often are compared to national brands on the basis of packaging alone in the consumer's eyes. If the packaging were different, then private label would not be so competitive on the shelves.

While private label is traditionally recognized for its copycat packaging, there are innovative private label packages. Loblaw Companies Limited innovates in its generic packaging not so much for pizazz, but for cost savings. Some revolutionary packaging ideas have been adopted: freeze-dried coffee in a bag, detergents in poly bags, milk and orange juice in bags. The company aims for value in its products, trying first for top quality, or quality decreased to an absolute minimum. If necessary, Loblaws looks to other areas, including packaging, to effect cost savings: "A six-liter Tide box would cost us about 40 cents. (I don't know what P&G pays for the box, because of their volume.) But we can put six-liter poly bags of detergent out there at a cost of approximately 3 to 5 cents per bag," according to Robert G. Chenaux, vice-president of Company Brands, Intersave, Loblaw's buying and merchandising division (Chenaux 1981).

Dafoe & Dafoe, Brandford, Ontario, Canada, a producer of sanitary napkins, disposable diapers, tampons, and cosmetics, took the initiative in 1978 by introducing a four-color package of beltless maxi pads for the U.S. private label market. Instead of the conventional sealed box, this product was packaged in an expensive flip-top, reclosable paperboard box, beautifully illustrated with four or five processed colors with attractive graphics. The item was so successful that a national brand producer reportedly copied the format for its packaging of a similar product.

Stop & Shop Supermarkets has innovated with recycled paperboard packaging, converting its folding carton grades on such items as snacks, facial tissues, and cake mixes. This approach not only cuts down on packaging costs, but also helps preserve the environment while still offering the consumer quality packaging. Each recycled package displays a recycling symbol. There has been positive consumer acceptance and willingness to switch products to the recycled paperboard, according to the company.

Private label packers are said to becoming more innovative with coupon and label advertising on their packaging. "One of the real problems in this area," says Bill Ricks, president of Taylor & Sledd's Retail Division (a brokerage firm in Richmond, Virginia), "is that you don't normally have the volume in private label, which sometimes involves expensive changes in the label plates. Putting a 15-cent offer on a Richfood [a T&S private label account] can of green beans can be an expensive proposition, which Procter & Gamble can handle better. But this activity is starting to come about in private label." Ricks later mentions that instead of compromising on quality in generics, his firm looks for other ways to cut costs: "In dish detergents, for example, if you eliminate the push-pull cap, you reduce the unit cost three to four cents; and you don't necessarily sacrifice detergent quality. In aluminum foil, if you eliminate the aluminum tear stip, you reduce your cost there. In tea bags, if you eliminate the tags and possibly go into a bag instead of a box, you reduce cost.On macaroni and cheese, if you go into a pouch instead of a box, you reduce cost. Actually, the first stage of packaging this product is the pouch, so you just drop the box stage and go to a stronger pouch. In items that would normally be in glass, we've gone into cannisters, which reduce freight costs as well as the cost of glass" (Ricks 1982).

In a rather penetrating interview about packaging, H. Chazen, director of packaging at Woolworths, talked about the importance of private label packaging:

> The product that we set out on our counters is positioned in a package that becomes its suit of clothes, its protection, its cleanliness. Every merchandising function is served by the package; in fact, the product becomes totally dependent on the package itself. . . .
>
> We never design any package as a pure abstraction, because the design or whatever you put on that package has to serve the product. In terms of reality, the design must describe the product and cannot be just pretty for its own sake. The package must communicate to the customer; so immediately, you must have a frame of reference in terms of langauge, approach, color, size, etc. Also, a particular item can be psychologically tuned to a potential buyer: the mother influenced by a baby's picture on a disposable diaper package, for example. We try to address ourselves to a particular customer in their terms, i.e., a teen-age item directly appealing to a teen-ager. We don't do anything purely abstract; it's always a solution to the problem of selling a product. . . .
>
> We stay current with our packaging. . . . Packages these days for the most part are sealed. The best thing you can do is illustrate it in use. Without any words, you've told the story. Illustrations are used as a solution to a problem and not for their own sake. It's my tendency to illustrate more than most other people. . . .
>
> In our private label product lines, we do innovate quite a bit, but not in areas where there are extremely strong predispositions of a type of package. For example, some time ago, we introduced a blister card of flashcubes, when there was an industry expression of a package of six being called a six-shooter. This was arranged with the cartridges in a six-shooter case. They're General Electric cubes, which we designated on the package; but we designed the package and so it carries the Woolco name. It's one of those few instances where we identify the manufacturing source, because we feel in this case it lends credence to the product.
>
> Another innovative package is our new big bag of socks for a family. It's a family pack. Quite a while ago, we introduced a six pack of tube socks. It was an inventive package with a drawstring on top; and it's perhaps the most copied package in the industry. I've seen it on everybody's counters (Chazen 1979).

Chazen adds that Woolworths avoids a unified look in its private label packaging. That's too dull, he notes, indicating that his approach is more creative, up-to-date, appealing, and individual.

There are different ways to copy a successful national brand. Superficially, the private label retailer/wholesaler can adopt a package design that comes as close as possible without violating the national brand's trade dress. There also is a more subtle approach, picking up on the concept of package design as applied by the national brands, but adopting it to the private label product. Such a case is Caldor, Inc., Norwalk, Connecticut, with its nut line, which vies for shelf space with Planters. Caldor depends on its label to sell the Caldor with little media advertising support. An article in *Private Label* Magazine described this packaging strategy:

> Caldor's in-house artist/design Jack Jaser has worked with the supplier in creating a strong point-of-sale identity, telling customers what particular nutmeat is in each jar. "It's a neat look and easy to read. The oval design draws attention like a bullseye, almost forcing the customer to read the bold sans serif lettering," Jaser indicates. Labels also are color-coded so customers can perhaps subliminally relate to or remember the contents the next time they come to purchase an item they like. The label also includes Caldor's "rainbow logo" (similar to a stylized "C"). This thoughtful and inexpensive approach is juxtaposed against Planter's strong brand logo: sameness that ties most of its product line to a single color and design motif. While that name may be stronger in consumer's minds (reinforced by advertising), its label is not as effective as Caldor's in drawing customers to a particular item, such as peanuts, sesame seeds, mixed nuts, etc. There's another subtlety in the Caldor label: mini-ads that evoke responses from people, using charged words like "fresh," or "delicious" (Jaser 1979).

In the woman's hosiery category, private label packaging often adopts its own unique style. In K mart, for example, shoppers can select from the L'eggs egg-shaped packaging with subtle shading, the No Nonsense pouch display, or K marts' hosiery line—an explosion of colors and graphics, showing women enjoying the feel of their pantyhose.

Shoppers in the discount environment or in a supermarket look for price and convenience in women's hosiery; but in the department store, the shopper trades up to a better price line, according to Mike Goverman, executive vice-president, Pennaco Division of Playtex International Inc., owned by Esmark Inc., Chicago. Goverman says the private label line in a department store must look important:

> We don't suggest a package with a boom, boom, boom label, featuring a lot of words; instead, we prefer a subtle approach with large lettering, so that the customer can easily read the label. (Most customers who wear glasses usually don't when they're shopping, so a wordy label isn't important. Clarity and a descriptive label, easy to read, is.) We also recommend a graduated coloring, without any fancy name on the package. It's usually a name tied in with the department store, for example, "Belair by Broadway" (Goverman 1979).

In Bloomingdale's, New York hosiery buyer Mark Suss notes:

> For the past four years at least, we've been using these bright color packages, which will soon be changed to a more timely and chic design, something sedate and female and sophisticated with a clean look and very little writing. Our packaging itself is unique. Hosiery traditionally has been wrapped in paperboard packaging with a width of about six to seven inches across. Our packages are much more narrow and elongated, allowing for more goods to be displayed on the floor (Suss 1979).

PACKAGING COMPONENTS

The private label retailer/ wholesaler can take lessons from the national brand manufacturers when it comes to packaging products. Dennis J. Moran, executive vice-president of Siegel & Gale, New York, a package design and corporate identity consulting firm, lists eight components used by the brands to produce successful packages:

1. *Container Configuration*—the shape and image that a package communicates: how it communicates product attributes. Lever Brothers' Wisk laundry detergent, for example, conveys cleaning strength with broad shoulders and a solid masculine shape; dishwashing liquid containers convey gentleness to hands with a slim and feminine shape; Perrier mineral water conveys prestige with an elegant and distinctively shaped container.
2. *Brand Name*—an appealing and imaginative name that helps the product stand apart: Keebler's Zesta crackers evoke a taste sensation and Johnson Wax's Raid tells how that product works.
3. *Illustrations*—use of photographic or illustrative labels, whichever way is preferred. It should be executed professionally to show off the product (ideally in full color).
4. *Symbols*—to allow customers to identify with a symbol, particularly a human one, thus providing visual and identifiable elements to help the consumer remember and identify with the product.
5. *Typography*—not a multitude of type styles that could result in chaos; instead a customized logotype structured well to complement both the name and the product. Muellers' Egg Noodles, for example, convey an old-fashioned image. Other possibilities are imported, contemporary, western, or southern looks.
6. *Logotype*—the logo must be memorable and distinctive, representative of the product name, functioning well on the package and in other media. It must be designed carefully and creatively to span a full line of different items. The logo also must be positioned on the package so that it is noticed first.

7. *Functionality*—how the package dispenses and contains product. Lehn & Fink's Wet Ones use a pop-up disposable moist towelette dispenser; E-Z Time popcorn uses a self-contained popper; Liquid Plumber uses a self-applying drain cleaner.
8. *Mass Display*—how the product functions in a mass display. Standing alone, the packaging may be distinctive, but stacked among many shelf facings in a multiple exposure, it can fade from sight. This is overcome with effective use of color, graphics, and typography (Moran 1979A, pp. 64–66).

Most private label products tend to copy the national brand leader in a given category. Moran discussed the pros and cons of the look-alike strategy in packaging:

> It may be worthwhile to look at some of the reasons for adopting a "look-alike" stance of a national brand product:
>
> 1. To reassure the customer by a similar look that the quality of the private label product is similar or as good as the national brand.
> 2. To emphasize the economy image by the significant price differential between similar looking products.
> 3. To simplify the design of future house brand packages because guidelines have already been established by the national brand stance.
> 4. To establish in the consumer's mind the idea that all of the chains private label products are similar in quality to their national brand counterparts.
>
> On the other hand, there are certain drawbacks to "look-alike" packaging. For example:
>
> 1. The customers may *think* they are buying a national brand and be angered when they discover their mistake.
> 2. Some consumers may be annoyed that the private label is a copy of the national brand and decide not to purchase the private label goods.
> 3. In copying the stance of a national brand, a firm is denying its own identity.
> 4. In adopting a variety of private label stances that imitate the national products, there is no uniformity or cohesive look to the private label line. . . .
>
> In judging the best course to follow, if a retailer has a strong image in the marketplace, it is to his advantage to build on that image and market his private label products under his own distinct identity. The retailer's *reputation* in this situation will play a significant role in the buying decision (of customers).
>
> For those retailers who have a weaker image, it may be appropriate to adopt a house brand look that is similar to a national product. But this raises the following question: Would it not be better for the retailer to take immediate steps to strengthen his image in a manner that will aid future marketing efforts? The continuation of a fragmented private label packaging approach only worsens the existing identification problem (Moran 1979B, pp. 65–66).

National brand manufacturers have built-in safeguards to guarantee consistent packaging of the highest quality. Private label retailers/wholesalers, dealing with different sources of supply, do not have that protection. They must guard against packaging inconsistencies, especially with such printing deviations in color, logo, and placement.

Martic Zarett, president of Novel Lithographers, Port Reading, New Jersey, notes this trouble can result from:

- Poor liaison between the retailer and the manufacturer.
- Lack of packaging standards on the part of the retailer.
- Loose interpretation on the part of the manufacturer.
- Failure of both parties to recognize the importance of a more uniform "look."
- The failure of the manufacturer to insist upon tighter quality control by his printer.

"To compound the problems," Zarett continues, "each product supplier generally uses his own printer for his specific merchandise. Items displayed in a *single* category, such as hair care, baby products, etc., will probably be the collective output of several suppliers and as many printers. If there are even slight deviations in the physical appearance of a label or a blister card for example, the overall motivational effect of product line extensions will be less desirable. If major changes appear, the results can be disastrous."

To guard against this, he recommends adopting a comprehensive list of packaging standards, which could include the following:

- Standardization of distribution line, i.e., "manufactured for," "distributed by"
- A selection of PMS or other standard for color control
- Proper use of company logo
- Specification of paper or board
- Specification of finish
- Standardization of sizes for labels, blister cards, boxes, etc. (Zarett 1979).

Perhaps the trend of private label packaging toward a strong, identifiable brand image is best illustrated in the experience of Docktor Pet Centers, Andover, Massachusetts, which began in 1966. When a new management team took over six years later, it found packaging that "looked like every private label in the 1950s," according to one of the new partners, Eugene H. Kohn. The packaging, Kohn continues: "came in many different colors. We tried to design a new look, one that would effectively implement our strategy. We wanted a look that was different, uniform and denoted a professional quality, with a strong Docktor identification, and an up-to-date logotype—the Docktor name—used in a purple flag. This gave it a certain professional clean, highly identifiable look, one that would combat the former haphazard multicolored, nonimpressive look.

"We wanted an identity that would cross all category classifications, as opposed to the riot of color that existed in the competitive products. So we used one color, one look, one feel that worked in whatever products we carried—cologne mist, vitamins, fish food, or shampoo—whether it was for a dog, cat or bird. We created a dominant impression in the store that makes it look like everything was private label (Kohn 1982).

While that strategy may be too strong for most retailers/wholesalers, it does point out where private label is heading in packaging. Says Kohn: "I grew up in the advertising business in New York, working on Procter & Gamble products. So I got my schooling in the business of creating a brand and dealing with all aspects of the collateral material. When I came to Docktor Pet Centers, the brand became the Docktor store. What we've attempted to do is to position Docktor Pet Center as the brand; that's what we want to sell."

REFERENCES

Avischious, R. 1980. Private Labels: The Lifeblood of Shurfine-Central. *Private Label* Magazine, February-March, p. 15. E.W. Williams Publishing, New York.

Chazen, H. 1979. Packages Must Sell the Product. *Private Label* Magazine, June-July, pp. 38–39. E.W. Williams Publishing, New York.

Chenaux, R. G. 1981. Loblaw's Buying/Merchandising Muscle: Intersave. *Private Label* Magazine, August-September, p. 74. E.W. Williams Publishing, New York.

Diefenbach, J. 1980. The Power of Design in the Package for the 1980s: a Need for Top Management's Increasing Involvement. Grocery Manufacturers of America Annual Conference. (July).

Fame Marketing Corp. 1979. The FAME Story: Profit with Quality & Value. Dayton, Ohio.

Goverman, M. 1979. The Cadillac of Private Label Hosiery. *Private Label* Magazine, April-May, pp. 33–34. E.W. Williams Publishing, New York.

Grand Union Co. 1980. Annual Report, Elmwood Park, New Jersey.

Howard, M. 1981. Eaton's Private Label Comeback. *Private Label* Magazine, August-September, p. 86. E.W. Williams Publishing, New York.

Jaser, J. 1979. Caldor's Nut Line "Chews Up" a National Competitor. *Private Label* Magazine, April-May 1979, pp. 28–29. E.W. Williams Publishing, New York.

Kallach, A. 1981. The Rebirth of Private Label at Gray Drug. *Private Label* Magazine,February-March, p. 82. E.W. Williams Publishing, New York.

Kohn, E. H. 1982. Private Label is "Top Dog" at Docktor Pet Centers. *Private Label* Magazine, December-January, p.40. E.W. Williams Publishing, New York.

Margulies, W. P. 1979. Single or Multiple Private Label Lines. *Private Label* Magazine, April-May, pp. 40–42. E.W. Williams Publishing, New York.

Moran, D. J. 1979A. Learning Packaging "Tricks" From National Brand Marketers. *Private Label* Magazine, June-July, pp. 64–66. E.W. Williams Publishing, New York.

Moran, D. J. 1979B. Pros and cons on Private Label Packaging That Imitates National Brands. *Private Label* Magazine, August-September, pp. 65–66. E.W. Williams Publishing, New York.

Proctor & Gamble Co. 1979. Celebrating 100 Years: Ivory Soap As America's Favorite. Moonbeams (Special Edition), p. 17, Cincinnati, Ohio.

Rite Aid Corp. 1979. Annual Report. Shiremanstown, Pennsylvania.

Safeway Stores Inc. 1977. Annual Report, Oakland, California.

Suss, M. 1979. Merchandising Style-21st Century. *Private Label* Magazine, April-May, pp. 34–35. E.W. Williams Publishing, New York.

Zarett, M. 1979. You Can't Separate the Package From the Product. *Private Label* Magazine, August-September, p. 68. E.W. Williams Publishing, New York.

9

Private Label Pricing Strategies

Next to packaging, a private label's price can be the most eye-appealing to a potential customer. In the customer's decision to buy, pricing is perhaps the most important factor for a private label product.

Historically, private label's strategy of being priced lower than the national brands has been its primary selling point. Today, when private label can offer the customer equal or superior quality plus a price advantage, the product value to the customer is significantly enhanced. Pricing, therefore, remains the key to unlocking private label sales and opening the door wider to gross profits.

Profit margins built into private label are much higher than national brands, because the latter products carry with them costs not necessarily shared by a private label product. National brands are burdened by product development and marketing costs, including expensive advertising in national broadcast and consumer print media. Some manufacturers also support large sales forces for their product lines. Private labels merely copy a successfully established national brand and then are promoted inexpensively at the local level, mostly in newspapers, mail circulars, or store tabloids, as well as within the retailer's own stores through signage and special displays. Product costs also figure into the retailer's determination of private label pricing.

The private label retailer usually will price his own brands against a target competitor, either the leading retailer in his market or more likely against the product category leader in that market. In other words, private label pricing is targeted below the established market prices of national brands. The pricing differentials—private label versus national brands—can vary depending on the item or the category.

The retailer can realize a greater profit with private label. Associated Grocers of Florida, Inc., a retail-owned co-op that buys from the Shurfine-Central buying group, earns 1 to 2% higher profit margins on the Shurfine and Shurfresh labels over national brands. Georgina Perez, manager of the co-op's buying department, notes that these margins are minimum; "Price differentials vary within categories. In canned vegetables, a minimum spread of 2 cents unit differential is expected; while in paper and household goods, 15 cents is easily obtainable" (Perez 1982).

When Zody's, a 37-unit full-line discount department store chain operated by Hartfield-Zody, Inc., Los Angeles, structured a private label program for health and beauty aids, the price differentials went from a high of 33% down to a low of 10% with its profit margins set similarly, the overall profit aimed at about 33% versus comparable national brands' average margin of about 18%.

A drug chain reports that, in setting up its private label program, it was necessary to establish product categories with both low and high profit margins. Overall, its target margin was set at 45%, but for some items, like diapers, the profit dipped to 10 to 12%, while for other items, such as cosmetic beauty aids and cold capsules, it soared to 60%. The margins for some items, for example, toothpaste, may appear low (relatively speaking) at a 25 to 28% range; but when compared to the national brands' profits in toothpaste of from 5 to 10%, the private label margin is still quite respectable.

The basic rationale for private label pricing centers around the retailer realizing higher gross margins because of the lower cost factors involved, allowing him to just ride on a successful duplication of the national brand. Of course, the penny profits are just as important as the retailer's percentage profits. The customer first notices the price difference—lower for private label versus national brand; compares the private label packaging, which in many cases looks like the national brand's; then reads the private label ingredients to substantiate its quality versus the national brand.

Usually, customers in a supermarket, for example, make value comparisons based on the unit price of the private label against different competitive brands. They also check unit price differences in items sold by weights and measures (per ounce/pound/quart), by package count (number of sheets/bags/napkins), and by area (square inches/feet). When the private label item offers quality and quantity equal to or better than the brands—at a lower price—it is considered to be of more value to the customer.

While lower pricing is the primary consideration in private label fashion merchandise, merchants do not necessarily duplicate designer clothing. Instead, they create variations on a product or piece of merchandise—a unique style and color with its own price, from 10% to more than 100% lower than the national designer wear.

An important consideration in pricing—and, in fact, in carrying private label products—is the turnover rate. The ServiceStar private label program, run by American Hardware Supply, Butler, Pennsylvania which deals with some 3500 independent hardware and building supply dealers, operates under such a premise. Jim Marone, merchandise manger for private label, notes that "a hardware store's turnover rate is two to three times a year versus a food store that may have between 40 to 50 turnovers in product per year. We do get turns with disposable items. We've got private label in small areas: replacement vacuum sweeper bags, clothes lines, corn brooms, and a selection of thermos bottles." Private label also does well in the paint category: "There is brand name dominance in paints, but we're able to outsell them with our private label on a brand-by-brand basis. . . The margins on name brand paints average about 40%: but for private label the dealer can build in a minimum 50% profit margin" (Marone 1979).

The food retailer creates an adequate price spread between his brand and the national brand—not too small a differential, aimed at getting a higher profit margin faster, because profits also depend on product turns. If the customer is satisfied with the private label purchase, he or she will buy that product again at the "bargain" price.

For some product categories, such as health and beauty aids, the profit margins are higher than for other categories. Joe Healey (1979) vice-president of merchandise for A&P's Supermarket Service Corp. (health and beauty aids and nonfood items), says: "The retail price of private label is at least 20% lower than national brands. Our profit margins usually run 35 to 40% with the exception of promotions, at which time, we will discount private label. In contrast, national brands gross profits run approximately 26%."

Earl N. Pilgrim (1979) vice-president of purchasing for A&P notes: "A national brand item may have a 6 to 10% gross margin during a feature sale, whereas with private label, the margin can range from 20 to 25% on the same item. High volume results when the private label is displayed correctly with a proper mix in terms of retail price, shelf allocation, store traffic flow, etc.

In adopting generics, the pricing differentials can vary across the board, from fractional differences—pennies below the national brand—up to major differences—dollars apart. When FedMart, San Diego, Calif., a 70-store low-margin discount chain, started its Bright Yellow Wrap generic program in July 1979, the price differentials ranged from 5 to 10% on the low side up to 150% on the high side, averaging out to about 40% lower than the national brands.

Generics are not positioned as a profit margin category, but they can earn high percentage yields, in some cases better than the national brands.

King Soopers Discount, Denver, a 53-store supermarket chain which operates perhaps the largest generics program in the U.S. (550 generic items at last count) reports its average gross profit in generics is about 18%.

Western Grocers Inc., Denver, a wholesaler for some 200 independent and chain clients, indicates its margins in generics vary from 15 to 27%; while for health and beauty aids, profits can leap to 35% average and for some items edge up to 48% profit margin.

Chains can price private label an average 10 to 20% below national brands, while generics might average 30 to 40% below the national brands. The generics are adopted in most cases to serve as traffic builders and to generate sales volume. Profit is not a primary consideration, yet the profit margins can be attractive, as Foote, Cone & Belding (1979) discovered in a buyers' survey at different chains that had adopted generic products (Table 5).

The gross margins for generics were higher for four of these five product categories. Aspirin showed the most significant gross profit difference in favor of generics—17.4% versus Bayer's 2.6% profit.

In the past, customers have come to relate lower prices to poor quality; but through experience, education, and more exposure to consumerists' reports in newspapers and magazines and on radio and TV, today's shopper is better educated and smart enough to recognize that savings can be linked to quality merchandise. In today's marketplace of inflated prices, the good buy—a quality product selling at a reduced price—does not escape the alert shopper's attention.

Unfortunately, customers who stand to benefit most from the price advantage of private labels and generics remain committed to national brand quality. The low-income, the poorly educated, and people identified with ethnic groups, all still prefer higher priced national brands over the bargain store brands. They feel there is status in buying the national brand that adds to their self-esteem. Their preferences also could be traced to ignorance about the value inherent in private labels. These customers, exposed to heavy advertising, use the manufacturers' mes-

Table 5. Profit Margin of National Brands versus Generics

	Grape jam (32 oz) 12's	Paper towel rolls 30's	Aspirin 200's	Breakfast drink (27 oz)	Dry roasted peanuts (16 oz) 12's
Direct case cost					
Brand	10.20[a]	18.40[b]	22.19[c]	22.87[d] (15's)	13.55[e]
Generic	5.94	11.00	27.36[c]	10.47 (12's)	10.06
Unit cost					
Brand	0.85	0.61	1.84	1.52	1.12
Generic	0.50	0.37	0.57	0.87	0.83
SRP					
Brand	1.09	0.67	1.89	1.89	1.65
Generic	0.69	0.45	0.69	1.39	1.09
Gross (%)					
Brand	22%	8.9%	2.6	20	32
Generic	28%	19	17.4	37	24
Penny profit					
Brand	0.24	0.06	0.04	0.37	0.53
Generic	0.195	0.08	0.12	0.52	0.26

[a]Welch's Grape Jelly
[b]Kim-Clark (Teri Towels)
[c]Bayer Aspirin 200's/12's; generic aspirin 250's/48's
[d]Tang
[e]Planters

sage as their only orientation to shopping. A sign inside a store, promoting private label as a quality item at less cost or offering a money-back guarantee, does not necessarily change their minds, which has been convinced about the "superiority" of national brands. A lower priced item cannot always break their brand loyalty.

There is optimism about a consumer awakening with respect to pricing. As Bill Boggess, vice-president of merchandising and advertising at King Soopers Discount notes:

> I see a consumer shift, just like the consumer boycott of 1965. You take away a lot of the high cost of distribution and selling you something; don't play games with me like bingo and sweepstakes and mail-in refund offers, and coupons—just give me an everyday low price. That's what customers are thinking today. They're really responding in that respect. And as people become more intelligent about their shopping, there's a bigger place for private label and specifically generics.
>
> National brands are increasing their marketing and media costs—their TV expenditures and all of that to maintain their market shares. At the same time, they're not getting those increases, they're going to be forced to increase the cost of the product, which is going to create a larger spread among the everyday prices of private label, generics, and national brand.

Personally, I see more strength developing from the signs we see in the Denver market for private label and generics. You look through the brand preferences and consumer analysis, and you might see that last year customers didn't know or didn't have any brand preferences in 9% of the cases. This year it's closer to 11%. Five years ago, it was 3%.

Dick Wassenaar, head grocery buyer at Associated Grocers of Colorado, Inc., Denver, feels that

> the introduction of generics into the Denver market has made the consumer more aware of the price image, which makes them recognize the value of a house label, a controlled label, or a brand that is controlled by a given store or group of stores. They recognize that the quality of private label is equal to or better than the national brand.
>
> I've come to feel in the last two years especially that national brands have relaxed their quality in an attempt to hold the price down. But in the meantime, they've poured in so many dollars for their promotions that they've been forced to do it at the expense of the product's quality.
>
> In our cuttings of national brands versus our controlled label (Shurfine), we find in many instances—in fact the greatest percentage of times—that the quality of our controlled label has exceeded the quality of the national brand. The housewife is beginning to realize this and say, "Hey, I can save two, three, five cents on the house brand and have product quality-wise that is equal to or better than the national brand. So why should I buy the national brand?"
>
> I think the introduction of generics over the past two to three years, depending on what market you're in, has helped create this image with the housewife.

Associated Grocers has worked first to educate its retail customers, who buy from the wholesaler. Greg Gallus, corporate vice-president of merchandising, tells how

> We went out on a road show, where we took our private label, Shurfine, and the national brands. I think we compared 40 or 50 items one by one, everything from blind taste tests to straight-out cuttings and samplings. The retailers a saw where our brand in many instances was better than Del Monte. We grade our private label fancy. What grade does Del Monte go under? Del Monte quality. What is Del Monte quality? They call their product Del Monte quality, which is synonymous with what is suppose to be the best. But that's one thing we've done to educate our retailers. Now they have more confidence when they promote the private label. The national brands try to convey the message that they are one cut above private label; but they are not. . . . We've also encouraged individual stores to conduct cuttings within the store for consumers.

In contrast to this more aggressive push for private label and generics, there are some retailers who are content with a predominately national brand pricing structure.

King Kullen Grocery Co., Inc., Westbury, New York, a 55-store supermarket chain, maintains a program of 500 private label and 65 generic items. Rudy Becht, director of grocery merchandising, says: "We don't want to shove it down people's throats. We like private label. It gets our name into the consumer's hands; it's advertising—free advertising—for us. And we have excellent quality. In fact, of the top 10 best sellers in our chain, four items—apple juice, bleach, five-pound sugar, and green beans—are in private label."

Becht's argument for not pushing hard with private label is that

> it's not that much cheaper than the national brand, when the latter is on deal. In some instances, private label might be more expensive when, for example, the national brands come out with some special deal to move product out.
>
> The national brands offer bigger allowances than private label. You can't get the price spread on private label that you can on national brand; for example, it might be 50 cents per case allowance on private label versus $2.50 or more a case on national brands. The national brands deals come more frequently and there's more profit for us, because of customer demand."

He adds that he could buy private label a lot cheaper, but King Kullen insists on dealing with a single supplier for a commodity to insure consistent high quality. Some companies, he believes, deal with four or five packers for certain commodities and therefore do not maintain a consistent quality; but they do get the product cheaper.

Customer demand for national brand coupled with occasional double coupon offers from manufacturers for consumers make the national brand product mix more attractive for this retailer. But Becht admits that "some of the national brand manufacturers are not being realistic with their allowances. They have over-inflated prices and then come out with these tremendous allowances to bring the price back to something realistic, where it should have been in the first place."

PRICING FLEXIBILITY

Private labels give the retailer more pricing flexibility, because he owns and controls the label. National brands, unless sold on special deals, are priced rigidly and competitively within a given market. Private label can be priced at certain percentages or cents below the national brand in different product categories. Retailers have more say over how private labels are priced. The problem is that this can sometimes get out of hand. A retailer may want too high a profit margin and therefore mark up his private brand closer to the national bread, creating a small price differential.

"Fair pricing is important," says William A. Robinson, vice-president of private label sales at A&P:

> If you get a price spread too big, it destroys your quality connotation. If you get it too close, then what's the savings? You have to offer a reasonable amount of variety or you get lost on the shelf. You've got to go to those items or flavors that will get you an 80% level of buying, because 100% is ill-affordable in private label capability. You can't sell

> everybody everything all the time. Customers will change, because they like to change. Also, the item's characteristics come into play: in one market, you can't give it away, while in another area it sells and you don't know why. . . .
>
> As a rule of thumb in retailing, whether it's in private label or anything else, the merchant should never get greedy. If there's a fair share that's affordable to get, then the retailer is entitled to it. The day he starts to get greedy, tries to get it too fast, or too much of it, it will cost him more than he gains (Robinson 1979).

Retailers mostly calculate their national brand markups on a retail base price, since a cost–price basis would dramatize the markup in the eyes of the consumer. Asking or selling prices are more readily available and statistics are most often stated on a sales basis.

Private label pricing can be perceived as more like a markdown on the national brand selling price. One approach is to mark private label down so many cents from that level; another approach is to discount private label on a percentage basis below the national brand. The type of item often determines what kind of price spread should be adopted.

High demand products, those heavily advertised as national brands, maintain a strong consumer loyalty. Private label can experience difficulty penetrating categories such as coffee, cigarettes, and beer and so must maintain a wider price spread to entice customers away from the higher-priced national brand. It is a price sell, because private label cannot compete on a quality level; customers are already sold on the national brand quality. Generics, positioned mostly as a price sell, have been able to penetrate consumer loyalty in some of these categories. Consumers are asked to trade down for acceptable, not comparable quality. A tight budget often can affect such a buying switch.

When there is less customer loyalty to a particular brand—several national brands vying for equal market shares in a product category—private label can come in almost as an equal brand competitor on the basis of quality and also with a lower price at a smaller price spread.

There is no general rule about private label pricing. Each retailer has its own philosophy on how to structure markups or markdowns. But there are certain options open to the retailer. Private labels can be priced as:

- A regular price—traditional markup without a measure against the national brand
- A premium price—higher than the national brand, because the private label is of superior quality
- A competitive price—the same as the national brand pricing
- A price differential—below the national brand pricing
- A lost leader—sold at or below cost or given away in a coupon offer
- A discount price—buy one and get another free or promoted at a reduced price

The most effective pricing strategy for private label involves a balancing of these different strategies. Woolworth's does this very effectively, using different departments to draw in customers. Some products are featured with markups of less than 20%, while other items carry a 40% markup. "It's really a balance of pricing storewide that makes the difference," according to S. A. Tuohy, vice-president of merchandising:

> We have about 30 items in our ladies hosiery line, priced from 69 cents up to $3.99 for control top pantyhose. The quality we offer customers in this line is at least equal to the most famous of the advertised brands; while our prices are considerably less. Lab tests prove that our private label items are superior or, at the very least, equal to items selling at substantially higher prices. We pass the savings on to our customers, while making a good average profit on our private label line. And customers recognize the values offered and come back again and again for this product.
>
> Ladies hosiery is not a loss leader; we do have a 20% off sale on our entire line twice a year, which helps to build up customer enthusiasm. We nationally advertise the product in newspapers and on TV, plus use in-store point-of-purchase materials. . . .
>
> If you wanted to pick an individual item as most important in terms of dollar volume, it's probably our Pata Cake disposable diapers. This is a tremendous volume item; we do millions of dollars of business in this product. In fact, anything that is disposable or considered a consumable is an important sales item. Customers today must economize someplace. Not many people wash diapers anymore. So a disposable diaper that is made of good quality and good design, priced low, is an attractive purchase. Frequently, we sell our diapers at just above cost. We have all the styles of the national brands, including their special features. But our item is priced well below the nationally advertised brand. So people appreciate the fine quality we offer. They drive well out of their way to buy our diapers at the lowest price possible (Tuohy 1979).

While customer values are not always based on price, the price nevertheless weighs heavily on shopper's buying decisions. Private label often is placed side-by-side with its national brand counterpart to allow customers to see the quality and compare the price. The lower price of private label should be easy to read, not obstructed by old price stickers. Special signs used on shelfing displays will keep that lower price image in front of the consumer.

Walgreens, Chicago, runs three to four major promotions a year, the biggest one scheduled in January around its private label vitamins, followed by fall and spring "Buy 2 Sales," each for 10 days, offering two private label products at a specific bargain price or two for the price of one, when the profit margins allow it. The drug chain usually cuts 20% off its regular retail prices.

Duane Vogelsburg, president of Walgreen Labs, says: "The profit object is a 42–42% markup plus internal manufacturing profit. We keep ourselves as competitive as possible in the cosmetic area, where national brands take a command of the market through heavy advertising. Our products are priced about 20% below the national brands, but still fixed with a 42% markup. We also stay competitive with traffic builders: hot items sold at a low price (Vogelsburg 1979).

One of the benefits of private label is its pricing flexibility. Retailers control the pricing, since it is their brand. They can react in response to market conditions. Sometimes it can be a crisis, as in 1980 when Esther Peterson, special assistant to the President for consumer affairs, called on retailers to help ease inflationary pressures on consumers by placing a voluntary price ceiling on some commonly purchased food items. Major food retailers—Safeway, A&P, Giant Foods, Grand Union, Foodtown, National Tea, Fisher Foods' Dominicks, Schnuck's, etc.—reacted by placing a price freeze on their private label and/or generic products.

Retailers often establish a flexible pricing strategy with private labels to adapt to an unpredictable marketplace. So their pricing is not necessarily fixed at a rigid percentage level below national brands. The latter sometimes can be priced below private labels. Generics often are priced at the lowest level possible (along with a lower profit margin) and usually fixed in price at that level.

Of course, every retailer has his own strategy. In most cases, private labels sell best when they are priced below the brands. But private labels also take on a brand status that is, they sell quality as well as price.

Whatever the strategy, price remains a crucial factor in the customer's decision to buy private labels.

REFERENCES

Foote, Cone & Belding. 1979. Generics and Limited Line Stores: A State-of-the-Industry Report, New York (April).

Healey, J. 1979. A&P's Growth into HaBa and Other Non Foods. *Private Label* Magazine, June-July, p. 47. E.W. Williams Publishing, New York.

Marone, J. 1979. Private Label Housewares/Household Items: A Grab Bag Category. *Private Label* Magazine, October-November, pp. 61–62. E.W. Williams Publishing, New York.

Perez, G. 1982. The Private Label Buyer Speaks: A Private Label Uprise in Florida. *Private Label* Magazine, December-January, p. 65. E.W. Williams Publishing, New York.

Pilgrim, E. N. 1979. A&P's Corporate and Divisional Purchasing Strategies. *Private Label* Magazine, April-May, p. 13. E.W. Williams Publishing, New York.

Robinson, W. A. 1979. Troubled A&P Chain Gets Private Label Face Lifting, Part II. *Private Label* Magazine, June-July, p. 45. E.W. Williams Publishing, New York.

Tuohy, S. A. 1979. Woolworth's Lasting, but Not Timeworn Private Label Strategy. *Private Label* Magazine, June-July, pp. 34–35. E.W. Williams Publishing, New York.

Vogelsburg, D. 1979. Looking Behind the "100% Guaranteed" Walgreens Label. *Private Label* Magazine, June-July, p. 27. E.W. Williams Publishing, New York.

10

Private Label Merchandising Strategies

The package and price work together on the store shelf to sell a private label product, but the catalyst that clinches the sale is called merchandising. Private label merchandising involves presenting the product with good shelf position and facings, attractive promotional displays, effective in-store advertising, noticeable point-of-purchase materials (especially signage), and suggestive selling by employees. It is an orchestration of activity to avoid allowing private label to die on the shelf. Merchandising can range from a two-dimensional effort, where only the aisle shelves do the selling, to a three-dimensional push with depth achieved using signs, displays, in-store ads, pamphlets, banners, buttons, decals, tags, employee suggestive selling, closed-circuit TV commercials, live product demonstrations—all tied into the effort to sell, sell, sell the product.

In the past, private label programs have relied almost exclusively but mostly passively on in-store merchandising activity. More recently, this effort has been augumented with new marketing activities (discussed in the following chapter). The retailer/wholesaler continues to manage his private label merchandising efforts with one priority in mind: To convince the consumer that there are more value and savings in the private label product.

Space is at a premium in the retail store. Products that do not turn quickly or within a reasonable time should be weeded out of the product mix, allowing for new items to help boost sales. Usually, a food retailer/wholesaler will group products into major category groups or headings—health and beauty aids, general merchandise, canned foods, frozen foods, household chemicals, meats, produce, bakery. Within each category, there is product segmentation to accommodate changing consumer tastes and to allow for variety of selection targeted at different consumers. This overall product mix is usually dominated by national and regional brands. Private label is positioned against the product category leaders, usually the national brands.

A store layout depends on many interrelated factors, including market demographics, available space, shape of store, type of store (i.e., combination grocery—drug versus limited assortment), type of market segment (i.e., drug versus department store), traffic patterns, and store location (suburban mall versus city street). It would require several books to discuss these conditions fully as they relate to specific retail market segments and to the positioning of private label within each segment. This discussion, therefore, focuses more on overall merchandising techniques, which can be adopted by any or all types of retail operations, depending on their logistics.

Consumers tend to shop with predictable behavior. In other words, there are some fundamental "tricks of the trade," which can help boost private label sales through merchandising.

PRODUCT VISIBILITY

Most often, the front of the store receives the most customer traffic. Customers entering usually bear to the right. Also, their focus tends to bear right. A basic merchandising strategy for private label calls for placing the private label product to the right of the comparable leading national brand. In a vertical shelf display, the best position is at eye level or within easy reach, requiring no stooping or tiptoe stretching. If the product is very large, it should be nearer to the floor, so that it can be easily carried off.

In a horizontal strip of product facings, the ideal position for private label is in the center of the display for best visibility. When two national brands vie for category leadership, the private label product should be placed between them for best exposure.

A shelf talker—a sign asking the consumer to "compare and save" with the price difference between the private label and the national brand listed—often is placed on the shelf between these competing products to draw consumer attention to the value and savings realized in the private label product. Mass merchandisers do not usually run in-store comparisons of private label versus national brands, but do employ signs to call attention to "Our Own" brands. They also dramatize a display with mannequins wearing private label merchandise.

Private labels are almost always integrated or cut into the product mix by product category. On a product-by-product basis, private label's portion of space can be high or low—from one or two facings up to multiple or sometimes dominant facings in the category—depending on the product category. A frozen vegetable section, for example, might contain more private label selections than national brands, while a cosmetic department very likely will feature only national brands.

Usually, the rate of product turnover can be visually detected by the number of product facings; many facings often mean a high turnover. A retailer frequently will allocate shelf space in direct proportion to the percent of sales earned by the brand in that product category. Private label may also be allocated on its profit dollar contribution and may purposely be over-allocated to get better sales or to move new items.

In the merchandise mix, some products are in demand, while other items are purchased more on impulse than on consumer need. The selling strategies for each type of product are important to consider.

Staple items such as meat, bread, milk, clothing, aspirin, vitamins, laundry detergents, and paper towels are needed daily. Consumers shop a store for these items, often looking just for them. So these products can be located deep within the store in order to draw customers through the aisles, past impulse or incidental merchandise. Usually, however, private label items are simply stocked in their appropriate sections according to the store layout.

Unplanned purchases, the impulse items, are positioned in highly visible areas, well traveled by the shopper. High traffic areas include the front of the store, near a pharmacy, or close to a checkout station or a wrapping desk. When customers pass by or are waiting to purchase staple items, they look at impulse goods. Often their interest can change to a purchase of that product, especially if it is merchandised properly. Customer attention is frequently attracted to impulse items presented in a multifacing display. Retailers should follow the lead of national brands in the placement of private label facings, as special features or promotions.

Sometimes a retailer will introduce a private label demand product as an impulse item using, for example, a cents-off offer on the package. Conversely, an impulse item can be presented as a demand item, when it is advertised as a loss leader or at a special discount price.

One of the most effective merchandising techniques is the mass promotional display, feauturing many facings and shelves of one or a few products, usually offered at a special price. Some retailers believe that this type of display should be made uneven or asymmetrical, because customers psychologically dislike to disturb something symmetrical— a debatable strategy. Generic displays have capitalized on this format, massing together not only single products but the entire generic category of products, which all carry the same plain packaging. The effect has double impact, serving as a promotional display together with a built-in connotation of special pricing suggested by the no-frills packaging or an economic-sounding identity.

The private label promotional display is often featured as an end cap display at the front of the aisle. End caps may work better at the rear of the aisle, where no check lane lines can destroy traffic patterns.

Effective shelf positioning and promotional displays serve to attract and draw customer traffic. The carefully drawn planogram for aisle shelfing will position items in a product category by popularity with the less popular items placed below or above eye level.

Product categories often require different strategies in shelf layout. In an interview, Joseph Conte of Witco Chemical Corp. mapped out the strategy for powdered laundry detergents, recommending that the retailer offer a good range of product types in the popular sizes: phosphate, nonphosphate, all-temperature, cold-water, blue and white products—packed in 24/20-, 10/49-, and 6/84-ounce, and 3/10-pound 11-ounce sizes. Each product type should be stocked in three of these sizes, at least: preferably Giant 49-ounce, King 84-ounce and Family 10-pound 11-ounce packages. The selection should be enough to compete with the national brands, featuring the Giant size (most popular) at eye level. Each item also should have at least two shelf facings.

Three successful planogram patterns for this product are recommended:

1. Eye-level positon of the private label with national brands surrounding it.
2. Billboard display clustering private label items, positioned as the first items with the flow of customer traffic in a vertical-type arrangement.
3. Billboard display with the cluster positioned in the middle of the detergent section with national brands surrounding it, which allows for placement of private label items next to the fastest moving comparable national brands, so shoppers can make a price comparison.

The article also notes that retailers should not positon private label next to slow-moving national brands or fragment private label items by random positioning next to national brands of corresponding package sizes (Conte 1979).

Kenneth Foster of Acme Products Co., recommends putting first aid products, within the impulse product group, on multifacing displays:

> On the more popular adhesive bandage product codes (both sheer and plastic strips) you should have a minimum of two facings of each of the 1-inch 30's and 50's assorted, with a maximum of four facings of each of these stock code numbers. For the remaining first aid categories, multifacings should probably include two each on the 2- and 3-inch gauze bandages, 3 × 3 inch gauze pads, and both sizes of absorbent balls (65's and 130's). The facings in your planogram should be reviewed quarterly to determine if too much space is being devoted to a size which may not be selling in your particular market (Foster 1979).

Other factors come into play in an effective shelf display: selection or variety, color coding and separation, container size placement, inventory control, placement of signage, and policing the mix. One of the major shortcomings in any planned display is follow-up at the store level. Store personnel who do not follow the planogram to the letter and keep it rotated, current, and policed defeat the merchandising effort.

TYPES OF DISPLAYS

There are numerous ways to pull product off its usual shelf-aisle positioning into minor or major displays to show it in its most effective way—isolated and spotlighted. Some of the popular display methods include:

Shelf Extenders. Miniplatform extending out from a shelf to hold a few private label facings (sometimes shared with the national brand knock-off items)

In-Aisle Floor Displays. Product displayed in cut shipper cases (stacked) or prepacked shipper display furnished by the supplier

End Cap Displays. Massive displays at the front or rear end of an aisle, sometimes cross-referenced with another product (private label only or private label with national brand) that can be used with it: window cleaner with paper towels, for example

Check-Out Station Displays. Products in shelves or on hook displays positioned for impulse buying near the cash register stations

Floor Dump Displays. In aisle, end of aisle, or island location, where product is held in a cardboard or wire container or on a table

Case Displays. Meat and frozen or refrigerated foods and dairy products are displayed effectively behind vertical reach-in glass cases or in traditional coffin-case displays

Window Displays. Product stocked up front where passersby can see a bargain private label sale from outside the store or when entering or leaving the store

Wall Displays. A hanging display that almost frames the product

Wire Displays. Free-standing, sometimes rotating stands used for general merchandise items. Also, this display can be positioned as an in-aisle basket for a break in shelving

Pegboard Displays. Vertical displays that neatly arrange product in layers

Boutique Displays. Hosiery or vitamin center, showing items clustered in different sizes, colors, varieties, sometimes positioned against an adjoining national brand display: L'eggs or No Nonsense hosiery boutique versus a private label hosiery boutique. A product grouping of separated or integrated brands can be part of the aisle shelfing, an end cap display, or an island display

Store-sized Displays. Store-within-a-store display where products of one category are clustered into a specialty shop effect for walk-in or walk-through shopping: a bakery, nutrition center (including health foods and full vitamin line), generics section, etc.

Demonstration Displays. Live action, where store personnel or a hired professional demonstrator shows product to customers, offering free or sample packages, allowing them to taste or see the product in performance. In private label merchandise, such a display could feature product cuttings, comparing the national brand against private label or generic products

Cut Cases/Pallet Displays. For an economy look, product is stacked in its cut cases or piled on pallets, taken from the warehouse

Counter Displays. Especially effective at a cosmetics counter, deli stand, pharmacy, film counter, etc., where customers need service. The counter display can work as an impulse sell, while customers wait for service or browse

Special Displays. One-of-a-kind displays, such as Plexiglass vertical or cup-shaped fixtures, or even shopping carts

A retailer's creativity often comes into play with displays. About 10 years ago, Safeway Stores started a three-times-a-year shopping basket comparison display, showing one cart filled with Safeway S brands and a cart next to it filled with comparable national brands. Over the shopping carts, a large sign compares the total cost of the national brand cart with the cost of the Safeway brands, showing the amount of savings in dollars and percentage. Lately, success with this display has led the chain to adopt the display in four promotions per year throughout its 21 divisions nationwide.

This promotion shows customers what the contents of each shopping cart will cost, indicating a savings of as much as 20% with private label over the national brands. The carts are filled with only staple items, excluding perishables and produce. A typical cart can include aspirin, margarine, corn flakes, crackers, facial tissue, flour and cake mix, dry milk, cider, shampoo, soup, charcoal briquets, detergents, juice, dog food, and bathroom tissue.

Promotion of the "Comparison Buggies" is backed with an in-store flyer announcing the "Safeway Brands Event" and featuring private label items in price comparisons to national brands. The message stresses savings during "S Brands Stock-up Week," but also hits home on the quality aspect: "Look for the Safeway 'S' on the label. . . . It marks the finest quality and best value!" (*Private Label* 1979). Overall the effort has helped the chain to push private label volume up annually by half a percent, according to the company.

As part of its 75th Diamond Jubilee promotion, Peoples Drug, Alexandria, Virginia, promoted a sweepstakes contest, using a shopping cart filled with $75 worth of Peoples brand products. Entry blanks in the stores (as well as in several newspaper ads) offered customers a chance to win the products in the cart plus "a dream cruise to the Caribbean," with no purchase necessary.

The objective in most displays is to get additional facings for private label besides their regular shelf allocation. For customers, the display is justified as a promotion; for the retailer, the display serves to increase private label sales (and profits).

A mass merchandiser recently introduced a new line of household chemical products under its store label. The line was rolled out into its stores in a special gondola-style promotion, pulling the full line together in stacked, cut cases, sold alongside the knock-off national brands in one massive display. "Compare & Save" signs were used to show the price difference. The retailer cut the front end of the boxes at the top level to show the product stocked supermarket-style for a dynamic effect. The effort also was backed up with end-cap displays of the private label again sold against the national brand counterpart with price comparison signs.

After the introductory promotion, the product line was integrated into its respective department sections, again sold next to the national brand with price comparison signs. The retailer suggested that when national brands in a particular category lower their prices, that the store manager lower the comparable private label item "somewhat" to make the savings still attractive to customers.

The chain equipped its stores with signs for end caps as well as generic signs, indicating such phrases as "Discount Price, Shop Our Own Brands and Save!" or "Discount Prices, Our Own Brands Help You Fight Inflation," or "Store Brands Quality Tested, Value Priced," to place over the end cap displays.

END CAP STRATEGY

A drug chain's strategy in using five-shelf end caps called for 8.5 × 28.5 in. category heading signs at the top of the display (identifying the category) along with 4.5 × 8.5 in. shelf talkers to be placed between the national brand and private label products on the shelves. The end caps were placed in high-traffic areas within the cosmetic and drug departments, facing the front of the store.

As an example, the typical end cap for "Cough & Cold Remedies" was designed in the following fashion:

End cap sign, on top:	"Cough & Cold Remedies"
Top Shelf:	Contact caps with 3 facings, private label cold caps with 3 facings
Second shelf:	Bayer aspirin with 4 facings, private label aspirin with 6 facings
Third shelf:	Vick's Formula 44 cough syrup with 3 facings, private label extra strength cough mixture with 3 facings, Robitussin DM with 3 facings, private lavel DM with 4 facings
Fourth shelf:	Vick's Nyquil with 7 facings, private label cold formula with 7 facings
Bottom shelf:	Hall's Mentholyptus cough drops with 4 facings, private label Mentholyptus cough drops with 4 facings.

Compare & Save shelf talkers were used on each shelf between the national brand and the private label counterpart.

In this program, the retailer dispatched 90 compare-and-save shelf talkers with extras for price changes. The majority of the signs were to be used on regular and end cap displays, the remainder on mini-shelf extenders.

This retailer developed displays with national brand and its brands on the mini-shelves, sharing the space equally with a compare-and-save sign placed between them. The mini-shelves featured at least one national brand facing and one or more private label facings. Signs on the mini-shelf were usually changed once a quarter with new-color signs that featured different items keyed into the season.

The rationale behind the program was that the store's private label brands are of comparable quality to the leading national reference brands, that its products provide significantly greater gross profit to the store than the national reference brand, that its brand can be sold at retail at a substantially lower price, and that its brand has the capability of good sales volume.

K&B Drug promotes its brand of beer with an eye-catching mock-up of the product.

In the recent past, K mart has become bolder in merchandising its own brands, using shelf talkers that compare K mart brands against leading national brands. Shoppers' attention here is called to the value and savings of the private label over Miracle-Gro plant food.

Even with a cents-off offer on Listermint, K mart's comparable product offers consumers a greater savings.

In the middle of a Ragu Spaghetti sauce end cap display, A&P has placed its Ann Page elbow macaroni in a combination sell.

A ceiling banner tells FedMart shoppers that the FM brand is backed with a quality guarantee. If customers are not satisfied with the health and beauty aids item, the store will replace it with "a comparable national brand (if available) or a refund."

This shelf talker suggests that ShopRite customers compare and save with ShopRite's Stress Formula 600 over the national brand, Lederle.

Ralph's Grocery generic diapers are prominently displayed in this aisle dump display with bold signage announcing the savings.

Revco Drug, besides the regular savings on its brands, also gives senior citizens a 10% discount on private label vitamins.

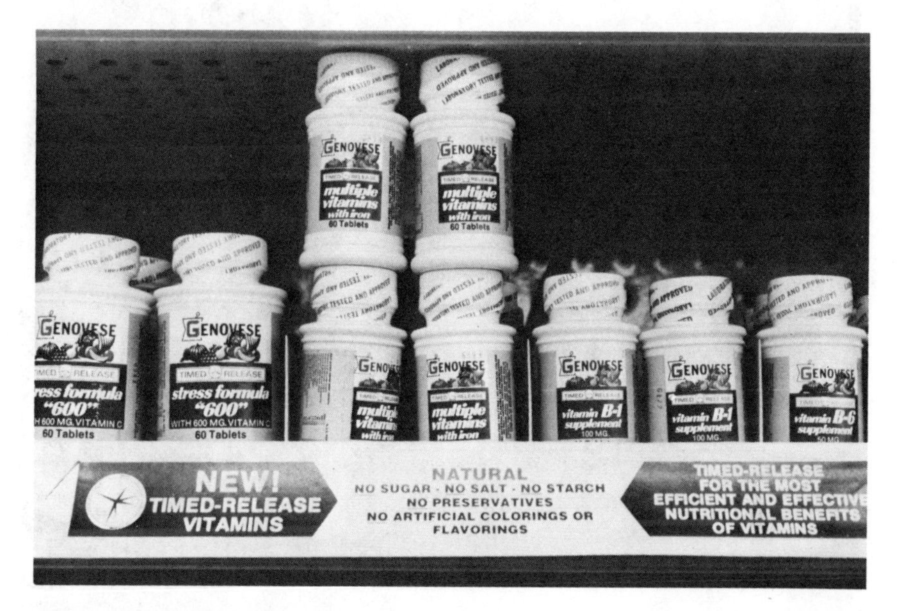

Genovese Drug (New York) advertises a new addition to its private label vitamin mix: time-release vitamins without additives.

Ralph's Grocery gives full-aisle treatment to generic Plain Wrap wine, beer, and liquor, using signage to advertise the savings.

Raley's deploys shelf extenders to highlight its brand of health and beauty aids. The mini-display is flagged with a shelf talker.

The bold comparison sign tells the story—up to 50% savings with the GNC brand at the General Nutrition Center outlet.

A&P displays its line of pantyhose in a hosiery boutique complete with fit information and the message, "Try A&P pantyhose. We guarantee a beautiful change, or your money back."

Here, Camellia Foods (Norfolk, Virginia) positions its brand of laundry detergent next to a complementary product, Purex bleach.

A General Nutrition Center store (New York) presents almost a library effect with the generous use of signs, including hard-sell savings messages, comparison signs (GNC brands versus national brands), and educational signs.

In this Marks & Spencer store in Canada, the St Michael's brand is advertised in a floor sign, calling attention to the foods section of the store.

K&B Drug (New Orleans) is not shy about promoting its brand of products, using a large overhead sign in this end aisle display.

Revco gives its own dandruff shampoo priority treatment in this shelf extension display, flanked with "Save" signs along with the message, "you need all the Revco you can get."

Raley's Supermarkets (California) have bold display signs to advertise the savings with Raley's brand of toothpaste over the leading national brand, Crest.

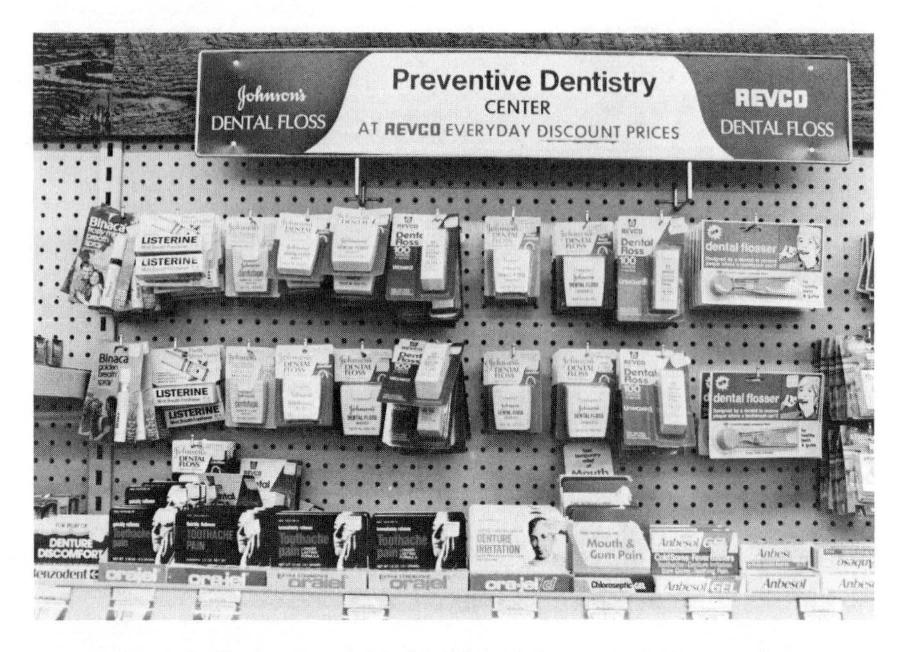

It is a combination sell, where Revco's brand cuts in with the national brand, Johnson's, in the special "Preventive Dentistry Center" at a Revco Drug store.

Stop & Shop positions its own latex gloves next to the national brand Playtex in this pegboard display.

A special floor display in ShopRite stores asks customers a pertinent question about hosiery.

Trash can liners under the Murphy's Mart label get special mass display treatment, featured as a special buy at $1.27.

A&P cleverly positions its Ann Page spices on a shelf extension platform in front of its own and national brand salad dressings. One product complements, does not compete against, the other.

This mini-shelf extension accents the Walgreen Dalai Musk cologne over the Old Spice Musk cologne. A "100% Guaranteed" underscores the private label sell.

Murphy's Mart capitalizes on the strong private label paint category with a full selection of latex flat wall paint and semi-gloss enamel. An information chart is provided for customers.

In this frozen food "coffin" display, Green Giant faces some strong competition from Ralph's private label selection of vegetables, attractively packaged with illustrations. A prominent sign hammers home the savings realized by shoppers.

Retailers like Safeway often provide film processing service in their stores as an incentive for customers to buy the store brand film. Here, Safeway 126 color cartridge film is featured along poles of the display.

Frequent paint sales are commonplace in retail outlets. Sears is no exception to the rule. Here, semi-gloss and flat latex paints are features with savings of $5 and $6, respectively, along with accessories, all under the Sears label.

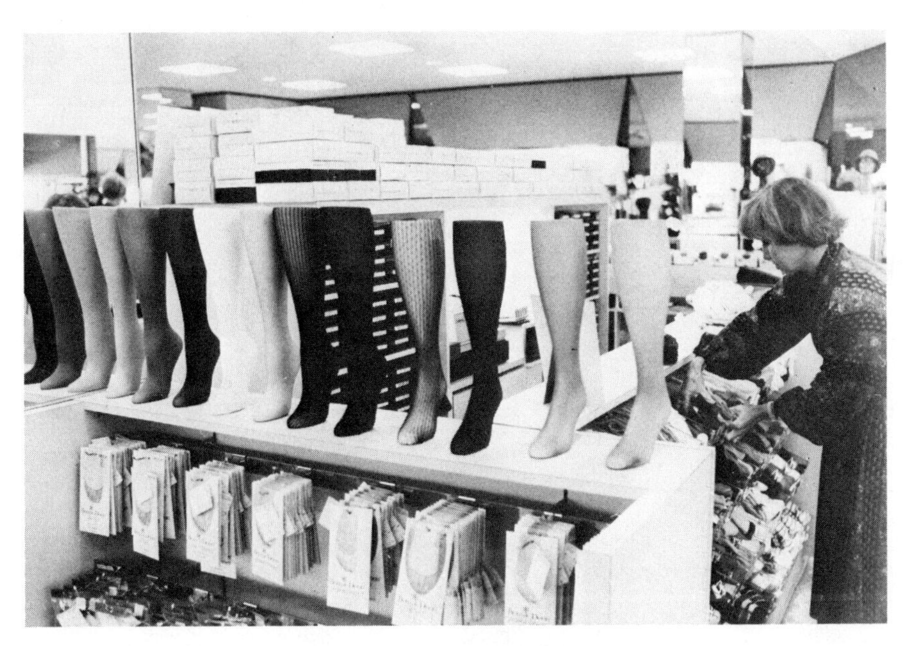

Leg manikins on a countertop at this Bloomingdale department store (New Jersey) allow for a display of different hosiery styles, all packaged under the retailer's store brand.

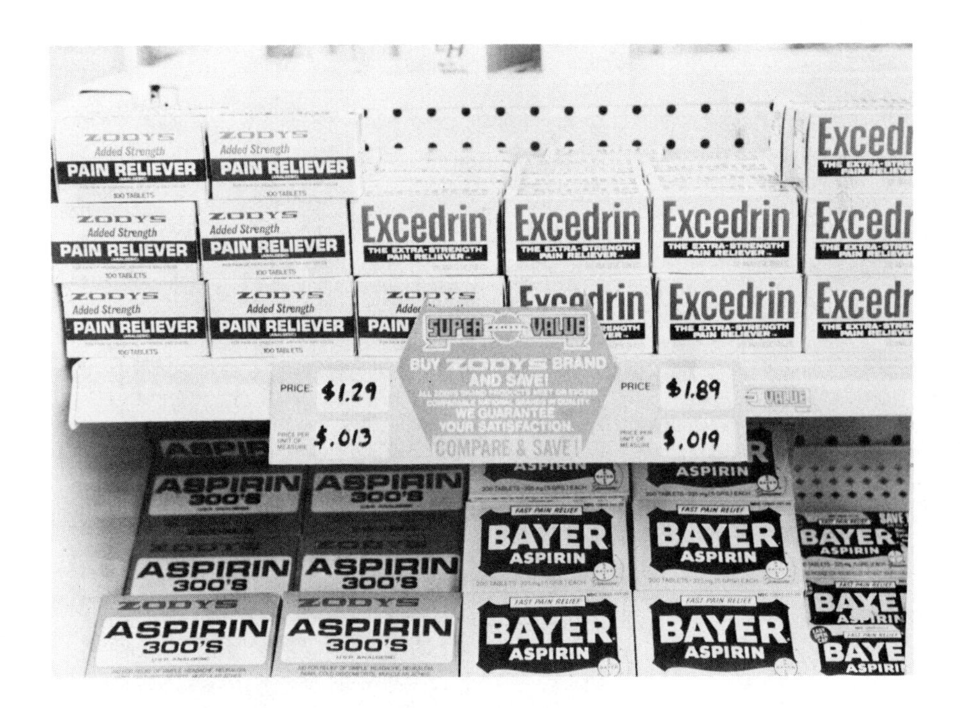

This compare-and-save shelf talker at Zodys (Los Angeles) measures the Zodys brand of pain reliever against Excedrin on a price and a price-per-unit-of-measure basis. The message says: "All Zodys brand products meet or exceed comparable national brands in quality."

One big private label seller is yarn. Here FedMart displays a pile-up of yarns in different colors in wire bins.

The comparison test sometimes carries right on to the label itself. Revco mass displays its Pearlescent green shampoo with the bottleneck message, "Try ours instead of Pert."

Safeway's standard grade Scotch Buy laundry detergent is positioned for easy reach, at eye level. A shelf talker clearly marks the price versus the national brand on the shelf below.

A special "2 for $1" sale backs this end aisle display of Stop & Shop paper towels: jumbo towel rolls at 50 cents apiece.

Gray Drug (Cleveland) spotlights creams and lotions in this special end-aisle display, where shelf-by-shelf Gray's brand is compared to a leading national brand in different product categories.

A bonanza of savings, most of them under the Longs label, is featured in this end-aisle display in a Longs Drug outlet in California. The shopper is oriented to a bargain display, including "sale price" or "low price" items.

AGGRESSIVENESS VERSUS SUBTLETY

The success of private label in-store promotional displays pivots on giving the customer a choice of products. This is accomplished by positioning private label items side-by-side with their national brand reference and by giving private label special additional display treatment. It is an aggressive merchandising tactic, promoted store-wide often with compare and-save signs that boldly describe the name, size, and price of the products compared. Sometimes ingredient or formulation comparisons are made, too.

Saul H. Schneider, prescription and drug director of K&B Inc., New Orleans, speaking at a merchandising panel at PLMA's 1981 spring meeting in New Orleans, when asked how his chain promotes private labels aggressively, responded: "We do it by emulating what is being done by the national brands. We're using point-of-purchase programs, shelf talkers, signs, window banners, etc. We're also tying in promotions with point-of-purchase displays in every department. When we promote vitamins, for example, it's on display in every department for that promotional period."

K&B groups companion items together under product groupings, such as in the cough-and-cold area: cough syrups, cough lozenges, nasal spray, and vitamin C. Says Schneider: "What has happened is that we're cross-merchandising private label lines in every area."

In effect, K&B flexes its merchandising muscle: Pain relievers are displayed not only next to their national counterparts, but also in the feminine hygiene sections, where private label diet items and vitamins also are featured. "With a little thought," he notes, "you can see how you can cross-relate items to get companion sales and additional sales."

Some retailers conduct sales contests within their operations, giving awards to managers with the highest sales and best promotional displays during a special promotion.

One retailer within the United Grocers (Berkeley, California) membership runs twice-a-year promotions, setting up its programs with points and dispatching judges to inspect each store's work and originality in product displays. United Grocers tracks store sales during the promotion, while its retailers run an inventory check at the end of the promotion to determine the winning store. Awards are presented to both the store with the top sales and the one with the best display. In a typical promotion, the retailer selects about 125 items to feature, creating shelf tags. The retailer explains: "We do supplies for four weeks, display for three weeks, then clean up with a hot sale. When the promotion ends, our supervisors take inventory, sales figures are checked—tracked electronically by our wholesaler—and we award prizes—gifts or vacation trips." The 1980 fall promotion of Bonnie Hubbard products netted this retailer a 30% increase in sales over the previous year.

Tom Thumb Supermarkets, Dallas, runs year-round private label incentive programs to help boost sales, giving awards to store managers for their merchandising and promotional efforts. Managers go all-out in developing effective merchandising effects: crepe paper letters to identify a product department, giant mannequin packages dangling over display cases, painted scenes over freezer cases, and wagon displays.

Such aggressiveness, however, is shunned by other retailers, who feel it's particularly insulting to both the consumer and the national brand to make price comparisons with signs. Instead they use other devices thought to be more subtle: "Try Our Brand" signs or special mannequins dressed in private label softwear or hosiery, for example. It is a matter of degree or attitude.

Bill Robinson, vice-president of private label sales at A&P, feels that

> private label has to be merchandised as compatible with the total operation. It can't be done at the expense of the operation. Side-by-side promotions—yes. But I don't think you can insult the consumer's intelligence by attacking her favorite name brand.
>
> A better approach to private label merchandising is what I call a flip–flop display, placing our spaghetti next to Ragu spaghetti sauce. If you took the traditional private label approach of putting our spaghetti sauce next to Ragu spaghetti sauce, I can tell you that nine times out of 10, the Ragu would sell out first. The following week, we would still have our private label on display. So instead, we put some of our macaroni or spaghetti with the Ragu and they both sell down. Why waste the first week of the promotion? We're trying to increase consumption of the commodity group. The name brand helps sell the private label, because they go together. One brand of soap powder can help the other brand of fabric softener. That's what we should do more of. The customer is smart. She knows quality. She'll buy something the first time on price. But no different than the national brand, a private label gets its repeat business on quality . . . .
>
> Another merchandising technique we've adopted is advertising a product commodity rather than the store brand private label. We do a moderate amount of this type of advertising. Coffee is a specific example (Robinson 1979).

Each retailer has his own merchandising strategies. With a flare for the dramatic, David Nichol, president of Loblaw Ontario (Canada), speaking at a generics seminar in Chicago, explained how his chain merchandises No Name generics, comprising some 300 items: "In our No Frills stores (limited assortment) where 50% of our noncommodity grocery sales are No Name items, we simply cut the cases and prominently display the items. In our 70,000-square-foot superstore, we cut pallets of No Name products right into the gondola. In addition, at our new superstores, we often use huge displays of No Name products cross-merchandised with deep-cut national specials."

Referring to one such display, featuring Coca-Cola surrounded by No Name snack items, Nichol asked his audience: "What does the largest display of Coca-Cola in the world look like? Like this. It's over 100,000 10-fluid ounces of Coke. We are selling this display for as long as it lasts for five cents a bottle plus deposit. A family can buy up to 12 bottles" (Nichol 1980).

According to Robert Gunn, founder and chairman of Gunn, Fish, Mead, Inc., New York, a marketing firm:

> a good annual promotion plan should be structured to approximately 2/3 of product at regular prices and 1/3 on promotions. . . . Many private label programs sell as much as 60% off price, which is a mistake. A strong promotion plan is keyed to: (1) generating trial purchase; (2) converting trial customers to regular users; (3) rewarding current users and encouraging pantry loading. To do this, you have to use a variety of devices over and above the price-off promotions. While price-off is certainly an extremely effective tool, if it is overused, the promotional price soon becomes the everyday price in the mind of your customer. When that happens, you will find that the only time you move any volume is when you lower your price. This is a situation we are now in the process of reversing for a major retailer through a structured promotional program which still utilizes price-offs, but also uses premiums, couponing, bonus packs, cross-couponing with other store brand products, and other techniques to round out the program (Gunn 1979).

A&P uses trial sizes to introduce new private label products to customers. The company also offers cents-off coupons, for example, A&P saltine crackers cross-couponed with A&P pantyhose or coffee with coffee filters.

One drug chain boosts health and beauty aid sales in private label by 50% through the use of sample-size giveaway packages of baby powder, baby shampoo, regular shampoo, toothpaste, mouthwash, and OTC cold and allergy relief remedies. Customers who purchased any health and beauty aid item at the check-out stand were given a sample size of the same product in private label. The checker explained that the customer could save more by purchasing the private label item, which is equal to or better in quality than the national brand. The private label items were guaranteed, with a money-back refund.

Camellia Foods, Norwalk, Virginia, has used cross-couponing for more than a year on its private label trash bags, offering 10-cents-off coupons inside the package, which helped to more than double the item movement with a 12% consumer response to the offer.

The options are endless on the ways to merchandise private label in the store. A retailer can adopt bag stuffers, telling consumers about the quality of private label products, including a coupon on their next private label purchase. The shopping bag itself can become a medium for private label advertising.

Circular handouts conveniently located in the store draw attention to special private label sales or new items.

Private label packaging can be flagged, tagged, or specially marked with decals or strips, attracting customer attention to a bonus pack, a refund or rebate offer, or a cents-off deal.

The store has advertising capability with voice-over ads announcing specials in private label or a private label sale. TV monitors with taped ads or helpful hints on using private label products, or even a demonstration of a cutting of private label against the national brand with consumer reaction to the taste, all serve as effective in-store advertising for private label.

Newspaper or store tabloids help to promote private label; brochures or pamphlets serve to explain the private label or generics program; charts or graphs with consumer information tied to private label ingredients or formulation are effective.

General Nutrition Center, Pittsburgh, Pennsylvania, a chain of over 750 health food retail outlets, specializing in vitamins, aggressively promotes its private label lines with signage and helpful information posters in each store. GNC's entire marketing thrust is contained in-store with point-of-purchase selling. A poster, for example, reads: "GNC Brands vs. National Brands. Compare our formulas with these and many other nationally advertised brands and save! You can save up to 50% when you buy the GNC brand." The poster includes the GNC brand items and prices listed next to comparable national brand prices.

The 160-store franchised Docktor Pet Center Chain, based in Andover, Massachusetts, creates a pet department store atmosphere, offering a complete line of animals and top-of-the-line private label products. Docktor seeks its own price point, often without a brand comparison; so its in-store merchandising strategy centers on offering better quality merchandise under its store brand name at a comparable price to national brands found elsewhere.

Regular monthly in-store promotions are conducted—win a free puppy, product or pet discounts, etc.—all backed with signage, ad slicks, displays, point-of-purchase and educational materials. Often livestock and products are promoted jointly. For example, the chain offers pet starter kits. Also, the company frequently includes regular aisle shelfing that promotes a "team sell," where the Docktor products are sold alongside a complementary national brand product: "Your Flea And Tick Prevention Team," featuring dog and cat shampoos, sprays, powders and dry bath under the Docktor label along with Zodiac tags and collars.

An extremely important part of Docktor's merchandising strategy is found in its store personnel, who wear white coats (useful to keep their clothes clean), helping to create a feeling of professionalism. In fact, many of the Docktor products are called professional: "Docktor Professional Skin and Coat Conditioner." This merchandising strategy is explained by Eugene H. Kohn, vice-president of Docktor Pet Centers: "The pet counselors in our store use suggestive sell for our private label. Our training is designed to teach this method. The compensation system is built around sales. In the extensive training process, they are told that the name on the door and on the products is the same. When they sell our product label, which is available only in our stores, it affords them the chance of capturing a repeat customer instead of having the customer go to the supermarket and buy a brand which is available in many locations (Kohn 1982).

EMPLOYEE INVOLVEMENT/COMMITMENT

One of the most critical areas in merchandising is employee commitment to the private label program. A customer often will ask about a product, and if the employee does not believe in the product quality, then interest and involvement are lost. The employee also should promote the product through suggestive selling. Lack of employee interest can be reflected in customer attitudes.

Employee involvement in a program entails convincing the employee that the private label lines are exactly what the signage and advertisements say: quality merchandise at a lower price.

When Gray Drug Stores, Cleveland, launched a "We're For You" promotion, which included a build-up of its private label skus, the chain conducted a special one-day seminar for all store managers, orienting them to the quality of the new Gray brands, the laboratory tests that back that quality, and the product guarantees. Suppliers of private label set up booths at the meeting to give managers a firsthand look at the products. There also was a briefing on the chain's merchandising strategies.

Gray followed up by giving some 3000 of its employees a special gift box, filled with seven different Gray brand products along with a questionnaire asking for their reaction to the products. The input was positive, including some good suggestions: Because one employee said she couldn't read a label too well, the packaging was changed (Kallach 1981).

FedMart, San Diego, California, has conducted seminar workshops to acquaint new employees, including people coming on board through acquisition of other stores, about its private label program. The suppliers are on hand with display booths for their products, while company personnel conduct film- and slide-lectures on the chain's philosophy about private label quality in order to reinforce employee commitment to that quality.

K&B Inc. of New Orleans launched its private label program with a point system for employees: "We paid the sales clerks for selling the private label merchandise," according to Saul Schneider, prescription and drug director:

> We had a simple system (when we started)—a double sticker, one indicating the price, the other indicating the PM that the sales person would get. They would tear that off and place it in a book. When they filled that out, the book would be redeemed by us for cash.
>
> We also have tied that into promotions, where we promote certain categories within a month, for example just promoting vitamins or cough-and-cold-related products and maybe pay double PMs for that period.
>
> People who attained a sales goal of X dollars over the sales period would be invited to a special dinner and awarded a certificate, pictures taken with the executives of the company. It was all necessary to kick off our private label program.
>
> We no longer do this, because private label areas sell well, so we don't feel we have to give those inducements. But it did start off that way in hard-hitting drives to make our people aware of the private label program.
>
> We also had a program where we would give or at a very special reduced price see that our employees had the private label, so they could use the product and get a better feel for it and be more confident in discussing it with customers when they came in (Schneider 1981, p.74).

Peoples Drug also works closely with employees to encourage private label sales. The chain has issued a four-page brochure outlining why its vitamins are important and offering suggestions on ways they can best sell the Peoples brand.

During the firm's Diamond Jubilee celebration, company executives visited stores looking for unusual displays or anything notable. Those people recognized received a certificate noting their extra effort. At the end of the promotion, Peoples selected 75 winners from a drum and treated them to a free weekend in Washington, D.C.

Walgreens, Chicago, now orients its employees to private label with a special 20-minute color videotape presentation, describing how private label helps to improve overall gross margins and build repeat sales. After outlining the selling strategies in product integration, pricing, tagging, and use of mini-shelf extenders, the presentation discusses different display strategies:

- drug and sundries racks, placed monthly and bimonthly
- vitamin displays—important, since 40% of the chain's private label sales come from vitamins
- basket fixtures, four or more placed monthly
- prepack displays, positioned for a month, featuring Walgreens branded products, providing better control since they are properly stocked beforehand

The presentation also offers clues to store personnel on selling private label, recommending a "low-key" personal approach. The sales person opens with a friendly greeting, offering to help the customer, even though the store is self-service.

In a slice-of-life exchange, the presentation shows how the salesperson can make a suggestive sell for private label. After finding out what the customer is looking for and what type of product, the Walgreens brand is mentioned as available in that product category. The salesperson then is instructed to:

1. Narrow the selection to a specific need, remembering that the values of the customer are not always determined by price.
2. Stress the features of the private label product.
3. Always place the product in the customer's hand.
4. Don't be pushy or present a high-pressure sell; instead, adopt a low-keyed personal approach.

The presentation also encourages employees to buy and use Walgreens products, allowing them a discount off the discounted private label price.

REFERENCES

Conte, J. 1979. How You Can "Clean Up" by Selling Private Label Powdered Laundry Detergent. *Private Label* Magazine, June-July, p. 56. E. W. Williams Publishing, New York.

Foster, K. 1979. Private Label First Aid Products Need Aggressive Marketing Tactics. *Private Label* Magazine, October-November, p. 30. E.W. Williams Publishing, New York.

Gunn, R. T. 1979. How To Increase Sales And Profits On Your Private Label Franchise. *Private Label* Magazine, August-September, pp. 62–63. E.W. Williams Publishing, New York.

Kallach, A. 1981. The Rebirth of Private Label at Gray Drug. *Private Label* Magazine, February-March, pp. 84, 86. E.W. Williams Publishing, New York.

Kohn, E. H. 1982. Private Label Is "Top Dog" at Docktor Pet Centers. *Private Label* Magazine, December-January, pp. 34–41. E.W. Williams Publishing, New York.

Nichol, D. 1980. Experts Critique Generics Impact. *Private Label* Magazine, June-July, pp.43–44. E.W. Williams Publishing, New York.

Peoples Drug. 1980. Peoples Drug: Leaders in Promoting Private Label: *Private Label* Magazine, February-March, pp. 48, 50. E.W. Williams Publishing, New York.

Private Label. 1979. How Shopping Basket Comparison Display Boosts Private Label Sales for Safeway. *Private Label* Magazine, June-July, p. 31. E.W. Williams Publishing, New York.

Robinson, B. 1979. Troubled A&P Chain Gets Private Label Face Lifting, Part II. *Private Label* Magazine, June-July, pp. 44–45. E.W. Williams Publishing, New York.

Schneider, S. H. 1981. PLMA Convention: Merchandising Is Not Limited to Retailers Only. *Private Label* Magazine, April-May, pp. 73–74. E.W. Williams Publishing, New York.

Walgreens. 1979. Looking Behind the "100% Guaranteed" Walgreens Label. *Private Label* Magazine, June-July, p. 29. E.W. Williams Publishing, New York.

11

The Key to Marketing: A Quality Image

How does the consumer perceive private label? In the past, private label's market image was projected primarily within the store. A store label was considered a price brand, offered as an alternative choice to consumers shopping the store for nationally advertised brands. The private brand for the most part was not advertised outside the store. Today, the new role of private label as a quality alternative to the national brand calls for a new strategy in marketing.

Retailers now realize more than ever that their quality private label lines can build and reinforce the store image. Private label's quality image directly relates to the store image, which the consumer perceives as an outlet for quality merchandise. Private label can reinforce that image through advertising and frequent and timely promotions.

Retailers of the old school (and there are some still around) thought that only national brand merchandise could project a quality image for their store. But there were some pioneering retailers who developed quality private label programs that the consumer came to recognize, trust, and support. Many of these retailers—Sears, Kroger, Walgreens—over the years established their private label as a brand, not necessarily national in scope, but in quality equal to the best that national brand manufacturers could offer. In some cases, their private brands were superior to the national brands.

Some retailers pioneered in marketing, beginning with mail order catalogs, then advertising in magazines and newspapers and finally in the broadcast media. A&P reportedly became the first food retailer to advertise on radio in 1924, talking about its brands of coffee and bakery items. In 1937, A&P launched *Woman's Day* magazine for the express purpose of advertising its private label lines. Eventually, that publication became one of the leading consumer magazines in the country (now under separate ownership).

Early in the 1950s, Shurfine-Central Corp., a Midwest co-op, became a user of regional TV, sponsoring what it believes was the first feature-length movie shown on TV. Its ads were focused on the Shurfine line of products.

PROJECTING THE MAJOR BRAND

The marketing strategies now being learned by some retailers were in practice decades ago by other merchants. By the 1950s, First National Stores, Somerville, Massachusetts, had become one of the strongest private label retailers in the country. The company was formed by a merger of three grocery chains in 1925, bringing together a number of private labels. The chain then evolved with different labels assigned to various product categories—coffee, canned vegetables, dairy. After World War II, those brands were consolidated under one label, called Finast (one of the predecessor brands) an acronym for the chain's name, First National Stores. Finast products stood for quality equal to the national brands. The chain also kept other brands with strong equity built into them: Somerville for standard vegetables, Richmond for extra standard products, Brookside Farms for dairy items. The company at the time also began development of a new label, Yor Garden, which represented not quality equal to the national brands, but the finest quality available: Blue Lake beans from the Northwest, for example. This extra or superior quality line of products became "almost a national brand in New England, as far as top of the line goes on fruits and vegetables as well as frozen foods," according to John W. MacNeil, former president of the chain (now vice-president of Norwegian Preserving, Inc., Waltham, Massachusetts):

> We adopted the quality standards of the brands for the Finast label. If we couldn't match that quality, we put it under the Richmond or Somerville label. Our private label philosophy then was that the program must gear itself to a superior consumer value and at the same time project itself into the other levels of production. In other words,

> Del Monte couldn't be active in standard peas; but our private label program allowed us to reach into the big value areas of production. With a multitier program, we could be successful in marketing the value of our various quality levels. . . . In essence, private label could offer the consumer a superior range of quality, which the national brands could not do.

In those days, First National Stores projected its major store brand, Finast, making consumers aware that that brand could be purchased in its stores. The consumer directly identified the Finast brand with the image of the store. "Below that level," MacNeil believes, "you can market the secondary labels in-store. You sell or market the concept and do your real merchandising inside the store: You advertise the quality image of private label, then sell the products in-store through space allocation, product placement, number of facings, use of end aisle displays, and effective use of store operations."

One of the major shortcomings of some retailers in private label marketing is the tendency of the private label buyer to become too price conscious. Says MacNeil:

> When the buyer nickel and dimes it and that philosophy spreads throughout the house, then it's symptomatic that they're out to squeeze private label: they keep the retails too close to the brands; the quality is reduced; and the basic value isn't there anymore. You can squeeze short-term gains out of private label by shopping around; but then you start to negate the basic quality theme that you've projected in your marketing effort for your major house brand. When that happens, the consumer recognized the change. Although individually, she may not be as smart, collectively, they're brilliant. They see the product, they taste it, they feel it, and they start to reflect on the downgrading of its quality to the downgrading of the chain itself.
>
> Buyers today must be very cognizant of the merchandising–marketing theme of private label and buy consistently with that theme. Some chains will literally go out of stock, if they can't buy according to the standards set by the chain. This is an awareness by the buyer that his policy is sound. You cannot compromise with private label quality. If you want to sell lower quality, then you get into a multitier program. You may emphasize the lower or higher tiers more in the store, while you sell the quality concept in your marketing effort. That's how you work the mix. You must be consistent and loyal to the quality concept of each of the tiers all the time. Private label takes self-discipline. It has to be marketed, has to be worked. No one will take care of your labels, but the merchandiser of the wholesaler or the chain operator. If the private label buyer is not forceful in the projection and protection of his own brand, then it's bound to be diminished in importance; and the national brands will quickly move in on any vacuum.
>
> The chains that do not have a good internal relationship between the private label marketing and merchandising staff and store operations will have a difficult time. This relationship is essential to the long-term successful private label program.

The importance of adopting and sticking by a philosophy was stressed by Glenn Fischer, Director of Procurement, Wetterau, Inc., Hazelwood, Missouri, a multidivision wholesaler at a private label workshop at FMI's 1981 convention:

A suggested philosophy statement might be as follows: "Our private label will be of equal or better quality than the best selling national or regional brands within our marketing area. We will return our customer, the retailer, a profit greater than the brands, and we will offer the consumer a recognizable value which will reinforce our identity. Our generic items will be of acceptable quality at the lowest price possible."

You must gain a commitment from every department within your organization and their objectives must be set to achieve these goals.

Your procurement or buying department should be constantly aware of the quality which you have available under your private label, as continuity of quality is important, because once a consumer is convinced to buy your private label, changes in quality are not readily accepted or appreciated. . . .While quality of generics is not as important as it is in your private label, the quality under generics must be acceptable.

Private label suppliers must be urged to develop long-range promotional schedules, not from the standpoint that an exact per-case allowance be made known, but awareness of promotional activity on particular items will exist on a preplanned schedule. Your procurement department must work in close coordination with your advertising department to guarantee and develop opportunities for private label products.

Your advertising department must support private label on a regular basis within the advertising media which you normally use. Again, advertising and procurement must work together to develop these opportunities.

The nationally accepted standard of approximately 80%−20% brand to private label works well in our ads and, in addition, once per quarter we tell our private label story by reversing these percentages 20% branded items and 80% private label items (Fischer 1981).

MARKETING DEFINED

The store is a place to achieve the objectives of marketing: filling the needs and desires of the consumer with guaranteed, satisfactory merchandise. Broadly speaking, marketing encompasses the entire flow of merchandise from manufacture to its sale in the store. Specifically, marketing refers to the retailers' efforts to research the marketplace (the competition, trends, product market share), then adapt his quality, pricing, product mix, promotional and advertising efforts to remain competitive.

Marketing is a sophisticated discipline, sometimes difficult to define exactly. It deals with market share, market potential, consumer attitudes toward a store and its products, sales forecasting, market analysis, new product feasibility studies, test market activities, advertising research, and promotional activities. When compared to the marathon pace of the national brands, private label retailers have barely learned to crawl in the marketing area.

Yet, today's private label retailer is becoming more involved in some of these areas, tracing market trends, national brand market shares, changes in the marketplace, consumer trend shifts, and advertising and promotional activity by the competition. The expense of costly and time-consuming market research studies forces most retailers to follow the lead established by the market leaders, the national brands. Private label is not a trendsetter in the marketplace. Generally, retailer and wholesalers tend to target not so much on the consumer as on the national brands, which, in turn, have set the consumer as their objective. Private label adopts a sort of once-removed marketing strategy. It is a strategy, however, that does not always meekly follow the lead of the national brands.

Private labels began their marketing effort mostly as a price brand, not standing on their own merit, but rather in the shadow of the national brand, using that as a reference point, offering the consumer equal quality but with the option of a lower price. While the quality was there, it was not marketed aggressively—not until recent years.

Today, private label also sells that quality image to the consumer, reinforcing the message with marketing clout. Retailers and wholesalers are exercising that clout in different ways with new marketing strategies in advertising, promotions, consumer surveys, and consumer test panels. Their marketing efforts no longer are restricted to local newspapers; now bold ads appear on highway billboards, on network television, and in popular magazines like *Time* and *TV Guide.*

The once-buried mention of private label in a newspaper ad is now headlined in bold print across 16 column inches, side-by-side with the leading national brands. Full-color sections or truck spreads feature nothing but private label. Retailers and wholesalers are stepping up the frequency of their private label promotions, backed with effective advertising.

Store employees and customers are now being recruited as part of consumer testing projects to measure their response to a new private label line, for example. Efforts are underway to involve the retailer more in primary market research: the self-generated analysis of his customers, giving up-to-date marketing data.

Retailers also are upgrading their secondary market research data, as more information becomes available from outside research firms as well as suppliers. Retailers/wholesalers now subscribe to computerized printout data of product movement in their markets. They also track warehouse product withdrawals to stores and with electronic scanners in stores receive stock sales on a weekly basis. Early in the 1970s, Selling Areas-Marketing, Inc., New York, began tracking private label product movement in supermarkets as part of its regular market research reports. In 1981, SAMI issued its first comprehensive generics study, showing its dollar volume exceeding $1 billion, while capturing a 0.6% share of annual U.S. food store volume in April 1981, climbing by 0.1% since November 1980. Actually, SAMI showed generics climbing by 155.1% since April 1979, when sales were only $452.1 million (SAMI 1981).

A. C. Nielsen Co., Chicago, began to collect data on generics in mid-

1978 and first released its report at the 1979 Food Marketing Institute's Convention in Dallas. Every other year, Nielsen completes a National Consumer Attitude Towards Product Performance Study, covering 1000 U.S. homes via WATS telephone interviews with consumers who have received premailed material. Additional questions were included in January 1979, covering awareness, purchase, and intent to repurchase generic grocery products. Six out of 10 consumers interviewed were aware of generics; and of that number, 44% had purchased a generic product. Of those who tried generics, more than 70% said they would buy it again. Another 16 points in the survey qualified that by saying it "depends on the product."

In its 1979–1980 National Study of Supermarket Shoppers, the research firm Burgoyne, Inc., Cincinnati, reported that 60.2% of consumers rated private label equal to national brands; and of the 37.8% who purchased generics, most were from larger families. Interestingly, the firm found than 60.9% of respondents pointed to the elimination of advertising costs as the reason why private labels are priced lower than national brands, as opposed to the quality not being as good or consistent (31.1%) (Burgoyne 1980).

For the first time in 1980, Towne–Oller & Associates, Inc., New York, began to track private label and generic health and beauty aid product movement from warehouse to food stores. In eight product categories, private label gained in all but two (mouthwash and shampoo) while generics gained across the board, according to second-quarter results—1981 versus 1980. While private label registered significant dollar gains—vitamins and tonics up 123.7% and deodorants up 89.7%—generics gobbled up spectacular gains—analgesics up 569.2%, nail polish removers up 741.4%, vitamins and tonics up 1772%.

The North-American Wholesale Grocers Association, New York, surveyed its membership recently to discover that 76% of the country's wholesale food distributors are now carrying generics, with sales up 60% in 1980. Some 138 NAWGA members responded; of the number carrying generics, 40% started in 1980, 12% in 1979, and 14% in 1978 (NAWGA 1981).

The data keeps piling up, mostly on generics, because it represents a new marketing phenomenon; yet researchers are also tracking private label as part of their reports. Their interest is sparked by the fact that generics have had more impact on national brand market share—eroding its commanding lead, as minor or secondary national or regional brands disappear.

Current economic conditions appear to favor products that represent a lower cost but an equal or acceptable value. Both private label and generics tend to grow in this climate. Consumers, too, have become smarter shoppers, looking for value for their dollar. It is not likely that they will

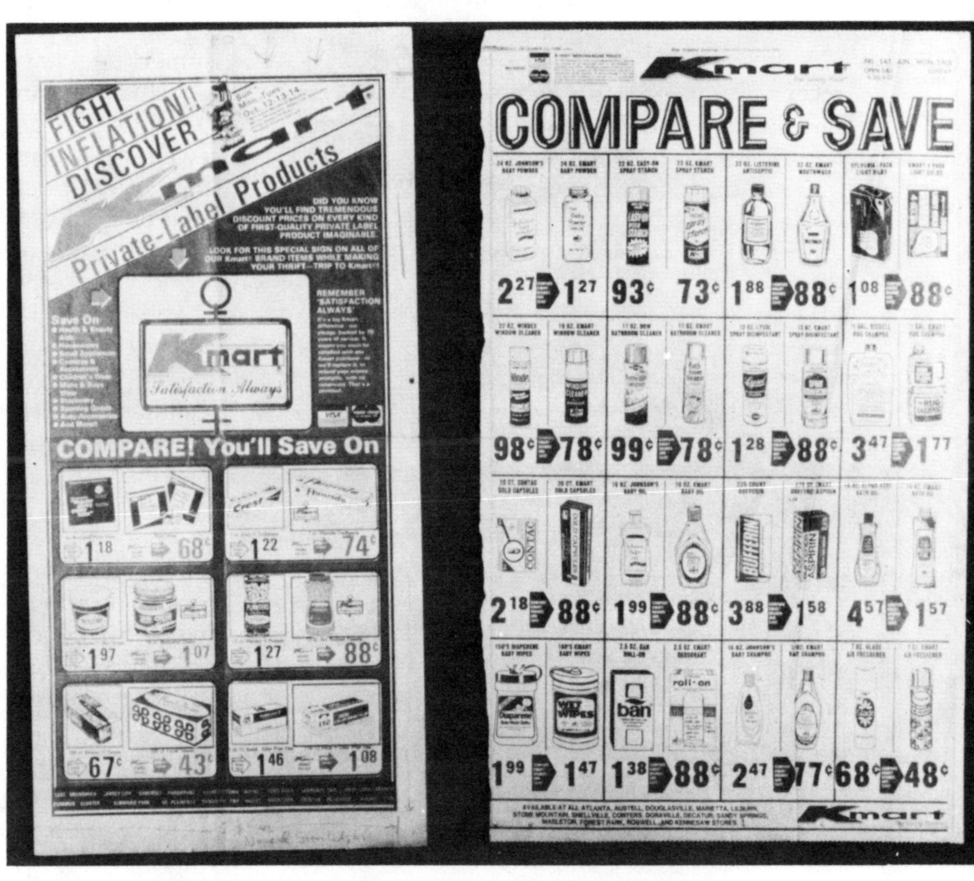

In one of the most impressive private label ads (left) ever run by K mart, a special four-page sectional, placed by a regional office, featured 57 different private label products, the most ever promoted in a single ad, including many items never before advertised. The other ad (right) shows a full-page compare-and-save pitch, matching K mart items against leading national brands.

Waldbaum's (New York) offers shoppers $5 worth of coupons to an amusement area in this tie-in promotion on its 10-pound detergent package.

ShopRite Consumer Buying Guide

Description: Baby Wash Cloths are a convenient soft towelette, moistened with a mild cleansing solution containing lanolin, to gently clean any part of baby's delicate skin after feeding or at changing time.

Storage: Keep lid tightly closed. Store at room temperature.

Directions: Snap open small cap, remove and discard foil seal. Tip of first sheet is exposed and ready for use. Pull sheet out at an angle and snap off. The next one pops up. If necessary to restart roll, pull up on cap ring to remove cover of container. Then pull up corner of center sheet of roll, twist it to a point, and thread it through dispenser hole in cover. It's as simple as threading a needle! Replace cover. Pull each sheet out at an angle. Dispose of each sheet after use.

Hints: Can be used for the whole family when away from soap and water. Handy for make-up removal, car trips, picnic, work or play.

Ingredients: Water, SD Alcohol 40, Propylene Glycol, Sorbic Acid, Sodium Monoxynol Phosphate, Oleth 20, PEG/75 Lanolin, Disodium Phosphate, Citric Acid, Fragrance.

Distributed By
Wakefern Food Corporation
Elizabeth, N.J. 07207 ©1979
Made in U.S.A.

The customer who buys ShopRite baby wash cloths gets a 50 cents bonus coupon on the next purchase of ShopRite diapers.

Coupon ads in newspapers are not uncommon for retailers, who sometimes carry the coupon offer onto in-store signage, as in this Stop & Shop 40-cents coupon discount.

Ralph's Grocery gives customers a discount on a national brand, Coke, when they buy Ralph's brand of peanuts.

automatically switch back to national brands when and if the economy improves. Stretching dollars can become habit-forming, especially when the consumer is satisfied with what is purchased.

Today, retailers and wholesalers are bolder about promoting their private label and generic lines. One buyer notes: "It's always of benefit to us if we're advertising a national brand to expose our private label brand to reference the price comparison and savings. . . ." The frequency of promotions has picked up sharply in recent years, as reflected in advertising trends.

Never before has a standard grade or acceptable quality product been advertised so aggressively or frequently. Generics literally steal the space and time of the brands; in fact, for some retailers, generics get top billing over the private label lines.

Private label advertising perhaps gets its greatest airing through promotions. Woolworth's, for example, features its private label items in promotions, cutting the prices to give customers an even better value on the already low price. Its newspaper ads are backed by strong in-store promotional treatment: extra displays, window signs, special setups near the front of the store. The company also advertises on TV and reaches a captive audience, its stockholders, through direct mail pieces featuring private label.

Department stores, when billing their charge or mail order customers, use enclosures, often tied to private label promotions. Even a 2% return on a mail circulation of 200,000 is considered good.

Stop & Shop Companies schedules two major private label campaigns per year in its supermarket chain, one in the fall and one in January, both featuring private label items. Then the chain can go for weeks or months not featuring any great amount of private label items. The company keeps an eye on national brand promotions and their effects on its private label market share. Stop & Shop stands ready to counter a national brand promotion with a private label promotion to maintain its market share.

Piggly Wiggly Corp., Jacksonville, Florida, conducts private brand sales four times a year, when its customers are offered something for nothing: "Red Hot" bargains, such as 59-cent gallon bottles of bleach at a "bonus saving special" of 9 cents; or free five-pound bags of sugar with the purchase of a four-pack of its 60, 70, or 100 watt soft white light bulbs. Loss leaders work as traffic builders, where items are offered at rock bottom prices or free; while the retailer gets the product on special deal by the carload at a favorable price. The effort is backed up with newspaper ads and end-aisle displays and signage.

The promotion can center on a product category, such as vitamins. Associated Grocers of Seattle, Washington, reports boosting its private label vitamin sales by 70% with a special back-to-school vitamin campaign, using a coupon ad in the regional edition of *TV Guide*, backed with local radio spots and in-store flyers. Its "Vita-Money" coupon offer of 25 cents off any vitamin purchase was a complete success.

Bill Matteucci, vice-president and director of merchandising at Matteucci's Super Saver Drugs, Great Falls, Montana, told a PLMA seminar on vitamins that his chain had relied on many newspapers, but was now switching to circular advertising mail.

> It's very expensive, but we believe in it. We direct mail in the neighborhood anywhere from 30 to 46 flyers a year—and in every one of the flyers, we will have a vitamin ad. Every month, we run a full page on vitamins. We coordinate this with our vendor at least three to six months ahead of time, so that our store managers know what's going to be on promotion and so that we have everything in the store when it's being promoted.
>
> Besides this, we have annual promotions. They follow our monthly and weekly promotions. Our end-caps have to be signed. Merchandise will sell spontaneously off the shelves, if you're signed properly—and not depending only on your advertising.
>
> All this can fail, if you don't get management commitment from the top level down to the store manager and the pharmacist. We have sales drives and contests within our stores for the pharmacists and store managers, centered around our private label vitamin promotions. The prize is a trip to Hawaii. It is a very expensive drive, but we feel it is very beneficial to our total commitment. (Matteucci 1980).

The co-op Shurfine-Central Corp. conducts three to six major promotional efforts yearly in addition to its continual daily and weekly allowances. A major effort can encompass from 200 to 400 private label items offered on allowances, tying in every possible media: newspapers, magazines, radio–TV, point-of-sale. Shurfine members can pick up materials from the co-op.

Roger Humbert, vice-president and director of merchandising, explains that this strategy is targeted to markets where the co-op's retailers operate:

> We don't go network TV, because we're not national in scope. Instead we buy network TV on a regional basis. Actually, we trigger the promotion, spending only a few hundred thousand dollars for a given TV show to put it on, while our retailers literally spend millions of dollars to supplement it. They not only buy TV where they're located, but also radio (we furnish the spots) as well as newspapers, handbills, mailers, magazine supplements, etc. We furnish the materials, they customize it.
>
> Today we do our own production work on TV specials, featuring stars like Wayne Newton, Julie Andrews, and Carol Lawrence. We go out into the markets and buy one hour of prime time in approximately 90 markets and air the special in prime time. This is used as a catalyst to trigger our retailers to get out there and do something.
>
> We do a lot of things differently from most advertisers in this market. I don't go to work with an agency like J. Walter Thompson or attempt to support a huge office. We work with a small agency. In many instances, we do much of the work ourselves. We wear a lot of different hats. For example, we produce our own shows rather than go to a Universal or 20th Century Fox. We do our own commercials; we attempt to do everything on a low budget.
>
> We work on the idea of possibly doing pilots, working with people who are looking

to get a start. We've built these kinds of relationships not only in the food business, but also in advertising and in the entertainment world. And in everything we do, we look for the best value (Humbart 1980).

A co-op recently presented its retailers with a selection of five major promotions and eight mini-promotions yearly, offering them the opportunity to exclusively push the private label brand. They can promote throughout the year or selectively. Each sale is scheduled for two weeks. The company's support includes ad art slicks and product slicks designed for most items on deal; free point-of-purchase kits with signs, banners, shelf-talkers, and danglers; and special treatment materials. For example, in a Big Top Days promotion, the store owner can order clown suits, hats and striped blazers for employees with balloons, lollipops, tissue balls, garlands, and ringmaster whistles.

To reinforce the message of its private label quality, Zodys, Los Angeles, began preparing a special presentation for the firm's semiannual merchandising seminar, scheduled a year after the launch of the chain's new private label program. To prepare material for the presentation, the chain worked through its marketing department and recruited store personnel to conduct a consumer survey on private label.

Over the weekend in January 1979, at two store locations, customers were intercepted and given a free package of 15 private label items. They also received a form to jot down their likes and dislikes about the products and whether they thought the private label item was better than the national brand. Within two to three weeks after trying the products the customers were contacted by phone and interviewed.

Phone interviews were conducted with 100 customers; of that number, a dozen of the most complete and interesting respondents were selected to participate in a consumer panel discussion. This exchange was videotaped and presented as a two-hour show for the merchandising seminar.

Frank Newman, divisional merchandise manager, notes that "random samplings were used in the survey to get a good cross-section of people—young, old, families, singles, ethnic groups, etc.—a good sampling of our customers. The results showed that no private label product, except toothpaste, was rated below 70% favorable. Most products fell into a range of between 80 and 100% favorable. . . . The toothpaste, however, failed because of its taste. This product since has been reformulated."

While the company used an independent consumer research lab, most of its own in-house resources were applied to the market research effort, according to Newman (1980).

Zodys relies heavily on tabloid advertising, where its weekly circulation can reach up to 3.6 million people. Other retailers and wholesalers mix their selection or are selective.

On the West Coast, for example, United Grocers in Oakland recently launched a multimedia advertising program, promoting the theme, "Local Girl Makes Good," using the message on its trucks, on radio, in newspaper ads, and point-of-sale materials.

Alpha Beta, La Habra, California, for the past several years has stuck to radio and TV advertising primarily, selling Alpha Beta brand as an idea or a group of products. The chain does not use print ads, where products and prices are listed.

In 1978, Certified Grocers of California Ltd., Los Angeles, launched an innovative outdoor advertising campaign designed to display its Springfield quality image, "Love the quality," using mammoth outdoor displays of individually painted billboards that were rotated monthly throughout Certified's primary trading areas. The campaign is said to reach more than 90% of all marketplace adults 35 times a year. The effort also is cost efficient. Posters and radio commercials supplemented the campaign. The billboards also help make customers aware of the new Springfield label design, which works to whet appetite appeal with, for example, slices of pineapple flowing out of a massive can.

REFERENCES

Burgoyne, Inc. 1980. Consumers Rate Private Label and Generic Quality "Equal to or Better Than" National Brands: Burgoyne. *Private Label* Magazine, August-September, p. 45. E.W. Williams Publishing, New York.

Fischer, G. 1981. Getting the Most out of Your Private Label (and Generics) Program. *Private Label* Magazine, June-July, pp. 56–58. E.W. Williams Publishing, New York.

Humbert, R. 1980. Private Labels: The Lifeblood of Shurfine-Central. *Private Label* Magazine, February-March, pp. 14–15. E.W. Williams Publishing, New York.

Matteucci, B. 1980. PLMA Fall Meeting: New Developments in Private Label Vitamins. *Private Label* Magazine, October-November, pp. 20, 24. E.W. Williams Publishing, New York.

NAWGA. 1981. 76% of Food Wholesalers Carry Generics, No-Frills Sales Up 60%: NAWGA Survey. *Private Label* Magazine, April-May, p. 65. E.W. Williams Publishing, New York.

Newman, F. 1980. Zodys Rejuvenates Its Private Labels. *Private Label* Magazine, February-March, pp. 29–30. E.W. Williams Publishing, New York.

SAMI. 1981. Generic Sales Top One Billion Dollars, Capture 0.6% of Food Store Sales. *Private Label* Magazine, June-July, p. 8. E.W. Williams Publishing, New York.

12

Fitting in Generics

Do generics fit in? Many manufacturers, retailers, and wholesalers still would like to see these standard grade or acceptable quality products, packaged in plain black and white, one-color, or multicolor wrapping disappear. Generics do not produce as much profit as private labels. This can vary geographically from high to low margins. They do not always carry a quality image. Also, they are handled differently at the retail level. A generics program has its own set of rules, many of which are still being written. Not yet 5 years old, generic products continue to seek their level in the marketing mix. Different theories or philosophies have evolved about how generics should be merchandized and marketed.

To some retailers generics represent a powerful marketing-merchandizing weapon, perfect for drawing in additional customer traffic; for others, generics are an uncomfortable but necessary evil, rubbing against their quality store image.

This controversial category developed as a trade reaction to consumerism, first introduced and still positioned as a low-cost, good value alternative to national brands. The consumer today needs and wants a price break. If that means compromising on quality, so be it. In fact, historically the consumer is not a stranger to compromised quality. As long as the quality of merchandise is good, wholesome, nutritious, acceptable, or serviceable—with the price set at a rock-bottom level—then generics do have a place in the market. Ironically, some manufactured generic products are of a quality equal to national brands, but are positioned at a lower price and as such are considered of lower quality.

Consumerist Ralph Nader, speaking at the 1980 PLMA Annual Meeting and Trade Show in Chicago, put his finger on the pulse of this issue: "Consumers should only have to pay for what they use. They shouldn't have to pay billions of dollars for promotional, nonfunctional advertising." Nader also warned his audience that "private label might want to get a little bit more pretty and have a little more frills. Maybe they will see a need for expanding the advertising and promotions. Soon the gap will be narrower and narrower. By interlocking yourself with consumer interests, you can prevent this from happening. Then the quality of the economy goes up, innovation goes up, and competition stays healthy" (Nader 1980).

Private label is evolving as a brand and as such is becoming competitive with national brands in terms of advertising and packaging. Private labels are getting "prettier"; the frills are inescapable, especially when the retailer/wholesaler must compete on the same quality level as the national brands. Meanwhile, generics, as an extension of private label, are filling in the gap of no frills—a plain look that conveys the message of being less expensive. In other words, generics are evolving as a private label.

Today's no frills mentality is evident in different areas—travel, real estate, foodservice, fashion/cosmetics—as part of a worsening economy. Generics are merely in step with the times. They represent products that give the consumer the lowest cost alternative. Consumers should be allowed to pay more for the hype or sizzle of national brands, promoted through advertising and packaging; they should be permitted to trade down in price but not necessarily in quality with private labels; and they should be offered a third choice—acceptable quality at the lowest possible price.

In a sense, generics sneaked in the back door of the retailing world, stirring up controversy over whether they should be added. Retailers/wholesalers still argue over the merits of a generics program or how to make generics presentable to the consumer. Attempts are underway to upgrade packaging and quality, to introduce discipline to the program—consistent quality, more attractive packaging, a private label name and a value (not price) image. Strong marketing support also is being applied. Yet generics appear to be strongest not when they attempt to duplicate private label or national brand activities, but when they stick to their initial thrust: cut-to-the-bone price, packaging, and sometimes quality.

Today's shopper is no longer as naive as some believe. No one knows better about *caveat emptor* than today's modern consumer. She is willing to try different products, willing to experiment to make a product work for her. If contents are not beautifully symmetrical, perfectly colored, evenly sized, does it matter when this product is used in a casserole or stew? Perhaps a little seasoning can help disguise an otherwise bland flavor. Generics test the shopper's creative abilities; in fact, they offer her a challenge to become ingenious. She does not always have to be led around by pampered senses with built-in guaranteed top quality. The fun of discovery, of making a lower priced bargain item work as well, of realizing a significant savings on something useful—all of this becomes psychologically more forceful and effective than just paying extra dollars for something expected. Generics satisfy consumers in this respect.

Edward H. Sussman, president of the No. 1 Marketing Group, Sharon, Massachusetts, pointed to performance as the consumer's most important consideration in the decision to buy generics. Distrust or questions over generic quality were of secondary importance, according to findings in a recent consumer survey of 1100 women in the Boston market.

Speaking at the PLMA's Second Annual Trade Show and Educational Conference, held in Chicago in October 1981, Sussman noted that the study focused on purchasing patterns in generic health and beauty aids. It was discovered that Black and Hispanic customers did not accept the generics as readily as their White counterparts, because the former groups felt generics were not specialized for their needs. Those women who bought generic foods felt they could alter that product's taste; but they indicated there was no such option with generic shampoo, for example.

Interestingly, he noted, many of the women could quote the exact penny savings they realized with generics, but could not quote the price they paid for the product: "The retail price may not have as much impact as showing the comparison saving, because that is the one she perceives as being put into her pocket. No matter how low the price is, they are paying that out of pocket. Paying out is a negative. Savings is a positive." Most respondents, he added, said they switched from national brand to generics mainly because of price (Sussman 1981).

DEVELOPING TRENDS

The story on generics is still being written. Much of its activity centers around testing and experimentation. The track record is too short to draw conclusions about its development. Generics do not have the long history of private label or national brands. Yet some basic trends in generics have surfaced, which by no means should be taken as law. Many retailers/wholesalers develop their own strategies, depending on different merchandising–marketing perspectives. Some common generic developments include the following.

- Products frequently are graded standard or acceptable quality; the move to extra standard or fancy in commodities depends on the season and product availability. Some nonfood items can be equal in quality to private label and national brand products.
- Packages are preferable in black and white or one color appearing as a band, stripe, or background in order to achieve a plain, economical look. Some retailers/wholesalers have packaged generics as another private label, using attractive graphics and a name (suggesting economy).
- Containers are sized to the leading national brand in a category or made larger to offer the customer more value; no more than one size per category is adopted, but there are some exceptions.
- Generics as a knock-off of the leading national brand or the top-volume mover in a product category can command a higher market share in that category.
- Products are priced at the lowest level possible, with the price fixed; usually no deals, coupons, or reduced prices are offered, since the customer must recognize the initial price as the lowest possible price. (Generics, however, can sometimes serve as a loss leader.)
- Products are sourced from different packers, although the recent expansion of generic activity has led to some "one-stop shopping" in certain general categories.
- Generics are frequently grouped together in a mass display, positioned in a high traffic area: products that sell mostly on impulse are better shown in multiple mixed facings, reinforcing one another as an economy sell. (A retailer who integrates generics into regular shelfing by category, sometimes will mass display generics in larger stores where more space is available.)
- Generic displays often are flagged with signage that stresses the savings in terms of percentage below the national brand.
- Items are sold honestly, telling the customer exactly what the quality is in the advertising, merchandising, and packaging.
- Effective use is made of aisle-long displays or store-within-a-store merchandising concepts to reinforce the low-price image with a stark, no-frills environment.
- Aggressive advertising supports generics, often featuring one or two items, especially introductions to the line, to make customers aware of a growing, diversified selection.

- The move is toward more consistent quality—if possible the best available at the lowest price.
- Products are being packaged more uniformly (product category to product category) in the same size containers, if possible, to realize savings in production costs.
- In-store continuing education program make consumers (including new customers) aware of generics quality and pricing through pamphlets and newsletters.

Generic development started in some basic grocery categories, including canned foods, prepared foods, paper items, and household chemicals. Eventually, the program was expanded to include health and beauty aids, frozen foods, prepared meats, produce, and general merchandise. Today, anyone starting a program can pick and choose with no restrictions on the type of products.

Generics have evolved into three types of packaging: a simple black-and-white label or *true generics*, listing only the generic name (i.e., tea); a *semigeneric package* or middle-ground treatment featuring some color and/or a specific brand identity (i.e., Topco's Tru Value, Pathmark's No Frills, Ralph's Plain Wrap); and *imitation generics* or merchandise marketed like generics but carrying a private label (i.e., Safeway's Scotch Buy, Kroger's Cost Cutter, or Winn-Dixie's Price Breaker).

The true generic label relies strictly on the mix of a white background with black lettering, sometimes including gray or a black stripe or symbol for distinctive graphics. This label is identified only by its generic name and, more recently also by the packer's name. These products are perceived by the customer to be available in any store and, by definition, are not true private labels, but instead packer labels (available to anyone) although the retailer/wholesaler sources, merchandises, and advertises them like his own brands.

The semigeneric label is distinctly claimed by a retailer or wholesaler, who stamps the generic line with a recognizable color design or color background, sometimes adding a distinctive name. Overall, the label is kept plain, mostly white or yellow in the background.

The imitation generic label is a private label, drawing on more sophisticated color and graphics, carrying a store brand name along with a guarantee of consistent quality at a favorable price. These products are merchandised like other generics labels, but frequently are integrated into all store aisles like private labels.

Of course, specific generic labels are difficult to classify. Topco's Tru Value, for example, is black-and-white, but has a brand identity—Tru Value—on the label. The label is plain white with distinctive black print and a unique type style with a rounded seal "Valu Time, Specification Approved" along with an explanatory statement about the product quality and its uses listed on the main panel.

Pathmark has adopted a blue-and-red stripe, flanking its "No Frills" identity on the label.

Loblaws Ontario avoided a white label, picking instead a yellow background with black printing. The category was called No Name, so no name appears on the label, except for the distributor's identity, Sunfresh Limited.

Ralph's Grocery, Los Angeles, picked a white label with blue lettering and a blue stripe, bordered with black for its identity. The category is called Plain Wrap, but not identified that way on the label.

Vons Grocery Co., El Monte, California, dubbed its generics "Slim Price," identified as such on the labels with a red tag and white lettering, all against a white background.

Plain white labels, sometimes with touches of color, have been adopted by a number of other chains and wholesalers: IGA's Much More, Weis Markets' The Way it Was, Foodtown's No Brand, Stop & Shop's Economy, Grand Union's Basics, Wakefern Food/Shop-Rite's Money Savings Brands (M$B).

Generics actually started in the United States as a semigeneric package. The concept originated that way in France in 1976, when Carrefour, a major retailer, introduced a private label line called Produits Libre (Brand Free)—a white label with a blue-and-red stripe plus the Carrefour logo. At the time, the trend in Europe was toward reduced brand names.

When Jewel Companies, Chicago, copied the Carrefour concept, it was adapted to Jewel's standard grade, acceptable quality products, identified as a generic private label family of basic bargains—the "no brand name" alternative. The chain already had a well-established top quality private label program. Jewel made the generic packaging plain white with a drab green and black stripe, admittedly calling it a dull, plain package. The firm said: "Since there is no fancy packaging or advertising and Jewel is able to buy standard grades in large quantities from manufacturers, our costs are less. These savings are passed directly on to you (the customer)."

Other retailers/wholesalers began to copy Jewel, picking up on its idea of a plain wrap, no-frills concept, but with variations in the packaging to distinguish their generic lines.

The U.S. orientation toward brands did not encourage a move toward "brand free" totally. Brand names did start to appear on the generic packaging, beginning with Valu Time and No Frills. (Recently, as generics have become more acceptable in the marketplace, there has been an increase in the number of packer label generics.)

In 1978, A&P became the first major chain to adopt generics in a true

A paradox in the making: "No Brand Brands." Many retailers have adopted a simple design package for generics without any brand name.

The generics phenomenon has spread to practically every product category—dairy, produce, meats, etc.

This end aisle display of Grand Union Basics generic items is promoted under the theme, Super Summer Savings.

Topco's Valu Time beer reportedly is a popular generic item.

Stop & Shop's Economy cola stretches out in multiple facings along a bottom shelf display.

Kroger's answer to generics is Cost Cutter—a yellow background label with black print and a black logo with red handled scissors.

In a center aisle display up front, Ralph's Grocery challenges customers to compare its Plain Wrap generic products with any similar national brand: "If you don't agree that Plain Wrap offers more value, we'll give you the national brand free."

Safeway promotes its private label "S" brands along with the Scotch Buy label, both offering the shopper savings.

Near the check-out station, Kroger displays Cost Cutter cartons of cigarettes as an impulse buy.

An independent grocer in Denver stocks one of the newest generic product selections: quick oats, supplied by Associated Grocers of Colorado, a wholesaler.

Stop & Shop's Economy generic label gets special shelf treatment with a sign advertising "another value choice."

A special health and beauty aids aisle display carries such generic items as hydrogen peroxide solution, isopropyl rubbing alcohol, white petroleum jelly, and baby oil.

A mass display of generics often features a mix-and-match selection, products drawn from almost every category.

Loblaw's promotes instant coffee with a special low price and a "satisfaction guaranteed" claim.

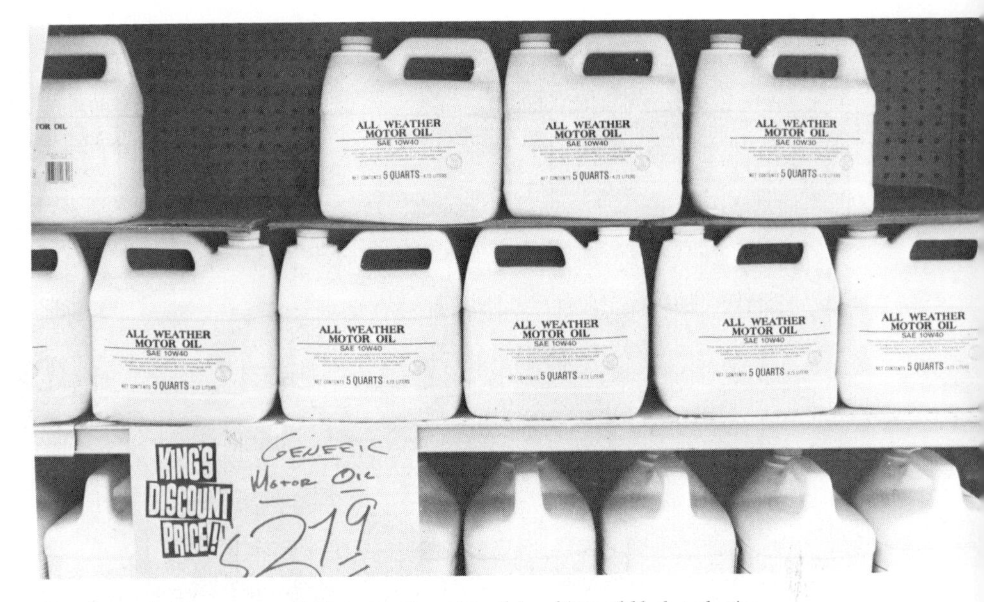

King Sooper in Denver mass displays generic motor oil in white and black packaging, using different color-coded hand-written signs on the shelfing.

This warehouse store in Denver, Shoppin' Bag, promotes generics with special shelf signs.

Stacked on a pallet, generic dog food alongside cat litter is promoted in the aisle of a FedMart store.

This Smith Food King outlet (Las Vegas) displays generics with comparison signs that ask shoppers why they should pay more for the national brand. Here, burger dog food at $2.49 is compared to Ken-L-Ration at $3.15.

Loblaws Ontario carries its no-name label into lawn and garden supplies.

Steinberg's distinctive shading of white, grey, and black on its generic products offers a stark contrast to the multicolored brand packaging that surrounds it. The generics are cut into regular shelf displays.

INGREDIENTS:
POIS, EAU,
SUCRE, SEL.

INGREDIENTS:
PEAS, WATER,
SUGAR, SALT.

PRODUIT DU CANADA

PRODUCT OF CANADA

PRÉPARÉ POUR/PREPARED FOR
AYGAL INC.
MONTRÉAL, QUÉBEC, CANADA

PEAS

CANADA STANDARD
ASSORTED SIZES

These peas may vary in colour, size or maturity.
They are wholesome and nutritious and are
suitable for use in salads and home made dishes.

100

19 fl oz 540 ml

Steinberg of Canada opted for a plain white label with shades of black and grey along with black print. The label honestly states exactly what product quality is represented.

Generics pop up everywhere, even in warehouse stores, where product is displayed in cut cases.

Generic refrigerated meats are a relatively new category being tapped by different retailers and wholesalers.

This customer's choice is not the Topco Food Club private label or the Coffee-mate national brand, but Topco's generic Valu Time coffee creamer.

Loblaw's No-name toddler diapers, packaged in bright yellow wrap, feature "no pins or plastic pants needed." The display vies for attention against the category leader, Pampers.

When retailers entered the generics competition, some did so rather gingerly, displaying a small selection of items in a corner. Eventually, as the line expanded, it was either cut into regular aisles or mass displayed in an aisle.

King Soopers (Denver) creates a special environment with black-and-white crepe paper and aisle-long displays of black-and-white generics under the Valu Time label. It is called a "Generic Store within a Store."

Huge billboard-like sign directs customer attention to FedMart's Bright Yellow Wrap selection and the savings realized when compared to national brands.

Yellow Wrap
FedMart's
Bright Yellow Wrap
No frills, simply packaged,
slight differences in quality.
Wholesome, nutritious, good tasting foods.
Dependable, efficient household products.
satisfaction or your money back
with national brands is not intended to imply they are
demonstrate amount of savings these products offer.
save
DOG FOOD

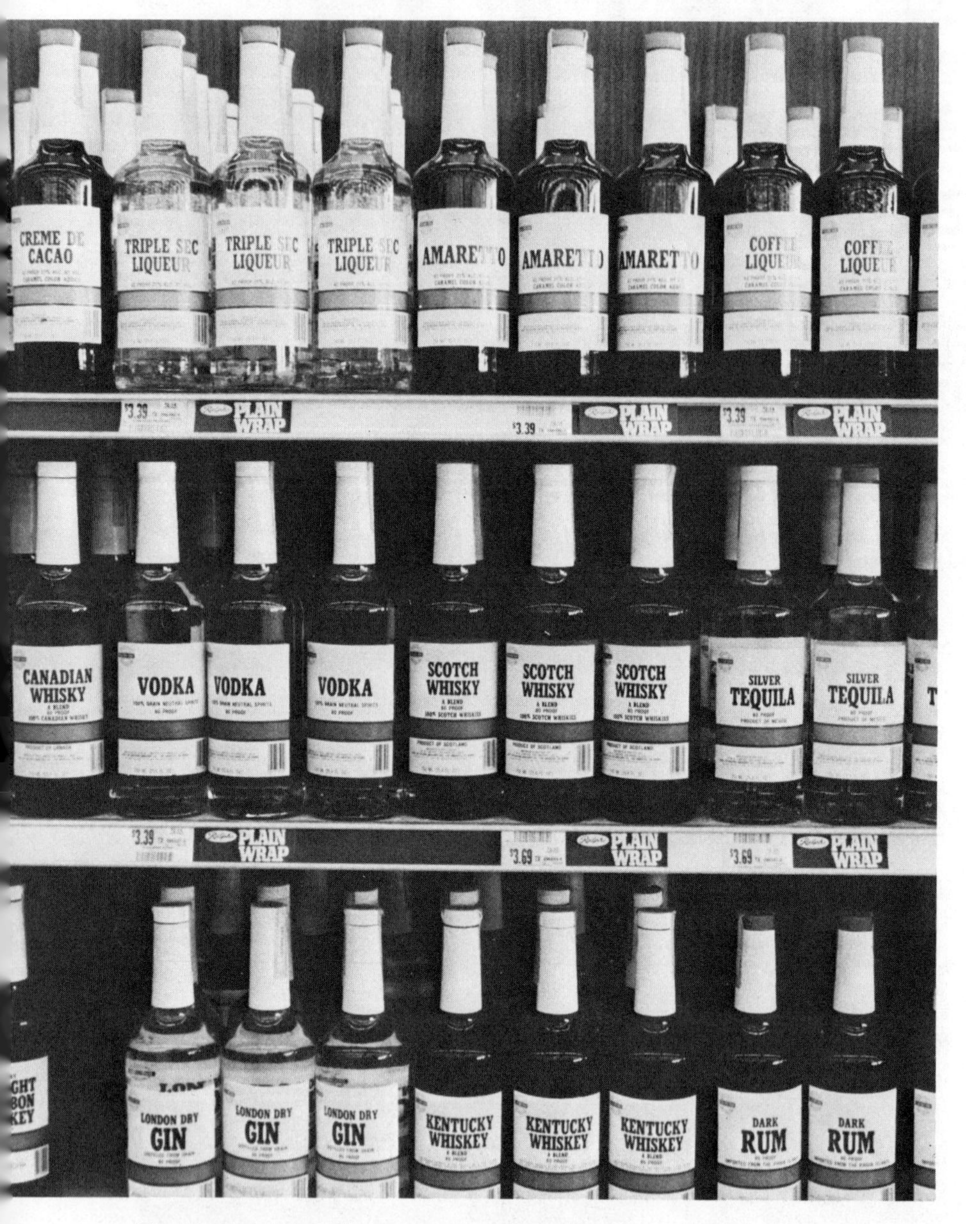

The generics fad attracted many customers, including Hollywood stars who reportedly stocked their home bars with Ralph's selection of hard liquor.

Like a TV commercial repeated over and over, Loblaws Ontario carries the "Save" message down the aisle of this special wire bin display, filled with "no-name" products. Signage is in attractive yellow with black print, exactly like the generic no-name packaging.

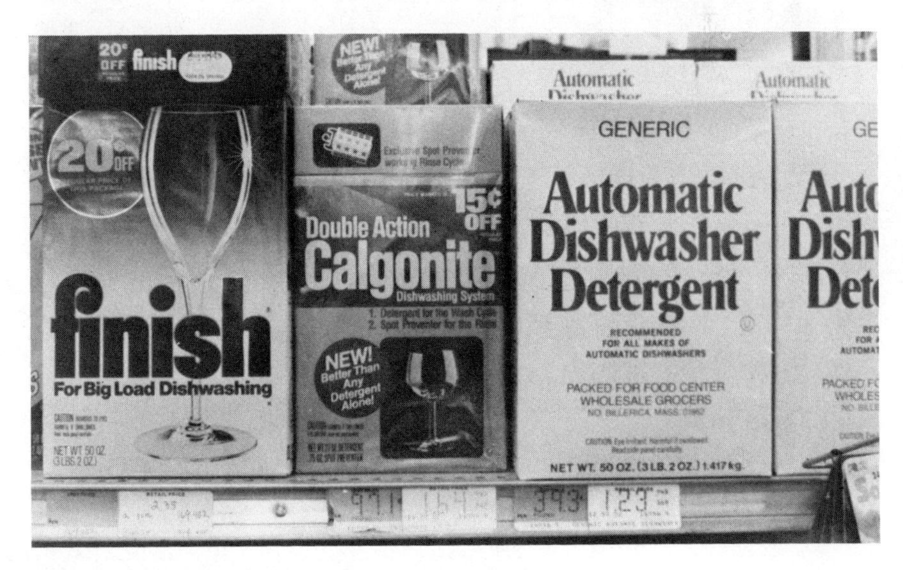

This generic label, plain black-and-white, is labeled "generic" with the distributor clearly identified on the front panel.

SLIM PRICE
100
TEA BAGS
Orange Pekoe and Pekoe Blend
NET WT 8 OZ 227 GRAMS
SLIM PRICE
CHUNKY
PEANUT
BUTTER
NET WT. 18 OZ. (1 LB. 2 OZ.) 510 GRAMS
SLIM PRICE
NCAKE
RUP
SLIM PRICE
UTOMATIC
HWASHING
ERGENT
oz. (3 LB. 2 oz.) 1.417 KG
SLIM PRICE
PURPOSE
UNDRY
TERGE
SLIM PRICE
SOYBEAN
SALAD OIL
PREPARED FROM PROCESSED SOYBEAN OIL
48 FL. OZ. (1½ QT.)
1.42 LITERS
70378 12693
SLIM PRICE
BABY
SHAMPOO
GENTLE TO EYES
FOR BABY AND
FAMILY, TOO
16 FL. OZ. (1 PT.) 473 mL
SLIM PRICE
SKIN
CARE
LOTION
SOFTENS AND
SMOOTHES SKIN
16 FL. OZ. (1 PT.) 473 mL
SLIM PRICE
TOMATOES
NET WT. 16 O
SLIM PRICE
BEER
SLIM PRICE
BEER
SLIM PRICE
BEER
SLIM PRICE
SAL
SLIM PRICE
MARGARINE
FOUR QUARTERS KEEP REFRIGERATED
SLIM PRICE
PORK & BEANS
NET WT. 15½ OZ.

A Denver grocer offers a wide selection of black-and-white generic items.

Vons (Los Angeles) debuted its generics line under the Slim Price label—a red tag logo against a white background.

King Soopers (Denver) in its frozen foods section give numerous facings to its Valu Time generic chicken and turkey pot pies.

Winn-Dixie Stores (Jacksonville, Florida) has consolidated different packer labels under the Price Breaker label, the chain's answer to generics. It is really a private label; the company says the grade is not standard but extra standard or fancy. Price Breaker is priced below the chain's Thrifty Maid label. Price Breaker has a yellow background with four-color illustration of the product and a white sunburst surrounding the name in red letters.

Jumbo packages of no-name bath tissue are stacked in cut cases right in the aisle of a Loblaw's store.

Dominion Stores (Canada) gives prime end aisle position to this display of its generic White Label personal products.

Without a calculator, the customer can recognize a big savings with Loblaw's no-name baby shampoo at 96 cents in a 500 ml bottle versus Johnson's 450 ml bottle at $3.59.

In King Sooper's Generic Store, customers find such items as filter cigarettes next to queen size panty hose.

Generic cat litter apparently is a string item in this pet food display, where the retailer otherwise stocks Hartz products.

generics label. It was black and white with A&P's sales and marketing subsidiary, Compass Foods, Inc., listed in the small print on products produced through A&P; while other generic items were sourced from packers outside the company. It was not really A&P's private label. But in 1981, A&P decided to switch to a imitation generic label, adopting the identity P&Q in green shading on a white background. A&P also began to identify itself as the distributor on the labels.

Richard Beazer, A&P's vice-president of national procurement, told participants at the 1981 PLMA trade show that a true generic label, which sells on price alone, couldn't last: "We feel that anything that sells strictly on price is a 'short-lived' product. Consumers are looking for a real value, the tradeoff between price and quality. The quality of the product must be consistent; the consumer will be more confident in a product or program if she knows that the store will stand behind it. By putting our identity on the product, we feel that this is our way of telling the consumer that we will stand behind our claims. . . .We've progressed into the P&Q label program—a single label to identify A&P's commitment to provide for the consuming public a value brand of product that we can guarantee the lowest price and consistent quality. To insure that quality, we have and are adapting a quality control specification for each and every product (Beazer 1981).

Handy Andy, San Antonio, Texas, another pioneering chain in this area, in 1977 introduced a true black-and-white generic line; but early in 1981 decided to switch to a yellow-and-black label, renaming the category, Smart Yellow Label, making it more of a semigeneric label.

Also in 1981, Lucky Stores' Eagle Discount Supermarkets in the Midwest launched a similar yellow background label with black print as its generic label. In 1982, that line was expanded chainwide to all Lucky operations.

FedMart, had already established a Bright Yellow Wrap generic program in 1980, its line identified by the yellow-and-black label.

This "yellow influence" traces back to Loblaws Ontario which first started a No Name yellow-and-black label in 1978. That influence is now being felt through its newly formed buying-merchandising arm, Intersave USA, which services Loblaw Companies' U.S. retail and wholesale operations (similar to the setup of Intersave Canada), which is changing the generic lines there to a yellow-and-black label, identified as distributed by Sunfresh Inc. These operations, National Tea Co., Peter J. Schmitt Co., and Western Grocers, if they had generic programs, operated them under a black-and-white true generic label.

While a trend does appear to be surfacing away from true generics, the white label is by no means dead. In fact, it is as strong or stronger than the other generic label types. Many packers are entering generic production with a white label, listing their firm. The experience of Associated Grocers of Colorado, also supports the white label approach.

As one of the largest wholesale members of the co-op, Shurfine-Central, Associated Grocers subscribed to the co-op's generic program introduced in 1978—an imitation generic label, called Thrift King, identified as an "economy brand." Thrift King was not unlike Safeway's Scotch Buy concept—a private label merchandised and priced like generics.

Greg Gallus, corporate vice-president of merchandising at Associated Grocers, explains "we moved very cautiously into that program. As a company, we felt a black-on-white label was the true generic route to follow; but we supported the 37 member warehouses of Shurfine-Central and their decision to go with Thrift King. Early in 1979, about six months into the program, however, we felt that we had made a mistake. So we started to go to outside sources for generic products (under a black-and-white label) that we could bring in very slowly.

"By the fall of 1979, Shurfine-Central had redesigned their thinking and also made a white generic label available to us. . . ."

The problem with Thrift King, according to Gallus, was that it was "nothing more than the introduction of another label. It was difficult to merchandise. It wasn't really the type of label that we would want to devote an aisle or a section to. Instead, you had to integrate it into your shelves for a price comparison right there. And that hurt the product. It is very difficult to cut into a store with 250 items—the number we had under Thrift King—and try to make the right impression or to get the right distribution.

"Some stores," he adds, "had tremendous luck, our warehouse type clients, for example. But the conventional size markets were having a difficult time with it. The brand identity was not to its favor; and perhaps we didn't push it as hard as we could have" (Gallus 1981).

MARKETING DOS AND DON'TS

With the benefit of nearly four years experience with generics, Robert Mendoza, grocery buyer and private label manager at Handy Andy Supermarkets, speaking before an FMI workshop on private label in 1981, offered some "valuable lessons" on how to handle generics:

- Don't jump into a program haphazardly. Key management people have to be involved from the onset when planning a generic program. Goals and objectives for an entire 12-month period are essential to the program's success; they should be reevaluated quarterly or at least every six months. One person should be given total responsibility for the program. Too many people making decisions on key merchandising questions leads to problems. But you need the input of all your buyers, because of their expertise. . . .

- Don't integrate generic products in with national brands and private label products. Generics should be merchandised together up front or in a high traffic area. This allows a customer to shop an entire generic section, pick up the products she needs and then proceed to purchase the rest of her items. One generic section has a larger impact and is more impressive. . . .
- Don't try to get rich on generics. At the same time, make money where you can. Some chains make as much as 30% in their generic category, others as little as 10%. . . . Be competitive where you need to be competitive. . . . There's not a whole lot of sections in your dry grocery department where you can make 18, 19, 20%. Make sure there is a comfortable spread between your private label and your generic products. You don't want to make your private label sales suffer because you're making good gross margins on those also. . . .
- Don't ignore your competitors. It's the worst thing you can actually do in generics. You need to shop his stores and see what he has to offer in his generics sections. Most importantly, see what he doesn't have. Here's where you can really get to him. Price your comparable items to be competitive with his and then make your better gross margins on items he doesn't carry. . . .
- Don't start out with several hundred items. Pick and choose your items wisely based on volume, based on profitability and demand. . . . You need to be in tune to what will sell, which may not necessarily be available in generics. One item that we found that sells well and that you can make good gross margin on is packaged seasoning mixes . . . you can make upwards of 40% on it. . . .
- Don't add three or four sizes of an item. . . . all you're doing is spreading out the sales for that one product. A good starting number is usually 100 to 150 items. . . . Make sure the schematics are updated with each item that you add and, most importantly, make sure that the store manager and key management people in that store are notified of the new item and the new schematic.
- Don't leave generics out of the ad and don't leave the shelf bare of shelf talkers and signs. If you want to be committed to the program, you should have at least some kind of institutional copy if not item and price in your ads. Also, signing sells products. It's got to be colorful. Use signs above the aisle to get the customer's attention as soon as she walks into the store and then smaller shelf tags and shelf talkers. It's got to be colorful. It's got to be informative.

Mendoza also cited the importance of educating all store management on implementing the generics program correctly:

> You need to make sure that they know what generics are, what kind of savings they offer to their customers, what the difference is between the generic and private label, what the difference is between your private label and generic and the national brand. Why is it that a store can sell a can of corn 10 cents cheaper than a national brand and 5 cents cheaper than a private label brand? If a store manager can't answer these basic questions for the customer, he doesn't know what the generic program is, or what it can do for his store. . . . Have cuttings in the store with your store mangers. Give them some products. Have them take it home, have them eat it, have them use it if it's a nonedible item, but let them know what it is.

He also recommended using the company's home economist as a "selling tool" for generics: "Set up a booth in the store with generics all around them, build some displays and let them sample it for the customers" (Mendoza 1981).

Generic displays are usually set up as a section from 35 feet up to a full aisle long (60 feet). King Sooper, Denver, a chain of more than 50 supermarkets, started its program in 1978 with about 24 feet of aisle space. Now its generics "store within a store" stretches across two or three aisles (up to 68 foot aisles) with the count approaching 500 items. Since the product lines have been expanded—up to 20% of warehouse movements—the chain also cuts generics into other sections wherever necessary: refrigeration and frozen food sections, packaged meats, bacon, orange juice, dairy items, pizza, ice cream, produce.

Its "generics store" was fitted into existing stores not by resetting the layouts, but by eliminating some "wasted space." Generics penetrated certain categories, taking over the facings occupied by some brands. That space was picked up by tightening the displays. Also, the chain cut back on its general merchandise section, eliminating some categories completely: spark plugs, windshield wipers, floor mats.

King Soopers' generics program led to some interesting developments within product categories, according to president Jim Baldwin:

> In the past, the preserve and jelly category has been a so-so or shrinking category. The consumption was almost static or decreasing. Two particular items that were very exciting for us were the 32-ounce grape jelly and the strawberry preserves. It was a cheaper quality product in generics, yet they just took off like a shot. We were ordering and we were out, and we were ordering again and we were out. Finally, we were caught up, but we knew full well that there was going to be a point where the consumer might expect the price to go up because of the value. We thought the consumer was loading up the pantry and that the sales curve eventually would go the other way. But it didn't.
>
> In my opinion, this was an example of creating consumption for different uses. It could be that more people are consuming strawberry preserves because of the low price point established in generics, or because of its 32-ounce jar. The package size was usually smaller in the brands. The generic item is of lesser quality, so the key had to be its value. . . . It may not be by design, but the consumer wants to save where she can in order to spend where she wants to. There's always that trade off.

He indicates that "in all our generics, we're looking for a lesser quality product at a price point that will attract new customers" (Baldwin 1981).

A better value alternative is what really sells generics, according to David A. Nichol (1981), president of Loblaws Ontario. Nichol's strategy with generic quality is different than most U.S. retailers/wholesalers. His No Name generics represent the highest quality possible within a product category—positioned as the best value in the marketplace. The packaging, distribution, or product formulation can be changed, if necessary, to produce higher cost savings over the national brands. As Nichol describes No Name quality: "In some cases, it's better (than the national brands); in some cases, it's the same; and in some cases, it's different, but always a better value.

From the start of Loblaws program in 1978, "we were after value," says

Nichol. "We have our own lab, which is instructed to test for value. They consumer-test products against the leading national brands; and then they tell the consumer the price and ask, given this price point and this quality, that you perceive in each product, which is the best value, which would you buy again. If the generic doesn't win that consumer preference test, it doesn't get on our shelf. That's why Loblaws has been so successful as opposed to our competitors."

He defines value as "a combination of price and quality. In the case of bleach, the leading national bleaches in Canada are somewhere around 6¾% in terms of acid content. We didn't think that was necessary, so we went to 6¼%. It tested and was found to be a better value, totally adequate."

Loblaws also realizes savings in packaging not by knocking off a national brand package configuration, as in a private label program, but by placing products in a basic grouping in the same container. As Robert Chenaux, vice-president of company brands at Loblaws Intersave Canada, explains:

> When you blow-mold 60,000 to 70,000 bottles of private label apricot shampoo then all of a sudden that market dies and conditioning shampoo takes over, then you've got yourself a packaging liability. We've structured it so that a product category can die, but we can still use the container to pack liquid detergent, baby shampoo, dandruff shampoo, cream rinse, etc.—all in the same type container, with some at slightly different sizes, but all out of the same mold. It's all standardized.
>
> We also realize a certain amount of savings by doing our own packaging. We're responsible for procuring the packaging and selling it to our suppliers. So we can have our own combination runs. In private label, there can be 10 labels with 10 different colors, which doesn't allow for a combination run; but we can get 10 No Name labels and run them on a combination sheet, getting the minimum price for a combination run. We take the sheet and cut it, sending the cat food label to the cat food supplier, the dog food label, etc. It's a penny here, a penny there; but in groceries, those pennies add up.

The chain also is testing new packaging ideas, such as poly bags for detergents or orange juice. Says Chenaux, "We sell milk in bags. Traditionally, orange juice has been sold in Canada in either tin or glass containers. Generic orange juice is now sold in the milk bags at a savings of roughly 20 to 30%" (Chenaux 1981).

Nichol believes his generics strategy is right versus the mistaken course taken by U.S. retailers. When generics were introduced into North America, he indicates, "they held the promise of protecting the North American consumer from the ravages of inflation . . . [yet, retailers have done] everything they can to destroy generics: the packaging is horrible, the quality varies all over the place from bad to abysmal, and their marketing strategy is to position it as garbage. 'If you can't afford good food for your family, we've got generics' " (Nichol 1981).

The approaches to merchandising generics vary from integration (cutting generic into different departments and product categories) to segregation (featuring generics as a section unto itself). The mix also varies from a small sampling up to a full complement, crossing many different product categories.

Ralphs Grocery's Plain Wrap program has evolved into a center aisle section, called the Super Saving Center, featuring mostly top-selling generic items. Richard Kester, vice-president of grocery division, describes it as "a conglomeration of ideas. We borrowed wire bins from Loblaws in Toronto, the center aisle concept from King Sooper in Denver, and some other merchandising ideas from other retailers to come up with this idea.

"The unique thing about this concept is that at the same time, we also promote national brands within the same section. The national brands are displayed for two weeks, then rotated with other national brand items; while the generics stay on mass display permanently."

This approach really represents a double exposure for generics in Ralphs, since the same generic items are also integrated into regular shelf displays to the right of the private label, which is positioned to the right of the national brands. This gives the retailer the option to promote generics en masse as well as a price comparison sell when integrated.

There is really no fixed pattern for generics. Yes, the quality in many cases is not equal to the national brands; generic vegetables may be uneven in length and mixed in size; some parts of the contents may be more mature than other parts; a paper item may be single-ply, a detergent may have less cleaning power, a cleanser may not include a perfume scent . . . yet, there are many similarities. In some cases, the formulations are the same as national brands or private labels. Some manufacturers refuse to touch generics in certain product areas, arguing that the product value cannot be compromised.

Retailers/wholesalers are becoming more aggressive in promoting generics. Recently, Supermarkets General Corp., Woodbridge, New Jersey, boldly proclaimed "The $ensible Alternative, The No-Frills Brand at Pathmark: Save Up to 39% over national brands." A full newspaper page pictured 12 different product categories, each featuring a leading national brand next to the No Frills knockoff, comparing price and size weight. Ten of the national brands had checkmarks, indicating "a warehouse price reduction," yet the price difference for generic was dramatic in each case. The ad asked customers to "compare the variety—over 180 products now . . . and still growing . . . compare the Taste—the difference is barely discernible in most cases. Nutritional value is equal to Fancy-grade items . . . sizes and colors of products may vary a little . . . satisfaction guaranteed or your money back."

The merchant also is more up front with customers in describing generic products. When First National Stores introduced its generic program, "Good 'N Plain" in 1981, its advertisement proclaimed:

> It's all in black and white. Good 'n Plain generic products come in white packages or labels, with black type identification. There are no decorator jars or reusable containers. Tea bags have no tags. Detergents have no free measuring cups or coupons packed inside. The beauty of Good 'n Plain products is the money you save.
>
> Good 'n Plain generic products are selected, tested, and guaranteed for value. All food items meet USDA standards for quality and wholesomeness, and there's no compromising of nutritional values. Household products are of good serviceable quality. Every Good 'n Plain generic product is tested in Finast's Quality Control Laboratory, and guaranteed to be what we say it is . . . Good 'n Plain.

The future of generics? Nowhere but upward, as long as consumers continue to demand them. A recent survey of the top 100 corporate chains, compiled by Chain Store Age Supermarkets, showed that 76.5% carry generics and that the one out of every four that do not carry them plan to do so in 1981. That means that 80% of the major chains will carry generics starting in 1982.

Business Week noted that no-frills products took 5% of the $200 billion grocery market and could capture up to 25% of the market in this decade, according to many observers. The publication hinted that food retailers are gaining control again over manufacturers.

REFERENCES

Baldwin, J. 1981. Denver Goes Generic: King Soopers' Strategy. *Private Label* Magazine, June-July, pp. 24, 26, 28. E.W. Williams Publishing, New York.

Beazer, R. 1981. PLMA Trade Show: The Pros and Cons of Generics: Issue of Quality Aired. *Private Label* Magazine, October-November, p. 16. E.W. Williams Publishing, New York.

Business Week. 1981. No-Frills Food: Power for the Supermarkets. March 24, p. 70. McGraw-Hill Inc., New York.

Chain Store Age Supermarkets. 1981. Generics Boon or Bane? April, p. 31. Lebhar-Friedman, Inc., New York.

Chenaux, R. 1981. Loblaw's Buying/Merchandising Muscle: Intersave. *Private Label* Magazine, August-September, p. 74. E.W. Williams Publishing, New York.

Gallus, G. 1981. Denver Goes Generic: Associated Grocers of Colorado's Strategy. *Private Label* Magazine, June-July, p. 30. E.W. Williams Publishing, New York.

Kester, R. 1981. Ralphs Grocery Gives 'National Brand Billing' to Private Labels. *Private Label* Magazine, February-March, p. 11. E.W. Williams Publishing, New York.

Nader, R. 1980. PLMA Fall Meeting: Nader Advocates Competition (Including Private Label Competition) for Well-Being of the Consumer. *Private Label* Magazine, October-November, p. 10. E.W. Williams Publishing, New York.

Nichol, D. A. 1981. Meet "Mr. Generics"—David A. Nichol. *Private Label* Magazine, August-September, pp. 78–79. E.W. Williams Publishing, New York.

Mendoza, R. 1981. Getting the Most Out of Your Private Label (and Generics) Program. *Private Label* Magazine, June-July, pp. 63–64. E.W. Williams Publishing, New York.

Sussman, E. H. 1981. PLMA Trade Show: The Pros and Cons of Generics: Issue of Quality Aired. *Private Label* Magazine, October-November, p. 18. E.W. Williams Publishing, New York.

13

Export Opportunities for the Manufacturer and the Retailer/Wholesaler

Traditionally, the private label business has created more importers than exporters among the ranks of U.S. retailers/wholesalers; and, at best, manufacturers have had little private label business domestically, and far less in foreign countries. Now, with the growth of private label, including the addition of generics, the potential for exporting private label becomes more attractive. Some plant closings by national brand manufacturers (provoked by the 1980–1981 recession) also open the way to more private label traffic abroad. Merchants, either through their own manufacturing capability or through their vast purchasing power, now have more lower priced goods at their disposal to sell to exporters or directly to customers abroad.

It is not surprising to see U.S. retailers/wholesalers begin to test or attempt to crack the export market. While some of them have been actively exporting for several years or even decades, the tempo has picked up in the late 1970s and early 1980s. Safeway, the country's largest supermarket chain, for example, has bought a "piece of the action" (9%

stock) in Allied Import Co., an import-export trading company composed of four Japanese retailers. AIC conducts trade among Japan, Korea, Taiwan, and Hong Kong. The deal was signed in late 1981. A year earlier, this country's second largest supermarket chain, The Kroger Co., entered a joint venture with The Daiei, Inc., Japan's largest food and general merchandise retailer. Both Safeway and Kroger intend to sell private label items in Southeast Asia, while importing products from the Orient.

Kroger's plans include selling such manufactured products as coffee, preserves and dry mix items to Daiei stores in Japan and Hawaii. Daiei, in turn, will sell its goods to Kroger's U.S. food and drug outlets.

Daiei also has exclusive rights to use various K mart trade names and trademarks under a license agreement with K mart Corp. K mart also has established a toe-hold in Mexico through its 44% acquisition of Astra S. A. The U.S. chain plans to introduce its K mart system into Astra's general merchandise stores.

Safeway reportedly opened its export department in 1979, selling products in Japan, Taiwan, Hong Kong, Singapore, and Malaysia. The company also entered markets in the Middle East and Peru. Safeway joins with four Japanese retailers in Allied Import Co. (Jusco Co., Chujitsuya Co., Izumiya Co., and Uny Co.—Jusco being the fourth largest grocery retailer in Japan) in developing trade. AIC members also will sell to Safeway in both the United States and Canada. In that latter market, Safeway now serves only eastern Canada, but is looking to expand into western Canada's food products market. The company operates some 106 manufacturing and processing facilities, including produce prepacking, bakery, dairy, ice cream, soft drink bottling, meat processing, egg candling, coffee and tea, fruit and vegetable processing, jam and jelly, and household chemical plants plus an edible oil refinery and a dressing and salad oil plant.

A&P, the third largest U.S.-based supermarket chain, formed Compass Foods Inc. in 1975 to pursue the export business as well as other outside sales of the firm's extensive line of private label products. Compass Foods had at its disposal the largest food processing plant in the world (the Ann Page plant at Horseheads, New York) plus detergent, coffee, nut, dairy, potato, and printing plants. In the recent past, this subsidiary had extended its marketing reach to some 30 countries. Its export catalog, describing the operation as "the most comprehensive food marketing program of its kind in the world," offers foreign customers some 8000 items. In its health and beauty aids catalog, Compass Foods lists more than 115 private label items.

The 1982 closing of the Horseheads plant has not curtailed A&P's export activities. The chain still manufactures and sources product for export.

"The export market for private label is in its infancy," according to

David Wells, special accounts manager, Associated Grocers, Inc., Seattle, Washington. "The potential is definitely there. It's proving to be a fruitful venture for us."

Associated Grocers, a member of the manufacturing food group, Western Family Foods Inc., began its export program late in 1980. Wells reports that first-year sales are approaching $1 million. That's barely a ripple in the $625 million volume of this wholesale operation; yet the potential for growth exists, as long as the exporter remains cautious, says Wells.

His firm deals direct with customers in Japan, Hong Kong, Singapore, and other Southeast Asian countries. The market in Japan is especially attractive, since the consumer there has been changing as far back as the 1950s, moving toward Western products and tastes. U.S. foodservice retailers already have established Japan as their second largest foreign market (Canada ranking first mainly because of geographic proximity to the United States).

Wells notes that the Japanese are receptive to Western ways. For example, corn pottage (corn soup) is now popular, corn being a commodity that the United States has a strong marketing edge in. Japan also is one of the most affluent countries in the world; its prime interest rate is a fraction of the U.S. rate. "The days of only fishheads and rice are long gone," he adds.

The exporter should be aware of new laws in different countries. Japan has stepped up sanitation standards governing food products. A law in the Philippines now requires that profits made in that country must be kept there. The exporter can get around this problem by shipping in canned goods, for example, taking a profit, then using the money to purchase Philippine products for export to the United States. In South American countries, there are inbound duties charged on goods and governmental fees charged to exporters.

While some exporters are successful, other find the going difficult. Potential exporters can run up against a tremendous amount of legwork in developing foreign markets; their ignorance of local laws and market conditions make the going rough; new trade barriers present problems; the growing competitive business abroad creates roadblocks; commodity buying can be tricky where a competitor might have the edge over a U.S. exporter who depends on U.S. crop and price conditions.

Some three years ago, Stop & Shop formed Marlboro Products Co. to flex its buying power in the export field. Buyers abroad were invited to take advantage of Stop & Shop's efficient distribution and purchasing system with a selection of some 1500 private label items—food, beverages, household cleaners, paper products, health and beauty aids.

Bernard Goldman, vice-president of international sales at Marlboro, reports however, that this program has not been too successful, since the company hasn't achieved the right volume. Exporting requires a tremendous amount of work, Goldman notes. It involves stiff competition, running up against fruit sellers from South Africa or Argentina and corn sellers from Australia. The job entails much paperwork; it requires tying up large amounts of capital. Also, there are shipping problems to deal with, trade barriers to overcome, and government red tape.

Generally speaking, exporters on the East Coast are more likely to deal with the countries closer to them—Europe, the Middle East, the Caribbean, and South America; while exporters on the West Coast will seek business in the Pacific—Hawaii and Southeast Asian countries, especially Japan. The longer the shipping route, the costlier the merchandise. Availability of commodities also plays a role in deciding where exporters develop markets. West Coast-based exporters have access to fruits and vegetables in California, especially tomato-base products and fruits like peaches and grapes; while the East Coast exporter is closer to crops like beans, lentils, greens, and apples.

Private label exporters can deal directly with customers abroad or through an export firm based in the United States. Wholesalers in particular are said both to supply export houses as well as to ship direct to foreign customers. Some prefer it only one way: Ralphs Grocery, Los Angeles, for example, deals with an export firm; while Associated Grocers of Seattle deals direct with foreign customers.

OBSERVATIONS OF A VETERAN EXPORTER

A veteran wholesaler involved in the controlled label export business for some 30 years, preferring anonymity, says that when markets first opened overseas, the going was much easier. As countries matured, however, government bureaucracy crept into the trade picture, creating restrictions on imports.

Today, this veteran says that private label is treated like an advertised brand in foreign markets, since people over there are not familiar with the labels. The market potential has grown appreciably, because private label costs less than national brands exported by the manufacturers. Without manufacturing capacity abroad, importers and traders in different countries look to buy the lowest cost products for resale in their countries or for reexport to other neighboring countries.

The trend, he notes, has been toward more competition abroad; in some markets, the previously inexperienced buyer who once looked strictly at price is now more quality conscious. (This view is contradicted by another private label exporter, who indicates that the buyer mentality in the Far East particularly leans toward price. There are cases where retailers sell end cap space at $1000 for display of imported goods.)

The veteran wholesaler also notes that Europe has limited appeal for the U.S. exporter, since competition there is stiffer with retailers and wholesalers already vying for business. Some of the larger European chains and wholesalers also import directly from canned fruit packers in California.

A relatively new market, the Middle East, has opened with the emergence of oil income and the influx of expatriates (Americans, Dutch, French, English, etc.) who shop for foodstuff that interests them. Also, the native population is beginning to develop taste for U.S. products. In foodstuff, the U.S. exporter has this market locked up, he believes.

This wholesaler noted further that the export busines continues to grow, but with ups and downs. One year, a particular country can be a big customer, then the following year weaken in business. The U.S. exporter, therefore, must be geographically diversified. Also, an exporter must carefully watch contract terms. He recommends using only letters of credit as the safest measure, carrying an obligation from a U.S. bank. While other more lenient terms can open up more business, they also are more risky. A site draft can be used, where documents against payment are held by a foreign bank—the bill of lading and invoices along with instructions on when to release goods and under what payment conditions. The problem with such an arrangement is that the importer receiving the goods can also be a customer of that bank and therefore be in a better position to work out a deal to his favor. An open account arrangement, of course, carries the most risk for a U.S. exporter.

Finally, this wholesaler was critical of U.S. Government involvement in exporting. He conceded that the Government does produce a great number of publications, conducts helpful seminars, and locates buyer prospects in different countries; but the information disseminated is old or dated. It really depends on the country involved and the personnel in foreign offices.

The best advice, he offers, is to go to the country and get the information firsthand. Importers, he says, travel through the United States looking for suppliers, telling them that *they* represent the biggest customer in a particular country. It is better for the exporter to visit the country and see conditions there, talk with the trade representatives, and check with steamship lines on just who does the biggest import business.

David Wells of Associated Grocers of Seattle, however, applauds U.S. Government aid in his development of an export business, referring to his own company's experience.

GOVERNMENT ASSISTANCE

Since the United States is a leading exporter, opportunities exist for both the private label retailer/wholesaler and manufacturer to capitalize in this area. Markets overseas are looking for "reliable sources of supply," according to Raymond E. Eveland, director of the U.S. Department of Commerce, International Trade Association (ITA), New Orleans District Office. Eveland, speaking on an export panel at the spring 1981 PLMA meeting in New Orleans, said "if a product is doing well in the domestic market, there's a very good chance there's a market for it overseas." He cautioned about the maze of legal, transportation, insurance, and other obstacles involved in exporting, all of which require expert advice.

J. Marc Chittum, industry program manager, Department of Commerce, Washington, speaking on the same panel, indicated that manufacturers often prefer to avoid the risks or complications involved in exporting; in fact, he noted a drop in U.S. share of world trade: "Out of an estimated 250,000 manufacturing firms in the U.S., only 25,000 of these are exporters. It's estimated at least double that number could export, if they tried."

The U.S. Government is now working to encourage more exporters to develop markets abroad, through efforts of the International Trade Administration. Chittum said that ITA works with companies to establish contacts, hold seminars, issues publications, answers inquiries, and provides counseling. ITA collects more marketing data than any other government agency, distributing more than 300 publications, he indicated. ITA also brings foreign buyers to this country to meet potential exporters.

Chittum outlined some specific ITA activities: conducting exhibits at foreign trade fairs, maintaining commercial officers both at foreign embassies as well as in its own district offices, operating a Worldwide Information and Trade System (established in 1980) to serve as a computerized information bank, locating proper financing for exporters, and so on. ITA works with three government entities in arranging financing: the USDA's Commodity Credit Corp. (CCC), the Import-Export Bank (X-M), and the Small Business Administration (SBA).

Under a 1971 law, the Domestic-International Sales Corp. sets up deferred income tax for a domestic company that deals in export trade; under the Export Trading Act, immunity can be granted from antitrust laws that would otherwise prevail in this country (Chittum 1981).

On the same panel, L. Clifton Gaston, ITA trade specialist based in New Orleans, said his office and others like it across the country stand ready to orient the exporter to foreign market potential. Gaston cited one market in particular, the Netherlands Antilles in the Caribbean, which does a thriving business in re-export trade to Latin America. In the first 10 months of 1980, he noted, that area purchased $10.7 million worth of health and beauty aids from the U.S. (Gaston 1981).

This cooperation was not always the case. Government bureaucracy in the past worked against the exporter. Also, the climate in the more industrialized European countries was not too receptive to U.S. imports.

L. Stephen Weiss, who helped develop an aggressive export program for Nysco, a manufacturer of pharmaceuticals and health and beauty aids, in the 1960s, remembers how in European countries,

> there was a sense of national pride, where the local government would give support only to local manufacturers. Countries, rebuilding from WWII, were not receptive to private label or contract manufacturing from the outside. The only import products they would consider were life-saving drugs.
>
> Also, at the time, the U.S. Government paid no more than mouth service to exports. The government was more interested in giving away stuff to impoverished or flood stricken countries. Their support to exporters left much to be desired.
>
> We were selling a new technology—time-release pharmaceuticals—to those countries. Our company was the first popular alternative to Smith Kline & French in this technology. The difference was the SK&F marketed their own brand, while we marketed our technology, adapting it to the needs of different countries, each with its own labeling requirements, color restrictions, import regulations, maximum strength needs, etc. (Weiss 1981A).

In the 1960s, contract manufacturing was a new concept overseas; in the 1970s, it became more acceptable as marketing organizations there began to seek other sources of supply. The reference to private label really didn't start until the late 1970s, according to Weiss.

In an article offering tips on exporting, Weiss, at the time vice-president of Rexall Drug Co., noted that the benefits to exporting can be not only more sales and profits, but also "exposure to new ideas, new technologies, new equipment, new products, and a panoply of new things (even people) to help your business or division grow."

The options open to the exporter include: shipping bulk for local repacking, semifinished goods for local processing and packing, and finished goods. This activity represents an extension of business with perhaps some modifications—changes in color, size, flavor—to accommodate the foreign customer.

Weiss noted that some of the nitty-gritty details include sending artwork by ocean freight, while special documents can be sent by freight forwarder; banking details can be handled by local banker; foreign government red tape can be handled by the customer. He recommended assigning someone to oversee, coordinate, and expedite the export activity, especially if it's a new operation, with support coming from top management. Other pointers:

- Contact a trademark lawyer and have your company name and trademarks registered in every country you do business with.
- Organize a file for sales leads, including contacts in the U.S. Department of Commerce's International Division, personal recommendations from other exporters and international executives, a bank's international department, trade publications, overseas suppliers, ad agencies, trade associations, consultants.

- Develop a well-illustrated catalog or brochure as a sales tool, with consideration of country preferences for type of product or size.
- Develop business references with the bank, commercial sources, or services to strengthen your reputation in the marketplace.
- Export credit terms can be started on a letter of credit basis and later loosened to an open account: "A well-drawn L/C offers you and your customer certain specific protection. Everyone involved knows what is to be shipped, when it's to be shipped, and the documents required to clear the merchandise into the customer's country and for you to get paid by the bank" (Weiss 1981B).

How do you find foreign buyers and good information sources for exporting? Ralph Behr, vice-president of Food Oils Corp., compiled the following list for *Private Label* Magazine:

T.O.R.S. (Trade Opportunity Referral Service)—A computerized direct mail service getting buyers and sellers in touch with one another. Write: TORS Coordinator, Export Trade Services, Foreign Agricultural Service, U.S. Department of Agriculture, Washington, DC 20250.

CONTACTS—A weekly newsletter to buyers listing U.S. firms and their products. Write: Export Trade Services, Foreign Agricultural Services Division, Room 4945-South, U.S. Department of Agriculture, Washington, DC 20250.

EXPORT BRIEFS—A weekly newsletter to sellers listing buyers who are looking for products. Write: Export Trade Services Division, Foreign Agricultural Services Division, U.S. Department of Agriculture, Room 4945 South Building, Washington, DC 20250.

FT 410 REPORTS—Foreign Trade Reports (FT 410) provides a statistical record of shipments of all merchandise from the United States to foreign countries, telling who buys what and where. There is a charge for this service. Contact your local U.S. Department of Commerce office.

Agency Sources

Eastern U. S. Agricultural and Food Export Council Inc., 2 World Trade Center, Room 5095, New York, NY 10047.

Western U.S. Agricultural Trade Association, 3600 Main St., Suite 1-B, Vancouver, WA 98663.

Southern U.S. Trade Association, International Trade Mart, Suite 338, 2 Canal St., New Orleans, LA 70130.

U.S. Department of Commerce—check phone directory under U.S. Government.

U.S. Department of Agriculture—check phone directory under U.S. Government.

Representatives

A.D.S. (Agent Distributor Service)—a Department of Commerce service that identifies foreign agents and/or distributors interested in your product. There is a charge for this service. Contact your local U.S. Department of Commerce office.

T.O.P. (Trade Opportunities Program)—a U.S. Department of Commerce service that computer-matches your company with overseas purchasers. There is a charge for this service. Contact your local U.S. Department of Commerce office.

COMMERCIAL NEWSLETTER—a service provided in most U.S. embassies located in foreign countries. They circulate this newsletter, listing U.S. firms by product. Many importers search the list for leads. Contact your local U.S. Department of Commerce office for details.

EXPORT CONTACT LIST SERVICE—The U.S. Department of Commerce lists more than 138,000 names of importing firms, distributors, representatives, manufacturers, and the like from more than 130 countries. Sheets of computer-typed mailing labels on your target companies can be mailed to you for a charge. Contact your local U.S. Department of Commerce office.

Pamphlets

A BASIC GUIDE TO EXPORTERS—a source book full of addresses, names, information, and good ideas. Write: U.S. Government Printing Office, Washington, DC 20250.

HOW TO DEVELOP EXPORT MARKETS—a useful primer for export. Write: U.S. Department of Commerce, Washington, DC 20230.

SPECIAL REPORTS—a valuable listing of more than 200 specialized reports and publications you can order from the U.S. Government. Write: U.S. Department of Agriculture, Foreign Agricultural Services, Information Division, Room 5918-S, Washington, DC 20250.

FOREIGN AGRICULTURE CIRCULARS—a catalog of specialized publications for marketing specific commodities (meats, fruits, dairy products, etc.). Write: Foreign Agricultural Services, Information Division, Information Services Staff Room, 5918-South, U.S. Department of Agriculture, Washington, DC 20250.

THE EMC—YOUR EXPORT DEPARTMENT—a description of the services provided by export management companies and how to select one. Write: Office of Export Development, Industry and Trade Administration, U.S. Department of Commerce, Washington, DC 20230.

REFERENCES

Behr, R. 1981. Sources For Export Information: Where To Find It . . . Who To Ask. *Private Label* Magazine, June-July, pp. 69–71. E. W. Williams Publishing, New York.

Chittum, J. M. 1981. Private Label Firms Briefed on Possibilities of Export. *Private Label* Magazine, June-July, p. 68. E. W. Williams Publishing, New York.

Gaston, L. C. 1981. Private Label Firms Briefed on Possibilities of Export. *Private Label* Magazine, June-July, p. 68. E. W. Williams Publishing, New York.

Weiss, L. S. 1981A. A Pioneer in Private Label Export. *Private Label* Magazine, June-July, pp. 75–76. E. W. Williams Publishing, New York.

Weiss, L. S. 1981B. Exporting: An Overview. *Private Label* Magazine, June-July, pp. 72–74. E. W. Williams Publishing, New York.

14

The Future: In the Hands of the Consumer

The private label industry is alive with activity and change. There's excitement and growth in every segment of the business. The retailer/wholesaler is adding new products, new lines; testing new merchandising and marketing techniques; developing new labels both on a corporate and on a generic level. Private label manufacturers are rolling out brand new categories, new packaging and product changes, and generics. National brand manufacturers have joined the ranks of private label, not only through more contract work in private label, but also in direct involvement through acquisition or start-up of companies devoted almost exclusively to private label and generic production. The broker is becoming more specialized in private label and also in generics. Markets abroad are opening for private label development. Most important of all, today's consumer now recognizes private label quality and the value of generics. Awareness and usage patterns are up considerably.

It is quite a turnaround from the past, when national brand manufacturers had private label literally muzzled. In practically all market segments, private label carried a second-best qualification—not really worth the time or effort. The cheaper bargain brand could never measure up to national quality standards. That image is dead in today's marketplace.

The retailing industry now has a new partner in business: the consumer. No longer does only the industry call the shots. It is no longer the national brands' world. It is approaching a more equitable situation, where private labels and national brands compete on the same quality level.

Without a monopoly on quality, national brands must offer the consumer something else, something of value—coupons, unadvertised brands at less cost, rebates or refunds, larger almost institutional-size packages with built-in savings, bonus packs.

Economist Robert L. Steiner, associated with the Federal Trade Commission's Bureau of Economics, speaking before PLMA's 1980 fall trade show, noted that "consumers and society are better off when neither retailers' nor manufacturers' brands dominate an industry but, rather when the two kinds of brands battle on reasonably equal terms—side by side—on the same retail counters." This retailing structure he termed "the mixed regimen," which he claims is much better than one where either national brands or private labels dominate the market. "It's best," Steiner said, "in terms of welfare, delivering some combination of reasonable prices, good product performance, a lot of new products, and variety of choice . . . a structure where both national brands and private labels are strong. People and society are better off under this structure, because it combines the benefits of the other two structures (national brand dominance and private label dominance) and it accomplishes these welfare goals because the two kinds of brands compete against each other vigorously and keep each other honest" (Steiner 1980).

In the supermarket segment, recent market studies show private label and generics far from achieving the level of dominance that national brands now command. SAMI data put private label share at about 17% and generics at about 1.6%. That is less than one-fifth of the total market; and yet there are exaggerated claims pointing to the overthrow of national brands. A dated mentality about suppressing private label and now generics continues in the marketplace.

For example, Opinion Research Corp., an Arthur D. Little Co. based in Princeton, New Jersey, in its latest in-depth consumer shopping behavior study (released in June 1981) reports in a press release that "brand name products may be in jeopardy as inflation-squeezed shoppers reach for more store brands and generics."

Completely oblivious to the quality standards set by private labels, ORC says: The study "reveals that inflation has cut such a wide and deep swath through all family income levels that cost is fast becoming the deciding factor in determining product selection. The quality differences offered in the past by nationally advertised brands, suggest ORC, may no longer suffice to keep the consumers from reaching for Brand X or worse—the unbranded 'generic' product."

What disturbs ORC is the fact that nearly half of the buying public (48%) says "it is purchasing store or distributor brands more often today as against two or three years ago. Forty-nine percent report more frequent purchase of the 'generics'—products plainly packaged and devoid of the usual trade names or trademarks."

The implication is that customers must trade off from national brands, going from bad (private label) to worse (generics). No credit is given to the consumer for being a lot smarter today—forced to be smarter because of a worsening economy.

Bon Appetit Magazine concluded in its special Trendsetter Tracking Study, Wave II (Fall 1980), prepared by Audits & Surveys, that national brand market share is "steadily eroding," based on "substantial" gains in consumer awareness and usage of generics. In polling 2150 of its readers, *Bon Appetit* showed 62% had tried generics, 32% were aware of them but hadn't tried, and 6% were not aware of them. This compared with the fall 1979 report of 1826 readers, where 49% had tried, 39% were aware but didn't try, and 12% were not aware. The report also showed frequent usage of generics up from 1979's 11% to 1980's 16%: women working full time going from 10 to 20%, 18- to 34-year-old women going from 11 to 19%, college graduates or better going from 13 to 19%, and respondents in the Southeast going from 4 to 13%.

In a listing of five criteria, respondents in the study ranked national brands first, store brands second, and no-frills third for all criteria. In three of the categories—taste, dependability, and price—national brands were favored by a wide margin over the other two categories; but in nutrition and value, national brand's marginal lead was trimmed substantially nearer to the other two categories: in nutrition—54% rated national brands high, 40% chose store brands, and 26% chose no-frills; in value—51% chose national brands, 45% chose store brands, and 31% chose no-frills.

A slowdown in the growth of generics was documented in a special report by A. C. Nielsen Co. The study, designed "to factually and objectively illustrate and comment on the true impact of generic labels," actually found that generic sales share in all supermarkets doubled since the fall of 1978, up from 2 to 4%. The decline occurred only in supermarkets handling generics, attributed to the fact that the original chains that picked up generics are larger and more aggressive in marketing generics, while the late-comers in 1979 and 1980 are smaller and not so committed. As a result, there's been a dilution of the total volume of supermarkets handling generics, bringing about a loss in sales share, down from 14.2% to 12.0% (Parks 1981).

Nielsen went on to analyze these data:

> while share of market in total supermarkets has doubled over three years, availability is 2.6 times greater which validates the fact that new distribution has not been as productive as that initially achieved.

> This diminishing rate of return or softness in marketing productivity is further borne out by the back-to-back doubling in the number of stores handling generic labels over the last three years. Helping to explain this reduced rate of return is the fact that the average supermarket taking on generics has decreased from nearly $7 million in annual sales to just over $4 million. Accordingly, the stores most recently taking on generic lines are somewhat smaller than the typical supermarket that generates $5 million of cash register sales per year.
>
> With respect to the future, there are (as of January 1981) still some 14,000 supermarkets that are evidently taking a wait-and-see attitude toward handling generics.

Nielsen went on to show that generics had no impact on category size and direction in paper, food, and household products and "despite their collective volume advances of plus 65% from 1979 to 1980, for example, they have failed to stimulate the physical size of the market which is off by nearly 1%."

Nielsen noted

> since no physical growth has been sparked by generics, what has happened is that gross cash register receipts, adjusted for inflation, have simply been reduced. This has occurred because the same amount of total category products has been sold both pre and post generics, but at a lower price per unit. The question which logically arises is: have retail organizations improved their profit margins as they have traded customers down from generally higher-priced private label and name brand entries to generics? As is so often the case, one question leads to another: have participating supermarkets truly calculated their return on investment by adding expenses such as the cost of shelf space, display area, newspaper ads and other media support activities to their basic marketing costs for generic products?"

Lower cash receipts, lower ROI, brought on by generics! Apparently the retailer/wholesaler has little to gain in continuing generics; those 14,000 stores on the waiting line can factor these data into their decision on whether it is go or no-go. But they should also consider another important factor in retailing.

There are some unwritten laws that help any retailer/wholesaler succeed—and profit—with private label and generics. One law is that they should never become greedy; they should always offer the customer value—equal or acceptable product quality with a savings that can be valued: not a few pennies, but a few dimes, quarters, or dollars cheaper. Another law is that the customer is always right. Today's consumer wants generics; many need generics to keep their budgets intact. These laws cannot be plotted, or charted, or weighed against a data base.

It is unfortunate that a newspaper like the *Wall Street Journal* can pick up Nielsen's report (and current SAMI data) with the headline "Generic Goods Aren't Selling as Fast" and in the copy report: "The reason (for the decline), both researchers say, is that much of the growth of generics is due to the increase in the number of stores stocking them. That number is peaking, so growth is slowing."

In acquiring Simpsons department stores, Hudson's Bay of Canada has created a new label, Beaumark, for major home appliances. (Simpsons previously carried Sears brand under a licensing agreement.) The Beaumark label is being positioned as a national brand, each appliance carrying a green seal that assures customers that the product has been tested for quality by The Retail Research Foundation of Canada.

The question is "Is Steinberg phasing out its private label cone cups or does this display suggest that private label outsells the Imperial brand?"

Eaton of Canada imports the finest leather women's shoes under its Eaton Raphael label—a fashionable item equal to the finest in footwear but at half the retail price.

In the past couple of years, Eaton has opened trade with China, importing these house coats, expertly hand-sewn, but retailing at a bargain price under the Eaton label.

A&P's 1982 strategy is to put more emphasis on its primary A&P brand and less emphasis on manufacturing (except coffee). Eight O'Clock Coffee, one of the chain's oldest brands, continues strong, not only in A&P outlets but in non-competitive markets, distributed by Compass Foods, an A&P subsidiary.

The choice is up to the customer: national brand versus private label. The former may look more sophisticated in its trade dress, but the latter has its own "brand" of sophistication with quality guaranteed to satisfy the consumer.

The real story is that generics continue to sell fast and the slowdown is really ascribed to less aggressive newcomers, many of which take on generics defensively and do everything within their merchandising power to destroy them.

It is encouraging to see that the customer is not fooled. Awareness of the value of generics is growing. (Generics gets all this publicity, primarily because private labels have been around for a long time.) The Spring 1981 issue of *Everybody's Money*, a money management magazine sponsored by credit unions, puts no-name products to the test in its cover story, "Be A Name Dropper . . . It May Save You Money." The magazine called its workers and their children together for a taste test:

> We purchased seven foods: hot dogs, orange juice, tuna, hot chocolate, crackers (soda and graham) and fruit mix. In each case, we bought a brand name, a private label and two "brands" of generics (when available).
>
> The generics cost an average of 26% less than name brands, ranging from a 45% savings on one of the generic soda crackers to a paltry 1% on a no-name fruit mix.
>
> Compared to private labels, the generics cost an average 10% less. We save 26% on graham crackers, but one generic fruit mix cost 11% more than the private label, probably because it was packed in a small can.
>
> Each sample for our test was coded and prepared in the same way. Twelve coworkers and four children used a four-point visual scale (cartoon faces with expressions ranging from a wide smile to a frown) to rate the foods for taste and eye appeal.
>
> The results—Our tasters' ratings were as inconsistent as the price patterns.
>
> Our tasters thought the brand name graham crackers, fruit mix, and soda crackers were better looking and tasting than the generics or private labels. But they gave generic tuna the highest rating on looks, the brand name on taste. Similarly, the generic orange juice scored highest on looks, but the brand name was rated the best tasting.
>
> The private label hot chocolate beat out the others on taste; the brand name got the highest score on eye appeal. In the hot dog test, however, the brand name came in last in both looks and taste. Our tasters thought the generic hot dogs looked the best, the private label (house brand) tasted best.
>
> Except for two products, a generic hot chocolate and graham cracker, all food earned at least a "fair" score. More often than not, scores were given at every point along the scale—illustrating the differences in individual tastes.
>
> Several tasters pointed out that although they gave some generic foods a low score, they would use them as ingredients, for example, the graham crackers for pie crust crumbs.
>
> It's up to you—With this year's expected 10 to 15% increase in food costs, buying generics may help salvage your budget. But comparison shop. You may find, as we did, that some private labels are cheaper. Or a store may be offering a brand as a loss leader.
>
> So don't automatically snub old friends. But no-names can save money, and you may find that dropping a name may not mean dropping value.

Those prophetic words, "it's up to you," are what retailers/wholesalers are beginning to respond to. It takes time for change. When generics established a foothold in parts of New Jersey, Wakefern Food Corp., advertised its packer labels under the banner, "Money $aving Brand, A great new idea that ShopRite's had for years!" Its newspaper ad early in 1979 described these products as "little-known local and regional brands, put out by local and regional packers who don't have high national advertising costs and who have lower overhead. . . . For decades, ShopRite has sold these money-saving brands at prices that are as low or lower than the Johnny-come-lately 'no name, plain package' line that some other supermarkets are handing you." Soon afterwards, ShopRite introduced its M$B generic brand, in an ad section in late 1981, the wholesaler described its "Winning Combination . . . ShopRite Brands—quality at the right price . . . National Brands—for super variety, top quality and low prices (and) Money $aving Brands—our generic brand and your ticket to value and variety . . . check the price and discover extra value."

More and more retailers/wholesalers are offering their customers this choice: the alternatives of national brand, private label, and generics. Consumers are being oriented to think in those terms.

Private labels and generics are not out to destroy national brands. Instead, they work themselves into the competitive mix, where they take only a small part of national brand's so-called fair share of the market.

Customers are becoming more aware of private label, because merchants today recognize their value—not only for customers, but for the retailer himself. Private labels help to build store loyalty; they build customer continuity and confidence in shopping a particular store; they offer the retailer greater profits; and they serve as traffic builders with their lower price.

EXCITING DEVELOPMENTS

In the vernacular, private label and generics are where the action is. Today, manufacturers are bringing new sophistication to store brands.

There is innovation in packaging. For example, Food Oils Corp., Carlstadt, New Jersey, has introduced a "Safe" cap on its private label vegetable oils. It is the first pilfer-proof closure for this product. The roll-on cap, usually appearing only on branded products such as liquors, wines, and pharmaceutical items, replaces the ordinary screw cap. The new cap leaves a metal ring on the neck of the bottle, indicating that the product seal has been broken. It is also said to prevent air leakage and to insure a longer shelf life and a fresher product.

There is boldness in packaging. Chase Products Co., Maywood, Illinois, has introduced a line of generic insecticides, each container stating on the front panel: "This product is unconditionally guaranteed to be equal in quality and performance to national brands. If this product does not give satisfaction in use, return for refund or replacement."

There is refinement in technology. Chicopee, a division of Johnson & Johnson, is taking patents from its parent firm to apply to a new line of private label diapers—100% polyester facings with a compressed layer underneath designed to draw moisture away from a baby's bottom.

There is specialization being introduced. Several manufacturers are now introducing incontinent pants (adult disposable diapers).

There is expanded selection. Wagner Juice Co., division of Westin Inc., Cicero, Illinois, now has a complete line of private label or generic juices: apple, orange, grapefruit, prune, grape, apple cranberry, cranberry cocktail, orange–pineapple. The first three also are available in low-cal versions.

The list could fill another book. There is secondary packaging being introduced. Plastics are now being introduced: film wrapped items, polyethylene bags, polypropylene containers. There are new personal products—generic feminine napkins, disposable douches, nail polish remover kits. Manufacturers are developing trial size packaging, for example, American Safety Razor Co., Staunton, Virginia, has a line of 5 oz trial size deodorant soaps available—knock-off of Coast, Dial, Dove, Safeguard—for private label packaging.

Generic drugs are now manufactured by many large drug firms, capitalizing on a potential market as patents on name brand drugs run out. At this writing, Dr. Arthur Flanagan, former medical director at Warner–Lambert Co.'s Parke–Davis operation, was about to organize the Institute for Generic Drugs to provide doctors and pharmacists with back-up information about generic drugs and possible side effects. Dr. Flanagan wants support from generic drug makers to get this project off the ground.

An argument can be made that private label will not succeed in a newly developed product category unless national brands first develop the market. Two recent product development stories support this point.

In 1980, Minnetonka, Inc., a Midwest manufacturer, developed the product Softsoap, a liquid soap dispensed from a plastic container. Minnetonka took a commanding market share as a regional manufacturer, but within a year its market share dropped dramatically as numerous manufacturers copied the idea, producing the product under their brands or under private label. At last report, retailers indicate that it is still too early to predict the potential market for this product. Some indicate that liquid soap will not develop as a viable category until national brand manufacturers start a roll out of their test versions of liquid soap (Anon. 1982)

Weyerhaeuser Co., Tacoma, Washington, the leading manufacturer of private label disposable diapers, introduced an absorbent insert diaper pad into test market in 1978 as "Diaper Booster Pads." This new product idea soon was adopted by a number of retailers under their store brand names. But some of these retailers thought that their private label item would do much better when sold against a higher priced national brand. Weyerhaeuser complied by introducing a national brand, Diaper Doublers, in July 1980.

New private labels and generic labels keep appearing, as retailers, wholesalers and distributors realize the potential in profits and sales. Early in 1980, Wegmans, Rochester, New York, a regional retailer that had belonged to the buying group, Staff Supermarket Associates, Jericho, New York, began phasing out of the Staff controlled private label program, developing instead a Wegmans private label line. In 1982, Smart & Final Iris Co., the wholesale warehouse store subsidiary of Thriftmart Inc., Los Angeles, introduced a Smart Buy generic line to complement its Iris fancy grade private label program. In 1982, F.A.B. Inc., (formerly Frosty Acres Brand) Norcross, Georgia, the co-op buying/merchandising group for both foodservice and retail distributors and chains, debuted a colorful Five Star generic label for its retail members with possible application in the foodservice area.

The private label business continues to grow and change. Private label is not for everyone, by any means. In the mid-1970s, for example, The Southland Corp., Dallas, the country's leading convenience store operator (7-Eleven stores) began putting private labels on almost everything in order to convey to the public a price image and to project the idea that convenience stores do not "gouge" the consumer. But in recent years, this company has found that private labels work as well as other brands. Since its stores are limited in space, the private labels are being phased out. This has meant dropping its large private label volume in cheese and soft drinks, as well as fast food items (corn dog, pizza, Danish pastry, pickles), health and beauty aids, hosiery, and so on. The chain is keeping some private label stock: condiments, frozen concentrate juices, Luv/It paper products (napkins, towels, toilet tissue), Super Shade sunglasses, and miscellaneous items. Southland also is keeping its private label foodservice products, such as 7-Eleven sandwiches; postmix soft drinks, including the Big Gulp 32-ounce drink; and Hot-to-Go Coffee. In addition, the company operates milk dairies under nine different names, all carrying a common logo design, linking them to Southland. This chain of 7000 stores also has a private label stake in another product, which interestingly accounts for the greatest share of store sales by principal product categories, that is, self-service gasoline under the 7-Eleven logo. Some 2500 stores in the chain now sell this product, which accounts for an estimated 25% of total store sales.

The trade press continues to talk private label and generics down; but consumers are slowly learning the truth about these alternative brands. It is up to the retailers, wholesalers, and distributors to maintain top quality standards for their products. The brand manufacturers will guarantee that quality on their products; but the guarantee with private label and generic products rests with the people who distribute and sell these products. When they fail to support fully their private label program, who else will? The group that stands to lose the most from such a failure is the consumer.

REFERENCES

Anon. 1982. Is it 'No Soap' for PL Liquid Soap? *Private Label* Magazine, April-May, p. 64. E.W. Williams Publishing, New York.

Audits & Surveys. 1981. Trendsetter Tracking Study, Wave II. (June). *Bon Appetit* Magazine, New York.

Everybody's Money. 1981. Be a Name Dropper . . . It May Save You Money. (Spring issue, pp. 5–6). Credit Union National Association, Madison, Wisconsin.

ORC. 1981. Brand Name Products May Be in Jeopardy as Inflation-Squeezed Shoppers Reach for More Store Brands and Generics According to New ORC Marketing Index Study (June). Arthur D. Little Co., Princeton, New Jersey.

Parks, J. 1981. Generics in Supermarkets: Myth or Magic? A.C. Nielsen Co., Northbrook, Illinois.

Steiner, R. L. 1980. PLMA Fall Meeting: A Plea For Stronger Private Label Market Share. *Private Label* Magazine, October-November, p. 12. E.W. Williams Publishing, New York.

Wall Street Journal. 1981. Generic Goods Aren't Selling As Fast. November 21.

Appendix **1**

Private Label Listing by Distributor

Included here are leading organizations that own or control their own labels, commonly referred to as private labels. These firms operate as supermarket chains, food wholesalers, retail distributors (including co-ops of retailers and wholesalers or broker-owned operations), and food-service groups (serving their membership of independent foodservice distributors). The list is a sampling of their important private labels. An asterisk indicates the top quality private label line; but in many cases, top quality also is carried under other labels to define different product categories.

Since the distribution system is often complex, there is a great deal of overlapping activity. For example, wholesaler Fleming owns its own retail and foodservice labels (the latter under the Fleming name) and is licensed to supply other private labels, owned by IGA and Piggly Wiggly, to stores under those names in its markets. Broker Taylor & Sledd distributes its private label Pocahontas to both foodservice and retail customers. T&S also handles its customer wholesaler or retailer private labels and generic lines—for example, wholesaler Richfoods' Richfood private label and Econ generic label. In addition, T&S distributes black-and-white generics to its other customer accounts. Foodservice distributor group

Frosty Acres distributes its Frosty Acres and Garden Delight labels to both foodservice and retail accounts, besides providing a new three-color generic label to retail customers. Frosty Acres also handles independent foodservice distributor members' private labels—for example, Capital Foods' Golden Age label.

There are a number of major retailers and wholesalers not listed here because they carry private labels owned by a co-op: The Cullum Companies and Affiliated Food Stores, both of Dallas, carry private labels supplied by Shurfine-Central; King Soopers Discount of Denver carries labels supplied by Topco Associates.

SUPERMARKET CHAINS

Albertson's. Inc., Boise, ID
Albertson*
Janet Lee*
Good Day
"No Name" yellow and black label generics.

American Stores Company, Salt Lake City, UT
Acme Markets, Inc.
Acme*
Louella dairy
Lancaster meats
Virginia Lee bakery
Ideal canned and frozen
Econo Buy generics
Alpha Beta Co.
Alpha Beta*
Econo Buy generics
Skaggs Companies, Inc.
Skaggs*

Bi-Lo, Inc., Mauldin, SC
Bi-Lo*
black and white generic

H. E. Butt Grocery Co., Corpus Christi, TX
H-E-B Brand*
Village Park
Park Lane health and beauty aids
generics

Dominion Stores Limited, Toronto, Ontario, Canada
Dominon*
Richmellow coffee and tea
Anniversary ("superior quality") cookies/ice cream
White Label generics

First National Supermarkets, Inc., Cleveland, OH
- Edwards-Finast*
- Richmond
- Yor Garden*
- Brookside Farms
- "Good 'N Plain" black-and-white generics

Fisher Foods, Inc., Bedford Heights, OH
- Heritage House*
- Shoppers Pride household chemicals
- Fancy Farms meats

Giant Food Inc., Landover, MD
- Giant*
- Heidi bakery items
- Aunt Nellie's canned goods
- Kitchen Queen deli items
- KISS ice cream
- Economy Line generics

The Grand Union Co., Elmwood Park, NJ
- Grand Union
  - Grand Union*
  - Basics generics
- Weingarten
- Big Star

The Great Atlantic & Pacific Tea Company, Inc., Montvale, NJ
- A&P Supermarkets
  - A&P*
  - Ann Page
  - Jane Parker
  - Our Own Tea
  - Eight O'Clock coffee
  - P&Q generics
- Plus Discount Foods
  - Plus

Jewel Companies, Inc., Chicago, IL
  - Jewel
  - Cherry Valley
  - Mary Dunbar
  - Jewel Maid
  - Jewel T
  - Royal Jewel
  - Hillfarm
  - Park
  - PaPa's pizza
  - Osco health and beauty aids
  - No Name generics
- Star Supermarkets
- Jewel T Discount Stores

Kohl's Food Stores, Milwaukee, WI
Kohl's*
Daisy Fresh
yellow-and-black generics

The Kroger Co., Cincinnati, OH
Kroger Food Stores
Kroger*
Avondale
Embassy
Kandu
Cost Cutter generics
Market Basket
Market Basket

Lucky Stores, Inc., Dublin, CA
Lucky/Eagle/Food Basket/Kash N' Karry
Lady Lee*
Harvest Day
Villa
Hi-Class pet food
Gold Seal liquors
yellow and black label generics

FedMart Corp., San Diego, CA
FM*
"Bright Yellow Wrap" yellow-and-black generics

Fred Meyer, Inc., Portland, OR
MY-TE-FINE*
Fred Meyer* health & beauty aids/auto supply/soft goods
Certified* drugs/vitamins
Turf King* garden products
Eve's* ice cream/candy/other perishables
BFD* designer jeans/running shoes/tee and sweat shirts
Sonny Boy food
Danbee nonfood
black-and-white generics

Pantry Pride, Inc., Fort Lauderdale, FL
Pantry Pride*
black-and-white generics

Publix Super Markets, Lakeland, FL
Publix*

Ralphs Grocery Co., Compton, CA
Ralphs*
"Plain Wrap" blue-and-white generics

Red Owl Stores, Inc., Hopkins, MN
Red Owl*
Harvest Queen*

Brimfull grocery
Valdor frozen/dairy
black-and-white generics

Safeway Stores, Inc., Oakland, CA
S Brands* ("finest quality")

Bel-air	Edwards	Sea Trader
Brocade	Lucerne	Su-purb
Captain's Choice	Manor House	Town House
Country Pure	Mrs. Wright's	Truly Fine
Cragmont	NuMade	White Magic
Crown Colony	Party Pride	
Empress	Safeway	

Scotch Buy ("good quality") generics

Blossom Time milk	Dalewood margarine
Dairyland milk	Oven Joy bread
Dairy Glen butter	Piedmont shortening

Steinberg Inc., Montreal, Quebec, Canada
Steinberg Supermarkets
Steinberg*
Orchard King ("choice") canned goods
Ice Castle ice cream/soft drinks
Our Own corporate label
black-and-white generics
Miracle Food Mart
Miracle Food Mart
Valdi Discount Foods

The Stop & Shop Companies, Inc., Boston, MA
Stop & Shop*
Sun Glory
Our Own corporate label
Economy generics

Supermarkets General Corp., Woodbridge, NJ
Pathmark Supermarkets
Pathmark*
No Frills generics

Vons Grocery Co., El Monte, CA
Vons*
Slim Price generics

Waldbaum, Inc., Central Islip, NY
Waldbaum*
generics

Weis Markets, Inc., Sunbury, PA
Weis*
Big Top
Carnival soft drinks
Dutch Valley snacks
"The Way It Was"* generic label health & beauty aids (national brand equivalent)

Winn-Dixie Stores, Inc., Jacksonville, FL
Thrifty Maid* (canned goods and commodities)
Arrow household supplies
Sunbelt paper products
Crackin' Good snacks and desserts
Tropical jellies and preserves
Astor groceries (oils, tea, etc.)
Price Breaker generics

WHOLESALE GROCERS

Associated Grocers Inc., Seattle, WA
Western Family*
Penny Smart generics

Certified Grocers of California Ltd., Los Angeles, CA
Springfield*
Gingham
Special Value
Prize
generics

Certified Grocers of Illinois, Inc., Chicago, IL
Raggedy Ann* canned items
Certified Red Label
Country Delight* perishables
House Delight household products
black-and-white generics

Farm House Foods Corp., Milwaukee, WI
Farm House

Fleming Companies Inc., Oklahoma City, OK
True Value*
Good Value
Montco* (East)
Rainbow
black-and-white generics

S. M. Flickinger Co. Inc., Buffalo, NY
Super Duper

Malone & Hyde Inc., Memphis, TN
Hyde Park*
Register of Merit
Sav-Sum

Pacific Gamble Robinson Co., Seattle, WA
Standby* grocery/canned goods
Freshie canned goods

Spring Fresh detergents/paper items
Snoboy* frozen/perishable/deli
Snomaid frozen
Garden grocery
Mountie grocery
black-and-white generics

Richfood Inc., Mechanicsville, VA
Richfood*
Econ generics

Scrivner Inc., Oklahoma City, OK
Leadway*
Tru Gold
black-and-white generic

Spartan Stores Inc., Grand Rapids, MI
Spartan*
Gem Garden
Gem Orchard
Gem Pantry
Home Gem
generic black-and-white

Super Food Services, Inc., Dayton, OH
Fame*
Table Treat canned goods
Table King fruits and vegetables
Gard paper/dish detergents

Super Valu Stores Inc., Minneapolis, MN
Super Valu* grocery/bakery
Flav-O-Rite* foods
Chateau* nonfoods
Sally's*
Quality Plus* meats
Elf
black-and-white generics

Twin County Grocers Inc., Edison, NJ
Foodtown*
Budget Line yellow-and-black generics

United Grocers Ltd., Richmond, CA
Bonnie Hubbard*
black-and-white generics

Wakefern Food Corp., Elizabeth, NJ
ShopRite*
Farmflavor
Very Best

My Favorite
Elizabeth York*
Money $aving Brands generics

Waples-Platter Co., Fort Worth, TX
White Swan* canned vegetables/tea/creamers
black-and-white/yellow-and-black generics

Wetterau Inc., Hazelwood, MO
Sunset Inn* canned vegetables
Nature's Best* perishable foods, limited groceries
Foodland* edible groceries
Home Best* manufactured groceries
black-and-white generics

West Coast Grocery Co., Tacoma, WA
Duchess fruits and vegetables
Capitol pet foods
black-and-white generics

RETAIL DISTRIBUTORS

Alliance Associates Inc., Coldwater, MI (food broker)
Family Fare*
Qual Pak
Town Pride*
Farm Maid dairy/frozen foods*
Nature's Pick* canned foods*
Fruit Valley canned fruits*
Pet's Delight*
Kitchen Kettle soup*
Breakfast Bowl cereal*
Sea Maid canned fish
Cook N Fry oil/shortening

Federated Foods, Park Ridge, IL (private label distributor) grocery and foodservice
Red & White*
Parade*
Hy-Top
Fine Fare
Lead Way
Federated black-and-white (with stars) generics
Del Haven
Sun Spun

IGA Inc., Chicago, IL (co-op owned by grocery wholesalers/distributors, working as a franchise operation that provides services—not including product procurement)
IGA*
Royal Guest
Much More generics
Happy Host

Piggly Wiggly Corp., Jacksonville, FL (independent and chain retailers who join voluntary groups that buy from a common source or form co-ops that own their own warehouses)
Piggly Wiggly*

Shurfine-Central Corp., Northlake, IL (co-op owned by independent food retailers who operate regional distribution warehouses)
Shurfine* canned/frozen foods/health and beauty aids
Shurfresh* perishables (bakery/dairy)
Thrift King generics
black-and-white generics

Topco Associates, Inc., Skokie, IL (co-op owned by supermarket chains and grocery wholesalers)
Food Club* dairy/processed foods*
Top Frost frozen foods*
Topco household/health and beauty aids*
Top Crest general merchandise*
Top Fresh produce*
Gaylord
Gayla beverages
Dog Club pet foods
Top Spred margarine
Beacon beauty aids
Valu Time generics
Kingston
Dartmouth

FOODSERVICE DISTRIBUTOR GROUPS

All Kitchens, Inc., Lyndhurst, OH
All Kitchens (maroon band)*—fancy
All Kitchens (blue band)—extra standard
All Kitchens (green band)—standard

Bonded Food Co., Boise, ID
Golbon (green label)*—fancy
Golbon (red label)—extra standard
Silbon (blue label)—standard

CODE Inc., Pittsburgh, PA
CODE (red label)*—fancy
CODE (blue label)—extra standard
CODE (green label)—standard
CODE Yorkshire, Wellington, Nottingham coffees
CODE Chef's tomato products
CODE Carbohydrate controlled fruits

Federated Foods, Park Ridge, IL
Red & White*—top quality
Parade—top quality
Del Haven—secondary quality

Sun Spun—secondary quality
Our Value—third quality

Frosty Acres Brands, Inc., Atlanta, GA
Frosty Acres*
Frosty Seas* fish
Garden Delight
Hi-Pies
Tasty Taters

Nifda (National Institutional Food Distributor Associates,) Inc., Atlanta, GA
Nifda*—fancy
Chef-Pac—extra standard
Econo-Pac—standard

North American Foodservice Companies, Inc., Chicago, IL
Host Favorite (blue label)*—fancy
Host Delight (red label)—extra standard
Host Pak (green label)—standard

Nugget Distributors, Inc., Stockton, CA
Nugget (black label)*—top quality
Nugget (red label)—secondary quality
Nugget (green label)—third quality

Plee-Zing, Inc., Greenview, IL
Plee-Zing*—top quality
Partake
Little Momma

Pocahontas Foods USA, Richmond, VA
Pocahontas*—fancy and choice
Mount Stirling—extra standard
Wigwam—standard

Appendix 2

SAMI Studies on Private Labels and Generic Labels

Over the past decade, SAMI (Selling Areas-Marketing Inc.), a division of Time Inc., New York, has tracked private label sales and market share in food retailing. Its data now cover 45 major U.S. markets, representing 82.7% of total food store sales in the United States. The data include all product categories except produce and store-delivered merchandise, such as snacks and soft drinks.

In the past three years, SAMI reports private label sales alone have climbed by 55%, from $10.1 billion up to $15.6 billion, as of June 1982. Generics, which were added to the data base in 1981, helped boost total private label sales for this period by 76% (adding another $2.1 billion in 1982). This compares to national brands increase of 23% since 1979, from $64.1 billion up to $78.8 billion.

Data in the following tables focus primarily on 1981, giving a full report of the penetration and impact of generics on private label and national brands in a category-by-category analysis—dry grocery food and non-food, frozen and refrigerated, and health and beauty aids.

Table 2.1A. SAMI Private Label Study. National Share Trends by Product Department (Period Ending June 26, 1981)

	52-Week Share Point Changes												12-Week	
Department	1971 vs. 1970	1972 vs. 1971	1973 vs. 1972	1974[a] vs. 1973[b]	1975 vs. 1974	1976 vs. 1975	1977 vs. 1976	1978 vs. 1977	1979 vs. 1978	1980 vs. 1979	6/26/81 vs. 6/27/80	CURRENT ANNUAL SHARE	6/26/81 vs. 6/27/80	CURRENT 12-WEEK SHARE
Dry grocery: food	[c]	[c]	− .14	+ .48	− .04	− .98	+ .18	− .24	+ .13	+ .95	+ 1.15	14.85	+ 1.02	15.11
Dry grocery: non-food	[c]	[c]	+ .36	− .29	+ .38	− .45	+ .28	+ .52	+ .34	+ .97	+ 1.40	11.61	+ 1.47	12.41
Combined total	+ .25	+ .41	+ .02	+ .37	± 0	− .92	+ .20	− .07	+ .16	+ .94	+ 1.21	14.01	+ 1.13	14.37
Frozen & refrigerated	− .84	± 0	− .25	+ .29	+ .98	− 1.52	+ .50	− .30	+ .46	+ .43	+ 1.48	25.65	+ 2.93	27.32
Health & beauty aids	+ .13	+ .23	+ .24	+ .08	+ .26	− .19	− .05	+ .04	+ .18	+ .35	+ .47	3.57	+ .55	3.73
Grand total	+ .09	+ .35	± 0	+ .33	+ .11	− 1.00	+ .11	− .06	+ .26	+ .78	+ 1.19	15.77	+ 1.46	16.37

[a] = Year ending November 22, 1974.
[b] = Year ending November 23, 1973.
[c] = Not broken out by food vs. non-food.

Table 2.1B. SAMI Private Label Study. Total Private Label Share Trends by Product Department (Period Ending June 26, 1981)

52 Week Data			12 Week Data	
Current Dollar Share (%)	Share Point Change	Department	Current Dollar Share (%)	Share Point Change
14.85	+ 1.15	Dry grocery: food	15.11	+ 1.02
11.61	+ 1.40	Dry grocery: non-food	12.41	+ 1.47
14.01	+ 1.21	Total dry grocery	14.37	+ 1.13
21.84	+ 1.66	Frozen	23.48	+ 2.74
29.74	+ 1.05	Refrigerated	31.48	+ 2.92
25.65	+ 1.48	Frozen & refrigerated	27.32	+ 2.93
3.57	+ 0.47	Health & beauty aids	3.73	+ 0.55
15.77	+ 1.19	Total	16.37	+ 1.46

Table 2.1C. SAMI Private Label Study. Regular Private Label Share Trends by Product Department (Period Ending: June 26, 1981)

52 Week Data			12 Week Data	
Current Dollar Share (%)	Share Point Change vs. Year Ago	Department	Current Dollar Share (%)	Share Point Change vs. Year Ago
13.37	+ 0.47	Dry grocery: food	13.39	+ 0.41
9.33	+ 0.28	Dry grocery: non-food	9.85	+ 0.51
12.32	+ 0.41	Total dry grocery	12.42	+ 0.42
21.27	+ 1.23	Frozen	22.60	+ 2.13
28.99	+ 0.47	Refrigerated	30.34	+ 2.07
24.99	+ 0.97	Frozen & refrigerated	26.31	+ 2.20
3.12	+ 0.20	Health & beauty aids	3.22	+ 0.32
14.35	+ 0.47	Total	14.69	+ 0.78

Table 2.1D. SAMI Private Label Study. Private Label Generic Share Trends by Product Department (Period Ending: June 26, 1981)

52 Week Data			12 Week Data	
Current Dollar Share (%)	Share Point Change vs. Year Ago	Department	Current Dollar Share (%)	Share Point Change vs. Year Ago
1.49	+ 0.70	Dry grocery: food	1.72	+ 0.61
2.28	+ 1.12	Dry grocery: non-food	2.56	+ 0.96
1.69	+ 0.80	Total dry grocery	1.95	+ 0.71
0.57	+ 0.43	Frozen	0.88	+ 0.61
0.75	+ 0.58	Refrigerated	1.14	+ 0.85
0.66	+ 0.51	Frozen & refrigerated	1.01	+ 0.73
0.45	+ 0.27	Health & beauty aids	0.51	+ 0.23
1.42	+ 0.72	Total	1.68	+ 0.68

Table 2.2A. Special SAMI Study of Generic Label Penetration and Trends. Annual Volume and Shares of Generic Dollar Volume by SAMI Department[a]

Department	Total SAMI Volume[b]	Annual Generic Label Volume[b]	Generic Share (%)
Dry grocery: food	$49,754,706	705,402	1.4
Dry grocery: non-food	16,648,620	355,869	2.1
Frozen	8,942,769	43,518	0.5
Refrigerated	13,352,139	77,863	0.6
Health & beauty aids	4,653,751	19,806	0.4
Grand total	93,352,985	1,202,458	1.3

[a]National projection basis. Year ending May 1, 1981.
[b]In thousands of dollars.

Table 2.2B. Special SAMI Study of Generic Label Penetration and Trends. 12-Week Volume Comparison vs. Year Ago

	Dollars			Units		
Classification	Year Ago Volume[b]	Current Volume[b]	% Change	Year Ago Volume[c]	Current Volume[c]	% Change
Generic label	$ 171,159	$ 356,805	+ 108.5	304,874	553,692	+ 81.6
Regular private label	2,771,233	3,299,897	+ 19.1	3,933,213	4,118,386	+ 4.7
Total private label	2,942,392	3,656,702	+ 24.3	4,238,093	4,672,078	+ 10.2
All other brands	14,637,807	16,025,306	+ 9.5	16,419,693	16,183,901	− 1.4
Total	17,580,199	19,682,008	+ 12.0	20,657,786	20,855,979	+ 1.0

[a] National projection basis, all categories combined. The following number of SAMI categories were reportable for generic labels as of the period ending May 1, 1981: dry grocery: food, 144; dry grocery: non-food, 40; frozen, 28; refrigerated, 12; health & beauty aids, 22; total 246.

[b] In thousands of dollars.

[c] In thousands.

Table 2.2C. Special SAMI Study of Generic Label Penetration and Trends. 52-Week Volume and Shares of Dry Grocery: Food[a]

	Dollars		Pounds		Units	
Category	Annual Volume[b]	52-Week Share (%)	Annual Volume[c]	52-Week Share (%)	Annual Volume[c]	52-Week Share (%)
Dessert baking mixes	12,263	1.7	19,686	2.5	18,794	2.7
Muffin bread & roll mix	80	0.1	159	0.1	308	0.1
Pancake mix	1,590	1.2	4,683	2.0	2,342	1.8
Baking chocolate & bits	5,542	1.6	3,986	3.2	5,282	2.7
Baking extracts	224	0.2	196	1.5	398	0.5
Baking powder & soda	1,434	2.0	4,098	3.4	4,089	3.3
Coconut	541	1.0	375	1.3	467	0.9
Ready-to-spread frosting	112	0.1	115	0.1	111	0.1
Frosting mix—double layer	2,392	3.8	2,680	5.9	3,144	5.6
Marshmallows	1,266	1.9	2,147	2.4	2,515	2.1
Caramel corn	175	0.3	127	0.5	338	0.2
Pkgd. chocolate covered fruits	188	0.9	153	1.9	143	0.9
Pkgd. chocolate covered nuts	242	1.2	146	2.1	208	1.5
Pkgd. hard sugar candies	1,103	0.7	1,172	1.2	1,115	0.6
Pkgd. soft sugar candies	82	0.2	98	0.3	100	0.2
Pkgd. jellies	1,559	2.2	2,860	3.7	1,821	1.9
Pkgd. solid chocolate pieces	28	0.3	15	.05	35	.06
Pkgd. other chocolates	176	0.4	112	0.6	161	0.5
Pkgd. candy covered chocolate	74	0.5	40	.07	44	.06
Ready-to-eat cereal	10,269	0.4	11,143	0.6	10,426	0.5

(Continued)

Table 2.2C. *(Continued)*

Category	Dollars		Pounds		Units	
	Annual Volume[b]	52-Week Share (%)	Annual Volume[c]	52-Week Share (%)	Annual Volume[c]	52-Week Share (%)
Hot cereals	1,641	0.6	3,694	1.1	1,730	0.6
Cocoa	743	1.8	254	2.4	507	2.6
Milk modifiers	10,208	2.5	11,494	4.1	9,183	3.2
Regular coffee	17,323	0.7	7,834	0.9	5,510	0.8
Instant coffee	5,513	0.3	882	0.5	1,538	0.3
Catsup	11,561	3.0	28,665	4.3	16,168	3.8
Prepared mustard	2,445	1.9	7,325	3.7	4,463	1.9
Meat sauce	56	.04	52	.07	66	0.5
Italian food sauces	17,832	3.6	39,864	6.3	19,933	4.7
Barbecue sauce	2,895	1.6	5,651	2.5	3,797	2.0
Dry gravy seasoning sauce mixes	541	0.3	181	0.5	2,461	0.5
Vinegar & cooking wines	1,688	1.3	7,241	1.9	3,121	1.8
Misc. sauces	57	0.1	62	0.2	105	0.1
Whse crackers	10,867	3.9	17,949	5.7	18,541	5.1
Whse bread & cracker crumbs	48	0.1	56	0.1	80	0.2
Stuffing mixes	142	0.1	87	0.2	233	0.2
Pudding	1,250	0.5	1,033	0.5	4,238	0.6
Gelatin desserts	2,627	1.2	2,250	1.7	11,795	2.2
Dry topping mixes	10	.03	4	.05	33	.11
Dessert & ice cream toppings	593	0.9	708	1.5	741	1.0

Canned salmon	908	0.4	477	0.6	499	0.5
Canned sardines	652	0.7	382	0.9	1,354	1.0
Canned shrimp	76	0.1	11	0.2	42	0.2
Canned tuna	9,771	0.7	4,774	0.9	11,879	1.0
Corn meal	192	0.2	818	0.2	164	0.1
Family flour	3,313	0.7	21,351	1.0	3,719	0.9
Canned peaches	13,085	5.0	33,868	6.4	20,666	5.2
Canned fruit cocktail	2,726	1.4	4,904	1.6	4,938	1.6
Apple sauce	8,084	3.8	23,350	4.8	17,738	5.2
Canned apricots	1,092	3.9	2,343	5.5	1,406	3.6
Canned pears	6,465	5.5	13,669	7.0	9,041	5.3
Canned mandarin oranges	1,852	4.2	2,757	5.5	4,011	5.8
Pie fillings	1,735	1.4	2,364	1.8	1,818	1.9
Canned pineapple	4,277	1.6	9,115	2.1	7,557	1.8
Misc. canned fruit	5,626	10.3	11,451	14.6	9,088	12.6
Raisins	2,300	1.1	1,750	1.5	2,611	0.4
Dried prunes	386	0.6	446	0.9	258	0.5
Honey	3,874	3.4	3,778	4.1	2,570	3.6
Jams, jellies, preserves	26,738	5.7	49,611	9.5	25,658	6.4
Peanut butter & combinations	17,665	2.2	18,718	3.3	14,372	3.4
Tomato juice	2,444	1.8	10,248	2.4	3,699	1.2
Blended vegetable juice	527	0.3	1,944	0.5	698	0.1
Orange juice	1,583	1.4	3,184	1.1	2,046	0.8
Prune juice	350	0.4	855	0.5	424	0.4
Pineapple juice	356	0.4	1,085	0.5	401	0.3

(Continued)

Table 2.2C. *(Continued)*

Category	Dollars		Pounds		Units	
	Annual Volume[b]	52-Week Share (%)	Annual Volume[c]	52-Week Share (%)	Annual Volume[c]	52-Week Share (%)
Grapefruit juice	2,912	1.5	9,387	1.8	3,028	0.8
Apple juice	16,541	4.2	56,321	5.8	15,978	3.5
Grape juice	4,535	4.3	10,466	6.3	4,283	4.2
Lemon & lime juice	3,175	4.8	7,574	8.9	3,787	4.9
Single strength juice drinks	12,165	1.8	47,602	2.3	13,764	1.4
Pasta	22,760	3.1	47,721	4.8	34,445	3.4
Meat stew	818	0.8	993	1.0	662	0.9
Beef hash	1,250	2.1	1,320	2.5	1,408	2.4
Lunch meat	576	0.3	347	0.3	463	0.3
Sausage & frankfurters	942	0.7	779	1.0	2,494	1.1
Evaporated & condensed milk	12,334	3.3	26,726	4.3	32,127	4.2
Powdered milk	2,584	1.4	—	—	538	1.0
Coffee creamers	13,803	6.5	14,613	10.2	10,925	6.8
Wet dog food	12,829	1.7	62,516	3.2	64,457	3.0
Dry dog food	30,199	2.1	178,300	3.9	6,912	1.8
Semimoist dog food	4,935	1.7	10,340	2.6	2,298	1.8
Dog food snacks	855	0.4	1,734	0.7	940	0.4
Wet cat food	4,793	0.7	12,604	1.3	20,271	1.0
Dry cat food	2,213	0.5	6,366	0.9	1,015	0.4
Semimoist cat food	2,041	1.1	2,646	1.6	3,257	1.6

Pickles	9,964	2.2	20,972	3.5	11,331	2.9
Relishes	1,993	2.7	3,005	3.9	2,530	2.7
Peppers	155	0.2	102	0.2	292	0.2
Ripe olives	900	0.9	558	1.2	1,653	1.2
Spanish olives	1,699	1.3	1,199	2.3	1,558	1.4
Pork & beans	5,337	1.2	17,988	1.7	17,646	1.8
Canned chili	2,965	1.4	4,430	1.9	4,651	2.1
Canned pasta dishes	1,902	0.5	3,775	0.7	4,027	0.7
Dry packaged dinners	11,246	2.6	20,640	5.1	45,530	5.7
Mexican food	539	0.2	986	0.4	1,019	0.3
Instant potatoes	1,752	1.0	1,609	1.3	2,404	1.2
Mayonnaise	10,400	2.0	19,428	2.9	9,732	2.3
Spoonable salad dressings	5,322	1.8	12,165	2.9	6,083	2.4
Pourable salad dressings	3,107	0.6	4,450	1.0	2,920	0.5
Spices & seasonings	2,706	0.6	1,057	1.3	2,507	0.5
Salt	790	0.8	6,154	1.3	3,787	1.3
Pepper	6,237	4.9	2,366	8.5	5,520	4.5
Solid shortening	12,756	3.0	23,775	3.9	8,950	3.8
Cooking & salad oils	24,429	2.4	38,126	3.5	14,595	2.8
Popcorn	1,032	0.8	3,460	1.7	1,820	1.3
Whse potato chips & products	11,714	5.9	9,660	8.5	10,764	4.5
Whse corn snacks	6,275	7.2	5,839	11.5	7,136	6.0
Whse pretzels	1,491	4.6	2,171	7.1	2,173	4.3
Salted nuts	14,683	2.9	10,038	5.3	10,988	2.9
Dry toaster items	338	0.4	361	0.4	550	0.4

(Continued)

Table 2.2C. *(Continued)*

Category	Dollars		Pounds		Units	
	Annual Volume[b]	52-Week Share (%)	Annual Volume[c]	52-Week Share (%)	Annual Volume[c]	52-Week Share (%)
Misc. snacks & dips	55	.11	5	.06	21	.02
Whse regular soft drinks	21,867	3.1	107,600	3.8	48,202	2.3
Whse lo-cal soft drinks	1,158	0.4	5,448	0.5	4,288	0.4
Soft drink mixes	4,805	0.7	6,249	1.3	4,001	0.3
Breakfast drink mixes	3,749	3.5	4,284	5.1	2,520	4.9
Bottled water	473	0.6	7,917	1.0	992	0.8
Dehydrated soup	1,506	0.5	1,291	1.3	7,188	1.4
Canned soup	3,142	0.3	7,553	0.3	11,118	0.4
Granulated sugar	28,285	1.6	65,610	1.7	13,108	1.6
Brown sugar	897	0.6	1,601	0.8	800	0.5
Confectioner sugar	922	0.7	1,727	0.9	863	0.6
Maple syrup	6,936	2.4	12,746	4.4	8,153	4.0
Instant tea	839	0.8	110	1.2	586	1.1
Tea bags	15,257	3.8	6,410	7.4	12,820	4.5
Iced tea mix	8,398	3.9	8,998	6.1	9,941	3.8
Canned peas	8,714	3.5	26,709	4.6	26,739	4.3
Canned wax beans	546	3.4	1,791	4.6	1,792	4.2
Canned tomatoes	13,306	4.3	37,154	5.3	32,739	5.6
Canned potatoes	2,345	2.2	7,514	3.2	7,128	3.6
Canned beets	1,909	2.9	6,718	4.5	6,718	4.2

Canned lima & butter beans	325	0.6	801	0.8	805	0.8
Canned kidney & misc. beans	4,374	1.8	12,667	2.3	13,264	2.5
Canned asparagus	80	0.1	86	0.2	96	0.1
Canned spinach	1,284	2.2	3,262	2.7	3,474	2.7
Canned mushrooms	11,539	5.5	6,252	7.6	24,831	8.0
Canned sauerkraut	492	0.8	1,629	1.1	1,634	1.2
Canned carrots	888	3.6	2,792	4.2	2,804	3.8
Canned mixed vegetables	1,570	2.2	4,903	3.1	4,855	2.8
Canned corn	16,433	3.9	50,442	5.0	50,081	4.6
Canned green beans	13,779	3.8	45,015	5.1	45,015	5.0
Tomato paste	2,637	1.7	3,927	2.1	9,719	2.5
Tomato sauce	9,243	3.1	25,011	4.0	41,490	4.3
Tomato puree	388	0.9	1,211	1.3	668	1.1
Dried rice	7,270	1.7	22,486	3.0	7,331	2.1

[a] National projection basis.
[b] In thousands of dollars.
[c] In thousands.

Table 2.2D. Special SAMI Study of Generic Label Penetration and Trends. 12-Week Share Comparison vs. Year Ago of Dry Grocery: Food[a]

	Dollars			Pounds			Units		
Classification	Year Ago Share	Current Share	Share Change	Year Ago Share	Current Share	Share Change	Year Ago Share	Current Share	Share Change
Generic label	1.1%	2.0%	+ .9	1.9%	3.3%	+1.4	1.5%	2.5%	+1.0
Regular private label	15.2	16.1	+ .9	21.9	22.9	+1.0	18.6	19.3	+ .7
Total private label	16.4	18.1	+1.7	23.8	26.2	+2.4	20.1	21.7	+1.6
All other brands	83.6	81.9	−1.7	76.2	73.8	−2.4	79.9	78.3	−1.6

[a]National projection basis. 144 Product categories in which generic label volume was reportable as of 12 weeks ending May 1, 1981.

Table 2.2E. Special SAMI Study of Generic Label Penetration and Trends. 52-Week Volume and Shares of Dry Grocery: Non-Food[a]

Category	Dollars		Pounds		Units	
	Annual Volume[b]	52-Week Share (%)	Annual Volume[c]	52-Week Share (%)	Annual Volume[c]	52-Week Share (%)
Scouring cleansers	1,326	0.7	5,143	1.5	5,596	1.6
All purpose cleaners	2,702	0.7	4,552	1.1	3,122	1.1
Ammonia	400	1.2	3,224	2.0	766	1.3
Window cleaners	682	0.7	2,152	1.7	1,065	1.2
Bowl cleaners	927	0.6	1,334	0.8	1,537	1.0
Light bulbs	4,951	1.5	—	—	12,297	3.3
Furniture polish	58	0.04	44	0.07	50	0.06
Cat litter	4,935	3.1	66,458	5.1	3,121	2.9
Handle goods	240	0.3	+	—	154	0.3
Air fresheners	1,200	0.6	1,145	1.2	2,041	0.9
Disinfectants	31	0.03	30	0.07	24	0.04
Self-polishing floor wax	55	0.05	57	0.07	38	0.08
Charcoal	664	0.3	4,100	0.4	317	0.30
Charcoal lighter	158	0.3	283	0.3	141	0.3
Insecticides	32	0.01	19	0.03	23	0.02
Fireplace logs	995	2.6	—	—	1.035	4.4
Motor oil & additives	173	0.1	491	0.2	124	0.1
Dry cell batteries	150	0.1	—	—	219	0.2
Chlorine bleach	8,310	2,9	103,700	4.6	12,969	3.3
All fabric bleach	1,154	0.6	3,305	1.0	1,284	1.1
Fabric softeners	13,981	2.5	58,385	7.0	13,174	3.5
Starches	36	0.06	53	0.07	46	0.08

(*Continued*)

Table 2.2E. *(Continued)*

Category	Dollars		Pounds		Units	
	Annual Volume[b]	52-Week Share (%)	Annual Volume[c]	52-Week Share (%)	Annual Volume[c]	52-Week Share (%)
Laundry soil–stain removers	61	0.05	67	0.08	48	0.07
Coffee filters	2,120	4.5	—	—	2,373	4.2
Waxed paper	51	0.1	—	—	91	0.2
Paper & plastic cups	1,033	0.4	—	—	1,166	0.5
Paper & plastic plates	10,026	3.3	—	—	10,215	4.4
Moist towelettes	1,114	1.7	—	—	717	1.6
Disposable diapers	12,362	1.0	—	—	2,843	0.8
Sanitary napkins	1,592	0.4	—	—	847	0.5
Aluminum foil	8,523	2.4	—	—	12,108	3.7
Household plastic bags	53,203	5.6	—	—	43,132	7.1
Poly wrap	1,080	1.0	—	—	1,426	1.4
Toilet tissue	68,095	4.2	—	—	359,000	6.2
Paper towels	53,727	4.7	—	—	106,000	6.7
Paper napkins	19,908	6.3	—	—	27,628	6.6
Facial tissue	22,927	4.3	—	—	48,936	6.0
Hand & bath soaps	2,798	0.3	3,004	0.5	9,491	0.5
Bath additives	582	2.2	1,322	6.0	558	3.1
Light duty liquid detergent	17,156	2.5	61,830	6.4	29,235	4.9
Dishwasher detergents	5,773	1.9	14,828	3.2	4,727	3.0
Heavy duty detergents	30,515	1.4	81,866	2.3	21,562	2.2

[a] National projection basis.
[b] In thousands of dollars.
[c] In thousands.

Table 2.2F. Special SAMI Study of Generic Label Penetration and Trends. 12-Week Share Comparison vs. Year Ago of Dry Grocery: Non-Food[a]

	Dollars			Units		
Classification	Year Ago Share (%)	Current Share (%)	Share Change	Year Ago Share (%)	Current Share (%)	Share Change
Generic label	1.6	2.8	+1.2	2.7	4.9	+2.2
Regular private label	9.9	10.4	+0.5	12.3	12.7	+0.4
Total private label	11.4	13.1	+1.7	15.0	17.6	+2.6
All other brands	88.6	86.9	−1.7	85.0	82.4	−2.6

[a]National projection basis, all categories combined. Product categories in which generic label volume was reportable as of 12 weeks ending May 1, 1981.

Table 2.2G. Special SAMI Study of Generic Label Penetration and Trends. 52-Week Volume and Shares of Frozen and Refrigerated Foods[a]

	Dollars		Pounds		Units	
Category	Annual Volume[b]	52-Week Share (%)	Annual Volume[c]	52-Week Share (%)	Annual Volume[c]	52-Week Share (%)
Refrig. & frozen toppings	$ 786	0.3	738	0.5	1,117	0.4
Frozen sweet goods	232	0.1	223	0.1	295	0.1
Frozen pies	196	0.1	241	0.1	148	0.1
Frozen dinner bread & rolls	335	0.3	644	0.3	649	0.5
Frozen meat	50	0.03	22	0.04	25	0.05
Frozen fish	877	0.1	559	0.2	386	0.1
Frozen strawberries	302	0.4	418	0.6	668	0.8
Frozen orange juice	18,405	1.4	18,503	1.7	23,096	1.4
Frozen grape juice	390	0.4	424	0.6	566	0.5
Frozen fruit ades	244	0.2	402	0.3	585	0.2
Misc. frozen juices	368	0.2	386	0.3	515	0.3
Frozen potatoes	2,954	0.6	9,772	1.1	2,417	0.5
Frozen pot pies	3,816	1.9	6,619	3.0	13,250	3.2
Frozen single dishes	1,005	0.1	1,300	0.2	1,467	0.2
Frozen regular dinners	401	0.1	389	0.1	581	0.1
Frozen pizza	3,463	0.5	2,657	0.7	3,593	0.8
Frozen peas	1,772	2.1	3,563	2.7	3,017	2.1
Frozen corn	2,043	1.2	3,362	2.8	3,357	1.6
Frozen green & wax beans	1,520	1.8	2,793	2.6	2,377	1.8
Frozen mixed vegetables	1,763	1.5	3,405	2.0	2,968	1.7
Frozen lima beans	251	0.5	393	0.7	393	0.5
Frozen broccoli	894	0.6	1,259	0.7	1,787	0.7

Frozen spinach	96	0.2	225	0.2	360	0.2
Frozen cauliflower	493	1.1	736	1.7	732	1.2
Misc. frozen vegetables	176	1.6	441	2.6	342	1.8
Frozen vegetables deluxe	522	1.2	693	1.6	566	1.0
Frozen southern vegetables	125	0.1	252	0.2	202	0.2
Frozen waffles	39	0.03	47	0.04	75	0.05
Natural cheese	5,355	0.3	2,266	0.3	3,516	0.3
Processed cheese	29,812	1.6	19,032	2.2	21,276	1.9
Cream cheese	2,766	1.0	1,898	1.2	3,836	1.1
Refrigerated yogurt	1,046	0.4	1,868	0.7	3,750	0.7
Hot dogs	6,065	0.5	5,608	0.7	5,407	0.6
Lunch meat	13,987	0.6	9,368	1.0	10,767	0.8
Bacon	6,737	0.6	6,546	0.9	6,544	0.9
Margarine	9,563	0.7	21,163	1.0	19,743	1.0
Misc. dough products	246	1.0	—	—	305	0.9
Refrig. salad dressing and sauce	29	0.1	42	0.3	21	0.1
Refrig. juices & drinks	2,123	0.3	8,291	0.4	2,036	0.3
Misc. refrigerated items	134	0.1	174	0.1	264	0.2

[a]National projection basis. Period ending May 1, 1981.
[b]In thousands of dollars.
[c]In thousands.

Table 2.2H. Special SAMI Study of Generic Label Penetration & Trends. 12-Week Share Comparison vs. Year Ago of Frozen and Refrigerated Items[a]

Classification	Dollars			Pounds			Units		
	Year Ago Share (%)	Current Share (%)	Share Change	Year Ago Share (%)	Current Share (%)	Share Change	Year Ago Share (%)	Current Share (%)	Share Change
Frozen[b]									
Generic label	0.2	0.8	+0.6	0.4	1.3	+0.9	0.4	1.3	+0.9
Regular private label	21.8	23.0	+1.2	30.1	31.4	+1.3	31.7	32.3	+0.6
Total private label	22.0	23.9	+1.9	30.5	32.8	+2.3	32.0	33.6	+1.6
All other brands	78.0	76.1	−1.9	69.5	67.2	−2.3	68.0	66.4	−1.6
Refrigerated[c]									
Generic label	0.3	1.0	+0.7	0.5	1.3	+0.8	0.4	1.3	+0.9
Regular private label	25.7	26.9	+1.2	26.0	27.9	+1.9	27.3	28.6	+1.3
Total private label	26.0	27.9	+1.9	26.4	29.2	+2.8	27.7	29.9	+2.2
All other brands	74.0	72.1	−1.9	73.6	70.8	−2.8	72.3	70.1	−2.2

[a]National projection base, all categories combined.
[b]28 Frozen product categories in which generic label volume was reportable as of 12 weeks ending May 1, 1981.
[c]12 Refrigerated product categories in which generic label volume was reportable as of 12 weeks ending May 1, 1981.

Table 2.2I. Special SAMI Study of Generic Label Penetration and Trends. 52-Week Volume and Shares of Health and Beauty Aids[a]

Category	Dollars		Pounds		Units	
	Annual Volume[b]	52-Week Share (%)	Annual Volume[b]	52-Week Share (%)	Annual Volume[b]	52-Week Share (%)
Baby powders	$ 736	2.0	885	5.3	683	3.0
Baby oils, creams and lotions	923	1.3	839	4.3	730	1.6
Spray deodorants	127	0.1	71	0.3	104	0.1
Roll-on deodorants	178	0.1	28	0.3	225	0.3
Stick deodorants and pads	31	0.03	4	0.06	26	0.05
First aid antiseptics	231	0.7	512	4.8	551	1.9
First aid products	3,763	2.6	—	—	4,889	4.1
Shampoo	3,951	0.8	6,191	3.3	4,393	1.6
Hair spray	96	0.1	46	0.1	93	0.1
Hair conditioning rinses	745	0.4	1,135	1.5	781	0.7
Toothpaste and powder	1,200	0.3	690	0.6	1,496	0.4
Mouth wash	1,412	0.8	2,809	2.7	1,451	1.5
Tooth brushes	74	0.1	—	—	279	0.4
Antacids	95	0.05	60	0.20	80	0.04
Internal analgesics	1,373	0.3	—	—	1,492	0.6
External analgesics	1,307	2.9	2,777	6.2	2,205	4.5
Cough remedies	15	0.01	4	0.02	10	0.01
Laxatives	57	0.1	—	—	82	0.2
Vitamins	2,422	1.9	—	—	1,142	3.0
Shaving creams	133	0.2	128	0.5	106	0.2
Razor blades	410	0.2	—	—	316	0.2
Hand and body creams and lotions	521	0.6	558	1.9	558	1.1
Cosmetic and medicated skin aids	6	0.01	3	0.03	11	0.03

[a]National projection basis. Period ending May 1, 1982.
[b]In thousands of dollars.

Table 2.2J. Special SAMI Study of Generic Label Penetration and Trends. 12-Week Share Comparison vs. Year Ago of Health and Beauty Aids[a]

Classification	Dollars			Units		
	Year Ago Share (%)	Current Share (%)	Share Change	Year Ago Share (%)	Current Share (%)	Share Change
Generic label	0.3	0.6	+0.3	0.5	1.0	+0.5
Regular private label	3.5	3.7	+0.2	4.6	4.7	+0.1
Total private label	3.8	4.3	+0.5	5.2	5.7	+0.5
All other brands	96.2	95.7	−0.5	94.8	94.3	−0.5

[a] National projection basis, all categories combined. 22 Health and beauty aids product categories in which generic label volume was reportable as of 12 weeks ending May 1, 1981.

Appendix 3

First Gallup Study on Private Labels 1981

The Gallup Organization, Princeton, New Jersey, conducted its first private label consumer survey in 1981 under the sponsorship of the Private Label Manufacturers Association, New York.

Gallup, surveying 1500 consumers who were interviewed in 300 sampling locations and projected out to the U.S. adult population, found that one-half of the population perceived national brand quality higher than private label, while 43% thought private label was of equal or higher quality. Also, eight out of 10 Americans (78%) believe that private label pricing is lower than the national brand, while roughly 22% feel that private label pricing is much lower than national brands.

The following four tables are taken from this study. Table 3.1A for perceived quality shows that private label in specific product categories—vitamins and over-the-counter non-prescription drugs, plastic wrap and bags, and household cleaning and laundry items—has received good quality endorsement by consumers: 48, 49, and 47% of respondents, respectively, feel private label is good or better than national brands in these categories, while 34, 39, and 42%, respectively, say national brands are higher in quality for those categories.

Table 3.1B shows that across all product categories, consumers recognize the competitive advantage of private label pricing over national

Table 3.1A. Perceived Quality of National Brands Compared to Private Label

	National Brands							
	Higher			Not Higher				
	Total (%)	Much (%)	Somewhat (%)	Total (%)	Same (%)	Lower (%)	Don't know (%)	Total (%)
All Products	50	15	35	43	39	4	7	100
Vitamins and over-the-counter non-prescription drugs	34	11	23	48	44	4	18	100
Plastic wrap and bags	39	11	28	49	46	3	12	100
Household cleaning and laundry products	42	13	29	47	43	4	11	100
Beauty aids (shampoos, skin care, and shaving needs)	46	14	32	41	37	4	13	100
Paper goods (toilet tissue, napkins, towels)	50	15	35	43	37	6	7	100
Food and beverages	51	14	37	41	38	3	8	100

Table 3.1B. Perceived Price of National Brands Compared to Private Label

	National Brands							
	Higher			Not Higher				
	Total (%)	Much (%)	Somewhat (%)	Total (%)	Same (%)	Lower (%)	Don't know (%)	Total (%)
All Products	78	22	56	15	9	6	7	100
Food and beverages	76	19	57	17	10	7	7	100
Beauty aids (shampoos, skin care, and shaving needs)	71	24	47	17	10	7	12	100
Paper goods (toilet tissue, napkins, towels)	71	18	53	20	13	7	9	100
Household cleaning and laundry products	70	17	53	21	14	7	9	100
Vitamins and over-the-counter non-prescription drugs	67	25	42	16	10	6	17	100
Plastic wrap and bags	67	15	52	21	14	7	12	100

brands. National brands are rated the highest in price in the vitamin and drug plus the health and beauty aids area.

In the trade-off between perceived price and quality, that is, in value (Table 3.2), four out of 10 Americans regard private labels as a "good value" over national brands: they rate the quality higher than the price they must pay for the products. One in 10 Americans think of private label as an "extra value," that is, it offers much higher quality than the price at retail. Three in 10 Americans (37%) rate private label as a "fair value," that is, "you get what you pay for," where quality and price of private label are relatively the same as national brands. Only one in six (16%) rate private label a "poor value," that is, quality is lower than the price.

In a comparison of private label versus generic quality (Table 3.3), Gallup found that the public positions private label closer to generics with respect to price. Interestingly, food and beverages get a higher rating for private label over generics, versus manufactured items, such as paper goods or plastic goods. National brand and private label quality are positioned closer together over generic quality (Table 3.4A), while national brand pricing is perceived as the highest—higher than private label and still higher than generics (Table 3.4B).

Table 3.2. Value of Private Label Products

	"Extra" value (Quality *much* higher than price) (%)	"Good" value (Quality higher than price) (%)	"Fair" value (Quality same as price) (%)	"Poor" value (Quality lower than price) (%)	Don't know N/A (%)
All Products	9	30	37	16	8
Vitamins and over-the-counter non-prescription drugs	15	25	26	12	22
Beauty aids (shampoos, skin care, and (shaving needs)	10	29	31	14	16
Household cleaning and laundry products	7	31	33	16	13
Food and beverages	7	30	37	17	9
Plastic wrap and bags	7	29	35	14	15
Paper goods (toilet tissue, napkins towels)	8	28	38	16	10

Table 3.3. Perceived Quality of Private Label Compared to Generics

	Private Label							
	Higher			Not Higher				
	Total (%)	Much (%)	Somewhat (%)	Total (%)	Same (%)	Lower (%)	Don't know (%)	Total (%)
All Products	38	8	30	47	37	10	15	100
Food and Beverages	36	7	29	47	37	10	17	100
Paper Products (toilet tissue, napkins, towels)	32	62	26	49	39	10	19	100
Beauty Aids (shampoos, skin care, and shaving needs)	30	6	24	46	37	9	24	100
Household cleaning and laundry products	28	5	23	51	42	9	21	100
Vitamins and over-the-counter non-prescription drugs	27	5	22	46	38	8	27	100
Plastic wrap and bags	27	5	22	51	42	9	22	100

Table 3.4A. Perceived Quality. Positioning of Private Label, National Brands, and Generics

	All Products (%)	Food, etc. (%)	Cleaning, etc. (%)	Paper, etc. (%)	Plastic Wrap, etc. (%)	Vitamins, etc. (%)	Beauty Aids, etc. (%)
Private Label, National, Generic, *Same*	22	22	26	23	28	26	21
Private Label and National, *Same*; Generic, *Lower*	11	10	8	7	9	8	9
National *Higher* than Private Label; Private Label *Higher* than Generic	25	24	18	23	16	16	19
National *Higher*; Private Label and Generic, *Same*	14	14	13	14	12	9	14

Table 3.4B. Perceived Price. Private Label Compared to Generics

	Private Label						
	Higher			Not Higher			
	Total (%)	Much (%)	Somewhat (%)	Total (%)	Same (%)	Lower (%)	Don't know (%)
All Products	61	10	51	26	15	11	13

	National vs. Private Label		Private Label vs. Generics	
	Higher (%)	Not Higher (%)	Higher (%)	Not Higher (%)
All Products	78	16	61	26

Appendix **4**

Brand Preferences of Foodservice Operators

In foodservice markets, many operators look to private label as their "national brand." The operator either positions his own labels as a national brand or joins a foodservice distributor group, which positions its corporate labels as national brands.

The national brands, while popular among foodservice distributors and operators, by no means dominate this market. *Institutional Distribution* Magazine discovered this attitude in a survey article, "How and Why Operators Buy," published in 1981. The following table shows that operators do not "always" buy by brand in certain product groups. In fact, canned and frozen vegetables and fruit get a weak rating in brand purchasing.

Table 4.1. Percent of Foodservice Operators Who Purchase By Brand (By Product Group)

	Percent of Respondents		
Product Group	Always	Sometimes	Never
Canned vegetables	21.5%	54.6%	23.9%
Canned fruit	23.2	51.9	24.9
Condiments	39.5	43.8	16.7
Shortenings, oils	56.4	30.9	12.7
Breadings, mixes	43.6	39.3	17.1
Soups	54.0	32.1	13.9
Crackers, cookies	49.2	37.4	13.4
Canned main courses	44.0	37.1	18.9
Canned fish and seafood	37.5	43.3	19.2
Canned or dry desserts	36.3	45.8	17.9
Frozen vegetables	26.3	47.5	26.2
Frozen fruit	22.4	47.5	30.1
Frozen meat	43.9	38.8	17.3
Frozen poultry	38.4	39.7	21.9
Frozen fish	44.9	40.4	14.7
Frozen shellfish	35.6	42.8	28.6
Frozen entrees	48.1	36.2	15.7
Frozen cakes and pies	56.0	33.7	10.3
Frozen coffee whiteners	35.8	33.9	30.3
Frozen toppings	52.3	31.4	16.3

Source: *Institutional Distribution* Magazine, p. 74. Restaurant Business Inc., New York.